Religion, Culture, and the Monstrous

Religion, Culture, and the Monstrous

Of Gods and Monsters

Edited by
Natasha L. Mikles and Joseph P. Laycock

LEXINGTON BOOKS
Lanham • Boulder • New York • London

Published by Lexington Books
An imprint of The Rowman & Littlefield Publishing Group, Inc.
4501 Forbes Boulevard, Suite 200, Lanham, Maryland 20706
www.rowman.com

6 Tinworth Street, London SE11 5AL, United Kingdom

Copyright © 2021 by The Rowman & Littlefield Publishing Group, Inc.

All rights reserved. No part of this book may be reproduced in any form or by any electronic or mechanical means, including information storage and retrieval systems, without written permission from the publisher, except by a reviewer who may quote passages in a review.

British Library Cataloguing in Publication Information Available

Library of Congress Cataloging-in-Publication Data

Names: Mikles, Natasha L., 1986- editor. | Laycock, Joseph, 1980- editor.
Title: Religion, culture, and the monstrous : of Gods and monsters / edited by Natasha L. Mikles and Joseph P. Laycock.
Description: Lanham : Lexington Books, [2021] | Includes bibliographical references and index.
Identifiers: LCCN 2020050652 (print) | LCCN 2020050653 (ebook) | ISBN 9781793640246 (hardcover) | ISBN 9781793640253 (epub)
Subjects: LCSH: Religion and culture. | Popular culture—Religious aspects. | Monsters in popular culture. | Monsters. | Culture.
Classification: LCC BL65.C8 R4466 2021 (print) | LCC BL65.C8 (ebook) | DDC 202/.16—dc23
LC record available at https://lccn.loc.gov/2020050652
LC ebook record available at https://lccn.loc.gov/2020050653

ISBN 9781793640260 (paperback)

∞™ The paper used in this publication meets the minimum requirements of American National Standard for Information Sciences—Permanence of Paper for Printed Library Materials, ANSI/NISO Z39.48-1992.

Contents

PART I: THINKING WITH MONSTERS

1. Five Further Theses on Monster Theory and Religious Studies — 3
   Natasha L. Mikles and Joseph P. Laycock

2. Reiterations: On Tellings, Variants, and Why Monsters Always Come Back — 17
   Douglas E. Cowan

3. Horror and Bible (Six Theses) — 29
   Brandon R. Grafius

4. A Biological Model of Monster Flaps — 41
   William Blake Smith

PART II: MONSTERS GUARDING THE GATES

5. The Idea of Evil and Messianic Deliverance in the Satpanth Ismaili Tradition of South Asia — 63
   Wafi A. Momin

6. Ghost Stories from *Tales of Retribution*: Understanding Elements of Seventeenth-Century Japanese Ghost Stories — 79
   Frank F. Chu

7. Of Monsters and Invisible Villages: *Nags myi rgod* Tales of the Tibetans of Gyalthang — 97
   Eric D. Mortensen

8	Godly Aromas and Monstrous Stenches: An Analysis of Buddhist New Year Fumigation Rituals in an Indo-Himalayan Borderland *Rohit Singh*	117
9	Man, Yeti, and Mi-go: The Transgressive History of a Monstrous Word *Lee A. Weiss*	131
10	The Mesopotamian Demon Lamaštu and the Monstrosity of Gender Transgression *Madadh Richey*	145
11	Topophilic Perversions: Spectral Blackface and Fetishizing Sites of Monstrosity in American Dark Tourism *Whitney S. May*	157

PART III: MONSTERS TEARING DOWN THE GATES

12	Finding Bigfoot: The Anthropological Machine and the Generation of Monsters *Timothy Grieve-Carlson*	171
13	Thomas Jefferson: The First Cryptozoologist? *Justin Mullis*	185
14	Shapeshifters and Goddesses: Gods, Monsters, and Otherness in the Mysticism of Gloria Anzaldúa *Stefan R. Sanchez*	199
15	The Monster Within: Rape and Revenge in Genesis 34 *Leland Merritt*	213
16	"Monsters among Us": The Cathartic Carnage of *American Horror Story* *Heidi Ippolito*	225
17	To Eat or to Be Eaten—*CHEW*: A New Study between the Beast and the Sovereign *Elena Pasquini*	237

Bibliography	251
Index	273
About the Editors and Contributors	279

Part I

THINKING WITH MONSTERS

Chapter 1

Five Further Theses on Monster Theory and Religious Studies

Natasha L. Mikles and Joseph P. Laycock

In *The Bride of Frankenstein* (1935) the mad Dr. Pretorius toasts, "To a new world of gods and monsters!" The line has an uncanny quality to it because while we seldom acknowledge the relationship between gods and monsters, we seem to understand it intuitively. Perhaps we don't talk about this connection because both these terms are rich with assumptions about both ourselves and the societies we live in. Colloquially speaking, gods are often thought to represent the best of us—the lofty ideals toward which humanity aims and the source of its ultimate salvation. Monsters, on the other hand, are generally conceived as the worst of us—the dark force that preys on others, a twisted moral authority, or a sadistic pleasure in the suffering of others.

But, as we elaborate below, the terms "gods" and "monsters" do not refer to phenomena that exist "out there" in the world. When we use these terms we often reveal more about ourselves than the thing we are describing. It is this semantic slipperiness that makes these terms both *useful* and *dangerous*. *Useful* because each term quickly communicates a constellation of meaning. In one word, the speaker not only expresses their appraisal of a phenomenon but also encourages others to understand the phenomenon through the same perspective. *Dangerous* because we often forget that such terms are, above all, second-order categories deployed to organize the world according to the speaker's viewpoint. To forget this is to accept as ultimately real—and therefore uninvestigatable—the world constructed by the speaker.

Religious studies as a field has a lot to say about gods; fewer scholars of religion, however, have had anything to say about monsters. It is possible that religious studies has neglected monsters, in part, to preserve a dichotomy that isn't really there. Once we start to theorize what the term "monster" actually means, it quickly becomes apparent that many of those beings dubbed "gods" are also monsters, and vice versa. Sometimes all that separates a god from a monster is a dedicated PR team.

Consider the book of Job where God not only revels in his creation of chaos monsters such as Behemoth and Leviathan but also appears monstrous himself in his cosmic indifference. Timothy Beal (2002, 48) writes, "Job's identification with the monstrous against God ultimately leads to God's identification with the monstrous against Job. God out-monsters Job, pushing the theological horror one monster step beyond Job's wildest expectations." As stated in the television series *Lovecraft Country* (2020), "The Bible is full of demons and monsters." In tantric Buddhist and Hindu traditions, divine beings draped in skulls and dripping with blood are a constant presence, using their fear-inducing visage to inspire a practitioner to greater meditative insights. Many of these beings were once themselves monstrous antagonists to the Buddhist order who could only be subdued via the wrathful actions of an enlightened being. A tantric "origin story" relates how the formerly devout Buddhist practitioner Rudra becomes an enemy of the Dharma, killing thousands upon thousands in a misinterpretation of tantric principles. He can only be stopped by the frightful nine-headed buddha Vajrapāni, who bests the demonic Rudra in battle, consumes and, eventually, excretes him as a newly christened defender of Buddhist dharma. Looking at the actions of both the bloodthirsty Rudra and the wrathful, cannibalistic Vajrapāni, it is hard to differentiate between the demonic and the divine. A similar story is told in the tale of Hārītī—a child-eating demoness who was brought to the Buddhist path through a compassionate trick played by Gautama Buddha. Having stolen her youngest child and hidden him under a rice bowl, Hārītī experienced the hardship she inflicted on other mothers and vowed in the future to only protect children. She now is worshipped as the special protector of children, and statues to her can be found throughout China, Japan, and India. Despite their "monstrous" origins, these figures are celebrated as divine beings who can aid one on a Buddhist path.

Gods and divine beings are also more likely to inspire "monstrous" actions than monsters. A public practice in parts of China during the Sui and Tang dynasty was to burn one's finger as an offering to the Buddha. Rather than an extremist outlier, the action is inspired by the twenty-third chapter of the *Lotus Sutra*, which tells of a great bodhisattva who burns his body as the ultimate offering to a Buddha; historical records and other contemporaneous writings show that such a practice was frequent enough to warrant comment and public condemnation. In a particularly famous essay, the writer Han Yu cited such public self-immolations to declare Buddhism a barbaric religion that had no place in the Chinese court.

Hārītī demonstrates that if gods can be monsters, monsters can also become like gods. On a recent cross-country road trip, the authors stopped at the Fouke Monster Festival, where locals and interested tourists gather to celebrate a hairy wild man living in the swamps around Fouke, Arkansas, who has reportedly been seen since the 1940s. Fouke is not a large town—in the 2010 census, the small town thirty minutes from the Texas border reported a population of only 859—and visitors approaching on U.S. Highway 71 would pass a sign that reads, "Welcome to Fouke: A Community of Faith, Family, and Friends." This creature, however, has become something of a mascot for the community. After inspiring the popular docudrama horror film *The Legend of Boggy Creek* (1972), Fouke began hosting a local festival called "Monster Days" that was re-imagined in 2013 as The Fouke Monster Festival. Resident Rick Roberts turned an ordinary gas station near the center of town into "The Monster Mart"—which is impossible to miss as one drives through Fouke on highway 71. The Monster Mart houses a museum where visitors can see casts of the monster's footprints, newspaper clippings, and other relics. Eventually, the stretch of 71 that runs through Fouke was officially renamed "Monster Expressway." Held during the height of the COVID-19 pandemic, the 2020 Fouke Monster Festival featured a moment of silence for the victims—which included the current owner of the Monster Mart's brother-in-law—and a plethora of jokes about Sasquatch "social distancing" in the swamp.

Times of crisis often inspire monsters to take on "pinch-hitting," doing the work of gods. Early in the COVID-19 pandemic, Japanese children and adults alike painted, drew, or otherwise formed depictions of Amabie—a chimeric *yokai* or supernatural being with three legs and a bird's beak. According to legend, Amabie arose from the sea and declared that those who looked upon a picture of her in the midst of a pandemic would be cured of their illness. As the novel coronavirus spread across Japan and cities were forced into lockdown, many began taking Amabie at her word, drawing her image. Not only were such images posted on doorways and in windows, but it became common to share drawings on Twitter and other social media. Within the course of a few weeks, Amabie had become a sort of mascot or collective spirit for those suffering from the confusion, pain, and fear of the pandemic.

The poet Ogden Nash wrote, "Where there's a monster, there's a miracle." After our visit to the Fouke Monster Festival, we were no more certain about the alleged existence of a species of great ape living undiscovered in North America than when we arrived. But we did observe rituals to honor the dead, the acquisition of material sacra, and bigfoot hunters recounting their personal experiences with things that filled them with both terror and awe. Above all, the festival seemed concerned with an almost totemic creature and what Mircea Eliade called (1963, 192) "the sacred history of the tribe." Perhaps we overlook these details of monster culture because we prefer the dichotomy between gods and monsters to be crisp and clear, unlike the murky swamps and waters from which the Fouke Monster and Amabie emerge.

All of these entities and the traditions that surround them are fodder for the essential questions that motivate this book: How can monster theory enhance religious studies? And what can religious studies offer to the burgeoning field of monster studies? Despite the long list of books that currently fall within the realm of "monster theory" the seminal text of the field is still Jeffrey Jerome Cohen's 1996 essay "Monster Culture (Seven Theses)." The reason for this is obvious: Cohen's essay is a *theory* of monsters—*all* monsters, from stigmatized foreigners to giants of the Middle Ages to giant ants of Cold War cinema—and the theses are written such that a scholar can readily deploy them to interpret whatever strange creature they have encountered. In fact, applying Cohen's theses to the Fouke Monster in the 1970s, the sudden devotion to Amabie in 2020, or the "barbaric" self-immolators of Tang Dynasty China would be a fairly simple exercise.

But religious studies is its own sort of monster—a chimeric mish-mash of various disciplines, and a reflection of the repressed hopes and fears of nineteenth-century Europeans. And so, more than twenty years after Cohen's watershed essay, we offer five *more* theses that can enhance and expand the conversation around the nebulous subject of "monsters." These theses draw from conversations at the 2019 "Gods and Monsters" Conference at Texas State University and the articles these scholars produced. Ultimately, they are meant to expand the theoretical tool-kit for thinking about those beings deemed "monsters" especially as they intersect with those beliefs and practices deemed "religious."

THESIS I: MONSTERS ARE A SECOND-ORDER CATEGORY

In the preface to his study of monsters, anthropologist David D. Gilmore (2003, ix) writes, "Monsters share certain characteristics no matter where they appear; they are always aggressive, gigantic, man-eating, malevolent, bizarre in shape, gruesome, atavistic, powerful and gratuitously violent." We dissent from such a universal definition of monsters as many of the entities explored in this book do not meet all or even most of these criteria. Wafi Momin's contribution to this volume discusses the Daityas and Dānavas of Hindu mythology, who, while they are often described as "demons," resemble the gods and can be either sinister or virtuous. Are they monsters? Stefan Sanchez interprets Chicana writer Gloria Evangelina Anzaldúa's experience of being inhabited by a "Shadow-Beast," a part of herself that seeks survival at all costs. Is the Shadow-Beast a monster? For that matter, is Anzaldúa herself a monster by virtue of her visionary experiences and her marginalized social status?

Perhaps a better question is, "Who has the authority to declare something a monster?" Cryptozoologists assume that what the layman experiences as a "monster" is actually an undiscovered animal to the initiated. In the film *Jurassic Park* (1993) when a teenage girl cries, "Don't let the monsters come over here," paleontologist Alan Grant reminds her, "They're not monsters, Lex, They're just animals." Conversely, it has long been recognized in the history of religions that one person's god is another person's monster. Of his trip to the holy city of Benares, Mark Twain wrote, "The town is a vast museum of idols—and all of them crude, misshapen, and ugly. They flock through one's dreams at night, a wild mob of nightmares" (Quoted in Eck 1998, 18). Although Twain did not explicitly use the word "monster" here, "nightmare" seems sufficient: Hinduism, for Twain, is a kind of "monster-olatry."

So how do we apply the monster theory when there is no definition of a monster and when the monstrous status of these entities is often contested? This question mirrors a well-known problem in religious studies—in fact *the* problem in religious studies: What constitutes "religion?" Furthermore, what business do scholars have going about slapping the label of "religion" onto the beliefs and practices of other cultures where such a category has not existed? One of the most enduring answers to this problem comes from J. Z. Smith (1998, 281–2) in his essay "Religion, Religions, Religious" in which he concludes: "'Religion' is not a native term; it is a term created by scholars for their intellectual purposes and therefore theirs to define. It is a second-order generic concept that plays the same role in establishing a disciplinary horizon that a concept such as 'language' plays in linguistics or 'culture' plays in anthropology. There can be no disciplined study of religion without such a horizon."

Monsters, then, are what monster theorists study! This sounds tautological. In fact, it echoes the final sentence of Cohen's (1997, 20) essay in which he asserts that monsters invariably confront us to demand "why we have created them." So why designate something a monster? There is only one legitimate reason for a monster theorist to call something a monster and that is as a basis for setting up a comparison between various entities. In a different essay, Smith (1990, 51) explains, "Comparison, in its strongest form, brings differences together within the space of the scholar's mind for the scholar's own intellectual reasons. It is the scholar who makes their cohabitation—their 'sameness'—possible, not 'natural' affinities or processes of history."

"Monster," therefore, is an organizing principle that brings together the various entities and traditions examined in this book (and the assorted scholars who study them). By deploying the category "monster" in this way and setting up this comparison any number of fascinating insights may arise. But the comparison is still *our* doing: The monster theorist must take responsibility for any "sameness" she perceives in the beings she studies. We all know what happens when those who make monsters refuse to take responsibility for their creations.

THESIS II: MONSTERS IMPLY AND (PARADOXICALLY) PRESERVE CATEGORIES

Not only can the designation "monster" serve as a basis of comparison but to call something a "monster"—both in popular usage and in the theoretical sense—is to imply a comparison with the typical, the quotidian, and the normal. For Gilmore (2003, 174), the sin qua non of monsters is that they are larger than they ought to be: "No matter how monsters differ otherwise, no matter where they appear, monsters are vastly, grotesquely oversized." Accepting this criterion for the sake of argument, something can only be a monster in comparison to some non-monstrous analog that is appropriately sized: The term "monster truck" is only meaningful if we have some understanding of what constitutes a reasonably sized truck. Other criteria of monsters are likewise comparative: They have too many heads or too few eyes compared to a "normal" specimen. To call a serial killer a "monster" likewise implies a lack of something—a conscience or a soul—in comparison to other human beings. Thus, whatever criteria of monstrousness are invoked, they are nearly always dependent on some preexisting category.

Furthermore, the "monster" frequently functions to preserve and reify those categories to which it is adjacent and from which it is excluded. Cohen's (1997, 6) third thesis states, "The Monster is the Harbinger of Category Crisis." For Cohen the monster is "a form suspended between forms that threatens to smash distinctions." In our reading of Cohen, these beings do not threaten distinctions because they are monsters; they are deemed monsters because they threaten distinctions. To quote Smith (2004, 269) yet again, "The 'other' emerges only as a theoretical issue when it is perceived as challenging a complex and intact world-view. It is only then that the 'different' becomes the problematic 'alien.'" The monster resolves the problem of the other by sweeping outliers off the table and quarantining them from the categories that they challenge: What the "No Good Scotsman" argument does to preserve a claim, the monster does to preserve a taxonomy. Accordingly, when someone labels something (or someone) a monster, we should ask ourselves what categories they are seeking to preserve.

What then of chimeras that appear to totally defy categories? Cohen cites the creature from *Alien* (1979) as an entity that resists any zoological taxonomy. We suggest that even the most imaginative monsters, paradoxically, function to reinforce a preexisting worldview. This is the function of monsters theorized by Victor Turner in his study of frightening masks used in tribal initiation rites in Africa. Previous theorists assumed these masks creatively confounded features of humans and animals because these "primitive" people "drew little distinction" between themselves and animals. In other words, monsters manifested in their culture because the categories that they used to understand themselves were weak and nebulous. Turner (1967, 105) writes, "My own view is the opposite one: that monsters are manufactured precisely to teach neophytes to distinguish clearly between the different factors of reality, as it is conceived in their culture." In explaining this theory, Turner quotes William James, "What is associated now with one thing and now with another tends to become dissociated from either, and to grow into an object of abstract contemplation by the mind. One might call this the law of dissociation by varying concomitants." Thus tribal monster masks are not an admission of weak boundaries between humans and animals; by associating horns, claws, roaring, or howling first with animals, then with monsters, the abstract concept of "animal-ness" becomes further reified and distinct from the human.

Let us return to the monster from *Alien,* which Harvey Greenberg (1991, 90) dubbed "a Linnaean nightmare" because its bizarre biology and parasitic lifecycle would have confounded Carl Linnaeus, the eighteenth-century father of biological taxonomy. But imagine an edgy life science teacher screening this film in conjunction with a lecture on the phyla of the animal kingdom. Would the students conclude that the creature proves biological categories are arbitrary and meaningless? Or would the mental exercise of trying to pin down the creature, or sort out its features into categorizable components, become a rehearsal for thinking about the world through the lens of biological taxonomy? This is the paradox: it seems possible for monsters to inculcate and entrench categories even as they appear to challenge them.

Finally, what of monsters that are truly "wholly other." Lovecraft's Cthulhu, for example, is so alien that his lair of R'lyeh is not even subject to the laws of Euclidian geometry. Can beings of pure chaos reify order? Well, technically, yes. These beings point to the most significant categorical distinction of all—that between worldly and otherworldly, knowable and unknowable, profane and sacred. For such theorists as Eliade and Durkheim, this separation between sacred and profane was the very essence of religion. Even when monsters transgress these boundaries, they paradoxically demonstrate their realness. This is why monsters that inspire awe are often the most interesting to scholars of religion. Cthulhu is what Eliade called a "hierophany"—an eruption of the sacred into our realm (Beal 2002, 183).

THESIS III: MONSTERS ARE PHENOMENOLOGICALLY ACTUAL

Cohen's first thesis states, "The Monster's Body Is a Cultural Body" (1997, 4). This may be good and well for analyzing fantastic creatures from horror films or folk tales. But what about Bobby Ford who was treated for shock at a Texarkana hospital after a monster attempted to break into his home? (Blackburn 2012, 59). Were the Fords firing their shotguns at a "cultural body?"

Jeffrey Kripal has analyzed the experiences of Whitley Strieber, whose encounters with beings he calls "visitors" in 1985 sparked a nation-wide interest in alien abduction. Kripal (2014, 898) vents his frustration with monster theory in making sense of the visitors:

> Enter "monster theory," which looks at the narratives and images of the monster throughout Western history as a kind of recurring deconstruction and reconstruction of cultural and social categories. Here the monster is taken seriously, but only, as far as I can tell, as an unconscious Foucauldian discourse, Derridean deconstruction, or postmodern materialism.

Kripal, of course, does not believe that Strieber encountered literal extraterrestrials (Strieber has no firm theory as to what the visitors actually are) or that a Sasquatch will one day be discovered in the swamps near Fouke. But he does call attention to the fact these entities are "phenomenologically actual" and that people who experience these encounters are sometimes never the same. Kripal frames Strieber's experience as a "litmus test" for religious studies: If we cannot produce a satisfactory interpretation of his encounter in 1985, how can we interpret Teresa of Avila's vision of being impaled by an angel or Lingza Chökyi's fearful encounter with the Buddhist Lord of the Hell during her supposed death and resurrection? As Kripal (2014, 907) puts it "We either put up here, or we shut up there."

Monster theorists must acknowledge that many of the entities they examine are *experienced* daily by people all over the world. These experiences are not always a life-altering encounter like those described by Strieber. Often they manifest in the imagination as a feeling of dread or wonder. At the Fouke Monster Festival, bigfoot hunter Jerry Hestand of the North American Wood Ape Conservancy told the audience, "It's all good and fine talking about it here in the daytime. When you're in the woods at night, it's scary. You'll hear an armadillo or something out there in the dark." Hestand was being very honest in divorcing his intellectual understanding of what lurked in the dark from the experience itself. Daily experiences of monsters often have this quality of being real and unreal simultaneously.

Robert Orsi (2016, 159) articulates this sense of nonhuman entities as both real and unreal in his discussion of *The Exorcist:*

> What makes *The Exorcist*, written by Catholic, Jesuit-educated William Peter Blatty, so terrifying for Catholics brought up in the middle years of the century is their—*our*: I have never been able to bring myself to see the film—deeply embodied sense of the really realness of the supernatural, good and evil. In this sense and in this context, *The Exorcist* was a documentary, "based on a true story," as Catholic gossip at the time maintained, rather than a work of fiction, although of course Catholics also knew it was fiction.

Orsi's explanation that the demon portrayed in *The Exorcist* is "really real" is a needed corrective to a massive body of literature in horror studies that assumes the actual concerns of this film are "domestic, psychosexual, and biological" (Badley 1995, 44). While the film may serve as a metaphor for social anxieties or be laden with certain psychoanalytical dynamics, for many audiences, it is a film about the human encounter with a demonic reality. (For more on this problem and how religious studies might breathe new life into horror studies, see Brandon Grafius's essay in this volume.)

This call not to explain away the demon serves as metonymy for Orsi's argument in *History and Presence* that religious cultures consist of webs of relationships between human beings and the "extra-human" (saints, gods, ancestors, etc.) whose sacred presence is experienced. Orsi (2016, 64) warns against historiography that tries to interpret religious cultures while bracketing out the gods:

> Constraints on the scholar's imagination become, by means of his or her scholarship, constraints on the imagination of others, specifically those whose lives the scholar aims to represent and understand. There is a double intellectual tragedy here, for once their reality is constrained by ours, they no longer have the capacity to enlarge our understandings or our imaginations. This is the price of ontological safety.

This warning about ontological safety applies double when religious studies intersects with monster theory. As Orsi (2016, 29) states, "Presence is a fearsome thing."

The answer, we feel, cannot be to accept reports of monsters at face value or to retreat to a position of epistemological nihilism in which making sense of these narratives is impossible. Rather we suggest that when looking at the kinds of encounters discussed by Kripal, monster theorists should seek an approach that Orsi calls "the tradition of the more." In his essay, "The problem of the holy" Orsi (2012, 90) rejects the notion that what Rudolf Otto called "the holy" is sui generis and affirms that it is a function of cultural formation. At the same time, there is a remainder to this experience that these interpretations cannot capture that Orsi calls the "2 + 2 = 5 factor" of religious experience. This "more" challenges the authority of naturalistic explanations and without attending to it the theorist cannot really understand her object of study. While not all objects of monster theory possess this 2 + 2 = 5 factor, many of them do. Certainly, monster theorists in the field of religious studies should consider the phenomenological realities of these entities and practice some epistemological modesty in interpreting them.

THESIS IV: MONSTERS CAN BE THE CENTER OR THE PERIPHERY

At the Fouke Monster Festival, we met Jay "Smokey" Crabtree. Jay was a celebrity at the festival because his father, J. E. "Smokey" Crabtree, had one of the most famous encounters with the monster and played himself in *The Legend of Boggy Creek*. In a recorded interview from a previous festival, Jay stated, "Let's be honest, this [the monster legend] is the only reason anybody comes here." Like many small-town cryptids, the monster has now become a source of local pride, identity, and of course, tourism dollars for Fouke, Arkansas. A nearly identical transformation took place in Point Pleasant, West Virginia, where a bridge disaster in 1967 that killed forty-six people was preceded by dozens of sightings of a bipedal winged entity dubbed "The Mothman." Today, Point Pleasant features an enormous bronze statue of the Mothman in the center of town, and its annual Mothman Festival has inspired several small towns with local monster legends and struggling economies to follow suit. Michael E. Heyes (2020, 47) writes that "on some level, Mothman *is* Point Pleasant."

This use of the monster as a source of communal identity is nothing new. Gilmore notes the "festival dragons" of France and Spain, which are loved and revered as well as feared. The French town of Tarascón takes its local dragon legend—the Tarasque—as a source of civic pride (Gilmore 2003, 193). In his classic study of totemism, Durkheim (1995, 380) describes Wollunqua, a mythical snake so large that its head is lost in the clouds: "But although Wollunqua differs in some respects from ordinary totems, still he has all the distinguishing features of one. He serves as a collective name and emblem for the whole group of individuals who see him as their common ancestor." We could just as easily say that the Fouke Monster, Mothman, and the Tarasque have likewise become totems for their respective communities. Or as Heyes (2020, 46) puts it, "Clearly, monsters can be on the inside looking out just as much as on the outside looking in."

We agree with Heyes that this function of monsters has been overlooked because theories of monsters tend to focus exclusively on fear and horror, assuming monsters to be outsiders and agents of chaos rather than sources of identity, community, and order. If we can accept the categorization of a giant snake-ancestor as a monster, than Wollunqua is the opposite of a "chaos monster." During the dreamtime, Wollunqua traveled the world sowing "spirit-children" that are currently incarnated as human beings. Indeed, Durkheim theorizes Wollunqua was invented to give a common ancestor to the Uluuru phratry, most of whose tribal groups had various species of snake as their totems: As a "super snake totem," Wollunqua exists to embody social harmony.

But our other examples of totemic monsters *were* scary until they weren't. Mothman and the Fouke Monster were absolutely terrifying to witnesses when sightings of these creatures first began (as indicated in police reports from Point Pleasant in 1967 and Fouke in 1971.) And in some versions of the Tarasque legend, the monster is ravaging the countryside until Saint Martha charms it using holy water and *leads it into the city*, where the people of Tarascón slaughter it (Ingersoll 1999, 171). Today, the dragon appears on the city's coat of arms, using one of its six limbs to shove a peasant into its mouth. So there is a tendency for monsters to begin on the periphery and move toward the center: outsiders are transformed into insiders and monsters become gods.

This transformation of the monster parallels—on a communal scale—the sort of transformation experienced by Whitley Strieber as his understanding of the visitors changed from demonic antagonists and violators to transcendent beings bringing *gnosis*. Here the two faces of the monster become interchangeable in what Kripal (2014, 907) calls "the traumatic-transcendent." But it was Otto who first noted a connection not only between fear and transcendence but also between the phenomenological experience of demonic dread and the sociological phenomenon of a moral community. He (1923, 140–1) wrote, "Whence comes this most surprising of all the facts in the history of religion, that beings, obviously born originally of horror and terror, become *gods*—beings to whom men pray, to whom they confide their sorrow or their happiness, in whom they behold the origin and the sanction of morality, law, and the whole canon of justice?" It is good to remember this the next time we see a television interview with a shaken witness describing their sighting of a creature that should not exist: Today's terrifying encounter with "the wholly other" may be tomorrow's social and moral order!

THESIS V: MONSTERS HAVE SOCIAL CONSEQUENCES

Sociologists William and Dorothy Thomas (1928, 594) wrote, "If men define situations as real, they are real in their consequences." On September

23, 1954, police were summoned to the Southern Necropolis Cemetery in Glasgow because hundreds of children armed with stakes and knives were swarming the graves. The youths said they were searching for "a vampire with iron teeth" that had already eaten two children. Even after police intervention, the vampire hunting continued for another two nights. According to a retrospective that appeared in *The Scotsman* on March 18, 2016, many blamed the behavior on an American horror comic called "The Vampire with Iron Teeth." (Others countered that a beast with iron teeth also appears in Dn 7:7.) In response Parliament passed the Children and Young Person's (Harmful Publication) Act of 1955, restricting what content may appear in children's comics. The law is still on the books today.

The so-called "Gorbals vampire" incident—which has since inspired a play and a mural—was hardly an isolated phenomenon. Folklorist Bill Ellis (2000, 207) notes that it occurred in the same neighborhood where large crowds gathered in the 1930s to hunt for Spring-Heeled Jack (an entity further discussed in this volume by Blake Smith.) Similar vampire hunts famously occurred in North London's Highgate Cemetery between 1963 and 1974. In the wake of sightings of Mothman and the Fouke Monster, there were also large-scale monster hunts with armed hunters searching the wilderness. Like the children in the Glasgow cemetery, these hunts seem to have been driven more by curiosity and fun than public safety concerns, but they disrupted the ordinary patterns of life (and certainly inspired hoaxing). Joseph Laycock (2009) has suggested that monster hunting elicited a kind of Durkheimian "collective effervescence" that contributed to Mothman assuming his role as the town's totem.

But what happens when the hunters are adults in deadly earnest and the "monsters" being hunted are people? This, of course, was the case with the long history of anti-Semitism, the witch-trials of early modern Europe, and the persecution of daycare workers during the Satanic Panic of the 1980s and 1990s. It is also the case with contemporary "QAnon" conspiracy theorists, who claim that Donald Trump is waging an invisible war against a cabal of "deep state" Satanic pedophiles. An FBI memo from May 30, 2019, identified extremists driven by these conspiracy theories as a domestic terrorism threat.

These kinds of moral panics are perhaps the best argument for why monster theory matters. Significantly for religious studies, the most dangerous monster hunters are invariably seeking monsters whom they perceive as the religious other, motivated by a nightmarish parody of religious ritual. David Frankfurter (2011, 83–4) writes, "Lynching, burning, dismemberment, gassing, torture, drowning, exposure, cremation—these are the methods that follow when we conjure evil cults. These are the acts, I would argue, that have historically followed when a community 'awakened' to some evil conspiracy."

But the social consequences that result from the appearance of monsters (or rumors of monsters) are not uniformly bad. In his famous study, Timothy Beal (2002, 6) draws a distinction between "demonized" monsters and "deified" monsters. Demonized monsters challenge the social order but paradoxically reinforce it as the community rallies against them. "Deified" monsters appear as a manifestation of the transcendent or the holy that calls the accepted order into question. Natasha Mikles (2020) has discussed how the experience of Returners—Tibetan individuals who reportedly die, descend to hell to view its horrors, and return to publicly share their tale—forces a re-evaluation of readers' and listeners' categories of monstrosity through the Returner's encounter with the "deified" underworld lord Yama. The appearance of deified monsters, therefore, functions similarly to historical moments that Orsi calls "an abundant event." An abundant event consists of a "density of relationships" between humans and extra-human presences in which the imagination becomes "unlocked" and the givenness of the "real" can be called into question. Consider the following passage:

> In the presence of this figure, people's imaginations become larger and more efficacious in their actions upon the world. . . . Much becomes possible that otherwise was not. Time may becomes fluid. Past / present / future, as they are, as they are hoped for, and as they are dreaded may converge. Spatial boundaries, between here and there, oneself and another, may give way. Relationships also come under the power of the unlocked imagination, relationships between heaven and earth, between the living and the dead, among persons as they are and persons as they are desired to be by themselves and others. In the abundant event and all that follows it, a certain kind of intersubjective receptivity and recognition may become possible, on earth and between heaven and earth, an awareness of being seen and known, of seeing and knowing, so focused that in certain circumstances it may seem intrusive and threatening; in others, deeply compassionate and supportive. (Orsi 2016, 67)

"The figure" here is the Virgin Mary and Marian apparitions such as those at Lourdes and Fatima are Orsi's prime example of an abundant event. But he could just as easily be talking about the presence of Strieber's visitors who likewise unlock time and precipitate a "density of relationships." Kripal (2014, 915) notes that many people report encountering the dead during their abduction experiences. Aliens may be the most prominent example of contemporary monsters that "unlock the imagination." This is why the presence of these beings—as experienced by various contactees—has led to the formation of numerous "UFO religions" such as the Aetherius Society, the Raelians, and Heaven's Gate.

Exorcism is likewise an "abundant event" in which the presence of a demon elicits a web of relationships (both between exorcist and demoniac and between the divine and demonic forces whose presence are felt) (Laycock 2020). This glimpse of the transcendent following the manifestation of a demon is what Blatty (1974, 10) meant when he said his novel was about "the mystery of goodness." This ability of exorcism to elicit a re-assessment of reality is also why the practice lends itself to all manner of political agendas and projects of social control (Possamai 2014).

TO A NEW WORLD OF GODS AND MONSTERS

Not all monsters have two parents, but many do. The Tarasque was said to be the offspring of the Biblical Leviathan and another creature called Onachus. In the Prose Edda, Loki and the giantess Angrboða sire the Fenris wolf, the Midgard Serpent, and Hel, ruler of the underworld. The chapters that follow are likewise the terrible and wonderful spawn of monster theory and religious studies. In the preface to the 1831 edition of *Frankenstein*, Mary Wollstonecraft Shelley (xii) wrote, "And now once again I bid my hideous progeny go forth and prosper." We do the same in the hopes that upon confronting these strange beasts the reader will experience a transformative encounter, or at least discover an interesting specimen for further study.

Chapter 2

Reiterations

On Tellings, Variants, and Why Monsters Always Come Back

Douglas E. Cowan

Consider the myth of the happy ending.

One of the most common misconceptions of the horror genre is that things turn out alright in the end: the monster is destroyed, the evil spirit banished, the alien ships are shot down. Always double-tap, life goes on, and hope springs eternal. Though not writing about horror movies specifically, for example, religious studies scholar Darrol Bryant argues that "the profoundly spiritual significance of film" is precisely this return to normalcy, the movement from chaos and confusion to the "experience of order and harmony" (1982, 112). Surveying Stephen King's *oeuvre* (at least pre–*Pet Sematary*), literary critic Deborah Notkin concludes that among all the monstrous uncertainties of everyday life, King's work "sounds a note of hope to counter them," to remind us that "hope is never lost" (1982, 142). In fact, for her, this enduring sense of hope constitutes King's "primary theme" (142). And, finally, in *Danse Macabre*, which still holds up as one of the premier surveys of the American horror genre, King himself writes that "it's this feeling of reintegration, arising from a field specializing in death, fear, and monstrosity, that makes the danse macabre so rewarding" (2010, 14). Although all three authors wrote these words more than a generation ago—in King's case, long before such novels as *Desperation* (1996), *Duma Key* (2008), *Under the Dome* (2009), and *Revival* (2014), storyworlds that explicitly challenge any notion of a happy ending—the necessity of a felicitous return to consensus reality retains a strong hold on interpreters of horror culture.

There's just one problem. It doesn't happen to be true.

It, whatever *it* is, always comes back.

Indeed, lest we make too much of what we might call the happy ending fallacy, especially in terms of King's work, it's worth paying attention to what he wrote in *Danse Macabre* just a few pages prior. "I believe that we are all ultimately alone," he declares, "and that any deep and lasting human contacts are nothing more or less than a necessary illusion" (2010, 12)—an illusion that keeps us reaching out for connection, to be sure, but illusory nonetheless. The Losers' Club may have formed in the face of Henry Bowers, and, whether in the childhood timeline or the adult, battled. It together in the sewers beneath Derry, but eventually each of its members must go their own way—alone. Here, King sounds a note much more in keeping with one of his most prominent literary influences, H. P. Lovecraft, whose own best-known story opens with the words: "The most merciful thing in the world, I think, is the inability of the human mind to correlate all its contents" (1928, 139). If we knew how bad things really were, the dark prophet of Providence warns, it would surely drive us mad. Thus, "darkness," for which, in this context, we can easily substitute *fear*, "is our natural condition. Light is the intruder, a temporary island of security in a larger, largely uncharted ocean of dark" (Cowan 2018, 264). This is one of the principal reasons why It always comes back.

This chapter looks at the monstrous *It* through the lens of its reiterations, its two differing versions, and asks, among other things, what is gained and what is lost when a novel as long, intense, and intricate as *It* adapted and necessarily abridged for the screen. What happens to the monsters when they are in front of us, rather than the products of our imagination? More than that, though, it considers the issue of reiteration in the larger context of King's work. While this chapter focuses mainly on *It*, discussing any of King's work in abstraction or isolation is a mistake. Over forty years of novels and short fiction, he has not written *stories*, so much as he has created genre-bending, densely interconnected *storyworlds*, a narrative constellation held together by the gravity of similar concerns, common locations, and, more than anything else, a commitment to asking questions rather than providing answers.

Many horror writers and directors thrive on the suspense generated by making readers and audiences wait for the monstrous reveal, by keeping questions alive while the answers remain obscured. The moment whatever it is that scares us finally steps out from the shadows and into the light, the glimmer of an answer is revealed. Indeed, for philosopher Noël Carroll, this is one of the main reasons for the persistent popularity of horror: our ongoing need to solve the mystery, to find the answer, to see what happens in the end (1990). Shirley Jackson's *The Haunting of Hill House* ([1959] 2006) and Ridley Scott's *Alien* (1979), which is basically a haunted house movie set in space, are both master classes in this technique. (Full disclosure: Scott's opus remains my favorite movie of all time, while Jackson's novel is the only one

I've had to put down at night—*It* included—afraid that I wouldn't be able to sleep.) Lovecraft's "At the Mountains of Madness" ([1936] 2001), on the other hand, builds tension in the story only so long as the Shuggoths and the Mi-Go are not in the literary frame, as long as they leave us wondering, questioning. Once the otherworldly monsters are revealed, the horrific *frisson* Lovecraft so extravagantly created simply evaporates before the answer they represent.

While the gradual reveal and its narrative sidekick, foreshadowing, are time-honored techniques in horror, they are often overdone, precisely because they give too much of the answer away. This is what happens every time you watch a movie trailer and come away thinking you've seen the best of the film, or figure out the gist of the plot from the back cover of a paperback novel. In a great many of his works, including *It*, Stephen King operates in a very different register. He tells us exactly what's going to happen, more often than not *how* it's going to happen, and then dares us to follow him anyway. That which we think is the answer is only the deadfall we must cross to get to the deeper questions.

In *Pet Sematary*, for example, a story King himself considered too horrifying to publish when it was first written, we know the essence of the plot from the moment Louis Creed tries to save poor Vic Paskow to the first mention of Route 15, the busy highway that runs just a few yards from the Creed family's new home in Ludlow, Maine ([1983] 2006, ix–xiii). We know that two-year-old Gage Creed is going to die, crushed beneath the wheels of a truck "so big and long that for a moment Louis couldn't see his house across the road" (1983, 20). We know what's going to happen at the Miqmaq burying ground, the place beyond the deadfall. We know all this, and we follow King anyway—because we're still asking "How can this possibly happen? And what does it mean?" Notwithstanding its rather naked plea for a sequel in the final scene, the 2019 big-screen adaptation of *Pet Sematary* changed the original story in what is arguably the most fundamental way possible. While the death of any child is a nightmare, by choosing to sacrifice an adolescent to the narrative rather than the toddler—Ellie, played by twelve-year-old Jeté Lawrence, dies on the road rather than her little brother Gage—directors Kevin Kölsch and Dennis Widmyer altered the one thing that made King tuck the manuscript in a drawer, and vow never to take it out again.

This brings us to the issue of tellings, variants, and why It always comes back.

As I have written elsewhere, "following the work of folklorist A. K. Ramanujan (1991), a *telling* describes a story for which we have no identifiable *ur*-text, while *versions* or *variants* describe storyworlds for which there is an established original" (2019, 32). Although, for example, their respective plots are separated by three-and-a-half centuries, *The Blair Witch*

Project (1999) and *The Witch* (2015) are both clearly *tellings* of the Hansel and Gretel story. It is true that particular cultural iterations of famous fairy tales become canonical, often in our culture through their saccharine and bowdlerized Disney adaptations (see Cowan, 2019, 37–49). The point, though, is that we have no unambiguous original to which any later Hansel and Gretel telling can be definitively compared. On the other hand, while redemption stories and coming-of-age tales are as old as our history as *Homo narrans*, Rob Reiner's *Stand By Me* (1986) and Frank Darabont's *The Shawshank Redemption* (1994) are *versions* or *variants*, because both have recognized sources on which they are based and to which they can be profitably compared. For the former, it is King's novella, "The Body," while for the latter, it's "Rita Hayworth and the Shawshank Redemption," both from the *Different Seasons* collection (1992). More on the latter below. This distinction between tellings and variants is important because of the analytical approaches it suggests, the distinctive questions each poses for interpreters, and the critical limitations that are distinct to each. This is particularly useful for an author such as King, both in terms of his prodigious literary corpus, and for the innumerable adaptations of his work.

More than anything, *tellings* often involve us in a hunt for the *ur*-text, as though getting "back to the original" will somehow solve the interpretive problem of the story. It won't, but that isn't the point. If we consider stories as social phenomena—and in terms of the way they circulate and are recirculated as part of popular culture, we certainly should—we have to bear in mind one of Émile Durkheim's most basic *Rules of Sociological Method*. That is, "when one undertakes to explain a social phenomenon, the efficient cause which produces it and the function it fulfills must be investigated separately" (1982, 123). Indeed, as classics scholar Eric Csapo points out, "Origins do not explain why any event or experience"—or, in this case, the literary origin of any particular Stephen King story—"was considered significant enough to merit so many retellings. What has to be explained is not the event behind the myth, but the criteria of social selection, and not the moment of conception, but the process of preservation" (2005, 161–2). That is, what a story meant originally is not what it means now.

If the monster is really gone, why continue to tell the story?

Conversely, precisely because they have an identifiable source text, *variants* present us with three fascinating analytical problems. First, there is the temptation to engage in fidelity criticism, something that is especially true with a beloved literary antecedent such as *It*. Next, when we are faced with televised or cinematic adaptations of this literary text—or, as in *It*'s case, with both, though separated by nearly a generation—the question often becomes one of the "authorized version," which one is "correct," a process that highlights, among other things, the prominence of the visual over the literary in our culture. Deriving from these, finally, is the analytical power of difference, the magic of comparison as a way of tramping deeper into the barrens of our horror story favorites. Let's consider each of these in order.

From dismal attempts that reduce a high fantasy masterwork like *The Dark Tower* (2017) to a ninety-minute run-and-gun (Yes, I'm talking about *you*, Nikolaj Arcel) to equally dismal efforts by King himself to bring his work to the screen (think *Maximum Overdrive* [1986]), or from films that have been nominated for the industry's highest honors (*The Shawshank Redemption*, *The Green Mile* [1999]) to those that occupy beloved spots as "one of the creepiest movies we've ever seen" (*Misery* [1990]. Full stop), arguably no modern author has been adapted for television and cinema more often, or less consistently, than Stephen King. Although it seems as though his views have softened in recent years, it's well known that King himself despised Stanley Kubrick's adaptation of *The Shining* (1980). Kubrick added a number of elements to the story (e.g., the famous "blood-fall in the elevator" scene, and the "All work and no play" text on Jack's typewriter), while he changed others so drastically that, for many fans, the entire story was rendered almost meaningless. Instead of sacrificing himself in the boiler room so that his family can escape the malign influence of the Overlook, Jack dies in the hotel's hedge maze, his face locked in a frozen rictus as he tries to kill Danny. As with *Pet Sematary*, there is no more fundamental way to change the story of Jack Torrance. "Movies do not 'ruin' books," write John Tibbetts and James Welsh in their introduction to *The Encyclopedia of Novels into Film*, so much as they "misrepresent them" (xix; see Cartmell 2012; Desmond and Hawkes 2006)—although it's also clear that Tibbetts and Welsh believe many books have been ruined in just that way.

Put simply, fidelity criticism compares later variants of a particular story to their common original, and interrogates the differences. For many of those who pursue this kind of criticism, however, because we have an identifiable original, the belief is that this antecedent should always control the ways in which later versions and variants are allowed to interpret the text. The novel, short story, poem, what-have-you is expected to provide the limit case for artistic license on the part of screenwriters and directors. Thus, in practice, fidelity criticism is often little more than a matter of measuring the movie against the book, and noting where the filmmakers have inevitably fallen short. Indeed, "in this instance, the goal is usually to demonstrate the superiority of the literary original over the cinematic imitation" (Cowan 2019, 33).

Fidelity criticism of this kind, though, essentially asks the impossible. Faithfully reproducing an author's vision of the text, never mind in a manner that will accurately reflect the numberless ways in which fans have imagined their favorite stories, is, quite simply a Sisyphean task. If you doubt this, ask yourself how many times you've groaned aloud when a film studio or television network announced who is (or isn't) going play this or that character in the next iteration of your favorite franchise. It's well known, for example, that Ann Rice was *not* happy when Tom Cruise was cast as the vampire Lestat, and the interview with Rice that was included with some DVD versions of the film sounds more like special pleading than an honest attempt to clear the air. And, as though anyone needs reminding, *It* is a *very* long, very detailed book that includes a number of intricate, interconnected storylines. My mass-market copy is nearly eleven hundred, almost onionskin-thin pages long, each crammed with what seems at times like impossibly tiny print. By definition, filmmakers can't include everything. In *It*, for example, two of the novel's most powerful scenes—the differences in the way Mike and Richie understand It's arrival in Derry (727–8), and King's brief cosmology of It (965–7)—are omitted entirely in both the miniseries and the films. Indeed, precisely because of these omissions, an important aspect of the novel—the religious socialization of the main characters, especially Mike, who attends the fundamentalist church on Neiboldt Street, and the ways in which this socialization inflects the different Loser's experiences of Pennywise—is ignored in the variants (see Cowan 2018, 73–4, 190–2). This is worth pointing out because it highlights the principal shortcoming of fidelity criticism: you can't please everyone, and, so, the question becomes: *should* the source text always control the ways in which it is adapted?

Try this thought experiment. If you've read *It*, and you read it before seeing either the television or film adaptation, pause here for a moment, and reflect on Pennywise. How did you imagine him? How did you picture him when you first read the novel? "There was a clown in the stormdrain," King writes simply, moments before little Georgie Denbrough disappears into that place where everything floats. "In fact he looked like a cross between Bozo and Clarabell ... there were funny tufts of red hair on either side of his bald head, and there was a big clown-smile painted over his mouth" (1980, 12). Did King's description become the essence of "the dancing clown" for you, or was it simply the canvas for your imagination, a hasty sketch, perhaps, filled in with splashes of color from the palette of your own coulrophobia? Now ask yourself how and whether this image of Pennywise changed when you saw him onscreen—played either by Tim Curry (1990) or Bill Skarsgård (2017).

As pattern-seeking creatures, we have evolved a number of cognitive "shortcuts" that serve our quest for survival as a species. Among these, the *availability heuristic* tells us that the more easily we can draw an example of something to mind, the more likely we are to think that thing either true or significant. If your introduction to Pennywise was through the novel, for instance, then his onscreen portrayals may be distinctly at odds with your own imagined clown. For me, Curry's Pennywise would have been significantly more menacing had he kept his native Cheshire accent (no Carrollian pun intended), rather than affect an American whiskey-and-cigarettes rasp. Skarsgård's drooling, wall-eyed interpretation of King's most famous villain, on the other hand, was quite simply terrifying, in no small measure because it added to the image of Pennywise that had already formed in my mind from the novel.

If a film or television adaptation cannot, perforce, do everything, asking what it *has* done with the story is only one part of the interpretive question. In its positive aspect, fidelity criticism encourages fans to compare the literary antecedent with its cinematic or broadcast siblings as a way of understanding the entirety of the story more deeply. Quite reasonably, both the 1990 miniseries and 2017 film focus on the relationships between the different members of the Losers' Club. Each does so, however, in a very different way.

Watching the miniseries, it's easy to imagine *It* as a story told in flashback. Certainly, that's the mise-en-scène established by director Tommy Lee Wallace. We are introduced to most of the characters as adults, and we learn something of their background and their desperate adventures that summer through a series of flashbacks. We don't quite see the famous *Scooby-Doo* "wobble transition" for each character, but it's close. Initially broadcast only two evenings apart (November 18 and 20), it would not be difficult for miniseries viewers to keep track of the character relationships, and maintain some sense of narrative continuity—especially since the miniseries was produced in the first flush of *It*'s literary popularity. If you've read the novel, however, and especially if you're a Stephen King fan for whom *It* remains one of the most engrossing reads ever, this flashback style could easily feel artificial. In its literary form, *It* is not a flashback story, but one of the parallel narratives. Indeed, these are almost parallel universes, separated by thirty years, but bridged by shared horror, recovered memory, and the dread certainty that It has come back.

Andy Muschietti and his screenwriting team of Chase Palmer, Cary Fukunaga, and Gary Dauberman chose to separate these chronologies, largely disambiguating the childhood narrative from the adult timeline, presenting the former as *It* in 2017, and the latter two years later as *It: Chapter Two* (2019). Critics were split on how successful that strategy turned out to be, but I was able to keep track only because I was familiar with all previous versions, and the flashbacks Muschietti included in *Chapter Two*. That is, maintaining a sense of narrative connection over a couple of days is one thing, trying to keep that same connection intact for two years—without having to devote an inordinate amount of time catching the audience up—was quite another.

The problem here is that it is all but axiomatic that, for many viewers, Muschietti's version will be their first introduction to Pennywise and the Losers' Club. King's prodigious output and his popularity have remained fairly steady throughout his career. Indeed, mistakenly thinking it something of a put-down at the time, Harold Bloom, the so-called dean of American literary criticism, concluded that "King will be remembered as a sociological phenomenon" (3). That is "he will be known for the fact that millions of people loved his books and found something meaningful in them" (Cowan, *America's Dark Theologian*, xi). Thus, it's worth remembering the dozens of his other novels and short stories, as well as their inevitable adaptations, have appeared since *It* first hit the bookshelves in mid-September 1986. It's not unlikely that many viewers who watched the miniseries from the family couch will be sitting in the theater with their own children as the latest version unreels. When I saw *It* in a packed theater in September 2017, a significant number of those in the audience had not yet been born when either the novel was released or the miniseries first broadcast. This was their primary encounter with the "clown in the stormdrain," something that brings us to the analytical problem of the authorized version.

One of my favorite Stephen King anecdotes, and one he clearly loves to tell, is recorded in the author's notes to *The Bazaar of Bad Dreams*. Sent to the store one day by his wife, novelist Tabitha King, as he searched for "batteries and a non-stick frypan," he was approached by an elderly woman. "She was a Florida snowbird archetype," he tells us, "about eighty, permed to perfection, and as darkly tanned as a cordovan shoe" (King 2015, 447). "'I know you,' she said. 'You're Stephen King. You write those scary stories. That's all right, some people like them, but not me. I like uplifting stories, like that *Shawshank Redemption*'" (King 2015, 447). We can only imagine King peering down from his towering height as he pondered how to respond. Eventually, he simply told her, "I wrote that too." "No, you didn't," she replied, before whirring off down the aisle on her motorized cart.

This is the problem of the authorized version.

It seems reasonable to suggest that more people will see a movie than read the novel on which it's based. Indeed, "given the supply-side nature of modern popular culture, it's almost axiomatic that, having seen the movies, millions of people around the world now feel no need to read the book" (Cowan 2019, 34). This isn't the case for all people, of course. Some will watch Skarsgård's Pennywise at their local cineplex, then download the novel to their mobile device while the car warms up in the theater parking lot. Others will scour basement shelves and dig through boxes in search of a dusty paperback copy they are sure they'd seen somewhere. Indeed, "one would like to believe," write Tibbetts and Welsh, "that movies might serve as a stimulus to reading—even if viewers end up reading the likes of Stephen King" (xx). They are clearly less than sanguine that about this, though, and herein lies one of the principal concerns of those committed to their form of fidelity criticism: that the beauty, grandeur, horror, choose-your-noun, of the literary forerunner will inevitably be rendered pale and ghostly no matter how well the product is rendered onscreen. For those who have not read, or do not read the novel, the film will, by default, become the "authorized version" of the story. Rather than simply take this approach with *It*, we can use it to interrogate many of King's storyworlds.

How many people watching the 2019 version of *Pet Sematary* would be surprised to learn that in the novel it's Gage who dies on Route 15, not Ellie, and that the story ends with Rachel Creed returning from the Miqmaq burying ground, rather than killing her husband at the base of the deadfall prior to a ghastly family reunion. "A cold hand fell on Louis's shoulder," King writes. "Rachel's voice was grating, full of dirt. '*Darling*,' it said" (1983, 562). That's it, that's how it ends—with a question rather than an answer. How many people would be shocked to learn that, however, iconic Jack Nicholson's film portrayal has become, the Jack Torrance of Stephen King's *The Shining* is really nothing like the Jack created by Stanley Kubrick. In the former, Jack arrives at the Outlook already seriously deranged, the latter charts his gradual descent into madness. "The problem becomes even more acute," as I point out in *Magic, Monsters, and Make-Believe Heroes*, "with revised or director's cut versions of popular films." Transiting for a moment from Derry, Maine, to a grimy Tatooine spaceport, "for those of us who thrilled to the original *Star Wars* in 1977, Han Solo (Harrison Ford) will always have shot first in the Mos Eisley bar, no matter how George Lucas digitally manipulated the scene when the film was rereleased a generation later" (2019, 35).

Which of these, then, is the correct variant, the right version, the real story, as it were? I want to suggest that this is the wrong question. Not just a little bit wrong, mind you, but entirely so. Among other things, it assumes that we are passive recipients in the storytelling process, a theoretical perspective that still occasionally lurches out of the grave to which it was quite rightly consigned decades ago. While the *storyworld* may exist on the page or the screen, the *story* takes place in the interstitial spaces between us and the book, the movie, the play, the videogame—you get the idea. Interpretation is never just about what we see. It's always an interaction between what is presented and what we bring to that space. It's the relationship we form with the text, whether that's "the scariest book I ever read" or a newly released film version of that same book. And, sometimes, it's not even the story elements themselves, but other, more emotional connections. For example, it's well known that the sewer entrance scenes in the 1990 *It* miniseries were filmed in Vancouver's famous Stanley Park, an area I know well from my own childhood, while the covered bridge featured in the 2017 film (known locally as the "Kissing Bridge") is just a few miles from where I live now, and lies along one of my regular motorcycle routes. King has often been criticized for the extraordinary, if mundane, detail in his work. Do we really need to know, for example, that it's "Blue Rhino propane" that many of his characters use to fire up their grills (e.g., *Bag of Bones*), rather than just "propane"? Yes, I think we do, because details such as these bind us to the story, they increase the everyday resonance, which allows the horrific questions to worm their way in almost unnoticed.

Which brings us to the power of difference and the magic of comparison.

"Comparison," writes historian of religions Jonathan Z. Smith, "has been chiefly an affair of the recollection of similarity. The chief explanation for the significance of comparison is contiguity" (1982, 21). That is, as pattern-making creatures, we have evolved to look for sameness, to rely on similarity as the background against which the threat of difference stands out. Because difference often makes us uncomfortable. Difference puts us on edge. Difference, we have learned, can kill us. This is precisely the "fifth-business" genius of Stephen King. He creates storyworlds in which everything is normal, unremarkable, routine to point of seeming humdrum—until one thing changes. "An invisible dome appears and cuts off a small Maine town (*Under the Dome*); a reclusive writer of genre fiction discovers an alien spacecraft buried for millennia on her property (*The Tommyknockers*); a strange, compelling figure arrives in town offering the one thing you think you need the most (*Needful Things*)" (Cowan 2018, 34). Or, as though we can hardly credit the sight, "There was a clown in the stormdrain" (King 1980, 12).

In one of his most oft-cited essays, "In Comparison a Magic Dwells," Smith encouraged scholars, critics, and commentators of all stripes to see the value of *difference* as an analytic tool, as a particularly useful way of looking at things, rather than an impediment to understanding them. For him, the significance of comparison lies in *explaining* the differences between versions and variants, not in simply pointing out their similarities and moving on, or complaining about their inconsistencies as though that solves the problem. "Comparison," he writes, "is, at base, never identity" and "requires the postulation of difference as the grounds of its being interesting" (Smith 1982, 35). This, finally, is why It always comes back.

"Swear to me," says Bill Denbrough, pleading with the other members of the Losers' Club after their final battle with It in the childhood timeline of the 1990 miniseries. "Swear to me that if it isn't dead, you'll all come back." In terms of what we might call *reiterations*, this simple, desperate request presents us with one of the principal realities of the horror mode, and what many would argue is one of its main attractions: the horror that appears and reappears—whether, for example, as a generational horror (e.g., *It*, or *The X-Files* episode, "Tooms" [1994]), as some kind of horrific contagion (e.g., *Ju-On* [2002], *Ringu* [1998], and such films as *It Follows* [2014]), or a horror that must be faced regularly to be kept contained or at bay (e.g., *The Cabin in the Woods* [2011], or King's masterful short stories, "N." and "Rainy Season").

As the miniseries Mike Hanlon explains to the surviving members of the Losers' Club when they gather as adults, there's a pattern to the horror. Whatever It is recurs in "thirty-year increments," each of which "corresponds to a huge disaster in Derry's history." In 1960, there was "the big fire at the Black Spot Club," and thirty years earlier, "an explosion down at the old ironworks." Three decades before that, the turn of the century say "the massacre at Drake's Creek." A quick flashback to ten-year-old Mike. "The biggest mystery is how 265 settlers just disappeared without a trace." Later, after It has been defeated once again, and the others have departed Derry, some for the last time, Mike writes in his journal that "the nightmare is over."

There's just one problem. It doesn't happen to be true.

King might have written that "Sometimes They Come Back" (1978), but the reality is that we know It's coming back, because it always comes back. This, as much as anything else, is the cosmological constant in the King storyverse. The nightmare is never truly over, because the sun will always go down again. We will always peer into the shadows, cast sidelong glances at the stormdrain, and shiver slightly as we watch for the "yellow eyes," "the sort of eyes [we have] always imagined but never actually seen" (King 1980, 12). Sometimes it appears as an enormous highway patrolman taken over by the malevolent entity, Tak (*Desperation*), while at others it rises up as *Duma Key*'s Perse, "something much older and more monstrous" than any of our pale mythologies (King 2008, 591). Perhaps it is Atropos, the trickster figure in *Insomnia*, whose underground lair is stocked with souvenirs and trophies gathered from the numberless millions whose life-cords his rusty scalpel has severed. Wandering those labyrinthine passages, we catch sight of "the sneaker of a little boy named Gage Creed" (King 1994, 726). How much further need we look to find an old paper sailboat, its paraffin coating cracked and soiled, as though it had spent time floating in a sewer?

To be clear, in conclusion, I am *not* suggesting that these are all the same entity, as Jeffrey Cohen's oft-cited, but deeply flawed "seven theses" of *Monster Theory* (1996) would have it. I would not argue that King imagines them as the same entity, but, rather, that each is a way of embodying the inevitable return of the nightmare. If science fiction is the great literature of "What if . . . ?" horror is the genre that asks more than any other: "What if we're wrong?" What if the monster isn't destroyed? What if it isn't gone? What if it comes back? When we consider the difference of reiteration—which is nothing more or less than what happens when It does come back—arguably the most important principle is enunciated by King himself. "I didn't want to write about answers," he tells his Constant Reader in *Just After Sunset*, "I want to write about questions" (2008, 538).

And, one such question, put simply, is: Does it ever really go away?

Chapter 3

Horror and Bible (Six Theses)

Brandon R. Grafius

Of course, the Bible is full of monsters, from the chaos-beast Leviathan to the demonic satyrs that haunt city ruins, from the giants who stalk the promised land to the Midianites who swarm like locusts.[1] And the monsters are only one piece of the horror that's present in these pages. There's war and bloodshed, more than a few rapes, torture, and many other events intended to shock and terrify. All overseen by a God who sends floods to the world or to the enemies of Israel, and promises to consume the world in a climactic battle of Good versus Evil that will leave most of humanity writhing in a lake of fire. As Steve Wiggins has argued in a recent essay, while many scholars have looked to Gothic Romances for the origins of modern horror, a strong case can be made for the genre's origins as lying instead in the sacred scriptures of Judaism and Christianity (Wiggins 2020).

That the Bible contains horror should be a statement beyond refute; while it might seem surprising at first, the evidence that horror is one of the important elements of both Testaments is strong indeed. But for generations, scholars have been able to interpret these texts without the use of monster theory, horror theory, or discussing horror movies at all. So what do we gain from this approach? What can biblical scholars versed in horror contribute to the debate that wasn't already uncovered either by biblical scholars or scholars of horror films?

In this chapter, I intend to trace the developing discipline of the Bible and horror, focusing on how it emerged from academic monster and horror theory to create its own identity. After this groundwork has been laid, the chapter will propose six "theses" for the study of Bible and horror, following in the footsteps of Jeffrey Jerome Cohen's influential essay (Cohen 1996).[2] Through this exploration, the essay will propose that biblical scholars appropriating horror theory for their work have a unique contribution to make to the study of both the Bible and the horror film, contributions with implications for the wider culture beyond their specific disciplines.

BRINGING RELIGION INTO THE HORROR

Jeffrey Jerome Cohen's seminal article "Monster Culture (Seven Theses)," first published in 1996, laid the groundwork for much of the scholarship on monsters that has been done in recent decades. Cohen's essay offered a way of reading monsters that viewed them as representations of the fears and desires of the culture that spawned them, a walking metaphor of difference, boundaries, and possibilities whose meanings can never be fully contained. Cohen's essay, along with a handful of other influential works on monsters and the horror genre, served to establish horror scholarship as a serious mode of study within academia, one with enormous potential for exploring a range of cultural issues.[3]

Scholars of film and cultural studies have long noted the close connection between the realms of horror and religion, but have frequently paid less attention to religion than other elements. Often, scholars trained in other disciplines have viewed religion as a backdrop for horror, a textual detail that is interesting but not crucial to a reading of the film. For example, in Carol Clover's influential reading of *The Exorcist*, she notes that the film is "less about the possessed girl than about Father Damien Karras," noting that Regan is only important as she impacts "the tormented spiritual life of Karras" (Clover 1992, 87). However, for Clover this "spiritual crisis" points to "issues of intimacy and sexuality" (Clover 1992, 88), which for her are the real subject of the film. Of course, issues of gender are crucial to an understanding of *The Exorcist*, as Clover's discussion so thoroughly documents. Similarly, Noël Carroll's thorough, detailed treatment of the structures of horror narratives spends a great deal of time asking the question of why audiences are drawn to horror. Carroll mentions briefly that "the experience of supernatural horror in the arts is frequently analogized to religious experience," but quickly dismisses these connections as only working in "a vague and decontextualized way," finding the supposed connections to not be "reliable" (Carroll 1990, 165–7). Carroll even manages to discuss *The Exorcist* without reference to religion.

But more recently, scholars from religion and associated fields have brought their expertise to bear on the discussion. Douglas E. Cowan's *Sacred Terror* serves as a landmark entry into the field, a monograph on horror movies from a religious scholar who is well-equipped to discuss a wide range of films through the lens of William James's concept of the religious imagination (Cowan 2008). Cowan is able to move beyond the "vague and decontextualized" connections that Carroll finds to make a cogent argument for "the religious imagination" (not necessarily religion) as being foundational to horror narratives (Cowan 2008, 14–16). For Cowan, the questions asked by both religion and horror are the same, focusing on our "relationship to the unseen order" (Cowan 2008, 16). Cowan argues that horror finds unsettling answers to questions which religion raises—the difference is that horror keeps these questions open, while religion frequently tries to close them off by providing a definitive answer. Still, the questions are the same.

As with monsters in general, biblical scholars for generations have studied Leviathan, Behemoth, and other monstrous elements of the biblical text. But perhaps the first book from a biblical scholar to make full use of monster theory was Timothy Beal's 2002 monograph *Religion and Its Monsters*.[4] While grounding his work in biblical scholarship, Beal introduces ideas of the Freudian uncanny and references theorists such as Clover and Creed. He also paves the way for biblical engagement with horror films, as he juxtaposes concepts such as the biblical laws concerning blood with various versions of *Dracula*, seeking to dig underneath the surface to not simply point out when religion is being used in horror texts, but to analyze how similar thematic concerns can shed light on one another. While Beal's work was widely admired and is still frequently cited and used in undergraduate and graduate courses on religion, few scholars attempted to build off his work for the next decade. A notable exception is Amy Kalmanofsky's *Terror All Around: The Rhetoric of Horror in the Book of Jeremiah* (2008), which provides a detailed, exegetically grounded reading of specific passages of Jeremiah with a focus on the elements of horror present within them. She uses Jeremiah as a way to discuss the motif of the victim who becomes monstrous, and the way in which the rhetoric of horror can be used as a means of social control. She even introduces the idea of Daughter Zion as the Bible's Final Girl, appropriating the scholarship of Carol Clover in a highly creative manner (Kalmanofsky 2008, 25–9).

The last ten years have seen significant scholarly interest in the Bible and horror, frequently with interesting results. Noteworthy examples include Safwat Marzouk's *Egypt as a Monster in the Book of Ezekiel* (2015), which uses monster theory to argue that the supposedly firm boundaries between order and chaos in Ancient Near Eastern texts such as the *Enuma Elish* and *Atrahasis* crumble upon closer inspection. Rhiannon Graybill has used the framework of Carol Clover to explore the anxiety-filled construction of the masculine body in the book of Hosea (2016, 49–69), as well as reading the story of Jael and Sisera against the backdrop of rape-revenge and slasher narratives (2018, 193–205). And with increasing frequency, biblical scholars began to use insights from monster and horror theory in support of scholarship that was primarily concerned with other matters; this appropriation of monster and horror theory as supplementary theories marks another step forward, as they are incorporated into other methods rather than being viewed as an oddity.[5]

Furthermore, recent years have seen a broadening in biblical scholarship from narrow uses of monster theory to more wide-ranging use of horror theory. Whereas monster theory is focused on the figure of the monster, horror theory more broadly construed allows for analysis of a wider range of elements, with a particular emphasis on the narratives in which monsters may (or may not) appear. For example, Steve A. Wiggins (2018) has analyzed a large number of horror movies to explore the various ways in which the Bible is used, from talisman to exorcism manual to symbol of oppression. In this work, Wiggins moves from an analysis of horrific themes in biblical narratives to an exploration of the ways in which the Bible and horror films are engaged in a mutually interpretive relationship, each contributing to the ways in which we understand the other. I have explored how Numbers 25 reveals a similar set of anxieties to the 1980s cycle of slasher films, with both works demonstrating a need to reassert patriarchal control in the wake of societal upheaval (Grafius 2018). More recently, my work has attempted to introduce a wider range of horror theory into biblical scholarship, reading the House of David as a haunted house and comparing the *sotah* ritual of Nm 5:11–31 to Carrie's humiliations in the 1976 film (Grafius 2019).[6]

I would suggest that the output of horror-themed biblical scholarship is significant enough that it's time to reflect on its purpose. When biblical scholars employ theories from horror studies, what are we accomplishing? What insights do we hope to provide that can't be obtained through other methods? In the spirit of Jeffrey Jerome Cohen's article, I offer the following six theses as a partial answer to these questions.

THESIS 1: HORROR REVEALS ANXIETY

The primary reason to apply theories of horror to the Bible is the same reason we study horror in the first place: horror films reveal a tremendous amount about our fears and anxieties. For Freud, horror (as with most things) revealed fundamental structures of the human psyche that were cross-cultural and universal (Freud 2003, 121–61; see also Grafius 2017, 35–7; 2018, 15–27). For Freud, horror emerges from the stages of development which humans share, and which we try to leave behind as we grow and develop. However, we are frequently unsuccessful in leaving these prior stages behind; horror primarily frightens because it reminds us that we have not been completely successful in our development. For Freud, horror is one-size-fits-all.

Robin Wood's hugely influential article "The American Nightmare: Horror in the 70s" was among the first to explore this idea in connection with contemporary horror films.[7] Wood adapts Freud's idea of horror as "the return of the repressed": horror is what we try to push down, what we try to deny about ourselves, but nevertheless continues to come back in sublimated forms. So Wood is able to read the American horror films of the 1970s, such as Wes Craven's *Last House on the Left* (1972) and Tobe Hooper's *Texas Chainsaw Massacre* (1974), as critiques of the patriarchal family, and the repression that this structure requires to perpetuate itself. These films portrayed the patriarchal family as damaged and damaging, a nexus of control that was only held together by violence.

While this is not a new insight into the nature and structure of horror narratives, it gives biblical scholars the necessary warrant to approach biblical passages through the lens of horror theory. Just as uncomfortable truths exist in our society, truths that we continually try (unsuccessfully) to deny, the writers of the biblical text engaged in complicated processes of repression. However, because of the particular work that biblical scholars are engaged in, this thesis must be considered in conjunction with the second thesis.

THESIS 2: CULTURE HELPS TO SHAPE THE PARTICULAR FORM OF OUR ANXIETIES

For most contemporary scholars, the anxieties revealed by horror may have some universal elements, but are largely determined by the particular film's *Sitz im Leben*. This tendency also finds its genesis in Wood's work. Wood starts with Freud but complicates his idea of horror as universal with the inclusion of the Marcusian distinction between "basic" and "surplus" repression. Wood agrees with Freud that some degree of repression is necessary for society to function; there are some forms of repression that all societies share. This is the shared foundation of horror, the reason that there is a significant overlap between what differing cultures find horrific. However, there is also a surplus repression that each society adds on top of the basic, necessary repression. This surplus repression, varying from culture to culture, adds a culturally specific component to horror. In this way, we can understand horror as having elements that are both universal and culturally determined.

So as Wood reads the American horror films of the 1970s, he is careful to put them into the context of American culture; they are in some way reflecting the Civil Rights movements of the 1960s, and responding to the culturally conservative horror films of the 1950s. They represent institutional challenges to patriarchal constructions of race and gender that were not possible before the cultural movements of the 1960s. Similarly, the slasher films of the 1980s (inaugurated by John Carpenter's 1978 film *Halloween*) are a product of the Reagan revolution, demonstrating a return to patriarchal values and an uncomfortable attempt to regain the control over the family that was lost in the 1960s and 1970s. For Wood, while slasher films demonstrate a surplus repression that is rather common (premarital sexuality), they are most productively read within the context of 1980s America and its particular cultural values.[8]

Biblical scholars have been well-trained in specifying cultural contexts and not leaping to fanciful conclusions based on imaginary connections.[9] But this caution becomes particularly important when placing the Bible into conversation with a culture that's both thousands of years and half a world away. Many of the anxieties that are found in the Hebrew Bible are also reflected in contemporary horror films; discussing the Bible in conjunction with contemporary horror films can help to shed light on these anxieties and reveal them in more depth. But in addition to discussing the overlap of these anxieties, attention should be paid to the points of dissimilarity.

THESIS 3: HORROR IS USED FOR MANY DIFFERENT PURPOSES

All horror is not the same. This is reflected in the ever-increasing number of subgenres that fall under the umbrella of horror, which can vary widely in tone, style, pacing, and any number of other salient features. And within these varying strands of horror, the effects of horror are put to particular usages.

In the 1980s slasher films, discussed above briefly, the primary motivation is horror-as-social-control (Dika 1990). When characters are punished for misbehaving on screen, the audience receives the message that engaging in behavior such as premarital sex or drug use is dangerous. But other horror movies operate at a different level. The recent film *It Follows* re-interprets the 1980s slasher films, so that the horror is not premarital sex, but societal repression of sexuality (Barbera 2014). Here, horror is not a means of social control, but a means of exposing the injustices of society. And frequently, the rhetoric of horror has been used as a way to demonize others, to depict marginalized groups in less-than-human, monstrous terms.[10]

All of these uses of horror can be found in the Bible as well, along with many others. Amy Kalmanofsky (2008), for example, has explored how horror is used in the book of Jeremiah in an attempt to frighten the reader into correct behavior. And Safwat Marzouk (2015) has demonstrated that the monstrous imagery of Ezekiel is used in an effort to dehumanize the biblical writers' Egyptian enemies. When reading horror-themed biblical texts, we would do well to consider the purpose of the horror. To what purpose is this horrific imagery being put? To what ends is this author attempting to frighten his audience?

THESIS 4: BROAD DEFINITIONS OF HORROR ARE MORE PRODUCTIVE THAN NARROW ONES

In historical-critical studies, it is common for the scholar to define the parameters and methodology of the study with a high degree of precision, to ensure that the study's results can be seen as accurate. While this type of study has its place, a similar kind of methodological control is less helpful when using horror theory to read the Bible. Connections between disparate texts are generative when made well, and we should strive to make more of them.

As such, using a narrow definition to identify horror texts within the Bible is a less helpful procedure. While Noël Carroll proposed that horror must contain the presence of a monster (a debatable proposition), he also recognized that the presence of a monster was not a sufficient condition to classify a work of art as horror (Carroll 1990, 12–27). More important, both for Carroll and many subsequent theorists, is the response that horror attempts to create within the audience. Kalmanofsky (2008, 31–41) is able to use this idea to explore texts in the book of Jeremiah that produce a horrifying effect on the audience, even if they don't explicitly include the presence of a monstrous threat, such as the depiction of the devastated land in Jer 4:23–28.[11] When we broaden our definition of what can be horrifying, possibilities open up for our scholarship.

The purpose of these studies should be to make creative connections, to uncover meanings in the text that may be lying dormant, and to place these texts in conversation with our own culture. Horror can provide a bridge for doing that, as it offers us a template of concepts, narrative structure, and vocabulary that we can apply to the biblical text. But this works best if we are casting our net broadly, seeking to include texts rather than exclude them. This is why I prefer working with "horror theory," as opposed to the more narrowly defined "monster theory."[12] Monsters are a part of horror, but not the sum total of it, and looking at horror more broadly than simply focusing on places where monsters appear opens up more possibilities for connections. Our scholarship benefits from finding connections in unexpected places. Perhaps, the question shouldn't even be whether or not a particular text is or is not horror, but how it connects with elements of the horror genre.

THESIS 5: FIND THE CONNECTIONS, THEN ARGUE FOR THEM

As biblical scholars, we're starting to run out of productive things to say about Leviathan.[13] While much of the work has been interesting and has opened up pathways for readings of the Bible with horror, scholars also need to move onto other areas, to find connections with other biblical texts, and to explore ways that biblical texts are horrifying with or without the presence of a chaos monster. This means thinking creatively about the affects created by biblical texts, and delving more deeply into horror scholarship than the triumvirate of Carroll, Clover, and Creed. Their work is excellent and foundational but doesn't begin to cover the range of possibilities for horror scholarship. We should be seeking to identify an element of the text that seems horrifying, then argue for how it connects with the tradition of horror, using all of the scholarly tools at our disposal.

This approach opens up a wide range of possibilities for scholarship. Are there texts in the Bible that use time or location in a similar way to haunted house narratives? Places where the approach to structure is similar to a home-invasion horror film? Narratives where the view of the outsider allows us to draw connections with "hillbilly horror?"[14] Or how about passages in the Psalms where the psalmist feels under siege like the characters in *Night of the Living Dead*, or worries about the afterlife in a way that fits in with contemporary ghost stories? When we approach connections with horror this way, we open ourselves up to discussions that dig under the surface, and that can help open our eyes to features of both the Bible and horror movies.

THESIS 6: HOPE AND FEAR EXIST IN A DIALECTICAL RELATIONSHIP

One of the main differences between the realms of horror and religion is their point of emphasis: horror focuses on our fears, while religion focuses on our hopes. (At least, that's what the party line says for each of these realms.) But hope and fear are reflections of each other, both pointing to the same place. You can't talk about one without at least implying the other. These discourses may take different routes, but they both arrive at the same destination.

In his recent book on the "religious imagination" of Stephen King, applying William James's term to the extremely popular author, Douglas Cowan develops his argument that horror and religion both ask the same set of questions. Cowan remarks, "Both the stories we have labeled 'religious' and the other fictional storyworlds we create emerge from the same place in our imagination" (Cowan 2018, 15–16). The prophets cannot tell us about the hope of the world God is calling us into without describing the miserable state of the current world. And horror cannot frighten us with a depiction of an apocalyptic nightmare world, or a world where the monstrous lurks within the structure of the family itself, without suggesting the possibilities for a better world.

This is another way of saying that horror and religion are both about what matters to us most deeply. While religion and the Bible often (but not always) use the language of hope, and horror often (but not always) uses the language of fear, they are both talking about the same thing. They are both attempts to explore our deepest questions about our role in the universe, our relationship to the unseen order, how we should treat each other, and how we should live in the world. And those connections, on their own, are enough to make approaching the Bible through the lens of horror an intriguing task. With this warrant in place, our job as scholars is to make this conversation as exciting, surprising, and eye-opening as possible.

NOTES

1. Leviathan can be found in Job 40–41 and Ps 106:26, along with a handful of additional scattered references; the demonic satyrs (NRSV: "goat-demons") dance among the ruins of Jerusalem in Is 13:21; 34:14; the inhabitants of the land of Canaan are described as monstrous giants by the Israelite spies in Num 13:30–33; the Midianites are described as swarming monsters in Jud 6:1–6. Here and throughout this chapter, the translation and verse-numbering is from the NRSV unless otherwise noted.

2. This approach was also adopted by Dawn Keetley in her recent essay, "Introduction: Six Theses on Plant Horror; or, Why are Plants Horrifying?" in *Plant Horror: Approaches to the Monstrous Vegetal in Fiction and Film*, eds. Dawn Keetley and Angela Tenga (London: Palgrave MacMillan, 2016), 1–30.

3. While scholars will undoubtedly have their own list of important works, I would include Noël Carroll's *The Philosophy of Horror: Or, Paradoxes of the Heart* (London: Routledge, 1990); Carol Clover, *Men, Women, and Chain Saws: Gender in the Modern Horror Film* (Princeton, NJ: Princeton University Press, 1992); Barbara Creed, *The Monstrous-Feminine: Film, Feminism, Psychoanalysis* (New York: Routledge, 1993); Tony Williams, *Hearths of Darkness: The Family in the American Horror Film* (Madison, NJ: Farleigh Dickinson University Press, 1996; Updated edition Jackson, MS: University Press of Mississippi, 2014); and Barry Keith Grant, ed., *The Dread of Difference: Gender and the Horror Film* (Austin: University of Texas Press, 1996; Second edition 2015) as being the foundational works that introduced me to the nascent field.

4. One might also see Tina Pippin's *Apocalyptic Bodies: The Biblical End of the World in Text and Image* (London: Routledge, 1999) as an early forerunner, though she does not use theoretical work from the fields of monster or horror studies in the way Beal does.

5. Examples include Brad E. Kelle's use of monster theory in combination with trauma studies in, "Dealing with the Trauma of Defeat: The Rhetoric of the Devastation and Rejuvenation of Nature in Ezekiel," *JBL* 128.3 (2009): 469–90; Rebecca Raphael combines monster theory and disability studies in "Monsters and the Crippled Cosmos: Construction of the Other in *Fourth Ezra*," in *The 'Other' in Second Temple Judaism: Essays in Honor of John J. Collins*, eds. D.C. Harlow et al. (Grand Rapids, MI: Eerdmans), 279–301; Denise Kimber Buell, "Hauntology Meets Posthumanism: Some Payoffs for Biblical Studies," in *The Bible and Posthumanism*, ed. Jennifer L. Koosed (SemSt 74; Atlanta: SBL Press, 2014), 29–56. An overview of this literature is found in Brandon R. Grafius, "Text and Terror: Monster Theory and the Hebrew Bible," *CurBR* 16.1 (2017): 34–49.

6. Steve A. Wiggins has explored further possibilities for Bible and horror scholarship in his article "Good Book Gone Bad: Reading Phinehas, Watching Horror," *HBTh* 41.1 (2019): 93–103.

7. Wood's article has been reprinted (in slightly modified forms) in numerous anthologies, including in Wood's own collection of essays *Hollywood from Vietnam to Reagan... and Beyond* (New York: Columbia University Press, 2003), 63–84; and most recently in *The Monster Theory Reader*, ed. Jeffery Andrew Weinstock (Minneapolis: University of Minnesota Press, 2020), 108–135, with the title of "An Introduction to the American Horror Film."

8. There's been a significant amount of horror scholarship paying attention to the cultural particularities of horror films. Examples include Linnie Blake, *The Wounds of Nations: Horror Cinema, Historical Trauma and National Identity* (Manchester, UK: Manchester University Press, 2008); Sarah Arnold, *Maternal Horror Film: Melodrama and Motherhood* (London: Palgrave Macmillan, 2013), 115–53, who discusses the manner in which themes of motherhood is shifted from the original Japanese films to their Hollywood remakes. Michael J. Blouin has read *Cabin in the Woods* (2012) as intentionally playing with the dialectic of universal-vs.-localized horror in his article "'A Growing Global Darkness': Dialectics of Culture in Goddard's *The Cabin in the Woods*," *Horror Studies* 6.1 (2015): 83–99.

9. See, for example, Brent Strawn's discussion of Friedrich Delitzsch's methodological errors in Delitzch's famous "Babel und Bibel" lecture, in which Delitzsch argued for a Near Eastern precursor to everything in the Bible. Of course, some of his connections have proven valid with further study, but many did not take account of the specifics of time and culture. Brent A. Strawn, "Comparative Approaches: History, Theology, and the Image of God," in *Method Matters: Essays on the Interpretation of the Hebrew Bible in Honor of David L. Peterson*, eds. Joel M. LeMon and Kent Harold Richardson (Atlanta: SBL Press, 2009), 117–42.

10. Stephen T. Asma, *On Monsters: An Unnatural History of Our Worst Fears* (New York: Oxford University Press, 2009), 74–93, for example, offers a brief overview of "monstrous races" rumored to inhabit other lands in the ancient world.

And Edward J. Ingebretsen, *At Stake: Monsters and the Rhetoric of Fear in Popular Culture* (Chicago: University of Chicago Press, 2001), explores how societies use monstrous rhetoric to de-humanize criminals and other transgressors.

11. Kalmanosfky does use the presence of specific vocabulary as a marker of horror texts, but this is more a function of limiting her study to a manageable scope. She uses a broad enough range of terms that this does not serve as an overly restrictive criterion.

12. At least, narrow in one sense, in that "monster theory" only considers the portion of horror that directly involves the monster. However, the monster theory is extremely useful for looking at how monsters participate in a wide variety of genres, including fairy tales and historical reports, which may or may not be relevant to exploring themes of horror.

13. The scholarship on this beast is immense; recently, see Brian R. Doak's monster theory-influenced monograph *Consider Leviathan: Narratives of Nature and the Self in Job* (Minneapolis: Fortress Press, 2014); as well as the more traditionally historical-critical volume of essays Koert van Bekkum et al., eds, *Playing with Leviathan: Interpretation and Reception of Monsters from the Biblical World*, Themes in Biblical Narrative 21 (Leiden: Brill, 2017).

14. For generic features of haunted house narratives, see Barry Curtis, *Dark Places: The Haunted House in Film* (London: Reaktion Books, 2008); home-invasion horror is discussed in Michael Fiddler, "Playing *Funny Games* in *The Last House on the Left*: The Uncanny and the 'Home Invasion' Genre," *Crime, Media, Culture* 9.3 (2013): 281–99; an example of scholarship on "hillbilly horror" is Jacqueline Pinkowitz, "Down South: Regional Exploitation Films, Southern Audiences, and Hillbilly Horror in Herschell Gordon Lewis's *Two Thousand Maniacs!* (1964)," *Journal of Popular Film and Television* 44.2 (2016): 109–19.

Chapter 4

A Biological Model of Monster Flaps

William Blake Smith

Occasionally within a geographical area and within certain chronological constraints, a high frequency of monster reports will cluster together. Such a cluster of reports is commonly called a *monster flap*.[1] The term flap here refers to its less common meaning of "a state of excitement or agitation" and has been applied to public enthusiasm about questionable observations ranging from flying saucers to fairies, but also to monsters.[2]

Since the late 1990s, I've examined monsters through the lens of scientific skepticism. This approach asks the question of whether any claim can be verified through methodological testing to definitively say whether something is "real" in a material sense. However, this constraint ignores the vast amount of anecdotal data in the field of monsters that is untestable, but that suggests in many cases that the monsters are experientially "real," regardless of whether such stories have a basis in a material sense. There are certainly hoaxes, but, for the victims of these hoaxes, a robust spectrum of emotional experiences still takes place. This is true for cases when the root cause is misinterpretation, delusion, dream, or some other mode of perception, as well as when there is the possibility that something real was encountered. As a researcher, I have struggled with a dearth of effective models to explain how these monster flaps develop and how clusters of narratives arise around a particular monster in a particular area.

In the past two centuries, as communities such as these have reported monster encounters, a pattern of distinct phases has emerged. Various scholars have sought to understand these phases differently, including most prominently, Richard Dawkins's discussion of memes or "mind-viruses" and Bill Ellis's discussions of ostension and contemporary legends. Both of these models, however, have flaws that overlook crucial features of the development of a monster flap. In this article, I propose to present my own model that better explains how monster flaps work as living ecosystems that follow the rules of natural selection. I will then apply this model to several well-known monster flaps to demonstrate that, rather than isolated stories or incidences of mass hysteria, monster flaps can be more beneficially thought of as living systems where stories act as the individual nodes responding to natural selection.

A FEW MONSTER FLAPS

Since many readers may not be familiar with the monster flaps I plan to analyze, a brief introduction is in order to the four monster flaps that will form the heart of this article's analysis. While these retellings are necessarily brief and each monster flap could be described in greater details, such an introduction will provide necessary background information for the remainder of the article.

The Beast of Gevaudan

In the Gevaudan region of France from 1764 to 1767, many people were killed by what was reported to be a monstrous beast (referred to often as La Bête, or The Beast). Death-toll estimates range from 60 to more than 200 victims, all of whom were torn to pieces and then partially devoured. Rumors spread quickly that it was a werewolf or some other supernatural, man-eating creature. To stop the slaughter (or at least to hinder the public outcry), the French government sent hunters to slay the beast. Something terrible was loose in the region, and the proof could be measured in graves and maimed victims. While stories about the beast held that bullets would not harm it, the narrative was eventually concluded after the killing of two large wolves—one by huntsmen hired by the king and one by a commoner named Chastel. Although these were not the last wolf-deaths in France, the second wolf's death is generally agreed to mark the end of the monster's reign of terror.

Spring-Heeled Jack

In nineteenth-century England, the urban public was terrorized and thrilled by sightings of a man who could reportedly leap over walls, sported long metal claws, and could belch blue flame. His visitations spurred panic, and there were numerous attestations to his existence by witnesses in newspapers, with spikes in reports in 1837, 1843, and 1870. Victims (mostly women) were attacked (groped and clawed), and carriages were wrecked when the mysterious figure jumped out in front of the horses. The man (or monster?) was never caught.

The Mad Gasser of Mattoon, Illinois

In 1944, as World War II left many small towns deprived of the majority of their male citizens, the people of Mattoon, Illinois, were gripped by fear of a strange character who is said to have used a flit-gun (a bug-spray pump applicator) to deliver a load of noxious chemicals that induced coughing, partial paralysis, and nausea. For two weeks or more, the town became hypervigilant to strangers on the streets at night, to any strange smells, and any peculiar sensations. The police never caught a perpetrator, and the case is considered by some skeptics to be a case of *mass hysteria* (Johnson 1945, 177).

Mothman

In 1966 and 1967, the Ohio Valley—and especially the town of Point Pleasant, West Virginia—was a hotspot of UFO sightings. Amid that activity, sightings of a strange flying creature were reported. The creature, which came to be known as Mothman,[3] was said to be a humanoid with glowing red eyes that had a 10-foot wingspan and could fly as fast as 100 miles per hour. UFOlogists such as Gray Barker and John Keel scoured the region for stories and evidence. Keel collected his data into a narrative called *The Mothman Prophecies* (1975). His book concludes with the tragic collapse of the Silver Bridge that connected Point Pleasant to Gallipolis, Ohio. The collapse took place during heavy Christmas-shopping traffic and killed forty-six when their vehicles plunged into the icy Ohio River. Keel suggested that the tragic collapse was somehow foretold by, or related to, the associated Mothman phenomena.

PRIOR ANALYSIS OF MONSTER FLAPS AND OTHER NARRATIVE CLUSTERS

Clusters of narratives such as those described above are strange both for their content, but also for their mental "stickiness," so to speak. Each of these could have been a series of isolated stories that were told once over a beer and then immediately forgotten. Rather than disappear, however, they became complex narrative events that involved entire communities, local government institutions, and history. While many cultural theorists may have explanations for them, two cultural theorists, in particular, represent opposing ends of a theoretical spectrum that extends from biological to social: Richard Dawkins and Bill Ellis.

Turning first to Richard Dawkins, if such narrative clusters are "biomes" full of various story "lifeforms," then these social conduits could be said to respond to a set of selective Darwinian pressures. Evolutionary biologist

Richard Dawkins's book *The Selfish Gene* (1989) argues that it is more reasonable to view the gene, not the individual lifeform, as the primary unit seeking to be preserved through natural selection. Going further, he posits that nonbiological *things* might also be subject to natural selection. Defining a "meme" as a unit of culture,[4] Dawkins proposes that such units or individual ideas could be beneficially thought of as products of natural selection in much the same way as a biological organism. From this argument, the rather sidelined field of memetics emerged as the study of how these units spread and changed over time (Dawkins 1989). In analyzing the monster flaps discussed above, a scholar using a hardline memetic angle inspired by Dawkins would highlight the spread of the narrative like a "virus" that attacks its host's gullibility and naivety to create an incorrect belief (i.e., that monsters are real).[5] The virus then spreads to new hosts via retellings, largely unchanged.

However, the term "meme" has been criticized for its simplistic application of scientific principes to a cultural field. In his book *Aliens, Ghosts and Cults: Legends We Live* (2003), folklorist Bill Ellis considers the meme as a model for the spread of folklore and ultimately rejects it. According to Ellis, Dawkins is guilty of a naïve unfamiliarity with the work of folklore outside of biology for modeling such diffusion of ideas. Additionally, Ellis notes that Dawkins is inconsistent with actual natural selection in that Dawkins argues "religion" and other things he disagrees with act like viruses, while science does not:

> The core of the scientific method is reflexivity and response to rebuttal. Many of the notions behind the concept of "mind viruses" seem inadequately examined and deserve challenge. Such rebuttal must itself be reflexive and ready to concede value to the other side. But at minimum we should expect scientists to obey their own tenets when discussing cultural material. And if "memes" and "mind viruses" are to be discussed as organisms, even in analogy, we members of a 150-year-old discipline should insist on the scientifically recognized principle of priority in nomenclature. (Ellis 2003, 83)

Ellis proposes we term these stories "contemporary legends" rather than "memes" and encourages a focused eye on the social dimension of spreading narratives about monsters. Specifically, he relies on the concept of "ostension," which Ellis defines as "the literal acing out of a legend" (Ellis 2003, 162).

Ellis describes variants of ostension (pseudo-ostension, quasi-ostension, quasi-ostension) that account for deliberate hoaxes, misinterpretation, and lying for status about involvement in folkloric events. This folkloric model of ostension model could account for many aspects of behavior in cryptozoology such as organized bigfoot hunts as a form of re-creating sightings that have taken on mythic significance, such as the Patterson bigfoot sighting (and film) of 1967 (Coleman 1999, 197). Deliberately creating bigfoot tracks to create a belief in the existence of the creature is a form of quasi-ostension and also figures prominently in the hoaxing around the earliest bigfoot story, the 1958 track sightings by logger Jerry Crew that were eventually revealed to have been faked by fellow logger Ray Wallace after Wallace's death in 2002 (Buhs 2009, 242).

Ellis describes the outbreak of legends and ostentive behavior as "ostentive panics." He cites Veronique Campion-Vincent who proposed that such panics move from story into ostention prompted by a variety of factors including underlying stress and triggering events. A central part of Campion-Vincent's theory is the community's collective action that culminates in a *showdown* or climactic moment in which the legend is "fulfilled." The features of this particular panic model may be applicable in some kinds of urban legends, such as those featuring killers and cults with transgressive but scrutable motives or fully supernatural creatures such as vampires, but are rather difficult to apply to a cryptozoological monster flap in which the creature is a understood as a biological reality.

FOLKLORE COMPARED TO MEMES

Ellis and Dawkins are both describing the spread of story and behavior, but arrive at very different outcomes. Using memes as a model can show the transfer of information and behavior but its reductive explanation that memes are viruses that control or hijack behavior is overly simplistic. It ultimately disregards the effects of existing qualities of the receiver's mind in how memes change when passed on. By contrast, folklore models use methodologies such as cataloging motifs to identify not only the recurring story elements but also the rituals and other recurring behaviors that result in stories being passed on. However, by focusing exclusively on a social model of monster flaps in which the entire experience is socially constructed, the experiential element of the participants is overlooked entirely.

In the case of modeling monster flaps, Ellis eschews memes in favor of the term "contemporary legend," but I would argue that although folklorists define a legend as a story that someone, somewhere holds to be true, using the term *legend* has connotations of *fiction*. In a monster flap, we should assume that at the core of the story, an earnest experience has taken place. It's not that Ellis is dismissing the narratives so much as that folklore itself describes the spread of story without systematized consideration of psychological effects such as priming, bias, and other influences on human behavior.

By contrast, Dawkins provides technically specific language that pays special attention to how stories spread; however, his simplistic dismissal of memetic content he doesn't like as negatively connoted "viruses" that "infect," fundamentally undermines his argument. While my article is indebted to Dawkins and his original conception of a meme as a cultural unit that can be analyzed individually, I posit that he overlooked the complex relationship between the story (meme) and the complex role of the human mind in interpreting, changing, and spreading the stories and associated behaviors.

I attempt to use these two cultural theorists as a corrective to one another through recovering the original conception of narratives (memes) as a cultural unit responding to natural selection and demonstrating how it can be usefully applied to analyze the social patterns that develop around so-called monster flaps. Ellis pointed out that Dawkins neglected the scientific priority of folklore's "contemporary legend" as a unit of cultural transfer. Therefore, I am going to reach back further still to rely on a plant-themed metaphor for the spread of ideas. While natural selection generally involves, for most species, sexual reproduction, in recognition of the many cultural connotations associated with human reproduction, I will use the neutral plant world as the basis of my model and discuss the spread of story in terms of *pollination*. However, for more accuracy, I suggest we avoid the use of "seeds" (as in "a seed of doubt") for the spread of ideas and instead use the metaphor of *story germ*, similar to *cereal germ* in botany. In the following section, I will describe the process of story pollination, some possible factors that affect the process, and how such "pollinated" monster flaps follow a general life cycle that can be traced across different flaps.

A RE-ENVISIONED BIOLOGICAL MODEL OF MONSTER FLAPS

Humans tell stories for a variety of reasons, but told stories are abstractions. They carry wildly different levels of detail depending on who is telling them. It isn't always possible to tell if a story is literally a factual accounting or if it is exaggerated or even confabulated. The inscrutable nature of the storyteller's motivation in retelling stories and the lack of predictability of which stories will spread successfully makes researching their spread and effect both fascinating and frustrating.

The study of narrative considers the intent of the authors, the structure and symbolism of the story, and the way the story is received by the reader. There is, in short, an ecosystem of story. There is a storyteller, a presumed audience, and environmental circumstances of the telling. There are many factors at play that impact how effective a story will be at evoking emotion, accurately relaying a message, and sparking an urge in the audience to carry the story on by sharing it themselves: the storytelling skill of the teller, the attentiveness of the recipients, the aptness of the moment, the distractions at hand. In oral transmission, there are emotional reactions for all involved parties and the storyteller enters into a relationship of performance with their audience that creates a unique, relational arena in which the story develops (Bauman 1975). For the storyteller, success might elicit laughter, gasps, tears, or some other indicator that the story was well received; however, for our purpose, success is measured in how well the story spreads after this initial telling.

As highlighted by Dawkins and Ellis, there are many factors that determine why a story spreads successfully outside of the specific content of the story: Is the storyteller well trusted by the audience? Does the story contain strong emotional content or an important moral or ethical element? Does the story mean something special to the audience? Does the story strongly confirm community values or beliefs? How many people are hearing the story? Is it told in an elevator? In a break-room? In a church? Is the story being repeated by a trusted newspaper or a compelling news reporter on television or radio? Indeed, the *conduit theory* of Linda Dégh and Andrew Vázsonyi notes that the transmission of stories is not a given, but rather the result of an intricate evaluation and relationship between storyteller and story recipient (Dégh and Vázsonyi 1975). Once shared with an audience the story transmission might end, or it may be carried forward to another conduit, forming what I am calling a "narrative ecosystem." The narrative ecosystem is comprised of people and systems that facilitate the transmission of stories. These are nodes in a connected network that allows for both single and multidirectional spread of information. Within this network, the stories themselves behave like biological organisms and are subject to natural selection.

For natural selection to occur, three things are needed:

- a replicator that makes copies,
- a copying process that allows for some degree of variation in the copying,
- selective pressures that favor some of these variants over others.

Narratives and other memes surrounding monster flaps aren't literally alive, but they do resemble life in ways that seem to be more than mere metaphor. Most noteworthy is that stories change and some of these changes become more successful at transmission than their parents. These changes happen when the original narrative encounters the narrative ecosystem of the human mind. Children are a mix of the genes of two parents—alike, yet unique from their parents. Similarly, stories take on material from each host as they are reproduced in a narrative ecosystem.

Story is the fundamental unit of transfer in this model, the fundamental organism we are analyzing. The teller of the story says they have seen or experienced something unusual, often identified as a monster.[6] The story has to be passed on. Sometimes the story is told to explain some other peculiar behavior: *Why were you driving out of the woods so fast? Why must everyone avoid the old graveyard?* Sometimes the story is told because the experience was so odd or unsettling that it demanded someone else have a look: *This is going to sound crazy, but you won't believe what I saw in that cave. . . .* In this way, the story is told to other people in the community. It may be told to authority figures, such as law enforcement or clergy. It may be told to reporters. The nature of the audience receiving these stories may mandate further spread of the narrative as their own regulatory or vocational requirements demand. Police may file reports that become public.[7] Clergy or politicians may frame the story in some way to comfort or entertain the community, or they may contextualize the story within an existing framework.[8] Journalists and writers may post news stories.

Viral metaphors dominate discussion of the spread of stories, but the virus metaphor is flawed. A virus copies itself with high fidelity and turns the host's own cells into duplicates of itself. What happens in the spread of story is much more akin to *pollination* where the genetic material of two plants join to create a genetically new plant. In story transmission, incoming story elements mix with the narrative contents and tastes of the recipient's mind. If the story is repeated by this receiver it will take on the flavor and character of the new storyteller's experiences and storytelling style. Within each storyteller is a set of selective pressures (biases, world view, experiences, storytelling skill, etc.) which will affect whether they are likely to become pollinators themselves, and whether their retelling will strengthen or weaken the fecundity of the story network.

The story germ, once in the minds of recipients, *gestates* and becomes a new variant of the original story. Assumptions, biases, personal tastes, fears, and the panoply of mental qualities that make us all unique combine to form new memories that can then be dispersed as a new generation of stories. These stories may take multiple paths through a community but for our purposes we will reduce these to whether or not the recipient will share the story again. The method of sharing has an impact on the fidelity of the story to the original details. Oral transmission is very likely to introduce changes (mutations) to the story, whereas social media sharing likely might have a very high fidelity depending on whether the recipient forward the story intact as received or packaged with personal thoughts and interpretations introduced as preamble or commentary.

Mutations aside, the question is whether or not the recipients also share the story and thus expand the story network. Each person retelling the story becomes a new pollination agent themselves, and depending on a variety of factors may help increase the viability of their generation of story spread based on factors such as their social standing, narrative skills, and so on. If they do not spread the story or are poor conduits, their node may be a dead-end in the network. This is a simple binary outcome, but if enough receivers also become pollinators, there can be a geometric growth in the spread of the story.

It is important to note here that this is a story-based model, not a test of whether or not there really was a monster involved in the flap. Regardless of the reality of the monster, additional story nodes may surface that are *apparently* independent of the original account. It is difficult to determine whether these subsequent stories were influenced by the original story in circulation, but if one were mapping the story spread historically these new accounts become part of the ecosystem.

While the seed analogy is only a metaphor to help us understand better how stories about monsters spread, it also allows for some useful analogies to the world of farming that can better flesh out the narrative ecosystem. Not all communities or individuals are equally open to monster stories. There are cultural beliefs that may serve as strong prophylactics against belief in or spread of monster stories. Religious beliefs might be either conducive to miraculous aspects of narratives of the bizarre or cause the audience to reject them if their narrative content approaches blasphemy. Scientific materialism might cause individuals to reject narratives or frame retellings with disclaimers or explanations that diminish the spread of the story. The narrative fecundity of a community is therefore wildly variable depending on many factors.

Some people are highly connected socially and enjoy telling stories more than others. In viral terms, these people are referred to as *super spreaders*. In botanical terms, plants use a variety of strategies for spreading pollen. I will continue to favor non-virus metaphors and will call these network nodes *spreaders*. These can be individuals with large social networks and a propensity to tell stories. However, spreaders may also be community members whose roles involve sharing information. Religious leaders, politicians, social workers, and a variety of other roles have the dissemination of information as a key part of their function. The media is a particularly effective spreader in the story network. Newspapers, radio, television, motion pictures, podcasts, blogs, magazines, visual art, and books all can become nodes in the network of story. Some of these media take longer to produce and are less influential in the early parts of a monster flap.

A special kind of story spreader is the *harvester*. This is a person who collects a particular kind of story and shares it with a targeted audience who is specifically looking for this kind of content. In a monster flap, such people may help feed the flap while it is happening or may arrive later and help define the boundaries of what constituted the flap when it was active. Authors such as John Keel (Mothman), Loren Coleman (various cryptids), and Linda Godfrey (Dogman) have specialized in pouncing on monster related stories and providing contemporary magazine and news articles and later books that provide the reader with a curated crop of tales. Filmmakers such as Seth Breedlove (*Smalltown Monsters*) and television shows such as *MonsterQuest* also fit this harvester role.

A variant of the harvester is the *historian*. Historians try to provide evidence that the monster flap is not an isolated event, but rather is part of a long history of sightings in the region. It is tempting to think this approach is part of a naturalistic, materialist/evolutionary acknowledgment that monsters don't just appear out of nowhere and thus is grounded in science. However, many historians focus on the anomalous and try to cluster as many odd details about the flap's geographical and historical qualities as possible. Their role is to harvest stories that match the narrative's tone and content and their own opinions on the nature of the monster. For example, see Linda Godfrey's *The Beast of Bray Road* (2003), in which she anchors contemporary sightings of an upright canid "dogman" with Native American folklore of skinwalkers and wendigos.

Viral models of memetics don't account for the wildly divergent versions of narrative that emerge from the interaction of so many unique minds. The pollination approach accounts for a mixture of incoming story elements and the interactions of the recipient's mind to produce mutations within each new generations of story. There are internal and external selective pressures on any story's viability including such simple things as shyness and forgetfulness to misremembering to bragging embellishment.

These mutations may result in a flap where the inaccurate elements of the story are endowed with unexpected significance. It is worth taking a quick look at the non-monster media flap around UFOs in 1947. In June of 1947, pilot Kenneth Arnold saw some unusual aerial objects while flying near Mount Rainier in Washington State. When he landed, he reported the sighting and then flew on to an air show. The story of the strange, fast objects he saw was picked up by a wire service, leading to him speaking with reporters at *The East Oregonian*—a newspaper in the same town where the air show was held. He had described the group of objects as crescent shaped, with early drawings showing their details. But he also described their flight as being like a saucer skipped across water, and the craft themselves as saucer shaped. Despite these two differing versions of the story, the metaphor stuck and "flying saucers" were born. The Cold War made America nervous as it turned its eyes to the sky in search of Russian bombs, and suddenly the world's first "flying saucer flap" was underway. It really didn't matter that crescents aren't saucer shaped or that early drawings of his sighting showed crescent-shaped craft. Arnold's own book on the subject (originally published in 1952) included a photo of a boomerang-shaped model with the caption, "This is a photo of a model of the strange disk Arnold saw over the Cascades June 1947" (Arnold 1952, 162). The "flying saucers" name was mentally sticky and created a readily available mental template for unusual sightings in the sky. Subsequent sightings and fictional depictions would be overtly described as flying discs and flying saucers.

What are its nutrients of a story while it grows and develops in the mind of the pollinated host? In the ecosystem of story, the mind is the womb the story grows in, while *attention* is the primary nutrient. This is very significant as will be seen in the examples below of monster flaps and their lifecycles. As more people hear about the story, more individuals appear, including those who wish to "hunt" the monster and those who wish to debunk it. If the flap is compelling enough, and the location amenable, it is possible that many interested parties will converge and form an amplified network of story carriers. Sharing notes, anecdotes, images, and evidence with the investigators—either to prove or disprove the monster—will reinforce the strength of the story, even if they do not experience anything themselves. The story is repeated widely, and new experiences quickly folded into the narrative.

Concurrent with the added interested parties feeding the monster flap with their attention, there are often organic additional sightings, which can (1) become part of the main narrative as supplementary evidence, (2) can spin off to form their own narrative, or (3) can end up ignored for a variety of reasons. For example, the two wolves killed in the Gevaudan case (see below), represent divergent conclusions to the outbreak and exist as their own stories within the wider context of that particular flap. In that case, the government solution to the problem now seems like an ineffective effort at damage control and casts the hunter Chastel as a people's hero out to protect his community.

Individuals will have their own circle of connections to whom they are likely to repeat their stories. If the story is successful (i.e., it has properties that make it highly shared) then it is possible that repeated versions from multiple sources (multiple monster witnesses, for example) will be shared with the same audience and this creates a strong reinforcement that the story is important enough to both believe and share.

WHAT ENDS A MONSTER FLAP?

The "end" of a monster flap is difficult to identify with precision because their boundaries are often hazy. If we concern ourselves with the story rather than the literal existence of the monster within the story, then the flap always has the potential to reactivate. Like a cold sore, shingles, or a frozen-cave creature in a 1950s horror movie, the dormant story can spring back to life and start the cycle once again. Often, within a post-flap community, it becomes economically important to monetize this potential. Recurring festivals celebrating the original events become an annual tradition.[9] Point Pleasant (Mothman) and Flatwoods (The Flatwoods Monster) in West Virginia, Fouke (The Beast of Boggy Creek) in Arkansas, and Bishopville (The Lizard Man of Scape Ore Swamp) in South Carolina have all embraced their monster heritage in festivals that both celebrate and monetize the monster narratives anchored in their respective communities (Laycock 2018).

Even if it is difficult to find any clear demarcation of the end of the flap, a key factor is "attention depletion." If attention is the life force of the flap, then losing it will necessarily "starve" the narrative cluster. A significant part of the story lifecycle in a flap environment is the repetition by media. The media's continued coverage is dependent on continued interest by the story-consumers. While the media may try to push a narrative on an uninterested public, that is not a sustainable model in an advertising-dependent journalism world. Attention needs a degree of novelty and the public's fascination demands new and interesting details. When those dry up, so does public interest. In these example cases, the end of media coverage closely correlates with the end of the flaps. I strongly suspect this is a causal relationship.

PHASES OF A MONSTER FLAP

With these important terms in place, I can now detail the stages of a monster flap (see figure 4.1). The stories that comprise a monster flap unfold over time, and it is likely that the arc of activity within the flap lifecycle represents a bell curve of activity rising, peaking, and then falling. The fuel of a flap is *attention*. Attention is not an unlimited resource, and continued exposure to the same story with no variation will deplete interest. The phases here are potentially overlapping, but unfold chronologically. Not every flap will have every phase.

The Phases

Instigation

This is the phase where the monster stories first start emerging in the community. This can be from oral accounts of the original witnesses, from reporting from official agencies, or other sources.

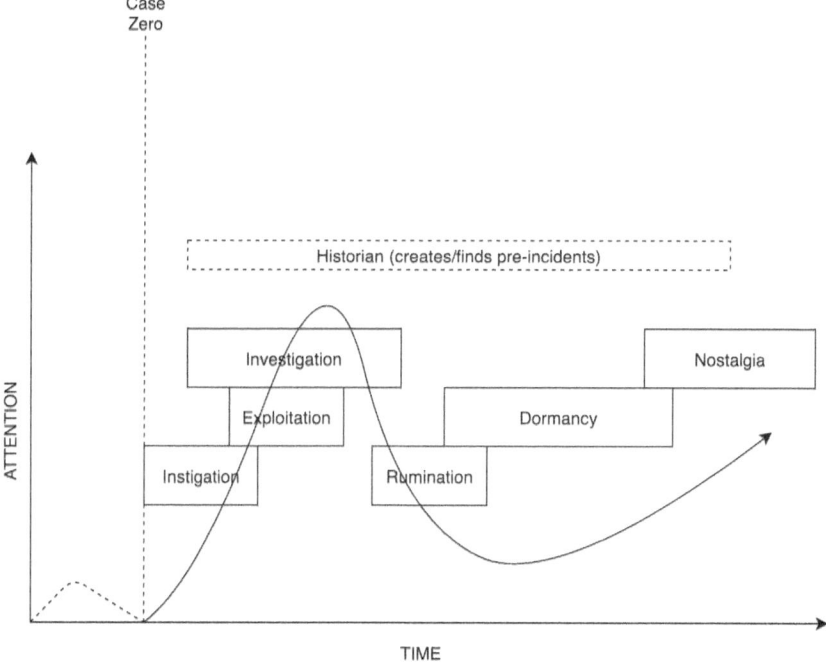

Figure 4.1 Created by Blake Smith.

Exploitation

This is the phase where the monster stories are picked up by media. This usually starts with local media and sometimes expands to national or global coverage. This phase spreads the story widely, often with a tone of detached humor or insincere inquiry.

Investigation

This is the phase where locals and outsiders come to investigate or explore the story through ostension or field work. Part of this phase is collecting and rebroadcasting the stories accrued during phases 1 and 2.

Rumination

This is the phase where the media coverage dies down and people ruminate on the events. There may be some retrospective media "think pieces" but generally the active flap is over.

Dormancy

Here, the community may occasionally be asked to cough up stories for notable anniversaries but in general the story cycle is in a state of hibernation.

Nostalgia

This is when the community decides to remember the monster flap by holding festivals or conferences to bring together witnesses and stories and possibly gain some economic benefit for the community.

Across these phases, the historian harvester can appear at any point and try to give extended historical context to the monster flap.

Natural selection—the idea that some stories are more "fit" than others and more likely to spread—remains an important feature throughout these phases. Not every story will pass on, and by the very nature of the "sexual" reproduction of stories, most stories will not pass on in exactly the same way. Having laid out this model and its associated terminology, I will now apply it to examine some notable monster.

THE BIOLOGICAL MODEL APPLIED TO REAL-WORLD EXAMPLES

The Beast of Gevaudan

The Beast of Gevaudan story begins with a failed attack on a young woman in the summer of 1764. The girl was not killed but described the beast [Instigation]. Soon after, the first death by the beast occurs. The story spreads. The attacks continue, vulnerable especially are the women who attend livestock in the fields of this region depopulated by war. A new technology is at play as well—the introduction of the gazette newspaper (Smith 2011) [Exploitation]. These papers build on the story adding or highlighting the most outrageous aspects of the beast's properties. Church leaders saw the attacks as evidence of God's wrath and contextualized it as such (Pourcher 2006). Eventually, the government becomes involved, and professional hunters, hired by the French government, kill a large wolf [Investigation]. The attacks don't end.[10] Eventually, another large wolf is killed, this time by a local named Jean Chastel, and soon after, the attacks come to an end [Dormancy]. In reality, the edges of such cases are forever a gray territory because the story doesn't need a living physical monster to inspire a resurgence of the narrative cycle.[11] The feedback loop between the sightings, the exaggerated coverage in the newspapers, and the heightened expectations of the locals and outsiders coming to hunt the creature(s) parallels the flap model proposed herein. The attacks of wolves didn't end when the second animal was killed, but there was obvious pressure from the Crown to stop both the killings and the *story* of the killings. When the second wolf was killed, it provided a tidy narrative conclusion to the story—and marked an attention-depletion for the "beast" narrative. Without the food of attention, the story withered and died.

The Mad Gasser of Mattoon

In 1944, as many of the young men of Mattoon, Illinois, were off fighting in World War II, citizens of the town were affected by a strange series of incidents. They began on August 31, when a couple awoke at night believing they had been affected by a gas leak [Instigation]. They report partial paralysis and a strange smell. The next night another citizen reported a strange smell late in the evening. When her husband came home that night from work, he spotted (and pursued) an unknown prowler. His description of the prowler and the incident of the strange smell were reported in the news. As the days unfolded, more reports came in of strange smells and mysterious prowlers. Newspaper reports fed the rumors [Exploitation]. The reports piled up until the police, frustrated and skeptical, issued several statements and policies to reduce panic. Roving gangs that had formed to look for the gasser were disbanded [Investigation]. Chasing police cars to try and help catch the gasser was made punishable by arrest. Statements from local chemical plants debunked theories of chemical leaks. The gasser's reign of terror ended after two weeks. Multiple efforts to stop the panic included editorial dismissal of the gasser hypothesis, efforts by the police to stop vigilante activity, and possible suppression/dismissal of subsequent police reports. A year later, *The Journal of Abnormal and Social Psychology* would publish an article titled, "The 'Phantom Anesthetist' of Mattoon: A Field Study of Mass Hysteria." It permanently associated the case with the concept of mass psychogenic illness (Johnson 1945). The short cycle of the tale followed the escalation pattern of story spreading, amplification by media inspiring further sightings, and the repetition until the cycle was broken. The end of the Mattoon Gasser flap came when the media stopped covering the reports [Dormancy]. The loss of attention once again strongly correlates to the end of the monster flap.

Spring-Heeled Jack

The precise history of Spring-heeled Jack is difficult to pin down because he appears early in the nineteenth century in London at a time when "ghost" type figures were still fresh in the public mind. In 1762, Londoners had been captivated by the ghostly events and poltergeist activity at Cock Lane in London (Cave, Forman, and Hicks 1989, 61–4), In 1837, numerous frightening "ghostly" attacks were experienced in the autumn and winter as a "bull" and later a "bear" before the assailant's form changed to that of "an imp of the 'Evil One'" (Bell 2017, 20), Jack's most well-known appearances take place in 1838 when reports of a villain that can appear in various guises and is assaulting women are sent to the mayor of London [Instigation]. It is very difficult to track down precisely where case-zero starts in this narrative because the story creeps into the public consciousness as part of a historical tendency toward ghost panics among the London public. Two cases in particular brought the Spring-heeled Jack story to the larger London population (Monstertalk 2013). Both took place in February 1838. On the evening of the 19th, Jane Alsop was attacked in the entrance of her father's home by a man pretending to be a policeman who claimed he had captured Spring-heeled Jack. When Jane went to get a candle, the man belched blue flame into her face and assaulted her. Nine days later, on the evening of the 28th, Lucy Scales and her sister were attacked by a man who shot blue flame from his mouth. Both cases were carried in the news, and many reports came in of the mysterious figure. In addition to the organic sightings by citizens of London and the journalistic coverage in the papers of the time, the figure became a popular character in fiction through the cheap pulp fiction periodicals of the time known as Penny Dreadfuls [Exploitation]. The sightings died out [Dormancy], but then resurged again in 1872 when sightings were reported in both the Peckham area south of London and in Sheffield in the middle of England. Sightings and reports abound in the 1870s, then the story dies again before resurging in the 1880s and again in the early 1900s. In each resurgence of sightings, the word-of-mouth reports and organic sightings are amplified by media and the viral cycle repeats. Perhaps no other case of monster flaps better displays the resurgent power of story after a period of dormancy. It is tempting to speculate, but impossible to prove, that these resurgences in sightings correspond to retellings of the previous events priming and shaping the experiences of a new generation of experiencers [Rumination, Nostalgia].

The Mothman

From late 1966 to the end of 1967, there were strange reports in Point Pleasant, West Virginia, about a man-sized bird with red eyes. November 16, 1966, gives us the initial report that heralds the outbreak when two couples are frightened by a red-eyed bird that chases them out of a local lover's lane known as "the TNT area" [Instigation]. These stories were part of a larger narrative of UFO sightings in the Ohio River Valley at the time and were being followed by several amateur UFO investigators and writers [Exploitation, Investigation]. After the initial sightings (and related police reports) the newspapers carried the story, and subsequent reports steadily came in. In addition to local news coverage, UFO/paranormal writer-investigators Gray Barker and John Keel both wrote articles and eventually books about the events. The story would even be tied back to folklore both as a form of cryptozoology and as a native curse (Keel 1975, 65).[12] From a narrative perspective, the story was wrapped up when the Silver Bridge collapsed, killing forty-six people right before Christmas of 1967 and the topic of flying man-sized birds took a backseat to the human tragedy for the community. It would not be the end of Mothman, as subsequent flaps of man-sized birds would be reported in Chicago in 2017 (Coleman 2017). While these sightings lacked many of the aspects of the Point Pleasant case fifty years before, they did carry forward the brand.

CONCLUSION

The goal of this chapter has been to organize some patterns I have observed during my own research into science and monsters. While I am deeply fascinated by monsters, I am equally fascinated by why people experience them. They serve many cultural and psychological purposes.[13] They scare us. They thrill us. Occasionally, they kill and eat us. But even when the monster is dead and gone, the story goes on and shapes the way we see the world, perhaps more literally affecting our perception that we understand.

In considering the ecosystem of stories as a biological model, the importance of attention in the story cycle became a critical property. There is a risk of tautology in that monster flaps are a product of story and we can't know about any flaps without story—because they *are* story. Modeling memetic transfer of story through a pollination model, rather than the virology model favored by Dawkins, has more aptness and less baggage. Ellis makes many excellent points about the nature of the spread of stories but doesn't distill the process down into a simple model. The biological described herein acknowledges the important work of folklore as an academic field and its work on studying the diffusion of stories. It also acknowledges the utility of the memetics model for describing cultural transfer. This is a hybrid model that avoids the pitfalls and connotations of "viral" terminology in describing how stories *actually* get transmitted and acknowledge the critical role that human minds have as the agar in which stories grow.

The most intriguing aspect of this research has been discovering the significance of *attention* in the narrative ecosystem. The economically driven sister field to diffusion studies is marketing. In 1997, nearly a decade before social media sites such as Facebook and Twitter appeared, business strategist and author Michael H. Goldhaber wrote that the world was shifting toward an "attention economy" (Goldhaber 1997). While a variety of factors may trigger a monster flap, I believe it is uncontroversial to conclude that it is attention, not monsters, that keeps the flap alive.

If it were only the telling of stories at stake here, the significance of monster flaps might be dismissed as unimportant. However, memetics and folklore both converge on the idea that stories don't just entertain us. Stories change our behavior. Stories are contagious whether they are literally true or not. Moral panics, whether localized or national, follow these same lines of transmission and can explode in behavior that is difficult to explain without the context of a network of narrative transmission and its impact on behavior. The familiar monster trope of the village mob with torches might just be one compelling story away from reality.

NOTES

1. It's difficult to say precisely what would constitute a *monster flap* from a numerical perspective. I'm going to constrain the definition to refer to three or more non-simultaneous reports within a close geographical area within three or fewer months. This feels numerically underwhelming, but the impact of a flap is easier gauged by the scope of the story's cultural reach rather than the quantitative number of sightings.

2. See Nickell's *Real-Life X-Files* (2001), Coleman's *Mysterious America* (2007).

3. Researcher John Keel hypothesized that the creature was an ultraterrestrial, a being that could travel from other dimensions into our own.

4. As seen in the spread of the idea of "meme" outside of Dawkins's original use in *The Selfish Gene* to mean "funny internet picture," the metaphor of highly infectious ideas is itself highly infectious and we now widely use the term "going viral" for the success of such images.

5. Dawkins himself became one of the greatest obstacles to acceptance of memetics when he followed-up on his idea with a 1993 paper titled "Viruses of the Mind." In this work, Dawkins rails against religion as an example of a dangerous "meme," identifying it as a "mind-virus." While Dawkins's personal disdain for religion is well known and has earned him a place as one of the "Four Horsemen" of Atheism, his claim that religion is a "harmful mind virus" is highly subjective and takes as a given the category of "religion" itself.

6. What exactly is a *monster*? For this model, a monster represents something unusual and possibly unnatural that generates menace, fascination, fear, and excitement. It might be a real animal or something else, but it exists within the perceptual realm such that it can be experienced to the extent that it generates narrative from those who encounter it. Stephen Asma says of monsters, "The monster is more than an odious creature of the imagination; it is a kind of *cultural category*, employed in domains as diverse as religion, biology, literature, and politics" (Asma 2016).

7. Such police reports are common to Bigfoot sightings where there is ambiguity around whether a monster, an animal, or a human prowler is to blame. Notable cases such as the Mothman of Point Pleasant, and the Lizardman of Scape Ore Swamp

involved police reports, but newspapers that report from police blotter often mention mysterious monster sightings. UFO cases also frequently cite police reports.

8. Here, I'm thinking of pastors who might explain the story as demonic, or politicians who might assure the public that there is no danger. Alternatively, some community leaders see economic opportunity in monster tourism and might actively promote such stories.

9. Good examples of this are the Mothman Festival of Point Pleasant, West Virginia, and the Bigfoot Daze festival of Willow Creek, California.

10. Skeptics of the supernatural assert that this is because the attacks were actually made by multiple wolves across the region.

11. Also, there had been previous and would be subsequent cases of mass wolf attacks but this one had the new newspapers amplifying and mutating the story in ways that promoted its spread.

12. Keel would reference Thunderbirds and the Garuda of India. He also tied the case to the "curse" of Chief Cornstalk (~1720s–1777). There is no known record of any curse utterances contemporary to the death of Chief Cornstalk (Laycock 2009).

13. On the functions of monsters, see Steven Asma's *On Monsters* (2016), Scott Poole's *Monsters in America* (2018), Christopher Dell's *Monsters* (2016), and Michael Meurger's *Lake Monster Traditions* (1988).

Part II

MONSTERS GUARDING THE GATES

Chapter 5

The Idea of Evil and Messianic Deliverance in the Satpanth Ismaili Tradition of South Asia

Wafi A. Momin

MESSIANISM, EVIL, AND THE SATPANTH ISMAILI TRADITION

The coming of an awaited savior to deliver the oppressed from tyrannical power or wicked forces is a motif found in many religious movements and cultic organizations through different ages. Such revolutionary currents are dubbed under a variety of labels, including millennial, messianic, chiliastic, and apocalyptic. They have tended to rally their supporters by fostering the vision of a new world order, promising emancipation from their present sufferings and the granting of rewards here on Earth (Landes 2000, xi–xii ff.). A noteworthy phenomenon within these currents is the intermingling of such motifs across religious lines—in some cases, even drawn from what are often viewed as irreconcilable worldviews—constructing in the process a harmonious conception of human history and its ultimate destiny. An interesting case of this cross-fertilization of messianic ideals is encountered in the long-awaited, tenth incarnation of the Hindu deity Viṣṇu, known as Kalki or Kalkin, and the adoption of this idea by many Muslim groups.

The doctrine of Viṣṇu's bodily manifestations (*avatār*s) as well as an exhaustive body of stories and customs surrounding it has long been recounted in Hindu scriptures, particularly in the epics of *Mahābhārata* and *Rāmāyaṇa* and the extensive body of Purāṇic literature. As per a generalized view of the doctrine, Viṣṇu has come to be associated with ten specific incarnations, moving from theriomorphic to anthropomorphic forms, which are distributed over a period of four ages (*yuga*s), with each subsequent age representing a gradual decline in the observance of religio-legal and moral norms (*dharma*). In these *yuga*s, whenever the evil powers are believed to have dominated and posed danger to the creation, Viṣṇu as the protector of life descended into the world to fight and exterminate them (O'Flaherty 1975, 175–237). He has, in consequence, remained an object of popular devotion all over India, while stories of some of his famous incarnations have repeatedly been told and adapted to different artistic expressions—paintings, theatrical performances, cinematic productions, and others.

The last of Viṣṇu's incarnations, Kalki, has yet to appear in the present and final *Kali* age, which represents the height of evil and moral degeneration. Varying details of Kalki's manifestation have been foretold in many Hindu texts according to which he will be born to a *brahmin*, Viṣṇuyaśas, in the village of Śambala toward the end of the *Kali* age. Riding a white-winged horse, he is depicted (in these prophecies) as leading an army to conduct multiple expeditions against heretical and cruel forces. These forces include those demons and humans whom (in some versions) Viṣṇu himself corrupted, in his previous incarnation as Buddha, by deluding them into a heretical doctrine (Buddhism and Jainism) so that gods could overpower them. Having annihilated those responsible for bringing about wickedness and injustice, Kalki will eventually herald the beginning of a new Golden Age (*Kṛta yuga*) and restore the balance of *dharma* (Norman 1908; O'Flaherty 1975, 231–7; O'Flaherty 1980, 38–45, 187–9, 200–4 ff.).

Over the centuries, there have been numerous claims to the status of the awaited Kalki emerging from within and outside of the Hindu tradition. Among Muslims, the doctrine has been employed by rulers and saints alike to serve their political project and preaching activities. In recent times, some Hindu observers have declared the Prophet Muḥammad as Kalki in a bid to foster communal harmony (Upādhyāy n.d.). The present chapter engages with the doctrine of the tenth incarnation as it was embraced and developed by a Muslim community from South Asia, namely the Satpanth (Nizārī) Ismailis. What makes for a worthwhile study of Viṣṇu's tenth manifestation in this branch of Islam is its treatment of the interconnected and multilayered notion of evil that the messiah is prophesized to exterminate. The problem of evil is further encountered within the community through the symbol of demonic figures—serving (at one level) as the functional other of the divine—which following the terminology in Hindu mythology are commonly styled as Daityas and Dānavas.

The Satpanth Ismailis of South Asia form part of the larger Shi'i Ismaili tradition whose followers are scattered amid many nations of Asia and Africa, as well as in sizeable numbers as diasporic communities in North America and Western Europe. The crystallization of their identity as "Ismaili" Muslims was the product of a long process of negotiations at the heart of which was the very nature of their religious heritage, articulated in terms of the practice of Satpanth (literally the "true path"). Broadly speaking, the beliefs and practices of Satpanth exhibited a rich interaction of ideas and cosmologies drawn from multiple religious streams, particularly those that are now tightly labeled under the categories of "Islamic" and "Hindu." This interplay is vividly seen in the eclectic character of literary works, doctrines, ritual observances, and social customs cultivated among the followers of Satpanth, all of which profoundly contributed to their deeply contested religious identity (Momin 2016).

A major literary production arising from Satpanth's evolution are the *Gināns*, a body of (mainly) poetic compositions of varying lengths dealing with doctrinal, cosmo-eschatological, socio-religious, moral-didactic, and other matters. Composed for the most part in Gujarati, Hindi, Punjabi, and Sindhi, they are attributed to the charismatic figures remembered in the tradition as proselytizers responsible for introducing the teachings of Satpanth to the masses of India (Shackle and Moir 2000). In the *Gināns*, we find a wealth of mythological and other stories bearing close resemblance to those appearing in Hindu scriptures (notably the *Purāṇas*) or to the Qur'ānic-Biblical narratives. The idea of evil and messianic deliverance occupy a central place in these stories and have continued to shape, over the past many centuries, the religious imagination of the Satpanth Ismailis, as well as some other groups that were historically associated with the Satpanth nexus but do not belong to the Ismaili cluster. Besides the avatāric conception, another important source of the messianic ideal fleshed out in the *Ginān* literature is connected to Islamic messianism, as represented by the notions of Mahdī (the "rightly guided one") and Qā'im (the "rising one") (Momin 2016, 141–52 ff.). It is, however, with the motif of Viṣṇu's incarnations, particularly the tenth one, that this chapter is concerned.

The teachings of Satpanth as expressed in the *Gināns* are time and again put forward by way of a code of conduct, which the adherents of (or aspirants to) the path are admonished to observe. At the same time, they are warned against unrighteous behavior, sinful acts and social iniquities which collectively constitute what may be called the evil imaginings of the *Gināns*, presented as an impediment to the attainment of the path's rewards. This overarching idea of "evil" covers the notion of moral and natural evil—what Paul Ricoeur has classified under the categories of *blame* and *lament* (Ricoeur 1985). The category of "blame"—one tied to sin and evildoing which warrant condemnation and/or punishment—is implicitly invoked in many compositions through the use of terms such as *pāp* and *gunāh* wherein it is posited as an unfortunate and undesirable human condition from which the audience of *Ginān*s is asked to be wary, seek forgiveness and work toward overcoming it (Shams 1952, *Ginān*s 26, 84, 98; Sadaradīn 1952, *Ginān*s 33, 146, 203; Imām Shāh et al. 1954, *Ginān*s 73a, 73b, attributed to Imām Shāh). Aside from such implicit reminders, the idea is more explicitly foregrounded in other compositions where the audience is directly alerted to the dangers of a host of "evil" actions and forewarned against their consequences. For example, in *Bāvan Gāṭī* and *Vīs Ṭol*, two thematically comparable *Ginān*s focusing on eschatological reckoning, the audience is cautioned about a series of sins, immoral comportment, and irreligious deeds which would bring about suffering to their perpetrators after their death either en route to their final destiny (as per the narrative of *Bāvan Gāṭī*) or on the Day of Judgment (in the case of *Vīs Ṭol*) (Sadaradīn and Imām Shāh n.d.).

The category of "lament," on the other hand, links evil with the experience of suffering (originating from diverse sources) and makes human beings its victims as opposed to culprits. It echoes more pronouncedly in those *Ginān*s which paint a bleak picture of the cataclysmic conditions engendered by the final and corrupt *Kali yuga* (*Kalajug*). In such *Ginān*s, even though the markers of maleficence are certain human actions, they are taken or predicted to come about as a *sine qua non* of the *Kali* age, which functions as a major driving force behind the moral breakdown in society. From this perspective, the sinister deeds and catastrophic signs repeatedly signaled as a consequence of the *Kali* age include quarrels between family members, reprehension of saints by their disciples, flouting of "caste" and religious norms, desertion of husbands by their wives for other men, affliction suffered by the righteous but fame attained by the hypocrites and so on. This thread of the *Kali yuga*'s dreadful consequences operates at two levels in the *Ginān*s. On the one hand, it takes the form of prophecies foretelling the sinister events about to befall, as evident from the use of "oracular" language in this instance. But, at the same time, it functions as a reminder of an actual state of affairs for the corrupt age has already begun and is well underway in casting its gloomy shadow. What we therefore see in some *Ginān*s is the space between these prophecies and the actual ramifications of the final age being somewhat bridged by creating a fear of the impending "great day" (*mahādan*), the ultimate day of reckoning, wherein some other signs compound the predicted markers of the widespread evil and suffering, for example, food and water shortage, lack of rain, earth becoming warmer, scenes of war, and so on (Shams 1917, esp. vv. 7, 18–19, 24, 28, 34–51, from *Vāek Moṭo*; Shams 1952, *Ginān*s 30, 43, 49, 50; Sadaradīn 1952, *Ginān*s 159, 168, 176, 180; Imām Shāh et al. 1954, *Ginān*s, 29, 38, 109, attributed to Imām Shāh). It is, however, not always the *Kali* age which is the source of wickedness in the *Ginān* literature. For instance, in one composition featuring a colloquy between Muḥammad and Jibrā'īl (Gabriel), the latter foretells how he would one by one take away from the world some cardinal virtues—blessing, generosity, modesty, faith, justice, patience, and so on—and the Qur'ān itself. The world being so deprived, this deplorable condition will herald the coming of the last day (*qiyāmat*). So, the absence of goodness resulting from the gradual disappearance of virtuous acts—or the source of evil in this case—ensues from the actions of an archangel associated with bringing God's revelations to Muḥammad (Shams 1952, *Ginān* 34).

In this manner, the overarching problem of evil in the *Ginān* literature plays out on two planes. When envisaged in the context of individual compositions, as outlined above, we find many cases of moral evil and suffering being indicated on their own with little or no direct connection drawn between the conditions of wickedness ensuing from the former or the darkness of a debased age leading to the latter. Furthermore, such insulated cases present us with some paradoxes. Evil is something connected to the wrongdoings of human beings about which they are warned, but they hardly stand a chance in overcoming them given the power exercised by the corrupt *Kali yuga*. Or, even though evil actions are despised by God, it is he (or one of his agents, such as Jibrā'īl) who causes evil (in different forms) to persist in the first place. However, when assessed holistically across the literature, this problem of evil subtly brings forth a tension through an overlapping space between *blame* and *lament*—between evil perpetrated and evil endured. As Ricoeur (1985, 636–7) has argued in a different context, this overlapping space may be seen, at a more abstract level, in the case of a punishment (of whatever kind) undergone for a sin and the resulting experience of suffering through guilt and pain, or how the fact of wrongdoing by one person, in its dialogical relationship, creates the condition of evil experienced by another either directly or indirectly. For Ricoeur, it further brings us to a more mysterious side of the enigma of evil, one that binds *blame* and *lament* in a dialectical structure, namely, the sense of belonging to a "history of evil" on the part of evildoers who find themselves entrapped in its dark power. To put it differently, the very wicked act which makes one its culprit also has the capacity of turning one into its victim.

I argue that when viewed in light of this dialogical intersection between *blame* and *lament* at the intra-Ginānic plane, we find an attempt in the compositions to offer a kind of resolution to the paradoxes associated with the origins of evil. These paradoxes are dealt with in different ways in which the agencies of a messianic savior (particularly Viṣṇu's tenth manifestation) and the demonic force (the anti-savior for the most part) play a paramount role. Although representing on one extreme the polarized forces of good and evil, these agencies also serve to bridge what at times come across as opposing categories of *blame* and *lament* by emerging in other cases as two sides of the same coin. In consequence, the idea of evil is sought to be addressed through such explanations as its necessity for human existence—it being a product of God's design or his playfulness for a larger cosmic end—and the liberating agency of Satpanth to lead people out of its clutches. To illustrate these points, I will focus in the next section on the dialectics of some specific texts dealing with the avatāric conception to show how the disparate threads of moral evil and suffering presented above come together to tell a larger story of the origins of evil and its annihilation by the savior god.

ANNIHILATING EVIL: THE *GINĀN* LITERATURE AND THE AVATĀRIC PARADIGM

The conception of Viṣṇu's incarnations, focusing especially on the tenth one, makes up an important facet of the Ginānic worldview. It essentially underpins the dialectics of several compositions of cosmo-eschatological and messianic-apocalyptic strain. There are, however, some compositions exclusively dedicated to the theme of the deity's *avatār*s and the annihilation of evil. Collectively, all these compositions foster the avatāric paradigm of the Satpanth's soteriological vision. In what follows, I will focus on the dialectics of two specific *Ginān*s bearing the name *Das Avatār* ("ten incarnations"), and qualified further as being the longer (*moṭo*) and the shorter (*nāno*) version. More precisely, I will follow through pertinent aspects of *Moṭo Das Avatār*, which is far more complex and elaborate in its description, and tease out the ways in which the notion of evil and messianic deliverance plays out in it; these aspects will then be compared with the narrative of the much shorter *Nāno Das Avatār* toward the end of the section.

The narrative of the longer version of the *Das Avatār* begins with some allusions to the primeval times. In particular, it glorifies the Godhead by invoking his cosmic creations, focusing on the fashioning of four *kalpa*s (a long cycle of time) and the *siddha*s ("demigods") that flourished in those aeons. In the last of the *kalpa*s, the Godhead brought forth four *yuga*s (another cycle of time), so as to manifest himself in ten bodily forms (Imām Shāh vs 1865/1808–9 CE, ff. 3v–4v; Imām Shāh 1923, 1).[1] From the outset, the idea of Divine Being is conveyed using a host of appellations, most frequently through the generic Sāmījī (from the Sanskrit *svāmī*, "lord"), but also with specific names such as Harī, Nārāyaṇ and Viṣṇu. The last three names along with others employed to refer to the Divine Being, as well as the overarching structure of the narrative itself, place the *Das Avatār* firmly within the worldview of many of the *Purāṇa*s, where Viṣṇu subsists as the *raison d'être* of all the creation. In invoking different appellations for the Lord, the narrative subtly plays with its audience's imagination, as if to foreground both his transcendent being—using abstract concepts such as Sāmījī, Shāh ("monarch") and *nirañjan* ("unstained one")—and his immanent state through the kind of well-known names just mentioned. His divine nature, in other words, is endowed with a certain elusiveness, both within and beyond the reach of experience. This is an important feature not only of the *Das Avatār* but many other *Ginān*s, where the Supreme Being's identity straddles between something well demarcated, or what at best is conjured by the familiar Indic and Perso-Arabic terminology reserved for the figure of Godhead. I shall come to the implications of this poetics of encountering the divine later in the chapter.

From here the text proceeds with recounting the story of each of the Godhead's incarnations, arranged in ten sections of varying lengths. In general, the main plot in each section revolves around a bodily manifestation of the Lord and the feat achieved during its tenure, either by slaying a demon or overwhelming the maleficent forces that ravaged the world order. While following this pattern, the stories also furnish details relevant to the background of a given incarnation, and (in many cases) even connect the dots of a grand cosmic saga. This includes making references to various threads of the larger avatāric paradigm and eschatological ideas, enunciated either in other sections of the *Das Avatār* itself or elsewhere in the *Ginān* corpus.

To take one example, the narration of the first incarnation, *Mach* (from *Matsya*, "fish"), first highlights the creation of Brahmā, presented as the true guide (*satagur*), from whose light the Divine Being brought forth the creation, life forms, division of different eras and so on. Thereupon, the story transitions to the birth of Sañkhāsar—born of Brahmā and presented as a demon—who steals the *Veda*s and thereby causes darkness to prevail. Upon Brahmā's pleading, Harī takes the form of a fish to rescue the *Veda*s, and chases Sañkhāsar down to different underworlds (*pātāl*), where he seeks refuge one after another before being caught and moving on to the next retreat. As Harī (in the form of fish) searches each of these places, he enquires from their "custodians" about the demon's whereabouts, who in return for disclosing this information earn a pledge (*qaul*) to be fulfilled by the Godhead himself. So, Mother Earth (*dharatī mātā*), with whom the demon finds a shelter early on, asks to be married to the Lord as her pledge. Harī grants the pledge by assuring that he would marry her at the close of four *yuga*s and the conclusion of his ten bodily manifestations, when innumerable souls would be delivered during the course of succeeding ages, and thus hinting at the upcoming time of great rejoicing—a thread that echoes in many other *Ginān*s. In this way, the honoring of each of the vows is assured in a forthcoming age, when the individual(s) in question is/are foretold the honorable, reincarnated life he/she/they would undergo, many of which then get embedded in the narratives of subsequent incarnations later in the text. Toward the end of the story, Sañkhāsar, having exhausted all possible shelters, hides himself in an ocean where the fish (Viṣṇu) rescues the *Veda*s by tearing open the demon's belly where they were kept (Imām Shāh vs 1865/1808–9 CE, ff. 4v–18r; Imām Shāh 1923, 1–7).

In Hindu scriptures, Viṣṇu's incarnation as a fish is generally associated with the flood myth when he saves Manu (the progenitor of the human race) and other life forms from a cosmic deluge (O'Flaherty 1975, 179–84; Dimmitt and van Buitenen 1978, 71–4). However, this motif is not the concern of the *Das Avatār*. Rather, it is another thread—albeit comparatively less widespread than the flood myth—which is employed in the text, apparently in line with its structural organization and narrative strategy whereby each section, as one of its major concerns, deals with the destruction of a demon or an evil power by the Godhead. The *Das Avatār*'s telling of the myth of the "stealing of the *Veda*s" follows, in the main, its central plot (O'Flaherty 1980, 99–102), though like many of the myth's variants, it weaves in its own threads. These include presaging some of the main characters and the reasons for their appearance in the subsequent stages of the "ten incarnation" drama; in this way, two central characters from the episode of the tenth manifestation are introduced right at the outset, as we shall shortly see.

The "demon" of the story, Sañkhāsar, as well as others mentioned in the text, are referred to as *daiñt* or *daṇav*, both terms used interchangeably. In Hindu mythology, Daityas and Dānavas—collectively also known as Asuras—form part of a class of demons frequently linked with the notion of evil and darkness. However, there is nothing inherent in their nature as a group which makes them "demonic," for the virtuous and sinister qualities strictly associated with gods and demons—on the basis of which they are then distinguished as good and evil—are found in them alike, with both groups constantly exchanging their "divine" and "demonic" roles. In fact, in physical appearance, Daityas and Dānavas are hardly distinguishable from gods and acquire their "demonic" function from the fact that they are portrayed as opposed to the latter with whom they are perpetually at war for the attainment of superhuman powers (O'Flaherty 1980, 57–93 ff.). This ambiguity pervades, at many levels, the *Das Avatār* (and other *Ginān*s), as may be readily seen in the birth of a demon (Sañkhāsar) from a god (Brahmā), or in the case of a virtuous demon, Pahelāj (Prahlāda of the Sanskrit accounts), who is guarded by Viṣṇu, in his incarnation as Narasiñha (man-lion), from the atrocities of his own father, Haraṇākañs (Hiraṇyakaśipu), perpetrated in reaction to his son's incessant devotion to Viṣṇu (Imām Shāh vs 1865/1808–9 CE, ff. 21r–30v; Imām Shāh 1923, 9–14).

The "evil" act committed by Sañkhāsar, which leads to his slaying, is the stealing of Brahmā's *Veda*s. In contrast to the stories of some other manifestations, the narrative here does not explicitly dwell as to why this act in itself warrants his killing and makes a "demon" of him, except for indicating that it brings about darkness (*añdhakār*). But, in the course of its narration, the text subtly lays out the saliency of the four *Veda*s as authoritative proofs (*pramāṇ*) in each of the four *yuga*s. Such hints operate against the backdrop of the *Veda*s' significance in the cultural landscape of premodern India, which (we may reasonably assume) formed part of the religious imagination of the *Das Avatār*'s audience too. Their rescuing, thus, symbolizes the protection of the very embodiment of a divinely ordained code; by stealing the *Veda*s, Saṅkhāsar becomes opposed to Harī who is the very source of that code. The ambivalence of "evil" in this episode is further compounded by the fact that those agreeing to reveal Saṅkhāsar's whereabouts do so only after being granted a pledge, even while fully recognizing from the moment they encounter the demon that he had in stealing the *Veda*s committed something wrong. This puts a "transactional" slant to the whole sequence of events, with the "moral" standing of those so favored by Harī (who is equally a part of the accord) hardly any better than that of Saṅkhāsar. The shifting burden of this "unrighteous" conduct balances itself out in the end when Saṅkhāsar entreats the Lord and earns a vow (*vacan*). The demon, as his vow, asks to fight the Divine Being until his tenth manifestation, which is granted. So, the continuity and persistence of evil in the form of a demon is ensured by the Godhead himself in each of his subsequent incarnations. This interesting motif plays itself out more explicitly in another composition *Muman Citaveṇī*, where the drama of ten bodily manifestations and the killing of a demon in each case are tied to the Lord's playfulness (*līlā*) (Momin 2016, 142–3). We are in short dealing here with a paradox consisting two aspects of the origins of evil—God incarnates to protect his devotees and the righteous people from a sinister power, but that power is what God himself makes possible. The subtle way in which these two aspects are reconciled in the *Ginān*s (alongside offering other resolutions) is the motif of God's larger cosmic design, his divine play.

Against this backdrop, we now turn to the discourse of the tenth incarnation forming part of the last (and longest) section of *Moṭo Das Avatār*. The narration opens with an indication of change in time, a transition from the third (*Dvāpara*) to the fourth and final age (*Kali*), before introducing the main characters of the story. The first protagonist introduced is the demon of the *Kali yuga*, Daiñt Kāliṅgā, who, having descended in Chīṇ Mahā Chīṇ (a reference supposedly to some place in China) and established his rule, is depicted as fully active in his mission all over the world. Thereafter, the authority of *Atharva Veda* is affirmed in the age of *Kali* when Brahmā (the archetypal guide) has manifested as the Prophet Muḥammad, Īshvar[2] as Adam, and Nakalaṅkī as the tenth manifestation of Harī who resides in the Arab region (Ārab Desh). At this point, Pīr Shams, a Satpanthī preacher, is introduced as the current manifestation of Brahmā who, after touring twenty-four countries, reaches the residence of Kāliṅgā, and taking a parrot's form goes to the demon's wife, queen Surjā, where a conversation ensues between them. The parrot first alerts Surjā of Harī's erstwhile (nine) incarnations in the previous ages when he destroyed nine demons, and forewarns her that in his last *avatār* the Lord will kill her husband. Disclosing his identity, Shams reveals that owing to her righteous (*satavañtī*) credentials he has come to show her the path of truth (*satapañth*), which alone will guide her to salvation. He further cautions Surjā and her close associates of the signs of the "great day" (*mahādan*), which will bring hardship and calamities upon those remaining oblivious to the path. The queen pledges that they will abide by the saint's teachings and entreats to be protected from the apocalyptic doomsday whose signs were just revealed to them. Pīr Shams, upon listening to their supplication, initiates Surjā and others into the practice of Satpanth and leaves them by promising to return at the time of a great war. Of Surjā's associates, the text mentions Kamlā Kuñvar (Kāliṅgā's son), Ajīyā and Vajīyā who feature in other *Ginān*s too. Surjā and Kamlā, who are among the central protagonists here, were so predicted to appear at the time of Godhead's first incarnation when their precursors revealed Sañkhāsar's whereabouts to him (Imām Shāh vs 1865/1808–9 CE, ff. 119v–125v; Imām Shāh 1923, 57–60).

The story at this juncture switches to Shams's arrival in Jañpudīp (from Jambudvīpa, a reference to India), followed by a brief account of his progeny's mission. It focuses particularly on a meeting between his descendant Hasan Kabīrdīn (a young child then) and the Lord (now frequently referred to as Shāh in the text), allusions to which are found in some other *Ginān*s. What is significant about this meeting is Shāh's conferring of a boon (*var*) to young Hasan for him to be the agent of the emancipation of innumerable souls (*anat karoḍ*) in the *Kali yuga*. To this burden of responsibility, Hasan expresses concerns given the atrocities of the age, but the Lord assures his assistance in the fulfillment of this duty. The boon in this way anticipates Viṣṇu's vow to Mother Earth, that of marrying her upon the delivering of innumerable souls in his last incarnation (Imām Shāh vs 1865/1808–9 CE, ff. 125v–130r; Imām Shāh 1923, 60–2).

The text then unveils the conditions of the awaited savior's advent by providing an exhaustive catalogue of the kind of sinister conduct and signs of physical calamities that I discussed in the previous section. In the proliferation of a corrupt state of affairs, what are dubbed as "great sins" (*mahā pāp*), the vicious designs of demons (Daityas and Dānavas) are fully at work, under the command of Kāliṅgā, who alongside the *Kali* age are portrayed as partners in crime for the decline of *dharma*. Alluding to the fulfillment of these signs, the time for the approaching battle is heralded all over the world, including the residence of Kāliṅgā, by the proclamation of Shāh's power and glory. This prompts the demon and his warriors to prepare for the war and depart for Jañpudīp after installing Kamlā Kuñvar on the throne. The narrative next graphically elaborates upon the preparations in Shāh's camp, providing intricate details of his warriors and weapons. In his camp, Shāh is joined by a multitude of supporters, the demigods and countless liberated souls of the earlier eras, the virtuous figures from Viṣṇu's previous incarnations, prophets, angels, genies, spirits, and many others. Shāh himself is portrayed as a majestic king riding his richly caparisoned horse, Duldul, and carrying a three-edged sword. Such is the extent of his army that when it sets off for Jañpudīp the whole world trembles (Imām Shāh, vs 1865/1808–9 CE, ff. 130r–150v; Imām Shāh 1923, 62–72).

Having stationed in Jañpudīp both the armies come face to face; Kāliṅgā attempts to create fear in Shāh's ranks through his magical tricks, and the Lord's warriors seek permission to counter by attacking his forces. At this point, Surjā and Kamlā arrive in Shāh's camp—having been commanded by Pīr Shams (who did return to Chīṇ to fulfill his promise) to leave the country and meet the Lord—and offer gratitude for being liberated through his mercy. Informed by Shāh that the time of Kāliṅgā's annihilation has come, they take permission to go to the latter's camp and implore him to abandon the idea of fighting the Lord of the three worlds. Ignoring their advice, Kāliṅgā boasts of his strength and claims to destroy their Lord with his forces. This angers Surjā who hits her husband's neck with a staff and knocks off his head. A panic erupts in the demon's camp leading to a formidable battle between the two armies. In the end, Kāliṅgā's forces are vanquished with the demon's head being trampled under Duldul's hoofs and thrown into Chīṇ; and so his city sinks. Having annihilated the arch demon of the age, the narrative moves to recounting the coming of the "great day" with its frightening calamities from which only the righteous believers are spared who now rule the world. The saga of tenth *avatār* culminates in Shah's fulfillment of his pledge by marrying Mother Earth who is now referred to as the virgin earth (Imām Shāh vs 1865/1808–9 CE, ff. 150v–171r; Imām Shāh 1923, 72–82).

The *Moṭo Das Avatār*'s telling of the tenth incarnation follows, in its basic plot, many a thread and symbol associated with Kalki's advent—the messiah's campaigns against heretics, his riding a horse with a lustrous sword, and his parrot acting as a messenger, for example. But the telling varies in numerous ways too. Even though the messiah has yet to come, who is not called Kalki but Nakalaṅkī (the "unstained one"), details of his manifestation have been narrated as if they have already happened. In fact, the language of the narrative constantly switches between past and future in order to recount events from mythical or remote period, from the time when the text was composed or modified (considering some variations in its manuscripts), as well as those about to occur. Also, instead of the *Kali* age being personified and eventually vanquished, in the *Das Avatār* it is Kāliṅgā who functions as the arch demon, the pivotal symbol of evil alongside the corrupting force of the last *yuga*. The savior is also referred to as Qā'im thereby invoking an Islamic millenarian ideal that is further cemented by occasional reference to Kāliṅgā as the Dajjāl, the "Antichrist" of the Muslims tradition. In this way, the messianic-apocalyptic image of the end time associated within Islamic and Hindu traditions somewhat blend in the soteriological vision of *Moṭo Das Avatār*.

The story revolves around three geographical spaces, Chīṇ (the residence of Kāliṅgā), Ārab Desh, Setar Dīp or Vīracā Shaher (the "seat" of Shāh) and Jañpudīp (the arena of actual battle and eventual rejoicing). The reference to Shāh's seat brings us to another connected issue, that of his identity. It is not until the end of the narrative that Shāh, the tenth *avatār*, is unequivocally identified as Murtaẓā 'Alī, Muḥammad's cousin and son-in-law regarded as his rightful successor by Shi'i Muslims. This contrasts with the narrative of *Nāno Das Avatār* where 'Alī is introduced as the tenth manifestation, Nakalañkī, right from the outset and further qualified (even if by an allusion) as being Sirī Salām Shāh (a probable, if opaque, reference to an *imam* recognized by the Ismailis), the manifestation of 'Alī himself. In fact, as per the narrative strategy of *Nāno Das Avatār*, every incarnation is plainly stated together with the evil power he annihilated in that form. Here, we do not find the threads of individual manifestations being woven in the way they are in the longer version. Rather, matter of fact statements are furnished concerning each of the incarnations, the demons killed by them and some other particulars—a kind of synoptic view found at the end of each section in (some versions of) *Moṭo Das Avatār*. The narrative of the shorter version as such only recounts that in his tenth manifestation Nakalañkī/'Alī will slay the demon with no other details, let alone any mention of Surjā/Kamlā or other protagonists of the longer version (Sadaradīn 1929). This contrasting narrative strategy has implications for approaching the identity of the savior figure (or any other protagonist) in the longer or shorter version of *Das Avatār* (or for that matter in other compositions); that is, specific meanings associated with these protagonists in many cases only become evident when such details as may be available about them are compared in light of the full range of threads enunciated throughout the *Ginān* corpus. Seeing in this purview, the reference to Setar Dīp (referring possibly to Iran) connects with those made in reference to the "seat" of the Lord in other *Ginān*s (such as Arab land, Iraq region, and the country of Delam) which collectively hint at some place west of India whence the savior will command his army for the great battle.

To conclude our discussion of the *Das Avatār* narratives, unlike the shorter version, it is in *Moṭo Das Avatār* that a number of threads connected to the saga of a Satpanth soteriological vision become somewhat apparent. Also, the problem of evil that otherwise presents paradoxes in different *Ginān*s is resolved here, in some ways at least, through the agencies of the divine and demonic, and the primordial battle between good and evil represented by them.

EPILOGUE: MESSIANIC EXPECTATIONS AND RENEWED INTERPRETATIONS OF EVIL

The idea of evil and messianic deliverance forming part of *Moṭo Das Avatār* (and other comparable *Ginān*s) is couched in what may be called mythic stories. The resulting mythic imagination works alongside a discursive formulation in the *Ginān* literature that invites its audience to constantly self-reflect and probe into the surrounding world in search of the recurrent, existential questions posed to it; in this way, the audience is led to find its rightful place in the world order by being wary of maleficent behavior and social inequities. What we therefore witness is a kind of dialectics that not only inform a given composition but also speak to and underpin the larger body of Ginānic worldview. The problem of evil and the connected thread of messianic expectations provide one such example where various facets of the problem need to be assessed in terms of the concerned (individual) compositions and the larger *Ginān* corpus.

Approached in this light, the Ginānic attempt at a resolution to the problem of evil on first glance presents us with some paradoxes. On the one hand, the category of moral evil—sin and evildoing—is depicted as a deplorable human condition to be constantly kept under watch and overcome by rising to the challenge, so to speak—a personal struggle for transforming one's conduct by following the prescribed teachings. On the other hand, these very sins, wicked deeds as well as human sufferings emanating from predicted calamities are part and parcel of a debased age over which one has no control—people are bound to fall prey to these evils save the fortunate ones, the righteous followers of Satpanth. In between these paradoxes, the agencies of the savior Godhead (in different forms) and a wicked demon furnish possibilities for carving some resolutions, particularly through an implicit logic of the necessity of evil as part of a divine cosmic design, and its persistence (including in a demonic character) by God's will toward the fulfillment of that purpose. These layered engagements with the problem of evil have been further enriched when the "elliptical" references to the savior-demon figures and the clash between them were subjected to other interpretative possibilities, something that has made the compositions part of a lived reality of the people concerned. Before closing this chapter, some examples of this continued engagement with the idea of evil and messianic expectations are in order.

The Ginānic ideas of the awaited savior and the annihilation of evil were given new meanings roughly from the middle of the nineteenth century when we see the followers of Satpanth engaging in new ways with the questions of their beliefs and practices, as well as that of their religious identity—whether Hindu or Muslim, and in the latter case, Shi'i or Sunni. These questions were contested through various platforms and often took the shape of heated debates and polemical exchanges, leading to their division in distinct sectarian groups. The teachings of *Ginān*s formed a bedrock to these debates which were subjected to new interpretations, reflecting the exigencies of a different era. While this quest for identity pulled those invested toward different ideological camps, a numerically dominant group argued that the message of Satpanth was nothing but Ismaili teachings passed down for generations, at the heart of which was the doctrine of a hereditary line of *imam*s ("spiritual leaders"). In their time, they argued, this line was represented by the Aga Khans, the proclaimed Nizārī *imam*s of Persian ancestry who had acquired sociopolitical eminence under the British rule in India. A prominent figure from this line was Aga Khan III, Sulṭān Muḥammad Shāh (1877–1957), also a notable Muslim leader of his time.

The intellectuals of this group sought to legitimize their position by arguing for the primacy of a living and present *imam*, who alone was not only the true Mahdi, the messianic figure whose appearance the Muslims had along been awaiting, but the tenth *avatār* of Viṣṇu whose advent was foretold in Hindu scriptures. What is more, they made even a bigger claim—the Aga Khan was the very savior whose advent had been predicted in the Bible, according to a reading of a section from Chapter 12 of the Book of Daniel, which alludes to the rising of the messiah in troubled times. Hence, the Aga Khan was presented simultaneously as the tenth *avatār* of Hindus, the awaited Mahdi of Muslims, and the messiah (Christ) of Christians, a truly global savior. As to the reference of troubled times, they held that it actually meant the events of World War I, and it was the Aga Khan who in his role as the savior worked toward bringing peace among different nations and religious communities, an invaluable and a widely acclaimed service for the cause of humanity. By and large, then, the demon of the *Ginān*s prophesized to be vanquished by the messiah was, as per this interpretation, accepted among some circles as the catastrophic times of World War I (Momin 2016, 219–43).

The provocative and pragmatic nature of this interpretation notwithstanding, many segments of the community have continued to imagine and speculate on the possible meanings of the Ginānic images of messiah and demon right through to the present. A noteworthy example in this connection may be seen in the work of a missionary and writer Abuali Alibhai Aziz (1919–2008). Through his scores of sermons (*wa'ẓ*) delivered all around the world, over the course of his long and distinguished career as a preacher in the community, Abuali Aziz more than anyone else has played a quintessential role in keeping the mythic imagination of the *Ginān*s alive by making it relevant and appealing to a new generation. The idea of the awaited messiah and the extermination of evil formed noteworthy themes in his sermons.

In some sermons, he saw the Ginānic war between the messiah and the demon as an impending clash between religion and communist powers, the latter viewed as a political system inherently inimical to any form of faith and doctrines associated with it. He held that although, during the years when he delivered sermons on this theme, it was Soviet Russia which represented the major communist power under whose regime many Ismaili communities suffered hardships, in time China would emerge into the paramount center of communism, the demon Kāliṅgā of the *Ginān*s. Furthermore, he interpreted Kāliṅgā's family members, Surjā, Kamlā, Ajīyā and Vajīyā (the last two taken as the demon's daughters), as different facets of the community's strength and resilience that will withstand the communist powers. So the motif of righteous forces, represented by the likes of Prahlāda, Surjā, Kamlā, germinating from and eventually challenging the wicked ones found a contemporary meaning in his sermons. In the end, at a time not too far in the future, the designated *imam*, Nakalaṅkī of the *Ginān*s, will deliver the community and other righteous believers from the mounting challenges and sufferings caused by anti-religious communist forces (Aziz 1982).

Indeed, the continued fascination and engagement with the motifs of demonic corruption and messianic deliverance bear witness to the fact that *Ginān*s are not dead texts, being relics of the past alone, but deeply inform the worldview and religious imagination of a living community. At the same time, they show how different segments of the community have creatively dealt with the long-debated problem of evil which takes human beings at the heart of something deeper within themselves, a constant battle between good and evil which they project on the outer world. For these reasons, we see a rich variety of forms and meanings that these ideas have taken in the life of the community, mirrored not only in literary and religious works but expressed in a variety of other ways.

NOTES

1. In Hindu mythology, *kalpa* denotes a day in the life of Brahmā, equalling 4.32 billion years. The concept of *yuga*, on the other hand, commonly refers to a cycle of four ages whose collective period adds up to 4.32 million years. In the Ginānic scheme of cosmic time, we generally find the idea of four *kalpa*s and four *yuga*s, though many *Ginān*s (including the longer version of the *Das Avatār*) often invoke the sense of several *kalpa*s and *yuga*s, implying indefinite time. The notion of *siddha*s also conveys the meaning of "perfected" beings that marked each of the aeons whose identity is given as Jakhs, Megs, Kinars, and Devs.

2. Although the text is not explicit, this seems to be a reference to Śiva as noted in other *Ginān*s.

Chapter 6

Ghost Stories from *Tales of Retribution*
Understanding Elements of Seventeenth-Century Japanese Ghost Stories

Frank F. Chu

This chapter introduces the reader to twenty-four Japanese ghost stories from the *Tales of Retribution* (Japanese: *Inga monogatari*)—a collection of supernatural stories published ca. 1660 (Reider 2001, 85) during Japan's early Tokugawa era by author SUZUKI Shōsan (1579–1655). Comparing this text with prominent works from earlier eras reveals how *Tales of Retribution* embodies changing understandings of Buddhism and Buddhist institutions in Tokugawa Japan and offers valuables insights into the putatively "supernatural" power of Buddhist institutions, particularly whether Buddhism was seen to be effective at laying ghosts to rest. This analysis is supported by a framework that breaks down the key components of each tale into *causation*, *manifestation*, and *resolution* as a method to map out narrative structures particular to the genre.

Through a detailed analysis of the fundamental components of the twenty-four early Tokugawa period ghost stories found in the *Tales of Retribution*, this chapter reveals how the larger Tokugawa period witnessed a widespread transformation in ideas concerning the efficacy of Buddhist ritual in subduing "ghosts" (*yūrei*). It shows how these earlier stories have themselves drawn from a pool of historical ghost story "matter"—as evidenced in the *Nihon ryōiki* and the *Konjaku monogatari-shū*—while also foregrounding significant additions made as they were adapted for new audiences in the eighteenth century. Toward this last aim, I show how the popular seventeenth-century ghost story of Kasane (whose tragic tale would eventually become the basis for the story of Oiwa) is composed of elements inherited from a number of earlier stories found in SUZUKI Shōsan's *Tales of Retribution*. This study, therefore, provides a critical grounding and much-needed context for future research into the more nuanced and complex stories of the Tokugawa regime's later years.

The Japanese word *yūrei* is most often translated into English as "ghost." For the purposes of this chapter, I will use the widely acknowledged definition offered by Japanese *yōkai* (monster) scholar KOMATSU Katsukiko, who presents a dictionary definition of *yūrei* as "the manifestation of a departed soul that cannot rest in peace" (Komatsu 2017, 134–5). I will also use this definition to identify stories featuring *yūrei* which, much like "ghosts" today, were known in premodern Japan by a host of other names, including *rei* (ghost), *ryō* (ghost), *bōkon* (departed soul), *bōrei* (departed spirit), *ikiryō* (living spirit), *mōja* (deceased person), and so on.

Of primary importance is an acknowledgment that the history of the development of ghost stories is indelibly tied to the history of Buddhism in premodern Japan. The first known references to ghosts, as we understand *yūrei* today, can be found in the *Nihon ryōiki* (the oldest known extant Japanese *setsuwa* ("myth and legends") collection), which was compiled by Buddhist cleric Kyōkai during the late Nara period (782–805) (Komatsu 2017). At that time Buddhism had already been practiced in Japan for hundreds of years (Bowring 2005, 16–17). The term the *Nihon ryōiki* is typical of Buddhist didactic collections in that it was written with the purpose of moderating or controlling behavior through warnings of karmic consequence (Nakamura 2014).

According to Komatsu (2017), the first appearances in literature of the word *rei* (ghost) date back to the twelfth century at the end of the Heian period around the time of the compilation of another *setsuwa* collection, the twelfth-century *Konjaku monogatari-shū* (*Anthology of Tales from the Past*). This grand anthology contains over a thousand tales, a large number of which are Buddhist didactic stories (Reider 2001). Throughout this chapter, I will contrast and compare elements taken from a number of these stories with those found in the SUZUKI Shōsan's *Tales of Retribution*—itself a Buddhist didactic collection (Tyler 1989, 94). This comparison reveals transforming ideas concerning the role of the Buddhist institution in its power to control ghosts—moving from having little to no power, to mixed ability, to being the most efficacious tool in quieting restless spirits—ultimately revealing the increasing role of the Tokugawa shogunate's *danka* system in structuring society.

CONTEXT FOR THE COMPOSITION OF SHŌSAN'S *TALES OF RETRIBUTION*

Most scholars consider early modern Japanese society to begin in the Edo period with the establishment of the Tokugawa shogunate. This period was ushered in by the decisive Battle of Sekigahara in 1600, which brought an end to Japan's tumultuous warring states period and began 260 years of relative peace and stability under Tokugawa rule. The feudal society of Tokugawa Japan saw the beginning, and eventual end, of Japan's isolationist policy (*sakoku* or "closed country") as well as the establishment of a strict hierarchical social class system. It is also considered a time when Japanese culture flourished preparing the ground for the development of popular culture products such as *kaidan* (strange and mysterious tales), which reached a peak in popularity during the mid-eighteenth century (Reider 2001, 79). Ghost stories were a prominent category within this genre and were widely enjoyed by the general population through a range of different mediums such as published novels and stage productions. A number of the more famous ghost characters, such as Oiwa from the well-received *Tōkaidō Yotsuya kaidan*,[1] have retained their popularity even today (Konita 2012, 10).

SUZUKI Shōsan came of age during the twilight years of Japan's Warring States period. Born into a warrior family in 1579 he served as a retainer in the army of Tokugawa Ieyasu (1541–1616)—one the three warlords who united Japan and the founder of the Tokugawa shogunate. Although he remained in service to the Tokugawa regime until his death in 1655, Shōsan was also ordained as a Buddhist monk in 1620. While on active military duty, he wrote a pamphlet promoting the superiority of Buddhism, and in his later years he composed a book denouncing Christianity—a shared target of criticism with the early Tokugawa shogunate. The Buddhist bioethicist Damien Kewon (2004, 285–6) explains that "his desire was to have a non- (or supra-) sectarian Buddhism declared the faith of the nation . . . (his) form of Buddhism was intended for all people, and so was designed to be suited to secular as well as clerical life."

Royall Tyler (1989), who has written on Tokugawa Buddhist ideologies, depicts Shōsan as believing that only by practicing Buddhism can the Shogunate construct its ideal of a harmonized society; however, for Shōsan, Buddhist practice has far more in common with the not explicitly religious notion of hard work than it does with more traditionally identified religious practice: all people working in harmony, each in his place, so that the shogun's rule should survive forever in peace. Shōsan addressed his teaching to all four classes of Tokugawa society (warrior, peasant, artisan, and merchant). On the one hand, he worked to implement Tokugawa propaganda; on the other, he preached a popular and inclusive form of Buddhism directed at the non-aristocratic populace. The *Tales of Retribution* was a work targeted toward a popular audience with the purpose of promoting ideologies the author saw as in support of both the Tokugawa regime and the Buddhist communities.[2]

A hiragana syllabary version of the *Tales of Retribution* was published posthumously in 1660 with a katakana version the following year (Reader 2001, 85).³ In the preface to the hiragana version it proclaims: "Here is a picture book called the Tales of Retribution, which was written by somebody named Shōsan. Children read it playfully and consider it to be just fun" (Sano 1929, 139). By contrast, the katakana version states: "(This) work was written as an expedient means to lead people to religious awakening and to record the manifest concept of cause and effect" (Yoshida 1962, 3–4).⁴ This publishing history reveals a range of frameworks for interpreting these stories—either as didactic stories or as "just fun." Both versions remained popular for readers of *Inga monogatari*, and their continued literary endurance remains noteworthy (Reider 2001, 85).

Noriko Reider's (2001) research on *kaidan* describes the *Tales of Retribution* as simultaneously didactic and entertaining. She emphasizes the playful side of the texts and how this fusion of the secular and didactic reflects the everyday reality of the era allowing for a wide reception of readers and audiences across Japan. As *yōkai* scholar Komatsu emphasizes, perhaps one of the most enduring elements common to all *kaidan* ghost stories is that they take place within the context of a range of social relationships circumscribed by the deceased individual's pre-death existence (2017, 141). My framework, therefore, builds upon the assumption that to a degree, the ideological, social, and political backgrounds of the era are often reflected in elements of these stories, especially in (1) the reasons given for why a ghost is unable to rest in peace, (2) the way in which it manifests, and (3) the methods behind the way it is dealt with. This narratological structure of *causation, manifestation,* and *resolution* will be used to identify key elements at critical stages of the stories analyzed. Although the *Tales of Retribution* has never been translated into English, or any language other than Japanese, it is beyond the capacity of this chapter to offer complete transcripts of my own translations. While conclusions are drawn from an analysis of the entire text, I have chosen to offer examples from key stories and then present them for discussion. For this work, I have used the 1914 version, which is accessible online through the Japanese National Diet library.⁵

DISCUSSION OF *YŪREI* PRIOR TO *TALES OF RETRIBUTION*—SOMETHING OLD, SOMETHING NEW

The earliest known references to *yūrei,* as we have defined them, appear in two of the 116 stories on myths and legends collected within the *Nihon ryōiki* (782–805)—Chapter 1, story 12 (1.12) and Chapter 3, story 27 (3.27). In story 1.12, a monk comes across a skull that has been trampled underfoot by passing men and animals. The holy man and his attendant, Marco, pick up the battered skull and place it in a tree. On New Year's Eve, a man's spirit appears before Marco and thanks him for respecting his remains. The spirit then leads the attendant to his home where Marco learns that the man was killed by his own brother (Nakamura 2014, 123). The narrative of story 3.27 is quite similar: Makihito, a layman, hears a voice calling out in pain during the middle of the night. The next morning, when Makihito goes out to investigate, he finds a skull in the forest surrounding his house. From one of the skull's eye sockets grows a bamboo shoot, which the man chooses to remove. Some days later, the skull, freed from agony, appears to Makihito in the form of a man and introduces himself as Otogimi of Anakuni village. After naming his uncle Akimaru as his killer, he leads Makihito to the home of his parents (Nakamura 2014, 260).

In breaking down these two encounters using our framework for analysis, we learn that, despite being a Buddhist didactic text, the Buddhist institution figures very little in the resolution of the *yūrei's* predicament: *Causation*—both stories demonstrate an unmet desire or incomplete goal that tethers the *yūrei* to this world. For example, in both stories the spirits feel the need to expose the truth behind their untimely deaths. *Manifestation*—instead of entering the Buddhist cycle of death and rebirth and transforming into another being, they retain their identities and remain the people they were before they were killed. They then appear in that form in front of witnesses. In death, they remain, in some way, bound to their remains. For example, when ill-treated, the skull suffers what seems to be emotional or physical pain. This fact seems to be at odds with other, more prevalent Buddhist ideas about reincarnation and bodily impermanence. *Resolution*—the witnesses are not required to be anything more than uneducated laymen; they appear to have been chosen because of the compassion they showed toward the remains of the deceased. The spirits did not ask the witnesses to help or alleviate their condition by, for example, assisting them to enter reincarnation. The story appears to end not through the use of Buddhist ritual or empowerment, but rather when the spirits are able to name their murderers.

Jumping forward in history by about four hundred years, we find a greater repository of ghost stories in the twelfth-century *Konjaku monogatari-shū* (*Anthology of Tales from the Past*). This sample is far more representative of the kind of historically embedded tales that Shōsan would have drawn upon in writing the *Tales of Retribution*. The *Konjaku monogatari-shū* is a collection of 1059 stories spread over thirty chapters. There are several theories of authorship, but it is traditionally thought to have been first compiled between 1120 and 1140 by Minamoto no Takakuni (1004–1077) (Kato 1979). The stories are routinely organized under three general principles: *Spatial*—by region of origin to emphasize the path which Buddhism took to

Japan (Tenjiku (India), Shintan (China), and Honchō (Japan)), *topical*—by either Buddhist or secular (*sezoku* in Japanese) themes, and *temporal*—into chronological order (Mori 1982, 147). Thirteen stories featuring *yūrei* appear among the forty-five tales of spirits and demons of Chapter 27 (Reider 2001, 82). Notably, Chapter 27 is part of the "secular" section of the regional volume for Japan.

Most editions of the *Konjaku monogatari-shū* available to researchers and the public today are based on the 1720 (first fifteen volumes) and the 1733 (second fifteen volumes) versions organized by Izawa Nagahide released during the mid-Tokugawa period. However, Inagaki Taiichi (1992) has identified multiple versions that had enjoyed varying levels of circulation and popularity between the fifteenth and eighteenth centuries. During Shōsan's life, we can find numerous books which have borrowed stories from the *Konjaku monogatari-shū*, such as historical collections by Hayashi Shunsai's (1670) *Shoku honchō tsugan*, Hayashi Dokkōsai's (1664) *Honchō doshin*, and more popular works, such as Fukakusa Gensei's (1664) *Fuso initsud*en, Fujii Ransai's (1684) *Honchō kōshiden* (Izawa 1992, 70–72). It is highly unlikely, therefore, that Shōsan went about compiling the *Tales of Retribution* without a robust appreciation of the tales collected within the *Konjaku monogatari-shū*.

Turning our analytical framework of *causation, manifestation,* and *resolution* upon the Chapter 27 of *Konjaku monogatari-shū* reveals a continuation from the *Nihon ryōiki*. Like the *rei* of the *Nihon ryōiki*, some strong feeling keeps them tied to the world of the living and it is resolved by a "secular" action; also like the *Nihon ryōiki,* the Buddhist institutions has no role in resolving the *rei*'s predicament in the *Konjaku monogatari-shū*. There is, however, evidence of Buddhist rituals being used on *rei,* albeit ineffectively. Looking first at *causation*—in nearly half of the stories there is no clear indication as to why *rei* manifest.[6] The remaining entries indicate a strong attachment to something in the realm of the living as the purpose of their appearance. For example, in Story 43, there is a rather novel tale where the death of a woman during childbirth becomes a very explicit reason for her transformation into a *rei*. Later versions of this tale become the basis for a specific kind of supernatural monster, the *ubume*, who comes to represent all women who have died giving birth thus sacrificing her identity as an individual (Komatsu 2017, 139–40).

Manifestation—Like the *Nihon ryōiki* the *rei* in the *Konjaku monogatari-shū* manifest as beings with supernatural power, though their abilities appear to be greater than those of the *yūrei* of the earlier work. Three stories depict the deaths of people after encountering ghosts: story 4, story 21, and story 20. Story four tells of a warrior dying in his sleep after using his bow to shoot down flying red clothes he assumes to be a *rei*. In story 21, a man enters into an agreement to deliver a box with a woman resembling a ghost under the condition that it remains closed. Although the box eventually reaches its destination, the man dies soon after his curious wife breaks her husband's promise by lifting the lid to peer inside the box. Story 20 offers a very unique manifestation of *rei*, it tells of the ghost of a woman intent on killing the person who had betrayed her; however, distinct from other stories in this volume, the woman in question is still alive albeit living in a distant prefecture. This kind of *rei* is called *ikiryo*, in which *iki* means alive, and has examples in other popular texts including an entry in the famous *Genji monogatari* (*The Tale of Genji*) from the early eleventh century.[7] Like the *Nihon ryōiki*, most of the *rei* from Chapter 27 manifest in corporeal form. In nine stories *rei* appear in human form and most bear resemblance to how they had appeared before they died.[8] Story 3, where the ghost appears as a child's hand on a wall, is a notable exception. In only two stories do *rei* appear as incorporeal: in story 27, when a silver bowl appears and is lost within the same dwelling it is thought to be the work of a *rei*; and in story 28, a voice thought to belong to a *rei* is heard singing an old song in praise of the cherry blossoms. Although both manifest as intangible phenomena, they are considered the work of unseen spirits tethered to specific locations.

Resolution—Finally, none of the stories mentions *rei* being dealt with in a way specific to any particular religion—Buddhist or otherwise. Although not explicit, it appears that if a lingering soul's attachment to the world, their body, or human society is resolved via a variety of germane behaviors, the *rei* will disappear. There are even two stories in which violence is used in dealing with ghosts. In story 3, after the chanting of Buddhist sūtras proved to be an ineffective countermeasure against a ghostly child's hand protruding from a wall, the author suggests "maybe an arrow would be more useful" (Sakakura 1981, 27). His advice proves fruitful, and the hand is successfully impaled to the wall. Somewhat less graphic, in story 30 a woman throws rice at several *rei* and soon manages to beat them away. Thus, like in the *Nihon ryōiki*, the Buddhist institutions remains largely absent in resolving ghost-related concerns.

In the *Konjaku monogatari-shū*, however, we see a clear development from the *Nihon ryōiki* in terms of the ghost's power—while still arising due to attachments to the living world, the ghosts have become more supernaturally powerful, moving objects and manifesting in corporeal form. The messages the writer of the *Konjaku monogatari-shū* imparts upon his readers are also richer and much more nuanced than those of the *Nihon ryōiki*. Strong emotional cravings cause *yūrei* to manifest; they can attach themselves to wealth, love, or even jealousy; ghosts are powerful and sometimes kill. While physical combat is occasionally effective, there still remains no concrete method for dealing with a troublesome ghost. The Buddhist institution appears briefly in the narrative, but is ultimately ineffective at dealing with ghosts, undermining the authority of the Buddhist institution over the spiritual world.

SHŌSAN'S *TALES OF RETRIBUTION*

Building on the *Nihon ryōiki* and the *Konjaku monogatari-shū*, Shōsan's *Tales of Retribution* contains no less than twenty-four stories which feature references to a dead person's soul returning with unfinished business to the realm of the living; although, he often names these spirits using terms such as *reikon* (*kon* has a similar meaning to the Christian concept of a "soul") (story 7); *bōrei* (*bō* meaning deceased) (stories 15, 16); *tamashi* (story 50); and *onnen* (deep-seated grudge) (story 12). There are also a few stories of reincarnation that do not name *rei* directly but are qualitatively similar enough to be included.

When looked at in total, the ghost stories of the *Tales of Retribution*, while boasting some elements unique to the Tokugawa period, share a continuity with earlier tales in the *Nihon ryōiki* and the *Konjaku monogatari-shū* especially under the categories of *causation* and *manifestation*. In *resolution*, however, *Tales of Retribution* reveals how the Buddhist institution is beginning to take on greater power as a force to handle supernatural spirits. Although not every story is resolved via a Buddhist means, roughly half of them are, allowing us to see the transformation of popular Japanese ideas of how to handle spirits.

Causation within the *Tales of Retribution* is primarily driven by familiar themes of jealousy (invariably women's jealousy), craving love, attachment to family members and, of course, murder—all themes that produced *rei* in the earlier literature of the *Nihon ryōiki* and the *Konjaku monogatari-shū*. In *Tales of Retribution*, we can further divide this *causation* into a number of subcategories; however, a strong emotional craving remains the primary cause. Story 1 tells of the vengeful *rei* of a woman killed by a lover who could no longer tolerate her jealousy; story 2 is also of a women driven by jealousy who upon her death becomes an inextinguishable flame bound to the cemetery where her remains rest; story 7 continues this trend by telling of a murderous wife who kills her husband's lover and, her jealousy unsatiated, becomes a *rei* upon death. Unsurprisingly, alongside jealousy, being murdered is the most apparent driver behind *rei* causation.[9] Interestingly, two stories even feature ghosts of slain animals.[10]

A less overtly impassioned, or perhaps less volatile, emotion-driving manifestation is the lament of the absence (or passing) of a family member. Stories 11, 16, and 17 tell of two incidences where spirits of deceased mothers return to feed and care for their living children for years following their deaths. Story 15 depicts a husband's spirit returning from death to treat his wife's illness. The spirits in these four stories are depicted as harmless, as are stories 38 and 39 which both feature men who failed to carry out their responsibilities before they died and therefore return as ghosts to fulfill their duties. These more wholesome emotional cravings add a new dimension to the *rei* narrative and reflect Shōsan's own philosophy of how people should orient themselves toward society.

Greed marks one of the more negative forms of craving that can drive causation. Stories 18, 19, 27, and 35 each feature a tale related to greed and, interestingly, all depict monks craving gold that they had accumulated in life. Story 20 even tells of a monk who becomes a *yūrei* after drinking himself to death. Stories 22, 45, and 55 give accounts of ghosts appearing following the failure of Buddhist monks to properly complete death rituals. This overlaps considerably with the *resolution* part of our analysis and will be covered in more detail later.

Among the causes of *yūrei* we see in *Tales of Retribution,* it is striking how many Buddhist monks become *yūrei* by falling prey to unwholesome worldly cravings, especially for money. Although attachment to property while alive is not a new causal factor,[11] this shift in focus toward monks as the subject of these cautionary tales could reflect popular attitudes or criticism toward the relative affluence enjoyed by Buddhist temples during the Tokugawa period and the methods by which they generated their wealth. For example, story 18 describes how temples lent money out to commoners at high interest rates, while the temples of story 19 charge commoners for performing funeral rituals. Such rituals had already become common place during the time when the *Tales of Retribution* were first published (Hur 2007, 196–215), indeed, stories 22, 45, and 55 all reflect the concerns of ordinary people over the quality of funeral rituals or the extent to which the Buddhist monks were qualified to lead them.

Like *causation,* the *manifestation* of *yūrei* in *Tales of Retribution* continues the models found in earlier literature, albeit as even more powerful entities with greater abilities. *Manifestation*—ghost stories in the *Tales of Retribution* can be placed into three main categories of how *yūrei* manifest: appearing as they had before death, transformation into a snake, and possession. Most *yūrei* appear in death as they did in life. At least fourteen stories feature this form of manifestation.[12] Special mention should be given to the rather gruesome tale of an *ikiryo* (living ghost): Story 50 describes a man who was on his way to visit a friend, when he passed a local cemetery and spotted his friend cutting off and eating the flesh of a corpse. The man pretended not to see and continued on his journey, but when he arrived at his destination, he noticed his friend in his home fast asleep. As his friend woke, he told the man of a strange dream he had just had of eating a dead body by the riverbank.

At the end of the story, Shōsan comments that "one should not doubt the soul leaves (the body), facing new life according to the rule of karma" (177). From Shōsan's use of the term *tamashi* (soul) in this story, he makes it clear that there is a soul within the human body that is carried into reincarnation. This is at odds with strict interpretations of the Buddhist system of death and rebirth,[13] but does, as Tyler (1989) and Reider (2001) claim, fit within a much simpler and widely understood narrative acceptable to the common masses of Tokugawa Japan.

In stories 1, 10, 20, and 63, the featured ghosts manifest as snakes. In story 1, when a jealous woman is killed by her lover, the story implies that her spirit immediately manifests as a nearby snake. Stories 19 and 20 are both about Buddhist monks dying and becoming snakes. Story 63 combines the snake and *ikiryo* narratives into a tale of how a maid's craving for sushi manifests corporally as a snake which, when attacked by a chef, causes similar injuries to appear on the maid. A similar tale appears in the *Nihon ryōiki* where a greedy monk is reborn as a snake after death (Ema 2004, 20). Although there is insufficient space to discuss the symbolism of snakes in Japanese mythology, in the *Tales of Retribution*, the snake comes to represent the most unwholesome emotions and cravings.

In no less than four stories the manifestation is incorporeal, but the *rei* gains the ability to possesses a living person.[14] People who are possessed by *rei* normally lose consciousness and become mediums for the spirit. One can be possessed by both human (as in stories 38 and 55) and animal ghosts (Stories 12 and 74). While possession is nothing new—it is found in story 40 Chapter 27 of the aforementioned *Konjaku monogatari-shū* when a fox possesses a human—what is new is that the *Tales of Retribution* reveal human ghosts with this ability. These stories became the archetypical basis for popular tales of possession by *yūrei* in the late Tokugawa period, one of the most enduring of which is the infamous tale of Kasane (Konita 2012), which will be discussed later.

Story 2 contains the only manifestation that fits none of the afore-detailed three types of possession, manifestation as a snake, and manifestation as a previous form. In story 2, the grave of a jealous woman continually erupts into flames and burns surrounding graves. It is debatable whether this is, strictly speaking, a manifestation, but from a didactic point of view, it vividly depicts the power of the scorned woman's jealousy.

As with *causation*, therefore, Shōsan's depiction of the *manifestation* of *rei* draws upon prominent elements from previous ghost stories in Japan. Where the *Tales of Retribution* deviates from the previous collections of the *Nihon ryoiki* and the *Konjaku monogatari-shū*, however, is in the large number of remaining stories where Buddhist monks try to appease *rei* by holding a *butsuji*, or a Buddhist ritual ceremony to appease spirits. There are nine stories that concern the supernatural power of Buddhist institutions, many of which are successful.[15] Buddhist rituals generally feature as a common and usually effective countermeasure against ghosts; however, to be strong enough they must be practiced properly. Story 55 holds that for a Buddhist monk to perform funeral rituals he must have the right mindset. Similarly, in story 22, a Buddhist monk appeases a *rei* by giving her a proper Buddhist name after death.

Building on the power of Buddhist rituals in dealing with ghosts, *Tales of Retribution* features three stories of people using Buddhist amulets to deal with *rei*.[16] Story 17 depicts how a protection amulet called a *goōhōinn*,[17] is effective against a ghost. However, when at last the amulet is removed, the woman's ghost is able to take her revenge. Similarly, story 36 tells of how a Buddhist amulet is successfully used to subdue a spirit, but with the added caveat that it would lose its effectiveness if taken off. Even so, in story 62 a man who craves the love of a girl and is murdered by the girl's father becomes a ghost with seeming immunity to both amulet and ritual.

Despite the general success of these Buddhist rituals, however, there are also exceptions in which the Buddhist ritual is ineffective. For example, in story 1, Buddhist power is depicted as only having effect within its own territory, that is, within a holy Buddhist site. Here, a monk of three years leaves the famous Buddhist mountain Kōyasan—where he had fled after murdering his ex-lover by drowning. Upon leaving the site, he is immediately attacked by a snake who is the rebirth of his murdered lover. Outside the protective powers of Kōyasan, the snake causes him to drown in a method reminiscent of his own attack on her. Similarly, story 7 features a jealous wife who returns from death as a vengeful ghost to attack her husband nightly, but against whom Buddhist rituals are ineffective. Resolution comes only after the husband becomes ill and dies.

Beyond these stories where Buddhist rituals are ineffective, much like the *Nihon ryoiki* and the *Konjaku monogatari-shū*, a significant number of the stories featuring *rei* in the *Tales of Retribution* are without real resolution. Eleven stories all lack the intervention of an external power that seems to be required to resolve the problems symbolized by *rei*.[18] For example, the ghosts of mothers who return to feed their children resolve themselves without external intervention, as do the stories built around unmet social or labor responsibilities. There are also three stories in which the ghost disappears after it has taken revenge.[19]

In summary, *Tales of Retribution* reveals the transforming beliefs concerning *yūrei* in Tokugawa Japan. Putting it in continuity with earlier literature like the *Konjaku monogatari-shū* and the *Nihon ryōiki* shows the increasing, but not complete, power of the Buddhist institution over supernatural forces like *rei*. These *rei* also become progressively more powerful over time—moving from merely ghostly apparitions to entities able to manifest physically to entities with the ability to possess people. While *rei* are always created out of a clear attachment to the living world, this transformation of their *manifestation* and *resolution* reveals a narrative of an increasingly powerful foe and an increasingly powerful religious institution to fight it. While the cultural change is not complete—many of the *rei* remain unresolved and the Buddhist rituals do not always work—*Tales of Retribution* provides an important insight into a transforming period of Japanese history and allows us to consider the influence of the Tokugawa shogunate's policies on changing Japanese worldviews.

TALES OF RETRIBUTION REFLECTING TOKUGAWA SOCIAL CONTEXT

In its stories of *yūrei*, *Tales of Retribution* reflects a growing power of Buddhist temples over local communities' affairs under the Tokugawa shogunate's introduction of the *danka* system. The transforming relationship between Buddhist temples and the local households of the time is succinctly summarized by Nam-Lin Hur in his seminal work *Death and Social Order in Tokugawa Japan: Buddhism, Anti-Christianity and the Danka System:*

> All families were required to be affiliated with a Buddhist temple, and everyone had to die a Buddhist and be given a Buddhist funeral. . . . The enduring relationship between a Buddhist temple and its funerary patron household, cemented from generation to generation through recurring rites and services related to death and ancestral veneration, gave rise to what is commonly known as the *danka* system (*danka seido* or *dankasei*). It was the *danka* system, more than anything else, that sustained Buddhist temples in Tokugawa Japan. (2007, 9)

As analyzed by Hur (2007), the *danka* system represented the cornerstone of Tokugawa's "anti-Christian" statehood policy, which provided valuable opportunities for Buddhist temples to extend their social and spiritual power. Shōsan was obviously affected deeply by this plan to introduce Buddhist temples as the cornerstone of Japanese society; in both his anti-Christian works and his later teachings he insisted, "priests would be held accountable for their temple patron's (*danka's*) conduct, just as the patrons would be held accountable for their priest's" (Tyler 1989, 99). The reality was often far from this noble ideal, however. Buddhist temples faced significant problems during the Tokugawa period, including accusations of corruption and hoarding wealth (Hur 2007, 244–76).

Although Shōsan's career peaked during the fledgling years of the *danka* system, he reflects a number of these early criticisms in the *Tales of Retribution* where we see Buddhist monks punished for acting inappropriately in a funeral. This is most apparent in the *resolution* stage, for example, in story 14, ghosts that could not get salvation came back to torture a monk to death because he performed their Buddhist funerals improperly. Similarly, as discussed above, the Buddhist rituals against *rei* are effective only *some* of the time. For example, again in story 7, the death rituals against *rei* were not only ineffective but also made the situation worse. The power and moral authority of the Buddhist institution portrayed in the *Tales of Retribution*, therefore, is incomplete and complex.

The incomplete power of the Buddhist institution against *yūrei* in *Tales of Retribution* is further demonstrated by the fact that Buddhist rituals also had the unfortunate potential outcome of manifesting ghosts if practiced incorrectly.[20] Story 22, by way of example, tells of how villagers banished the head of a Buddhist temple after he carelessly wrote an incorrect character during a funeral ceremony causing a *yūrei* to manifest. This story is a depiction of the interactions between relationships of power that characterized the roles of local village people and their local Buddhist temple. It also shows that funerary rituals performed by Buddhist monks were becoming commonplace among the general populace in early Tokugawa Japan. In *Tales of Retribution*, therefore, Buddhist temples are not omnipotent and lack the ability to deal with the fiercest *yūrei*.[21]

As the Tokugawa shogunate continued, Buddhist temples effectively kept their influential role in local communities, and the transformation we see beginning in *Tales of Retribution* becomes more evident in later popular works. Many of the elements discussed above —most notably the power of the Buddhist institution to combat *rei*—were extended even further into popular works by other authors of the Tokugawa period. Although we do not have a reference library of direct citations from authors, there is compelling evidence in the popularity and similarities between bodies of work to suggest that Shōsan's contributions to the *yūrei* genre live on in subsequent mainstream tales. As the populace began investing in the notion of vengeful spirits, Tokugawa authorities became concerned, as they held that all beings, including supernatural phenomena such as ghosts, were subject to their assigned space in a model society and should not be left unchecked (Hur 2007). These concerns were compounded by a growing realization that the popular narratives presented the Buddhist institution as having limited authority when dealing with the spirit world (ibid 310).

In support of this argument, Hur (2007) uses the example of the famous vengeful spirit Oiwa from the *Tōkaidō Yotsuya kaidan* written in 1825. Hur points out that Oiwa's story is based on the older tale of Kasane, a well-known vengeful female spirit from the seventeenth century (ibid, 310–11). He summarizes Kasane's story using a version published in 1690 called the *Shiryō gedatsu monogatari kikigaki* (*A Story of the Salvation of Dead Spirits*). Though numerous additions to the core story, this version gives a much more substantive account of the involvement of Buddhist ideology and its role in Tokugawan society; however, I will draw my examples from the *Yūrei jōbutsu no koto* (*A Story of the Salvation of a Ghost*), which was published in 1684 as part of the *Kokon inu chomon-shū*. This is the earliest known version of Kasane's tale with a simpler and easier to digest framework.

Far from just being the basis for other popular ghost stories, Kasane's tale enjoyed widespread popularity and a multitude of wonderfully varied and creative retellings as one of Tokugawa Japan's most enduring and beloved ghost stories.[22] Interestingly enough, the earliest record of Kasane's story can be viewed as a combination of several stories from the *Tales of Retribution*. It appears in Chapter 12 of the *Kokon inu chomon-shū* with the basic structure as follows (Konita 2012, 153):

- Kasane, a village woman, was drowned in a river by her husband, Yoemon.
- Each of Yoemon's subsequent five wives dies.
- Yoemon's sixth wife gives birth to his daughter, Kiku. Kiku's mother dies sometime after Kiku's thirteenth birthday.
- Kiku is possessed by Kasane's ghost who accuses Yoemon of murdering her.
- The monk Yūten is summoned to the village to save Kiku by asking her to chant the Amida Buddha's name to exorcise Kasane's ghost.
- Kasane departs Kiku's body and goes into reincarnation.
- Kiku said that while she was possessed, Kasane showed her *gokuraku* (paradise) and *jigoku* (hell).
- Yūten changes Kasane's Buddhist name, Myōrin to Ryokujōtei, and gives Kiku the name Fushōmyōhan.
- Kiku is then possessed by the ghost of Kasane's brother, Suke. Suke tells of how he was drowned by his mother, who then married Kasane's father and eventually gave birth to Kasane. Yūten delivers Suke into salvation and also gives him a Buddhist name.
- Yoemonn leaves his family and home to become a monk. He is received into paradise when he dies.

The scenes above are not unfamiliar. In terms of *causation*, Kasane's hatred of her murdering husband brought her back echoing story 1 from the *Tales of Retribution* where a man's murder of his wife is cause enough for her return. Murder, as mentioned before, accounts for the oldest record of *yūrei* causation in the *Nihon ryōiki*. Turning to *manifestation*, we see how an incorporeal

Kasane was still able to kill Yoemon's later wives, which aligns with what we learned of ghostly powers from story 17 of the *Tales of Retribution* where the ghost of a woman successfully killed a number of other women. Similarly, Kasane's bodily possession of Yoemon's daughter Kiku has precedent in stories 38 and 55 which both feature possession. In story 55 especially, we see parallels in mother's possession of her daughter.

Finally, in the *resolution* of *A Story of the Salvation of a Ghost, Kasane's Tale*, we see that Buddhist institutions have fully developed the power to compel dead spirits. Kasane receives salvation from the Buddhist monk Yūten and is correctly given a posthumous Buddhist name. A similar resolution is found in story 22 of the *Tales of Retribution* where another *yūrei* is granted salvation by a monk when he bestows upon her a proper Buddhist name. While not strictly a tale of ghosts, story 75 depicts a man who, much like Kiku, is also given the opportunity to see both paradise and hell while still being counted among the living. The witnessing of paradise and hell while alive was not new to the *Tales of Retribution*, it can be traced as far back as the tenth-century *Ōjōyōshū* (*The Collection of Rebirth Stories*) (Hattori 1975, 137).

Although the chanting of the Amida Buddha's name as a way of dealing with *yūrei* is not given in *the Tales of Retribution,* as speaks to the continued popularity of local Buddhist institutions, specifically those which promoted the Pure Land school of Buddhism. Beyond this, the tale has all the features of a generic story of vengeance and retribution, while also reflecting a broader Buddhist context which relies on causality to link the characters and events together. Although neither Kasane nor her ghost had ever met Suke, the accepted reason behind Kasane's death at the hands of her husband was the karmic consequence resulting from her mother having drowned her older brother. Caught in this relationship of cause and effect, it could be said that Suke's death caused Kasane's death and that Kasane's death then caused her to become a *yūrei*.

Putting the Kasane story in chronological line with *Tales of Retribution* and earlier Japanese ghost literature, therefore, we see the culmination of Buddhist organizations' power under Tokugawa shogunate's establishment of the *danka* system reflected in the popular literature of the time. It is firmly through the power of the Buddhist institution that Kasane's ghost is laid to rest. While this is only a case study, it is typical of other literature of the period that portrays the Buddhist institution as the most powerful force in challenging and controlling unwell spirits and ghosts.

CONCLUSION

When the ghost stories of the *Tales of Retribution* are compared to those of the earlier *Konjaku monogatari-shū* and even the eighth-century *Nihon ryōiki* through the literary framework of *causation, manifestation* and *resolution,* Shōsan's *Tales of Retribution* offers a much more expansive view on the supernatural power of the Buddhist institution. This is especially evident in the ways in which the author has fostered previously underdeveloped or absent components from the *resolution* stage, constructing the Buddhist institution as the primary force in challenging ghosts. The *Tales of Retribution* demonstrates a growing relationship between ghosts and Buddhist monks and their institutions. This reflects the way Buddhist temples had further expanded their power over local communities through the Tokugawa shogunate's effort to establish the *danka* system, as evidenced by the incorporation of such elements in later popular literature like the Kasane narrative.

Shōsan clearly aimed his work at a wide readership by incorporating into the causation of *rei* a rich spectrum of emotions such as jealousy, lust, hatred or greed, as well as dramatic manifestations like transformation into a snake and possession. While stories often also included monks or intervention by a local Buddhist temple that might have been effective, they may just have easily been flawed or ultimately useless. Although there is no record of how widely read the *Tales of Retribution* was at the time it was published, it is entertaining rather than overtly dogmatic elements are thought to have been largely welcomed by readers, and this is evidenced in how they have endured through incorporation into subsequent and surrounding stories. In short, the *Tales of Retribution* by SUZUKI Shōsan is a fascinating and revealing window into the historical development of ghost stories in Japan, as well as a gateway into developing a more robust and nuanced understanding of the wider role of the *yūrei* in Tokugawa popular literature, which normally reflects unique social-political characters of common people during the Edo era of Japan.

NOTES

1. Although undiscussed in this chapter, the *Tōkaido yotsuya kaidan was* written by Tsuruya Nanboku IV as a popular *kabuki* play in 1825.

2. Shōsan's other works are the two moral tracts *Mōnajō* (A safe staff for the blind) and *Banmin tokuyō* (Right action for all), the anti-Christian tract *Ha Kirishitan* (Crush Christianity) and two *kanazōshi* (books written in phonetic Japanese syllabary) (Tyler 1989, 94).

3. Katakana and hiragana are two components of the Japanese writing system along with kanji. Both katakana and hiragana are syllabary writing systems understood by wide swathes of the population, as opposed to the logographic system of kanji, which further contributes to Shōsan's intended desire of reaching a wide populace.

4. The publication of the katakana version was meant to reveal the true veracity of Shōsan's tales since hiragana version was believed by those who published

the Katakana version to have distorted and blurred the facts of the original (Reider 2001, 85).

5. *Inga monogatari* (1914) in Japanese Nation Diet Library: https://dl.ndl.go.jp/info:ndljp/pid/915767/4

6. For example, No.3, No.4, No.21, No27, No.28, No.30 of Chapter 27 *Konjaku monogatari-shū.*

7. Lady Rokujō of the *Genji monogatari* is a well-known *ikiryō*.

8. For example, No.2, No.11, No.20, No.21, No.24, No.25, No.26, No.30, No.43 of Chapter 27 *Konjaku monogatari-shū.*

9. *Inga monogatari* 12, 17, 74, and 81.

10. *Inga monogatari* 12, 74.

11. See *Konjaku monogatari-shū* No.2 in Chapter 27.

12. *Inga monogatari* No.7, No.11, No.15, No.16, No.17, No.18, No.22, No.27, No.32, No.35, No.36, No.50, No.62, No.81.

13. The "no self" concept of Buddhism emphasizes there is not an eternal soul that beings carry forth into rebirth in the system of reincarnation.

14. *Inga monogatari* No.12, No.38, No.55, and No.74.

15. *Inga monogatari* No.1, No.2, No.7, No.18, No.20, No.22, No.35, No.55, No.74.

16. *Inga monogatari* No.17, No.36, and No.62.

17. An exorcism amulet that combines Buddhist and Shinto features.

18. *Inga monogatari* No.11, No.12, No.15, No.16, No.19, No.27, No.32, No.38, No.39, No.45, No.81.

19. *Inga monogatari* No.27, No 45, No.81.

20. *Inga monogatari* Story No.22 and No.55.

21. *Inga monogatari* Story No.7, No.62.

22. For example, Kamiya Yōyūken collected the story in Chapter 13 of *Shinchomonjū* in 1749; the famous novelist Santō Kyōdan collected this story in his *Kinsei kisekikō* Chapter 2 in 1804 (Hattori 1975 133); another famous novelist Kyokutei Bakin recreated the story with the name *Shin kasane gedatsu monogatari* and published it in 1807 at Ōsaka (Ootaka 1985); same story was collected in *Sōmanikki* by Takada Tomokiyo in 1817; It was created in to *rakugo* by Sanyūtei Enchō as the title *Shinkei Kasane ga huchi* in 1859.

Chapter 7

Of Monsters and Invisible Villages
Nags myi rgod *Tales of the Tibetans of Gyalthang*

Eric D. Mortensen

Tales abound among the Tibetans of Gyalthang about wild creatures, "wild people" (Tib: *nags myi rgod*, Ch: 野人 *yěrén*),[1] that are only barely monstrous. They are capable of breeding with humans, imitate and invert human ways, and are described as primate like and dangerous but not often wicked; such creatures are described as very real and residing in their cliff abodes above invisible villages. In what follows, I will share some *nags myi rgod* stories that were told to me—or, more accurately in the idiom of folklorists, "performed" for me (and others)—during the course of fieldwork in the high-altitude rural villages of Gyalthang. There are myriad stories of monsters in the mountains; the entire landscape is animated with stories of spirits and mysterious beings, but the *nags myi rgod* hold pride of place in the storytellers' repertoires.

Performative tales invoke these creatures as irreducible, past the forested landscapes of Gyalthang, where they represent both the notions of what is "other"—out of the bounds of either the habitable or the imaginable—as well as the edge of what it might mean to be human. Replete with connotations of inversive behavior, *nags myi rgod* (locally pronounced *na nay gö*) serve as evaluative ciphers for the anxiety and identity signifiers vis-à-vis their habitation in close proximity to settlements. Simultaneously, and with some overlap, tales are told of invisible villages and formerly invisible villages that have been revealed via transgression of social norms. In one set of versions of a story, the *nags myi rgod* made the wondrous invisible village of Panlong uninhabitable.

The following story, interspersed with informational explanations, was told to me by a tradition-bearer, Ngawang Donden (August 2012), in the village of Geza. Ngawang Doden, a farmer, in no manner a professional or formally trained weaver of yarns, is an example of someone I would categorize as a "tradition-bearer" in that he is someone who other villagers identify as knowledgeable about traditional lore and local stories, and is someone who is locally respected and valued for his sharing of formative stories with younger generations—stories that help shape local identity and community memory.

> Panlong valley is a place you can hear but never see. People started to settle there. They set up racks to dry their harvests. Overnight, the racks and fields were destroyed.[2] Everything was inverted. This made it impossible to start a life there. The unseen creatures mimicked what they saw during the day. There were so many *nags myi rgod* trying to make primitive farm fields . . . like the Yi people.[3]
>
> *Nags myi rgod* have an armpit stone (*mchan rdo*), always hidden in their armpit, which they throw to destroy things.
>
> The villagers had an impossible life. They recognized the mimicry in the overnight destruction, so the next day they openly drank from a big pot of water and pretended to battle with wooden swords. Before they slept, they replaced the water with *arag* (hard alcohol) and replaced the wooden swords with real metal weapons. At night, the *nags myi rgod* drank the *arag* and killed each other with the swords. This made the *nags myi rgod* extinct—not all died, but many died.
>
> Today, in Geza, many families have the surname Panlong. They are refugees who moved down from that valley, which still exists. This was, perhaps, thousands of years ago. It's just a story. It was before Sumtseling.[4] Lucky people can see Panlong in a vision . . . part of the community becomes visible . . . this part became part of Geza.[5]
>
> *Nags myi rgod* think human faces are frightening, so they never look directly at their captives' faces.[6] So, when they catch someone, they look indirectly at them (over their shoulder) and tickle them to death. Sometimes *nags myi rgod* catch people, but never do anything with them or kill their victim until the sun goes down. People have a tradition of wearing jewelry or a mala or necklace . . . as that's how the *nags myi rgod* holds on to you . . . so as the *nags myi rgod* watches the sunset you slip out of your mala, etc., and slip away, leaving the mala behind.[7] One man caught by a *nags myi rgod* slipped away, leaving jewelry. He put his clothes on a log and watched from a distance. After sunset, the *nags myi rgod* realized it had only jewelry, saw the log with clothes on it, and shot it with its armpit stone, destroying the log. That's how people learned of the armpit stone.
>
> It is impossible to live in Panlong. Folks moved down to Geza but their names are still Panlong. There is no predetermined time or place where or when such stories are told. Random conversation leads to Panlong, which leads

to *nags myi rgod* stories. Panlong is said to be a wonderful place, suitable for farming and living but is impossible to live there because of the *nags myi rgod*.

People see large footprints or places where huge people rubbed their backs against trees. They firmly believe in *nags myi rgod* because they have seen these things. Today we rate animals on a scale of how protected and endangered they are—for example, pandas are A-protect, or B-protect. What would we give to *nags myi rgod*? Like the striped horse I saw on TV![8]

What does it mean for individuals to be refugees from an invisible dystopian village while facing current cultural, economic, and religious repression related to the land itself? In the context of this oral tradition, why, when, by whom, and to who are these stories of inversion and reversal told? After all, storytelling is a form of ritual. How can we most fruitfully explore and ask about the ritual efficacy of *nags myi rgod* storytelling, the "ritual" authenticity of storytelling, or the agency of the storytellers during *nags myi rgod* tale ritual performances? The answer to this set of questions is, in part, that we can explore the efficacy of the telling of monster stories through assessing the degree to which (and when and why) the stories are transmitted from generation to generation.

Even more crucial, although even more challenging, would be to assess the degree to which the contextualizing of the ambiance of the stories is conveyed, absorbed, and manifest in ensuing versions of the performances of *nags myi rgod* tales by succeeding generations. One of the reasons tradition-bearers were often eager to tell the stories to me—an outsider—was because they were simply happy that someone wanted to hear them. The land of Gyalthang is changing, with rapid infrastructure development, mining, and new roads. Fewer families hope for their children to remain in remote villages. What are the monster-human boundaries, and how do the performances of these stories contribute to local identity and inform upon the imagining of inhabitation of wildspace in this rapidly changing region? The understanding of the forests themselves is changing, as is the idea of traditional boundaries (however permeable) between "us" and "them." The differentiation between "us" and "the other" as defined by the very local landscape is a concept that is vanishing in Gyalthang.

TELLING TALES OF THE *NAGS MYI RGOD* IN GYALTHANG

To what degree are the performances of *nags myi rgod* tales subversive, intended for cultural maintenance, or simply fun for children?[9] *Nags myi rgod* tales are only rarely told as cautionaries—to frighten children about avoiding the high mountain tree line after dark, and the like. More commonly, they are told to explain the landscape and to share cultural identity markers vis-à-vis place. How can the variant *nags myi rgod* tales of Geza inform upon the interrelated dynamics of place, identity, lament, and memory, and, more to our purposes at hand, what can these stories tell us about the ways in which residents of Gyalthang understand the very boundaries of what it means to me human?

Gyalthang is a Tibetan region located in what is today northwestern Yunnan Province in the southwest of the People's Republic of China. Tibetans understand Gyalthang to be in southern Khams, which itself is the eastern part of the Tibetan world. Gyalthang roughly corresponds to Shangri-La County. Gyalthang is a multiethnic and multilingual place, with Naxi, Yi, Primi, Bai, Lisu, and Han peoples and languages, and several distinct Tibetic languages are spoken in neighboring deep-forested valleys between high snow peaks.

Between 2011 and 2020, I conducted more than two dozen fieldwork trips to various villages in and adjacent to Gyalthang, soliciting, recording, asking about, and listening to stories about *nags myi rgod* and other monsters in the mountains. Sometimes alone, but usually with a team of local colleagues, I recorded *nags myi rgod* stories in Geza, Langdu, Haba, Sanba, Nizu, Nixi, Jiedi, Nagara, Mulu, Ongshui, Dongwang, Yagra, Benzilan, Dechen, Shangrila, and many places in between. I typically worked with two or three local colleagues who accompanied me on these fieldwork trips,[10] camping and hiking, driving every backroad we could find, and spending many, many evenings sitting around crowded stoves working together to team translate and understand the stories.

Language is exceptionally local in Gyalthang, literally becoming unintelligible from one valley to the next, and our teamwork meshed well with the group endeavor that storytelling often turns out to be. Typically, on a first visit, we would arrive at a village and ask around for or follow a lead in search of the local storyteller and would inevitably be pointed toward the home of a tradition-bearer, who would welcome us around the family stove for tea, food, and stories of *nags myi rgod*. However, storytelling is not typically a process of one-to-one transmission. Rather, in short order the room would become crowded, with multiple generations of people, and sometimes more than ten voices contributing to the telling of the story. When reasonable, we would record the stories, but usually I would take notes by hand to be less obtrusive and keep the tellers more at ease. Thus, the stories were solicited; they were not stories I just happened to overhear. And they were chaotic performative events, full of interjections, arguments, laughter, and language barriers. All but two of the more than forty tradition-bearers I interviewed were men, and most were in their sixties, seventies, or eighties. These story performances were indeed times of transmission, as younger men in attendance (relatives, neighbors, etc.) would be utterly engrossed in the collective endeavor of storytelling, and young children would often be a part of the scene. Women and girls would often be present, listening, and occasionally involved in the collective verbal melee of the performance of the story. But women as community-recognized public-facing tradition-bearers—at least insofar as being identified as the best person to share stories with a foreign man—were rare. Most typically, elderly women would tell me that they knew the stories but were not themselves storytellers. We returned to many of our fieldwork sites several times and developed deeper relationships with storytellers in the areas between Geza, Nagara, and Dongwang. Indeed, some members of my shifting research team were locals from these villages, and our friendships over the past decades have made some of our fieldwork experiences deeply informal.

Nags myi rgod (literally: forest wild person),[11] are described as taller than an adult human, variously standing between eight to twelve feet tall, and are ape like (rarely bear like) and covered with hair. Their hair is brown, ruddy red, or grey, but is often two-tone and bidirectional—darker on the top half and lighter on the bottom half (or vice versa) and brushed or growing upward on the top half of the body and downward on the bottom half. They leave marks on trees, leave huge footprints, and make enormous nests of sticks and leaves just above the tree line. In some stories, *nags myi rgod* are capable of speech. Awang Doden (July 2017) told me the following story:

> In Kaygong—a place between Pemakarpo snow mountain and Dechen's big white stūpa—Gyalpo Jeongsay was king.[12] The king was friends with the *nags myi rgod*, and they shared a language. Gyalpo Jeongsay came from the east to Nduu (Dechen) for business. On the road back home his family rested and Gyalpo Jeongsay fell asleep on a rock. His children were playing with stones. A spider crawled out of their father's nose and vanished into a crack in the rock. Their father woke up and said, "You shouldn't have woken me. I was dreaming that I found a house with a roof of gold." The family decided that there must be a treasure beneath the spider rock. They dug down and discovered a copper pot (*zangs can*) filled with gold. Now rich, there was no need to return to their hometown. They bought land at Kaygong and Hongjiong. When? This was long ago, in Nyingmapa time.[13] They used 36 bulls to plough their new land—18 plows side-by-side! They were self-reliant, but Gyalpo Jeongsay's wife was unhappy because they had no neighbors. So, she hid a plow so that her husband needed to ask to borrow a plow, as he now had only 17, which was like a curse, and symbolized bad fortune. Later they started herding, with herds so large they could only keep track by counting the animals once on the way up to pasture and

once on the way down. The small stone hill where they did the counting is called Zhatsong chunyi,[14] and the pasture is called Nigö (*myi rgod*) ting.

There used to be many *myi rgod*, and the king became their friend. The *myi rgod* used to eat raw meat, as they did not know how to make fire. The *myi rgod* would hunt, the king would fry the meat, and the *myi rgod* would love it! The king's shepherd taught the *myi rgod* local human language but the *myi rgod* could not speak with fluency—they spoke like children. The *myi rgod*'s voices were loud. When the shepherd was out of salt, tea, or milled flour, he'd send the *myi rgod* to call out from the hill (just there, behind the middle school). The *myi rgod*'s voice was not very clear, but really loud. The shepherd could not bother to come all the way down because he was busy tending the king's herds. The *myi rgod* was huge. It had hair half up and half down and walked like a human but was two to three times as big. It had a weapon, a small stone, that it put in its armpit.[15] It used to rub the stone with oil all the time. It used the stone to kill big animals like tiger and deer, and when it threw the stone it would make a sound like a bomb. Maybe it had the stone when it was born.

Quantifying storytelling is problematic, particularly given the communal nature of storytelling and because of the added complication of the distorted effect my own presence as folklorist has in determining the occasion of storytelling performance, not to mention the vital issues surrounding whether or not such tales are "believed" (*yid ches*, or, as locals in Geza say, *bden bzung* "to hold the truth"). I have met four different people who have seen *nags myi rgod* and I know, personally, people who claim to be fairy refugees from invisible villages. However, incredulity, skepticism, and a sense of fun pervade occasions of storytelling. Children invariably talk smack to their grandpa if he begins to hold forth about monsters around the family stove, and my fieldwork partners, while genuinely full of respect for the wise elders of their communities, often refer to the tellers of *nags myi rgod* tales as bullshit artists. Nevertheless, according to many people in Geza, the enthusiasm and vibrance of storytelling have amplified over the past few decades alongside a return to augmented propitiation of local mountain and water beings. What Tibetans call *mi chos* (folk religion, or "religion of the people," as opposed to Buddhism) in Gyalthang has seen a subtle resurgence, correlative to the decrease in knowledge of Buddhism that came about due to the systematic dismantling of institutionalized religion at the hands of the Chinese state.

Folktales about *nags myi rgod* are religious performances. The ritual of storytelling, too, is efficacious, and it provides a sort of agency otherwise elusive for many who seek meaning-making alongside cultural revivification in the face of state-sponsored destructive mining, harvesting of forests, suppression of institutional religion, mandatory resettlement of remote village to valley floor roadsides, and new obligatory centralized boarding schools. Villages are empty of children for most of the year. A revitalization of folk religion is afoot in Gyalthang, and the stories of *nags myi rgod* are drenched with etiological anecdotes about the natural local landscape and reflections of local history. The performance of a *nags myi rgod* story is a world-making iterative act, full of wonder, fear, cleverness, transgression, ethics, and good humor. The verbs in the telling of these tales are rarely active, and the passive voice renders the story ambiguously agentless, its actors hidden.

Just as the lists of the possible results of divination texts reveal much about local anxieties and aspirations—the king dying, house fires, the arrival of strangers, and so on—listening between the lines of *nags myi rgod* story performances, analyses of the occasions of the tellings of tales, and the complexities of who is in the room during the joint-project of the tellings, can reveal much about anxieties and aspirations of local identity vis-à-vis the local landscape. And, by extension, just as the veracity or prophetic/diagnostic accuracy of divination is often less important than the act of soliciting or performing a divination in the first place, so too can storytelling be understood to be less about the content or the reality of monsters than the wonder and joy of the act of performing—and listening to—a story. Ambiance can become more valuable in understanding not just the so-called "function" of story, but also the folk-religious efficacy of the story's performance. The ambiance of the telling of folktales is revelatory. Combine the occasion and location of the story's performance with the mood of the telling, and stir, and we end up with much more information and arguably more valuable information than we gain simply through the story content alone.

The following story, from Sonam Tashi in Geza (July 2011), was told to much laughter:

> There was a hunter who had an old rifle. He played a nice flute. He made the *tsen* (here, mountain spirits) happy. In return the *tsen* helped him with his hunting. He played to make the *tsen* happy. A *nags myi rgod* came to listen. The hunter was frightened and dropped his flute. The *nags myi rgod* picked up and handed the flute back to the hunter. They were sitting by a cliff. The hunter (intentionally) dropped his flute over the cliff. The hunter then tried to run away as the *nags myi rgod* went to retrieve the flute. The *nags myi rgod* chopped down the surrounding trees with its armpit stone to keep the hunter from fleeing.[16] Again, it started copying the hunter. The hunter "smoked" his gun barrel (as if it were a pipe). The *nags myi rgod* tried it and the hunter lit the fuse. (The *nags myi rgod* was, of course, killed.)[17]

THE *SHERSHANG DUDU* AND THE ENVIRONMENTAL AND CULTURAL CONTEXT OF THE *NAGS MYI RGOD*

Nags myi rgod are not alone in the mountains of Gyalthang; the high-altitude forests and granite cliffs are home to various other monsters, from the short cannibals with their chins stuck to their chests (*sho ma nye*, or *ma ni og gyer*), to glowing lake bulls (*mtsho glang*), to giants and ghosts. Orgyan Dorje from Nagara related (November 2012) a tale about a flying monster, called the *Shershang dudu*, with folkloric relationship to *nags myi rgod*.[18]

> The *Shershang dudu* has very long (two-meter long) arms. It walks like a person.[19] The ruins of the creature's home still exist. A whole family of them lived long ago. It was not born from a person; it is a separate species. It was like a *nags myi rgod*.
>
> The *Shershang dudu* lived long ago, during the time of the Mu King of Lijiang ('Jang Sadam Gyalpo). It lived on *Mai yan goh* (holy) mountain . . . you can see its jagged peak from the pass. The *Shershang dudu* destroyed everything; it didn't leave villagers alone. It was afraid only when it saw children leading animals, because it looked like the kid had a lot of power, leading an animal, plow, etc. It never attacked anyone working in a field with an animal . . . only riders (it would take horse and rider together) or people walking.
>
> The *Shershang dudu* was finally destroyed by an eight-year-old boy from Ongshui. The boy filled a horn with gunpowder and added a fuse and left it outside. The *Shershang dudu* took it home and it exploded.[20] The whole mountainside came down, and the mountain burned. Even human-used pastures were destroyed by rock and mud from the explosion.
>
> Everyone was happy but the village headman of Ongshui was worried that the boy might overthrow him. So, he sent his men to capture the boy, put him in a box, and throw him into the river. The river carried him to the bridge by Benzilan. Firewood collectors by the river found the box. At the same time, the king of Sadam was riding by, and asked for the box, opened it, and found the boy inside. The king was thrilled because he had no heir . . . it was a gift from *shen* (local spirits). The boy became the king. Ever since, the river has been called the *gam chu* (box river). Now there are no monsters in Nagara. The king thought that since Tibetans threw him in a box, he didn't like them much. Nevertheless, he walked and built trails throughout the region, but always around, never across, farming fields. [*Vehemently!*] We did not pay taxes to 'Jang—we were conquered by Dewazhong [the Ganden Phodrang Gelug power in Lhasa, far to the west]!

In other accounts of this flying monster, it is described as much shorter than a *myi rgod*, and a distinctive species. Awang Doden of Dechen describes (July

2017) the *Sha shongshong* as "like a person with wings." The *Sha shongshong* lived opposite Chapü (*chab phug*) village, across the Yachu (*rdza chu*) (Mekong River), high in a cliff in a cave:

> People knew that he had a good pair of cymbals. The *Sha shongshong* would leave the cymbals on the road. Passersby would be curious and pick them up. The *Sha shongshong* would then swoop down and beat the person and take back the cymbals. He played this game often. One man made ice replicas of the cymbals and switched them for the real ones on the road. The *Sha shongshong* took the ice cymbals but they melted in the sun. A family in Nyinö village still has the cymbals.[21]
>
> The *Sha shongshong* caught a Nyinö village woman and took her to his cave. They had a baby. The *Sha shongshong* had wings and flew to find the best clothes and food for the woman. Her family wanted to rescue her. They hunted the *Sha shongshong*. They placed a trap on top of the *Sha shongshong*'s hill. They captured and killed the *Sha shongshong*. They then called to the woman, but she took their child and jumped into the Mekong, committing suicide. These stories are probably true. You can still find the cave but you can't reach it without wings. *Sha shongshong* are extinct now.

Compare this with the following tale told by Lobsang Dorje (May 2013) from Geza:

> A local girl was taken by a *nags myi rgod*. The details are shady—she later came back—she had a baby, hairy, not human-like. She had been kept in a high stone cliff where she got pregnant but she escaped and gave birth. The *nags myi rgod* came after her, making gestures that she should come back. She did not. He grabbed the child and tore it in half. He gave one half to the woman and took the other half home [the story was followed by laughter].[22]
>
> *Nags myi rgod* are giant. They have dark brownish-reddish hair, are very hairy: half up, half down. The direction of the hair on the top half of their bodies goes up, the bottom half hair goes down. They are gorilla-like.

Much about *nags myi rgod* relates to halves, to inversion, and to hybridity. They are something between human and ape, they can sometimes almost speak, their hair goes different directions on different halves of their bodies, and they live in liminal spaces between a magical world of the wild and human settlements. *Nags myi rgod* storytelling can be simultaneously fun and terrifying. The tales are full of *nags myi rgod* mimicking humans, frightened of but attracted to humans, wanting to be like humans.

The *Shershang dudu* and *nags myi rgod*, as described in stories, share overlapping folkloric valences. Both are considered frightening and dangerous, and both resemble humans in certain ways. *Shershang dudu* are "like *nags myi rgod* with wings," or are referenced alongside *nags myi rgod* only insofar as both are mysterious and wild and make life difficult for farmers. But *nags myi rgod* don't invert things because they are mean (although being tickled to death is, if you really think about it, no laughing matter). They do so because they mimic humans, wanting to be like humans. Or, more precisely, *humans* tell tales about *nags myi rgod* who mimic and want to be humans.

Nags myi rgod stories are also told throughout Tibet and the Himalayas, whereas *Shershang dudu* may be local to Gyalthang and adjacent regions. Another difference between the two creatures is that the *Shershang dudu* is understood to be a creature of long ago, whereas *nags myi rgod* are sometimes said to still inhabit the highest forests and sheer cliffs. Their stories are often told together, and elements of the narratives cross over and are borrowed into one another such that there is no rigid boundary between the oral accounts of the two monsters. Both are central in folktales that afford explanatory meaning to very specific outstanding or anomalous features of the local geography. In essence, both creatures are understood as local, as "ours." *Shershang dudu* are typically described as unique, singular creatures, who "lived just there, in that cave," even though the narrative structure and oral performative functions of the story of the *Shershang dudu* are remarkably similar wherever it is told. It is "ours" for everyone telling (or hearing) the story, which goes a long way toward connecting, in a shared identity, different tellers and listeners of tales in and from neighboring regions.

The geographic breadth of the performances of these hyper-local tales creates not incredulity, but community and shared intelligibility and identity. When someone from a nearby valley hears a tradition-bearer perform a specific *nags myi rgod* tale, it is generally not the case that the visitor reacts by claiming that the performer is incorrect—that the story actually took place in the listener's home valley, not "here." Quite the opposite, the typical reaction is one of solidarity of experience, of familiarity, and of a shared sense of "we have that story too," which, by the way, augments a sense for everyone in the storytelling room that *nags myi rgod* are plausibly real. Indeed, there is a particular sense when hearing a *nags myi rgod* or *Shershang dudu* tale that it is familiar, regardless of where it is being told, regardless of the specificity of the landscape in which it is inscribed, and regardless of whether the account of the monster is attested to by a storyteller who was an actual witness to the creature. Tradition-bearers who tell of their own personal encounters with *nags myi rgod* are, importantly, keeping something alive.

While this dynamic may be true for all sorts of folktales it may be particularly potent when the stories are about monsters. The "other"—the monstrous thing that lives past the invisible meniscus that is the boundary defining the "us"—is a monster that is shared. "We have that *nags myi rgod* story too."

Those who are familiar with the story as a tale that has been formative in terms of their own identity thereby identify as "us" and become more connected. The dynamic becomes one of shared identity through recognition of shared story. Ritual, with an intelligible syntax, can reactivate myth.[23]

THE CONNECTION BETWEEN *NAGS MYI RGOD* AND HIDDEN VILLAGES

Nags myi rgod tales and *Shershang dudu* tales are sometimes and, in some ways, related. However, to understand *nags myi rgod* stories—the ambiance of the occasion of the story performance, the importance of themes of transgression and mimicry, and why the tales are told—we must return to the veil. How, and in what specific ways, are *nags myi rgod* stories related to stories of invisible villages? What is it about the unseen and the unseeable that links the stories together in the repertoires of the tradition-bearers? *Nags myi rgod* and invisible villages are connected in that both sets of stories are central in conceptualizations of identity-construction in Gyalthang. It is not just an issue of the identity of a people vis-à-vis other "outsider" peoples (although such may well be a valuable interpretation of some of the stories and their ramifications). It is an issue of identity of humans vis-à-vis creatures that live in the wild,[24] the magical, and the unknowable landscape of the edges of the safe space, far from the warmth of the storyteller's stove.

Although *nags myi rgod* stories are widespread throughout Tibet and the Himalayas,[25] stories from the Geza region contain various descriptions of the invisible village Panlong.[26] In the stories, a mushroom gatherer or herder—often identified as a relative of the storyteller—would stop in wonder and hear the rushing water and agricultural sounds typical of village life, but the village could (at least initially) not be seen. *Nags myi rgod*, inhabiting the forests looking down on the bucolic invisible village, mischievously invert human farming efforts and hunting practices, making the village of Panlong uninhabitable, even for those lucky enough to break through the invisible meniscus and see or enter the valley with its perfect pasturage and farmland.

Nevertheless, Panlung remains fundamentally uninhabitable. The notion of the invisible resonates with the unseen and wondrous, and one theme central herein is the notion of transgression rendering the unseen seeable, the magically hidden space revealed *yet thereby* rendered unlivable. According to Lobsang Nongbu of Geza (September 2012, July 2015), Panlong is still invisible. Families in the region maintain the surname Panlong and consider themselves refugees from the invisible village. Panlong appears in many of the stories with the refugee element as the most common theme.[27] These invisible villages, locally called *zi göh* (or sometimes *yee göh* in Geza) are widespread, if occasional. The *zi göh* of the Nagara area is known as Zayzong, and the people from Dongwang tell of a local *zi göh* called Natöeyong. I would not be surprised if the concept of invisible villages extends far beyond the Tibetan regions of Northwest Yunnan.

In 2019, we hiked from Dongwang to Mulu, and found, on our route, the ruins of Tsenlong (a.k.a. Zayzong) village (see figure 7.1)—a formerly invisible *zi göh* inhabited by fairies, now abandoned.[28] Several (visible) villages in and around Gyalthang were formerly invisible, including, among others, Nizu and Yubeng. Sometimes villages are "revealed"/unveiled due to trickery, such as in the story of Yubeng, where a fairy person (*lhamo*) used to bring goods to the market of Dechen, then walk home, deep into the mountains. People wished to know where he lived, and thus pierced his bag of grain, followed the trail left by the grain trickling from the bag, and thereby discovered his hitherto unknown village. In the case of Nizu, a hunter followed a white pig to a rock face from behind which flowed a river.[29] There he killed the pig, which was a violation of hunting norms, as white wild animals are forbidden to hunters. Other *zi göh* remain invisible, such as Panlong, and Chyul (*bya yul*, "chicken land"), in the Benzilan area, which only chickens could enter or exit. Long gan yong village, above Nagara, remains invisible. According to Orgyan Chiling from Zoli (eastern Nagara) (July 2018):

> Only one in ten thousand people can see Long gan yong village, (a *zi göh*) between Nagara and Dongwang. People who walk near it can sometimes hear roosters or crying babies. Once, not too long ago, a tulku (reincarnate lama) could see it. A little girl saw a market and the lama interacting with the market. The lama asked the girl if she wanted a fruit. She said yes and ran toward the lama and the village disappeared. There is fruit and there are all sorts of treasures in the villages. There are people, with cattle, dogs, etc. The villages are just invisible.

Zi göh may well be related to the Tibetan Buddhist concept of *beyul*, or revealed paradisiacal valleys or lands or refuges, but may predate or have avoided a Buddhist explanatory gloss. Absent from the *beyul* category, though, are *nags myi rgod*. Great lamas can consecrate and open/reveal a *beyul*, and Tibetan Buddhist stories are dripping with accounts of the requisite pacification of demons (*bdud*, *srinmo/srinpo*) to make a space ready for the Buddhadharma. However, *zi göh* are not full of demons. Some traditionbearers insist that *zi göh* have no relationship with *nags myi rgod*—that the two sets of tales are separate. Others weave the stories together, as we can see in the weaving together of the *Shershang dudu* and *nags myi rgod* tales. Indeed, in some cases, *zi göh* are inhabited by wonderful beings, as in the

Figure 7.1 Tsenlong Village, Formerly a *zi göh*, Abandoned Since 2012. Photo by Eric D. Mortensen, November 2019.

case of Yubeng village. Yuzum Lobsang (July 2014), in Yagra, told the following story:

> The fairies lived there (pointing across the valley), high on the mountain side, but we could not see them.³⁰ They were beautiful and lived a long time . . . a really long time and did not get sick. But the fairies were intrigued by the humans here in the village, and they copied us. We did not know that they were there. They would watch the people build walls for houses, and they would try to do it too. When they watched people burn a dead body, the fairies burned a donkey, thinking that that what was they were supposed to do. But this was wrong, and it made their village visible. They had no choice but to come down. Now some people in our village have fairy blood . . . I do. Many people moved away from our village when it got dry.

Is veiling intended to conceal or reveal? Just as in the stories, when a box (containing a child, or in other Tibetan stories a captured god) is tossed into a river, the listener understands and expects that the box will be discovered and opened, so too, one might think, does the *zi göh* contain an imbedded anticipatory notion of revelation. However, there is an important counterargument to this seemingly clear narrative function of invisibility: not all *zi göh* have been unveiled. One conclusion, therefore, might be that *zi göh* are not merely tropes. It might be misleading to try to understand *zi göh* purely through the hermeneutic of narrative or folkloric functionalism, that is, seeing *zi göh* only through the lens of assessing their function in the story. *Zi göh* may be more than just the storytelling equivalents of allegorical expressions, meant to clue the listener into what is about to transpire. Rather, for the people of Gyalthang, *zi göh* exist outside of story. Sure, there are stories about them, but invisible villages do not only exist in folktales and are not merely used as explanations for ruins or for transgression and resultant moral revelation. Sometimes the stories seem to explain why and how a village could remain hidden deep in the high forests. But do as-of-yet veiled villages somehow serve, at least in part, as prognostic cyphers anxiously or yearningly anticipating that which is to come? The stories are about the mysterious, the dangers and the wonder of the unknown. They are about the places where "normal" humans do not live. Note that *zi göh* stories are never about becoming invisible.

CONCLUDING THOUGHTS: *NAGS MYI RGOD* AS NEXUS OF SOCIAL CHANGE

In Gyalthang, we see that narratives about *nags myi rgod* reflect, represent, and constitute something of a folkloric nexus for the complex social and cultural forces of the region. The understanding of the natural world around the people of Gyalthang is changing, and this change is reflected in their discussions of invisible fairy villages and monstrous creatures in the forests. As the children of Gyalthang are forced by government-mandated schooling into new forms of socialization far from the traditional knowledge holders of Gyalthang, they take on a new relationship to their home folklore traditions—one defined simultaneously by skepticism, lament, teasing, disinterest, and curiosity. Villages empty of children for significant portions of the year become the unlikely place to tell stories of women with half-human, half *nags myi rgod* children who are themselves taken away by powerful forces beyond the mother's control. It would be a mistake to look at this new situation of events as only destructive to local culture, a mistake that presumes cultures are static and unchanging until encounters with outside forces. In Gyalthang, the revitalization of folklore and folk religion challenges more normative definitions and understandings of Tibetan religions.

What, then, in Gyalthang, is a monster? Are they situational substitutes for fairy-like people? To what degree are the *zi göh* definitions of the unknown "other," even if it is a longed-for bucolic "other" space? To what degree are the stories reflections of the anxieties and fantasies of the community of tradition-bearers and their audiences of all ages? The monstrous is enticing, if dangerous. That which looks similar to us but is wild, and that wants to be like us but is reflected to mimic our worst natures and transgressions, is only barely visible, barely "other." At the bounds of what it means to be human in the lore of villages of Gyalthang lie narratives that explain inner wild-spaced identity, a maintenance of a sense of the value of mystery, and entertaining performances of beloved tales of *nags myi rgod*.

NOTES

1. Unless identified otherwise, all translations given in parentheses will be in Tibetan, transliterated according to the Wylie system.

2. The inversion of farm work is a central motif in versions of this story, although some storytellers provide more details than others. According to Awang Doden (July 2017) in Nyushu neighborhood in Dechen, *nags myi rgod* would watch people clearing brush to make a field, then come at night and chop stones with the workers' axes, ruining the tools. They would try to dig but they were too strong and would break the hoes. And "people would weed when the barley was medium high. *Nags myi rgod* would watch, and at night the *myi rgod* would weed everything, including the barley!" This core *nags myi rgod* tale is the most commonly recounted of the dozens of *nags myi rgod* stories I have heard. Although many published studies of "wildmen" are focused on proving the existence of the elusive cryptids, others focus on the phenomenon of fascination with the stories themselves or are published versions of tales. For comparison, see, for example, Werner (1922), Nebesky-Wojkowitz (1956), Vlček (1959), Kirtley (1963), (comparing Himalayan stories with those of Bigfoot/Sasquatch) Napier (1973), Siiger (1978), Das (1992, 229–31), (in Bhutan) Kunsang Choden (1994, 1997), Huber (1999), Doujie (2010), Childress (2010), (among the Rong of Sikkim) Capper (2012), Debenat (2014), Sykes (2014, 2016), Taylor (2017), Dhakal (2017), Taylor (2017). For a solid study of the history of cryptozoological fascination with Sasquatch, see Regal (2011). Kunsang Choden's 1997 work is perhaps the most valuable collection of tales in print, and many of the themes and structures of the Bhutanese Yeti stories are extant in the stories told in Gyalthang. For a Bhutanese version of the tale of inverting the fields and tricking the mimicking *nags myi rgod*, see Kunzang Choden (1994, 161–4). Kunzang Choden's story is about *mirgola*, who she differentiates from *migoi* [*myi rgod*], writing that *mirgola* "are said to be human-like creatures that live in the depths of the remote forests in the Himalayas. They are not to be confused with the *migoi*, which are believed to be much larger than human beings and have a mystical aura of fear and wonderment associated with them" (161). See also Dhakal (2017, 17–21). Note, also, that *myi rgod* "wild man" can refer to a bandit, as in *mi rgod byed pa*, "to behave as a wild person," that is, to rob (with odious connotations). In Dechen, adjacent to Gyalthang, *nags myi rgod* are also sometimes called *myi rgod gangs seng*, literally "white snow wild person." In Amdo (the vast region of northeastern Tibet), *myi rgod* are called *myi dred*, pronounced "ni dri," which can also be a name used for the Himalayan Brown Bear (*Ursus arctos isabellinus*). Villagers in Haba, on the southernmost edge of Gyalthang, refer to the creature as *Nadugu*.

3. This not-so-subtle derogatory comment about the (Nuosu) Yi people is reflective of a general negative view of the Yi people held by many Tibetans of Gyalthang. Nuosu Yi tend to farm on slopes instead of creating level terraces.

4. Ganden Sumtseling Monastery is a Gelugpa Tibetan Buddhist monastery and was the center of Gelugpa religious authority in Gyalthang from the late seventeenth century until its destruction in 1966. See Mortensen (2016).

5. Here, the meaning is that the part of Panlong that became visible is now part of Geza Township, a valley system of villages in the center of the region of Gyalthang. For more information about Geza (*skad tshag*) and its relationship with wider Gyalthang, see Mortensen (2019). Other versions of the story in Geza emphasize that Panlong is still there, and still invisible, but that several families relocated from there to Geza. Others in Geza insist that Panlong is visible as ruins. In the variant of the tale told in Dongwang (*gter ma rong*), the village where the *nags myi rgod* inverted everything was called Natöeyong, and the residents were thereby obligated to relocate, and settled in Nareshor in Gang gar (in Daocheng County, Sichan).

6. According to Bai Linde (a.k.a. Kelsang Dundrup), assistant director of the Buddhist Academy (Ch: *Fóxuéyuàn*) in Shangrila (July 2017), "*nags myi rgod* would wait until the sun would go down before eating people. They were scared of the face of people because people's faces have a light, a face brightness . . . like a spirit (*bla*), but not religious . . . we are different in animals' eyes."

7. In other versions of this story, the captive human would quietly and slowly cut off the end of their sleeve. A mala is a string of prayer beads, often carried on one's wrist or around one's neck.

8. Story told by Ngawang Donden (August 2012), in Geza.

9. According to Ma Zhishi (Geza 2014), who is originally from Xiangcheng in Sichuan, by way of Nagara, horse caravan traders tell *nags myi rgod* stories and miners tell the stories a lot. Lobsang Wangdu (2019) from Naraga confesses to having been terrified of *nags myi rgod* as a child, adding: "Boys and girls alike would be scared when walking alone in a dark forest on the way to pasturelands."

10. My research partners in these endeavors included several Tibetan friends, whose names I will withhold here due to the increasing political sensitivities in the region. Without their generous collaboration and knowledge, this research would not have been possible. Some tradition-bearers' names have also been changed herein. I also wish to thank the Faculty Development program at Guilford College, the Fulbright U.S. Scholars Program, the American Academy of Religion Individual Grant Program, and the Association of Asian Studies Summer Research Grant program for their generous support of this project. This essay is dedicated, with gratitude, to my research partner Ts, who knows how valuable the stories really are.

11. In regions of Tibet with scant or no forests, *nags myi rgod* are simply called *myi rgod*—"wild people."

12. Tibetan: *rgyal po 'jong sras*.

13. In other words, the events were before the hegemony of the Gelugpa sect beginning in the seventeenth century. Nyingmapa is a differing sect of Tibetan Buddhism that traces itself back to the earliest introduction of Buddhism to Tibet in the seventh century.

14. This place name is a bit of a mystery. Awang Doden suggests the Tibetan spelling of *ra tshang chu nyi* means, literally, something akin to "goat complete two water." An alternative possibility is the spelling *bcu gnyis*, which means "twelve." Awang Doden described the place as a small stone hill above two streams where people would count their animals en route to pastures.

15. The ubiquitous armpit stone (*mchan rdo*) is a central element of many *nags myi rgod* tales. Chamba Gyenee (Gendun) of Dongwang (*gterma rong*) (October 2012) described the *mchan rdo* as "black and shiny . . . egg-shaped but longer. The *nags myi rgod* I saw had a small one, about a full finger length long. Sometimes they keep a bigger stone under their right armpit." Cryptid-mania aside, *Sasquatch Field Guide*, a pamphlet published in Canada in 2016, explains that "rock-throwing might even be considered a form of 'communication'" (Meldrum 2016).

16. See, also, the first *nags myi rgod* story related at the outset of this chapter. Lobsang Wangdu of Nagara (November 2019) told a version where the flutist hunter escaped by leaving his hat on a tree as a distraction—the *nags myi rgod* destroyed the tree with its armpit stone. Interestingly, Lobsang Nongbu of Geza (personal conversation July 2018) told me that people of Nagara are renowned for their oral storytelling prowess: "When alone, men from Nagara will place their hat on a tree and talk to it to practice their oration skills. When they then speak publicly, everyone is extremely impressed."

17. For a Bhutanese version of this commonly told tale, see Kunsang Choden (1994), the story titled: "The *Zha* Collector and the *Migoi*" (156–9).

18. Although the etymology of this term is obscure, it most likely relates to the Tibetan *Shangshang*, a rendering of the Indic Garuda. The Garuda plays a central role in the religious (particularly the divinatory) traditions of the Naxi of Gyalthang and Lijiang. Shershang is the pronunciation of the term in Nagara. In Dechen the creature is called Sha shongshong, and in Chabé village on the Mekong it is called Sharchong dudu. The "dudu" may be a repetition of the Tibetan term *rtul*, meaning "intrepid/brave." Lhundrub Gyalthen from Jialigong (near Yagra) (June 2014) related a version of this story wherein the creature is given the name *Neyguh Sheungsheung*—a flying *myi rgod* with an armpit stone.

19. Sonam Chöphel, a tradition-bearer from Dröng ray village in Dongwang (October 2012), performed a version of this story wherein the *Shangshang dudu* lived on Gaizi Mountain to the north, could swing from branches and cliffs and "jump distances more than one hundred meters, and could lift a huge mill stone (it's still there, down by the river)."

20. Not surprisingly, other versions of this story offer acutely different details, even, as is sometimes the case in *nags myi rgod* stories, animalizing the monster. Lobsang Wangdu's (2019) version of this story describes Ongshui as a place "with lots of eagles that would pick up rice shoots and attack flocks. A kid from the Dranggo (*brag 'go*, "rocky mountain top") family attached a hot burning log to a sheep. An eagle picked up the log and flew with it back to its nest. The nest was destroyed. The boy kept doing this and burned quite a few threatening eagle nests."

21. Nyinö is the local Dechen pronunciation of the Tibetan *gnas nang*, literally "the inside/interior place."

22. Bai Linde (July 2017) related a similar version of this story but with a male hunter and a female *nags myi rgod* who sealed her human captive in a cave and fed him with musk deer until they fell in love. Gonpo Tsering (August 2017) from Amdo told a similar version but with greater emphasis on the man's escape from the cave by leaping from the cave mouth into a pile of leaves at the base of the cliff. Compare, also, with Dhakal 2017 "Yeti's Cave" (83–91). There are many versions of the story of a person being abducted by a *nags myi rgod* and together producing offspring. There are also tales of sexual violence perpetrated on human women by Yeti. See, for example, Dhakal (2017, 69–74). Other tales tell of humans (monks, nuns, hunters, herders) who have encountered *nags myi rgod* in their caves and either medically assisted the *nags myi rgod* or vice versa. Other stories emphasize *nags myi rgod* or Yeti as Buddhist practitioners or Dharma protectors—see, for example, Huber (1999), Capper (2012), Snellgrove (1995 [1957], 213), and Kunsang Choden (1997).

23. See Mortensen (1999).

24. Tibetans do express a relationship between "tame" and "wild," employing the distinction in the context of domestication, conquering, and "civilizing." David Gordon White, in his 1991work *Myths of the Dog-Man*, does a fine comparative job of unveiling for us the cynocephalic (dog like) nature of the "other," from the Indic worldview to the Chinese. On the taxonomic boundary of the human *v.* the animal and the concept of "wild" in Tibet, see Dotson 2019.

25. Stories of *nags myi rgod* are told throughout the Himalayas, the Tibetan Plateau and (as *yěrén*) in China. Many accounts of the Yeti exist in published form (see note 1, above), but although the Yeti is fundamentally a set of Central Himalayan tales (and most famously Sherpa tales from Nepal), themes overlap with the *nags myi rgod* tales of Geza, noting that the Sherpa are originally from eastern Tibet. See Bhandari et al. 2015. Published accounts of Tibetan epic and folklore contain mention of demons, ogres, and giants more so than wild people, and the Naxi tradition just to the south of the region is replete with tales of mountain gods and demons. Chinese bestiaries also contain mention of ogres and feral humanoids, and even of *yěrén* (e.g., Strassberg 2002). For a brilliant and detailed overview of *yěrén* in China, see Schmalzer 2008. Schmalzer's discussion of the *yěrén* in China is particularly salient with regard to the Tibetan *nags myi rgod* in light of her assessment of the political history of the notion of superstition (Ch: *míxìn*) and Tibetan credulity toward *nags myi rgod* tales and their tellings.

26. I am unsure of the Tibetan spelling of this place name. I have been told many variant spellings. Ngawang Donden of Geza (2012) wrote it for me in my fieldnotes as *sprang slong* (literally "causing beggers, begging"). It is locally pronounced Panlong.

27. According to Ma Zhishi (2014), who has lived in both Nagara and Geza, "the Zigöh people did not die. They watched human cremations in Nagara. When the Zigöh people did cremations (mimicking the humans) they became visible. When people from Zigöh came to Nagara things started moving around . . . like big logs. Although it is hard to believe, no way would so many people intentionally trick others by lying."

28. There is much confusion as to whether Zayzong and Tsenlong are the same place or are "sister" gorge villages (*brag 'tsho gsum*), grouped together as a set of three along with Bala (which was not a *zi göh*). The relationship between *nags myi rgod* and *lhamo*, in terms of their roles and functions in local stories, is a topic ripe for further exploration, and the category may well include other mysterious beings. In the cases of the *zi göh* described herein, the identification of the inhabitants of *zi göh* as *lhamo* and not as *nags myi rgod* may emasculate and unmonster the monstrous; who, after all, would want to say their ancestors were *nags myi rgod*? More likely, though, is that stories of *zi göh* were a separate type of tale than *nags myi rgod* tales, overlapping on the issues of inversion and transgression. The stories have eventually blended, if only occasionally. Plenty of *zi göh* tales have nothing to do with *nags myi rgod*, and many, if not most versions of the *nags myi rgod* tale involving the inversion of crops and the fighting with swords is told without the element of the village being invisible.

29. In some versions of this story, the hunter followed and killed a white bear, in other versions a deer. In yet other versions, the hunter was none other than the king of Gyalthang, which explains Nizu's incorporation into the region of Gyalthang. The "discoverer" of Nizu, according to Lobsang Wangdu (2019) was Nasidah (possibly reflecting Naxi family provenance, as in *Nàxī jiā*), who "could not look at Nizu directly . . . only out of the corner of his eye." The name Nizu has a disputed etymology (see Mortensen 2019) and may reflect the Tibetan *mig zur* "corner of the eye." Lobsang Wangdu disputes the view "from younger generation from Nizu who have been to college then returned" that the name means "beside (*zur*) Mu(li)," that is, the adjacent Muli kingdom.

30. Yangshwang Tsering of Nagara (October 2012, and reperformed July 2018) held forth versions of this story but of the village Zayzong, inhabited by beautiful fairy people. Humans could hear, but not see the village. It was in a spectacularly beautiful valley. The fairies were curious about humans, so they came down to Nagara to observe people, and saw the cremation of a deceased human, but thought the people of Nagara were burning a dog. The fairies' village was unveiled when they transgressively, though innocently, cremated a dead dog, mirroring what they incorrectly believed humans were doing. The inhabitants of Zayzong could thereafter be seen by people. According to Lobsang Wangdu's (2019) version of the story, Tsenlong (Zayzong) became visible because the dog was burned, and people from Nagara could see the smoke. Importantly, in none of the performances by Yangshwang Tsering, Yuzum Lobsang, or Lobsang Wangdu, did the *zi göh* story involve *nags myi rgod* in any way.

Chapter 8

Godly Aromas and Monstrous Stenches

An Analysis of Buddhist New Year Fumigation Rituals in an Indo-Himalayan Borderland

Rohit Singh

In her groundbreaking work, *Purity and Danger*, Mary Douglas provides an illuminating history and anthropology of the concepts of purity and pollution within diverse cultural contexts. She argues that whereas pollution eventually became associated with medicinal notions of hygiene and sanitation, many religions and cultures have historically conceptualized purity and pollution in terms of social order and stability. She presupposes that a given culture has historically envisioned itself as a "universe to itself" requiring that things have a place central to the cosmic maintenance. Douglas (2002, 5) posits, "ideas about separating, purifying, demarcating and punishing transgressions have as their main function to impose system on an inherently untidy experience." In other words, amid the uncertainties and dangers facing human cultures, concepts of purity and pollution present a semblance of order. They do so by creating conceptual places and boundaries ordering human relations, ritual practice, and social distinctions.

   I begin this chapter with Douglas's theories because they remind me to some degree of my own ethnographic observations made while researching Buddhist communities in the Indo-Himalayan border region of Ladakh in Northwest India. This borderland region in Northwest India, bordering Pakistan to the west and China to the east, is home to roughly 275,000 inhabitants with a population evenly divided between Buddhists and Muslims. Since at least the tenth-century reign of Nyima Gon, the first king of Ladakh, Buddhism in Ladakh has largely belonged to the Vajrayāna tradition found in most Tibetan and Himalayan cultural areas. Ladakhi Buddhists, like many Buddhists residing in Himalayan regions and the Tibetan cultural sphere, fear pollution (*dip*,[1] *sgrib*) as a threat to individuals, society, and various spirit beings thought to inhabit nature. Drawing on fieldwork I conducted in the region of Leh, Ladakh, between 2012 and 2013, this chapter explores two central questions. First, I ask: how do purity-based beliefs and practices reflect how Ladakhi Buddhists envision their relationship to each other and the gods and monsters residing in their local landscape? Second, because scent-based rituals serve ubiquitous means of appeasing gods or warding off demonic forces, I will ask: how does the perceived power of smell and smoke shape Ladakhi understandings of gods and monsters?

As this chapter demonstrates, Ladakhis view *dre* ('*dre*)—sinister supernatural beings that could be translated as "demons" or "monsters"—as intricately tied to, and direct byproducts of, pollution and social disorder. Conversely, they associate gods with cleanliness and social harmony. Further, the power of smoke, particularly the scent of incense, is pivotal for creating a purified atmosphere in which spirits and humans can coexist. Aroma, stench, and the production of odor constitute key dimensions of how Ladakhis imagine and describe purity and pollution, as well as the world of gods and monsters. This is especially the case during Losar or the Buddhist New Year. At this time, locals perform scent-based rituals to feed spirits, cleanse the abode of gods, and ward off evil demons. As a byproduct of these scent-based rituals, they ideally reaffirm shared moral values and strengthen their social bonds. As I examine the olfactory dimensions of religious life in Ladakh, I advance the following claim: Ladakhis use the ritual production of purifying scents as vehicles for ordering humans' relationships with the divine and the demonic, and with each other, thereby averting the polluting stenches, dangerous monsters, and social disorder. I will conclude this chapter by raising broader implications of this case study for academic research on gods and monsters. In particular, I will suggest how recent work on smell and scent theory can provide new questions and insights for the study of gods and monsters.

POLLUTION AND THE THREE-TIERED WORLD IN LADAKH

Before examining the scent-based rituals of the Buddhist New Year, I need to first give some background on how Ladakhis view their society as part of a matrix in which purity unites gods, demons, and humans. Locals believe that they reside within a landscape inhabited by humans and classes of spirit beings that may be divine or demonic in nature. Ladakhis refer to these entities as gods or *lha* (*lha*), and demons, ghosts, and other monstrous entities known as *dre* (*'dre*).

Gods, demons, and humans live together in a universe constituted by three interconnected realms: (1) the upper realm (*steng lha*) of the gods, a realm often associated with the sky and mountain peaks; (2) the middle realm (*bar sa*) where humans and animals dwell; and (3) the lower realm (*'og klu*), home to snake-like beings, called *lu* (*glu*). Beings in each of these three realms are believed to be in contact with each other. Each tier and their respective beings have a pivotal place in the maintenance of the local universe. Gods of the upper realm protect and aid humans so long as the gods remain placated. The *lu* in the lower realm protect the waters where they live and grant rainfall so long as they remain content. The humans of the middle realm have the pivotal role of harmonizing all beings in each realm through two means. First, by abiding by rules and restrictions concerning pollution so as not to contaminate any of the realms. Second, humans must perform rituals to cleanse any impurity people disperse into the three-tier universe and they must perform rituals to keep the spirits in each realm content. Incense and other aromatic substances serve as a potent force in these rituals because Himalayan Buddhists believe the sacred smoke disperses into all three realms for the benefit of all classes of beings.

This three-tiered universe is imagined as fragile as locals believe that human transgressions and demonic beings threaten to pollute this order. Pollution in any one tier threatens all three. The indigenous term for pollution is *dip*; this is a nebulous and ubiquitous substance created by anything seen to disrupt order in society or in nature. Body odors, negligence of social responsibilities, contaminating water, failure to perform rituals on specified dates, the mixing of saliva and so forth showcase the diverse sources of pollution or *dip*. For locals, purity rituals ensure that society and the cosmos maintain order and cleanliness, these rituals also preserve the world of the gods and prevent spirits from turning demonic. Once again, we must underscore the significance of scent. Vajrayāna Buddhist rituals employ a vast array of substances, sounds, and performances for various ends. Yet, smoke has a specific efficacy in purity rituals because of its perceived power to reach all the nooks and crannies of this three-tiered universe as ameliorating aroma for all beings to partake in. Certain mundane stenches on the other hand, have the same capacity to permeate the universe, but they pollute all spirits such as the *lha* and the *dre*, gods and monstrous creatures. Sanctified smoke is also viewed as the seminal product for ritualists to create because it is a force uniquely capable of purifying the *lha* and the *dre*, and cleansing the filth left behind by foul stenches. Before analyzing scent-based rituals, it is insightful to first ask what exactly differentiates the gods and monsters that encounter godly aromas or monstrous stenches?

LIVING IN A LAND OF GODS, HUMANS, AND MONSTERS

Buddhists in Ladakh divide all godly spirit beings into two general categories: beings who are supramundane (*'jig rten das pa'i lha*) and beings who are mundane (*'jig rten pa'i lha*). Supramundane deities are often associated with Buddhist monasteries. Monks invoke them during monastic rituals. Mundane spirits remain more accessible to the laity. Lay ritual specialists often work with these gods. One problem for Buddhists, however, is that these spirits are viewed as temperamental. They could be a god or *lha* one minute, and then a demon or *dre* the next. The categories of *lha* and *dre*, god and demon, are mutable and relative to the behavior of a given mundane spirit.

Gelong Thupstan Chostag, a monk from Ladakh's Rizong Monastery, has written a concise article detailing general characteristics of mundane deities. In his article, "Do Gods and Demons Actually Exist?,"[2] Gelong Chostag argues that different types of gods and demons exist, and humans must understand the nature of these beings to live in harmony with them. This article provides important insights into some of the perspectives underlying Ladakhi beliefs about local spirits. Describing the characteristics of mundane gods and deities, Gelong Chostag writes:

> In general, the gods are those who we call virtuous and beneficial to others. The demons are those formless beings that cause harm to others. However, between the two there is no division of good and evil in the strictest sense.... Sometimes these "gods" are virtuous and sometimes they cause harm. These demons are sometimes wicked and sometimes beneficial. Sometime after gods have been beneficial [to humans], later they cause harm [to humans]. Likewise, sometimes demons after first causing harm, it is even possible that later they will be beneficial to others. Therefore, the conceptualizing of both gods and demons from [the vantage point] of merely doing harm or being virtuous or evil... are all mundane superimpositions. Therefore, we say that they are mundane gods and demons. (dGe Thub bstan chos grags 1998, 66)

Gelong Chostag elaborated and clarified the above comments during an interview I performed during fieldwork. He argues that *"lha"* and *"dre"*—the Ladakhi/Tibetan terms respectively for gods and demons—must not be viewed as categories for beings with a fixed ontological status because both terms can be applied to a being depending on its behavior with respect to humans. If a spirit provides aid or benefit, denoted by the term *phanthog* (*phan thog*), the conventional label the entity is *lha* (god or goddess). Yet, if a spirit inflicts harm to humans, denoted by *nodpa* (*gnod pa*), the conventional label for the spirit is *dre* gods and demons, *lha* and *dre*, are formless beings whose classifications are based on behaviors that either benefit (*phanthog*) or harm (*nodpa*) humans. Because the behavior of mundane spirit beings may change, so too can their designations. When deities are unhappy, they turn demonic and inflict *nodpa* on humans. If a ritual specialist captures and tames a demonic spirit, the spirit being then serves as a protector god and provides *phanthog* for families and villages so long as Buddhists provide the deity with ritual offerings.

Gelong Chostag also characterizes many of the mundane spirits within Ladakh as fundamentally nature-based beings acting as landowners of specific geographic locations. If humans damage natural locations, then the spirit beings residing there become vengeful demons:

> People these days, for the sake of fulfilling their desires, dig up the earth, smash rocks, pollute the waters, cut up tress, and light fires. Likewise, they employ various chemicals. Because of disturbing the atmosphere and the elements with the fumes of these chemicals, non-human spirit beings like the earth spirits and local deities become agitated. And then terrifying adverse circumstance, the likes of which have never occurred before, arise: epidemics, diseases, untimely rainstorms, earthquakes, and hurricanes. Therefore, after giving up those things that cause harm to those formless beings residing in the natural realm, we should know how to respect nature. (Ibid., 66)

Ladakhis traditionally view their landscape as filled with natural abodes for spirit beings. These beings are offended and harmed when humans pollute their homes. Once their abodes have been polluted, spirits become demonic and act as *dre,* inflicting illnesses and natural disasters. Buddhists in Ladakh, therefore, traditionally value their landscape as part of a sacred ecology, the cleanliness of which ensures harmony between spirits and humans.

It is interesting to note that this permeability and mutability of the categories of gods and monsters is not unique to Ladakh or Buddhism. In *Religion and Its Monsters*, Timothy Beal theorizes monsters as paradoxical beings, simultaneously representing sameness and otherness, order and chaos, and the divine and the demonic. Surveying a vast array of data from *Enuma Elish*, Biblical literature, colonial depictions of foreign cultures, and modern monster films, Beal cogently argues that monsters may serve as embodiments of the other in contrast to which humans conceive of divine order, or monsters can appear in the world representing a revelation of the holy. As Beal (2002, 6) puts it, "The monster [is] often *both* demonized and deified, revealing a deep sense of ambivalence about the relation between the monstrous and the divine, and intensifying the sense of paradox." The paradoxical nature of the monster, as observed by Beal, manifests in Ladakh. This manifestation often involves the Ladakhi concept of pollution or *dip, a* human-derived substance capable of influencing the character of a given spirit, shaping it either into a godly *lha* or monstrous *dre*.

POLLUTION, GODS, AND MONSTERS IN LADAKH

The many Buddhists in the region believe that rivers and sources of water are the natural abode for mythical snake-like beings referred to as the *lu* (*klu*), the equivalent of the Indic *nāgas*. If humans pollute water sources, they risk offending or harming the *lu*. The *lu* are believed to retaliate by infecting the polluter with a form of illness (*nad*). Leprosy is one form of *nad* associated with offending the abodes of the *lu*. These beings may also punish villagers with droughts or floods. Locals believe that rituals of purity and atonement must be performed in such occasions to appease the *lu* and restore harmony in this society and nature. When content and happy with their human neighbors, the *lu* can serve as divine protectors, bringing about timely rainfall and bountiful harvest.

The above example dealt with the human relationship to the *lu*, believed to reside in the water or lower realms of the three-tier cosmos, the zone called the *ok lu*. I will also give an example how purity and pollution concerns relate to the gods of the *steng lha*, the top strata of the Ladakhi universe. Spirits of the *steng lha* may reside in a shrine-like structure called the *lhatho (lha tho)*. These *lhatho-s* are often placed atop mountains, homes, and castles. Locals fear that human-produced stenches travel into the atmosphere, offend the gods, pollute spirits, and defile their places of dwelling such as these *lhatho-*s. For example, if someone has not been ritually purified and they approach a sacred tree or household shrine to a god, their bodily stench offends the *lha* and the foul odor stains the spirit's place of habitation. Ladakhis I spoke with also claim that these foul smells weaken the gods' power to protect humans. These stenches risk transforming gods into demons who will inflict illnesses and cause natural disasters.

One anecdote told to me by an elderly woman reflects how locals broadly see gods as connected to humans via scent. She recalls one of her relatives was standing on the roof of his house next to the shrine housing the family god (*lhatho*). He was enjoying a cigarette. All of a sudden he found himself losing his balance and about to fall. He immediately put out his cigarette and invoked the name of the family god and asked forgiveness. She says he then miraculously recovered his balance and never smoked near the *lhatho* again. Many locals I spoke with emphasized that the gods of Ladakh are sensitive to smell. Further, just as stench pollutes gods, it is ritually produced smells that appease, feed, and purify them. Ladakhis view scent as a pathway for human contact with disembodied deities. When foul stenches from humans enter the atmosphere surrounding the abodes of spirit beings, such as cigarette smoke near a *lhatho*, the abode becomes polluted. Mary Douglas describes pollution as "matter out of place." Whereas Douglas referred to dirt and other forms of physical filth, in Ladakh the "matter out of place" with respect to the *lhatho* is viewed aromatically as the vapors from human pollutants that travel outside human spaces and materialize as stains and defilements contaminating the realms of local deities.

DIVINE AROMAS AS RITUAL REMEDIES TO MONSTROUS STENCHES

I observed during my fieldwork that scent-based offerings tended to be among the most pervasive ingredients of ritual life. The ritual production of scent is a ubiquitous practice in the region, taking place during virtually all domestic, monastic, and public ceremonies. The perceived power of smoke provides insights into how Ladakhis envision their relationship to each other and the world of spirits. Two scent-based rituals illustrate this point, one called *sur* (*gsur*) and the other the fumigation ritual of *sang* (*bsangs*). Before analyzing these ritual offerings, it is important to note that Ladakhis often refer to spirits as *driza* (*dri za*), which means "scent eaters." The reasoning for this designation, according to those I spoke with, is that spirits, unlike humans, lack bodies capable of eating food in the form of physical offerings. They can, however, indulge in the immaterial aromas emitted by ritual cuisines.

The first scent-based tradition I will examine is *sur*. *Sur* means "searing" and refers to different forms of scent offerings given to various beings through smoke from the "searing" of material offerings. In Ladakh, the common types of *sur* offered are classified as *marsur* (*dmar gsur*), or red searing, *karsur* (*dkar gsur*), or white searing, and *tsasur* (*tsha gsur*) or tsampa/barley searing. *Marsur* refers to the aroma arising from the searing of meat cooked to appease demonic beings who desire blood and flesh. *Karsur* are pure scent offerings made to the Three Jewels (Buddha, Dharma, and Sangha) and to monastic dharma protectors. *Tsasur* is offered during ceremonies for the departed. This substance consists of three white-colored ingredients (*dkar gsum*) and three sweet ingredients (*ngar gsum*).[3] This particular scent-based food is specifically associated with feeding the dead. Sweet smells of this food burning feeds and comforts departed spirits who roam during the eve of Losar. *Tsasur* is also offered during Buddhist funerals in Ladakh and throughout the Tibetan cultural world (See Gouin 2010, 27–8). Buddhists believe that after the departed enters the intermediary state between birth and death (*bar do*), the *tsasur* given during their funerals is the food that nourishes the dead until they take rebirth.

One elder in Leh told me a story demonstrating the power of *sur*. He recalls that his family once held a funeral for a relative thought to have had died in battle during the 1962 war between India and China which was fought in Ladakh. For forty-nine days—the maximum period in which one may remain in the *bardo* state—the soldier's family offered *tsasur* to his departed spirit. The elder recalled that, to everyone's surprise, his uncle returned home and explained that reports of his death were false. Yet, the uncle also told them that for forty-nine days he was unable to eat anything because he felt full. Additionally, he reported smelling sweet aromas wherever he went during that time. In sum, *sur* traditions demonstrate that Ladakhi Buddhists understand that certain aromas have the power to impact spirits residing in the landscape. Further, the power of scent-based ritual offerings connects both living and departed members of human society around shared responsibilities such as the caring of the dead through *sur*.

By far the most common of the scent-based traditions in Ladakh and the Tibetan cultural sphere is *sang*, a fumigation ritual using incense. *Sang* rituals aim to purify people, places, objects, and spirit beings through offering smoke from burnt juniper leaves and other pure-smelling substances. These same rituals of purification and atonement reaffirm the social ties and hierarchies associated with kinship, class, caste, and so forth. Annual *sang* rituals thereby create social and political cohesion and reinforce the belief in the necessity of purification. It is for these reasons that Samten Karmay has observed that purity, foundational to *sang*, is "one of the primary elements that constitute the basis of Tibetan culture," because beliefs about purification are intricately tied to Tibetan views on kinship, local deities, and sacred mountains. Moreover, annual *sang* rituals create social and political cohesion and reinforce the belief in the necessity of purification (Karmay 1998, 405). In his study of *sang* rituals to sacred mountains in Mongolia, Jared Lindahl argues that *sang* offerings address pragmatic concerns such as wealth accumulation, good weather, agrarian needs: these concerns are the domain of non-Buddhist specialists, but they are later appropriated by institutional Buddhist specialists who are believed to have tamed local mountain gods.[4] *Sang* ceremonies reinforce institutional Buddhist authority over the mountain deities who care for the pragmatic needs of local populations; *sang* rituals also reenact narratives about the conversion of Mongolia to Buddhism (Lindahl 2010, 226). For both Karmay and Lindahl, *sang* rituals are closely tied to authority and social stratification. While it is beyond the scope of this chapter to elaborate on this point, similar social dynamics are at play during *sang* rituals in Ladakh.

It is the perceived efficacy of its scent that gives *sang* its specificity as a purification practice in Ladakh and other Himalayan areas. As Tibetologist Giuseppe Tucci (1980, 199–200) observes:

> The *bsangs* [sang] exhibits diverse variations in its actual performance; its essential nature however, is always that of a *suffimen* [Latin for incense], a fumigation using aromatic and perfumed herbs . . . such as juniper. A purifying and atoning action is attributed to the sweet-smelling smoke of these offerings, which spreads in all directions. The fumigation is the basic element of these rituals.

Ritually produced smoke, as mentioned earlier, is viewed by Ladakhis to wield a unique power: starting from a specific ritual space, the smoke can diffuse in all directions, reaching the nooks and crannies of the three-tiered universe where all spirit beings can enjoy the divine aroma and in exchange, forgive humans for the noxious stenches they produced.

FUMIGATION RITUALS DURING THE BUDDHIST NEW YEAR

While fumigation rituals are performed all throughout the year, and daily in many Ladakhi homes, locals perceive Losar, the term for the New Year, as a particularly important period for performing *sang*. There are two reasons for this. First, from a sociological perspective, New Year ceremonies annually reaffirm the bonds and hierarchies connected to various social units such as family, clan, village, and caste. All social groups have roles to play in purifying the abodes of humans and spirits through the power of incenses. Second, the New Year rituals presuppose that with the passage of a given year, the old year becomes a wicked year, referred to as *lo nganpa* (*lo ngan pa*). The wicked year is one in which pollution or *dip* has come to pervade the world of humans and gods, contaminating family homes, villages, and the abodes of spirit beings. The same pollution that breaks down social bonds, engenders the presence of demonic forces, and threatens to transform a godly *lha* into a monstrous *dre*. To restore order and purity for the coming of the new year, to turn dirty monstrous beings back into gods, and ensure the stability of their three-tier universe, locals engage in various traditions, especially *sang* rituals.

During Losar, Ladakhis produce *sang* as part of larger ritual centered around the *lhatho* This offering ritual is called *lhasol* (*lha gsol*). Often a certain class of spirits called the *phas lha*, (*phas lha*), roughly translating as the clan god, constitute the chief object of worship. Often a layman, designated as a *lhardag* (*lha bdag*), serves as the priest during the Losar rituals taking place around a given *phas lha*'s shrine.

The collective community which this type of god protects and who are responsible for ritual practices to this deity are called the *phaspun* (*phas spun*). The *phaspun* are likened to a clan unit, although not bound by blood or descent, but rather by their shared connection to the spirit of their *lhatho*. Purity and pollution rules structure the relationship of the *phaspun* members to each other and their relation to the *phas lha* housed in their respective *lhatho*. Because they believe that their god becomes unclean, defiled by human *dip*, *phaspun* members annually cleanse and make purified scent offering at their *lhatho*, typically during Losar. As a byproduct of this, purification rituals reaffirm social bonds of the *phasphun* members.

Before I draw on first-hand observations and interviews with participants to provide a brief synopsis of the *lhasol* ritual, it is necessary to provide some background on the god called the *phaslha* and the clan unit of the *phaspun*. When I interviewed priests or *lhardag*-s about the origin of the deity they call the *phaslha*, they typically associate three points of origins. First, some were the restless spirits of the dead, such as the ghosts of dead kings or villagers, who became captured and domesticated in their respective shrines. Second, they could be *dre* or demons by nature, such as the fierce *tsen* (*btsan*). The *tsen* are often described as the departed spirits of corrupted monks. These demons were captured and forced to become oath-bound protectors of the *phaspun*. Third, the god could be a *lha*, indigenous to specific natural spaces such as mountain tops or ancient trees. Regardless of their point of origin, all spirits usually dwell in a *lhatho*. These shrines serve as a kind of totem for the clan unit of the *phaspun*. What exactly is a *phaspun* and are they bound together by their shared god? This question brings Ladakhi notions of purity and pollution into our analysis.

The *phaspun* members unite during major life cycle events, such as marriage, the birth of child, or the death of one of their members. Ladakhis believe that because these events disrupt or change the course of normal social relations, they yield significant amounts of pollution. Thus, a family of an unborn child or a deceased relative is ritually impure to the outside world for a given period of time. To eat or exchange food with this family during a period of impurity or to touch the corpse of their deceased relative risks spreading this pollution throughout society and the three-tiered universe. This polluting pandemic would weaken gods, engender demons, and transform otherwise innocuous spirits into monstrous beings. The universe and society would collapse in this noxious environment. Ladakhis believe that the impurity of life cycle events must remain contained by quarantining members of a polluted family.

Those affiliated with a family's *phaspun*, however, are protected from pollution via the power of their shared god, the *phaslha*. The *phaspun* can thus aid in caring for a newborn child, performing arrangements for a wedding, and most importantly for Ladakhis, disposing of the dead corpse. Those outside the *phaspun* must not engage in these functions because they lack support from the required *phaslha*. This makes the *phaspun* members reliant on each other to aid in the transitions associated with life cycle events. Key to their activities is the protective power associated with their god. If this god becomes unclean, however, it turns into a demon who will cause misfortunes for *phaspun* members and no longer ensure the purity of the clan. Here again, these dynamics point to how gods and demons relate to the purity and pollution in the human world; a spirit kept clean is a god, and a filthy spirit becomes demonic as the *phaspun* becomes defiled by impurity. The purity and pollution codes that unite the *phaspun* members to each other during life cycle events, therefore, simultaneously bind them to their shared god. To maintain this symbiotic relationship between the clan and the god, the *phaspun* annually reaffirm their social bonds through the ritual of *lhasol*.

The ritual purification of the *lhatho* and the feeding of the god are the two practices constituting the tradition of *lhasol*. In 2012, I observed three phases during one ceremony that are indicative of the sequencing of this practice. In phase one, an initial cleansing takes place before entering the presence of the *lhatho*. *Phaspun* members, especially the officiating priest, ought to bathe before the ceremony. Food that will be offered, such as wheat, bread, beer, and so forth, are ritually fumigated with juniper. This fumigation deodorizes these items with scent pleasing to the gods who will consume them. The *lhardag*-s who officiate the ceremony must also purify themselves with incense before they enter the presence of their god so that the odor of the body will not produce pollution. In the second phase of the *lhasol,* the male members of the *phaspun* gather to change the juniper leaves of the *lhatho*, while the *lhardag* circumambulates the *lhatho*, offering *sang* to the god. Other *phaspun* members present food and beer offerings to the shrine, while chanting *chod* (*mchod*), meaning "eat."

When I asked various *lhardag-s* why they made these offerings they gave four general responses: (1) the purified scent serves as an atonement offering to ask for forgiveness for any pollution humans produced; (2) the purifying smoke cleanses both the spirit and its physical abode of the *lhatho*; (3) because spirits are scent eaters (*dri za*) the fumigated smoke and the aromatic foods served as an annual feast for the *phaslha*; and (4) these practices serve as for payment the services rendered to the god during the past year and a guarantee that the spirit would continue to look after the *phaspun* in the new year.

While offering the food and incenses, *lhardag*-s typically recites a vernacular text called the *sangsol* (*bsang gsol*) or *Fumigation Worship*. The texts invoke the names of different *phaslhas*, names of village deities (*yul lha*), names of high lamas, and the names of dharma protectors (*chos skyong*) associated with different monasteries in Ladakh. After invoking these beings by name, the purified smoke is offered to them. Here the fumigation reminds a given *phaspun* that they and their god are linked to a broader network of spirit beings, and that purity is the foundation of this matrix.

The sanctified smoke, with its capacity to reach all beings in all the tiers of the cosmos, provides a shared sacred substance as it travels to different to nooks and crannies of the local landscape. Purification traditions in Ladakhi Losar reflect Mary Douglas's argument that "rituals of purity and impurity create unity in experience. . . . By their means, symbolic patterns are worked out and publicly displayed. Within these patterns . . . disparate elements are related and disparate experience is given meaning" (Douglas 2002, 3). The *lhasol* ceremony typically concludes with members of the *phaspun* feasting and drinking together. The ceremonial purification of the *lha* and its shrine thus reaffirms their unique social bond they have together.

The power of ritually produced incense to traverse locations, linger, and purify is not unique to Ladakh, but remains prevalent in many Tibetan cultural areas. Incense based rituals remain central to how many Himalayan Buddhists understand their relationship to their environment and the various beings resided within it. For example, in the current context of the COVID-19 pandemic, Tibetan Buddhists have been employing the *sang* rituals to purify the world of the novel coronavirus. Recently, members of the Druk Amitabha Mountain DGK Nunnery in Nepal have periodically broadcast livestream performances on Facebook. This ceremony is referred to in Tibetan as "*Nölsang*" (*mnol bsangs*). According to the Himalayan Buddhist tradition, this ritual originates from the figure Padmasambhava, who performed this ritual to cleanse the environment of pollutants disturbing local spirits who in their perturbed states proliferated the spread of infectious diseases and other calamities. Padmasambhava's use of ritual smoke cleansed these sprits and their abodes, thereby enabling a state of health and prosperity to manifest among the Tibetan people. As Himalayan Buddhists now employ these scented substances to ritually combat the COVID-19 coronavirus, they draw on long-standing historical traditions that invoke the power of sacred scents. These perceived powers include the capacities to placate spirits, travel and disperse vast distances into different realms, and ameliorate the devastation caused by pandemics. For these Buddhists, smoke serves as rope which strings together networks of humans, gods, and monsters all reliant upon the purifying power of *sang*.

CONCLUSION

I conclude my chapter by raising broader implications of this case study for academic research on gods and monsters. In particular, I suggest how recent work on smell and scent theory can provide new questions and insights for the study of monstrosity and its relationship to religious institutions and constructions of divinity. Examining monsters in the context of ancient Western societies, David D. Gilmore (2003, 41) identifies the Harpies as a unique species of foul-smelling monsters believed to "befoul everything they touched." Whereas the example of the Harpies describes a class of monsters having foul-smell as a key attribute, this chapter raises questions to how human-produced odors create pathways for individuals to relate to the beings within their cultural and religious imaginaries via the power of ritual. Spirits in Ladakh are believed to remain neutral with respect to humans, until foul stenches or ritually generated aromas bring humans into contact with spirits. Depending on whether the smells appease or offend a given spirit, it will either comport itself as a godly benefactor or a nefarious demon. For Ladakhi Buddhists, godly aromas and monstrous stenches do not originate from supernatural entities, but are rather the byproduct of human actions that either purify or pollute the socioreligious environment in which people and spirits cohabitate. My emphasis on the olfactory has been informed by historian Jonathan Reinarz's (2014, 1) observation that "smell is a cultural phenomenon. Members of past societies relied on smell to understand and engage with both their immediate environment and a wider world of meanings." Reinarz has cogently argued that smell provides key insights into how humans make their lives and world meaningful in relationship to stenches, odors, and various culturally significant smells. We have seen in this chapter how this has been the case with incense offerings in Ladakh. In short, the cultural categories surrounding smell are meaning-making symbols. Monsters, as Jack Halberstam (1995) has pointed out, also constitute meaning-making machines that provide lenses for viewing social values, norms, and hierarchies. In Ladakh, smell, monsters, and gods are intricately bound together as forces for constructing social order.

In his book *Sandalwood and Carrion: Smell in Indian Religion and Culture*, James McHugh examines Sanskrit perfumery texts. McHugh highlights that in Indic traditions, perfumers understand that the right combination of fragrance can be used to please gods, expel demons, project royal power, or manipulate erotic desire. Just as extraordinary powers have been associated with certain Indic perfumes, Ladakhis perceive the formulas used to make fragrances for scent offerings such as *sur* and *sang* to contain aromatic properties capable of placating spirit beings or purifying the landscape in ritual contexts. These smells and scent-based rituals underscore how locals remain concerned over pollution as a force responsible for personal illness, social disharmony, and the production of demons. Ladakhis use the ritual production of purifying scents as vehicles for ordering humans' relationships with the divine and the demonic, and with each other, thereby averting the polluting stenches, dangerous monsters, and social disorder. Based on this case study, I suggest that scholars of gods and monsters pay greater attention to the historical and social significance of godly aromas and monstrous stenches.

NOTES

1. Note on transliteration: Ladakhi is considered a "Tibetan" dialect. When using Ladakhi terms, I phonetically spell out the words approximating how they sound in the region. This often will not correspond with the central Tibetan pronunciation. When I first use a term, I will also place the Wylie transliteration in parenthesis.

2. Here, I am using my translations of dGe Thub bstan chos grags, "Lha 'dre zhes pa don du yod pa yin nam" [Do Gods and Demons Actually Exist?], in *Lo "khor gyi deb: Shes rig me long"* [*Annual Magazine: The Cultural Mirror*], editor Nawang Tsering Shakspo (Leh: Jammu and Kashmir Academy of Art, Culture, and Languages of Leh, Ladakh, 1998), 60–80.

3. In Ladakh, common white ingredients include barley, milk, and butter. The sweet ingredients can include sugar, apricots, nuts, and/or honey.

4. It is important to note that the categories "Buddhist" and "non-Buddhist" are, to a certain extent, constructed through the lens of European and American academic interpreters; they remain, however, useful designations to frame and interpret the expanding reach of Buddhist institutions into greater parts of Ladakhi life.

Chapter 9

Man, Yeti, and Mi-go

The Transgressive History of a Monstrous Word

Lee A. Weiss

In Lobsang Rampa's second book *Doctor from Lhasa*, published in 1959, the self-described lama—by his own account trained in Tibetan medicine, aviation, and trepanation—bemoans the destructive character of Western academic and scientific skepticism:

> What would happen to my old friends, the yetis, if the westerners got hold of them—as they are yet trying to do. Undoubtedly the yeti would be shot, stuffed, and put in some museum. Even then people would argue and say there were no such things as yetis. (Rampa 1990, 1)

It is worth noting that Lama Rampa, or Cyril Henry Hoskin, a plumber from Devon, likely never actually set foot in Tibet, and was probably not friends with any yetis. Belief in the yeti, however, is historically and geographically widespread throughout the Himalayas (Vleck 1964, 80–4), with regional gazetteers (Nag chu sa gnas srid gros 1992) and descriptions of mythical hidden-lands (Bkra shis tse ring 2008) warning of yeti and other wild animals harassing potential travelers. Another name for this monster, which occurs somewhat less frequently in Western sources is "mi-go" (*Tib. Mi-rgod*), which The *Tibetan-English Dictionary of Tibetan Medicine and Astrology* translates as "Wild and savage people" and as "raw, courageous men" (2006, 328). *Mi* is the Tibetan word for human, while the suffix *go* means wild and undomesticated.

The word first appears in the West alongside the accounts of mountaineers returning from Himalayan expeditions in the early twentieth century claiming to have seen inexplicable footprints, and heard stories about a mountain-dwelling man-like monster (Sawerthal 2017, 124–5). One early, and especially enduring, use of the word mi-go in the West occurs in the writings of horror author H. P. Lovecraft. In "Whisperer in the Darkness," published in 1930 Lovecraft (2010, 672) equates satyrs and wildmen with "the dreaded *Mi-Go* or 'Abominable Snow-Men' who lurk hideously amid the ice and rock pinnacles of the Himalayan summits."

The word occurs again in the poet and mountaineer Michael Roberts's 1937 poem *The Mi-go*. Robert's poetry was inspired by folktales exchanged by his Sherpa guides and attendants, who, he writes, "swore that they had seen them, white skinned and naked, but covered with thick hair." The first line of the poem reads: "Bind Jealousy and War, punish Greed, Torment your hideous Caliban and bind him, or send him, a puzzled scapegoat, to the outer darkness" (Roberts 1937, 193). These references to binding and to Caliban, the wildman of Shakespeare's *The Tempest*, are particularly interesting given the material covered below.

The doctor Reuchung Rinpoche (1976, 165) translates mi-go into English as "Ape-man," while medical texts translated and analyzed below provide descriptions and illustrations of mi-go (alongside conventional apes and primates) that are not exceptionally different from modern and Western accounts of yetis and abominable snowmen. Rather than focus exclusively on the literal ape-man, this chapter will examine the history and use of a single *name* for this monster. What can it reveal, not only about the idea of monstrosity in Tibet but also about the nature of monstrosity itself? The Western study of mi-go is inextricably linked with the yeti, and thus with monstrosity. However, the Tibetan use of the term, and the history of the word itself, is largely ignored and seemingly little understood. Therefore, understanding the genesis and early application of this word is essential to understanding both its meaning and its relationship to Western formulations of monstrosity.

Using a variety of Tibetan texts, this chapter examines the meaning and broader social implications of the word mi-go and considers these otherwise unexamined historical and moral contexts. These texts reveal a wide array of related meanings; in its earliest uses mi-go indicates wildness, thievery, and immorality. Later medical texts use mi-go as the name of an (apparently familiar) ape-like creature known in the Tibetan medical tradition, and some contemporary Himalayan folktales also describe a creature rather than a lawless human. Ultimately, these disparate uses of mi-go all revolve around the condition of being near, or adjacent, to humanity—of being something that has violated an essential rule or norm of humanity. Framed this way as an essential transgression of normative humanity, mi-go provides insight into Tibetan conceptions of human nature.

Conversely, by ignoring the multifaceted meaning of mi-go Western scholars have lost access to a subtle moral examination of human nature. Historical

Western engagement with mi-go (specifically yetis) has largely ignored any critical analysis of Himalayan attitudes and philosophies regarding the types of creatures we deem to be "monsters." This omission is consistent with a general tendency to exoticize and generally other Tibetans and the Himalayas; from Lobsang Rampa's friendly yetis, to Lovecraft's unspeakable alien fungi, endemic perspectives are ignored utterly.

Mi-go—like many types of monsters—signals a rupture, or transgression, of important social orders. The borders and liminal realms mi-go occupy are many, and are all interconnected with what it means to be—or fail to be—human. Significantly, the term mi-go is used *most often* to talk about humans, particularly in early translations from Sanskrit texts where it is used specifically to translate the word *caura* (thieving/thievery). In these contexts mi-go is used to describe barbaric or uncivilized behavior broadly: The incivility of excessive laughter, lack of meditative focus, the moral transgression of theft, are all understood as mi-go, as violations of a normative social order that governs what is acceptable and human. In short, mi-go—whether it refers to human that acts like a beast or a beast that is nearly human—denotes a monstrous, or socially transgressive, wildness. Understood in this sense, the mi-go provides valuable data for monster theory as a case study in the social function of a monstrous being from the Tibetan imaginary. More importantly, it opens the door to questions about the Tibetan understanding of what it means to be human.

MI-GO IN TIBETAN LITERATURE AND CULTURE

Before looking at examples of how mi-go has been used in Tibetan literature and comparing these to theories of monstrosity, it is important to understand the more subtle historical elements of the construction of the word. Especially important is the element of the word that implies the monstrous separation or violation of the human, the component of the word that makes it monstrous: *go*. "Go" indicates wildness and a lack of control; it is often amended to the names of animals to indicate undomesticated varieties. For example, yak (*g. yak*) and yak-go (*g.yak rgod*) distinguish domesticated and wild yaks respectively; *go* is also used in this way to describe wild-growing medical herbs (*rgod sman*) (Bialik 2018, 454–5).

Early uses of "go" conflate wildness with bravery and a professional soldier class in ancient Tibetan society.[1] A telling phrase from the Tibetan Imperial period (seventh to ninth centuries) refers to the "weak and the strong" (*rgod dan g.yud*) (Bialik 2018, 455). The influence of these early meanings can be seen in contemporary uses of mi-go as a descriptor for brave men and fierce warriors. "It appears that *go* as an adjective was used in OT

[Old Tibetan] sources in relation to human beings only in a clearly defined meaning 'aggressive fierce'" (Bialik 2018, 456). This notion of ferocity and aggression takes on a more critical tone when amended to "mi," though there are contemporary examples of mi-go used to indicate fierceness and bravery as positive traits,[2] the word tends to equate the fierceness with the lack of humanity or domesticity.

A particularly interesting and significant early use of the word mi-go in this context is found in the *Aryacaurividyanasananamadhāranī* (*The Dhāranī that Utterly Subdues Mi-go*), a short sūtra surviving only in Tibetan translation in the Buddhist canons, which contains a *dhāranī*—or short magical incantation—and accompanying ritual for subduing thieves, brigands, or otherwise wild men. The text opens with the Buddha and his principal attendant Ānanda traveling through the mountains of Videha:

> I pay homage to all the Buddhas and Bodhisattvas. Thus have I heard: At that time the Bhagavan was traveling with his attendant Ananda, going to Videha (Easternmost Continent). In the distance Ananda saw a horde of mi-go, a sight so fearful his hair stood on end. So, the Bhagavan spoke, saying: "Hear me and be purified mi-go. Hearing this you shall arrive at bliss, it is the Bhagavan who speaks, and bestows these words. Ananda, you are afraid of these mi-go? This statement of the Bhagavan is for when you are afraid, when those gone to bliss feel afraid. When these words are bestowed Ananda, you *will* overcome fear. Ananda! Now all within ten leagues are utterly controlled/subdued, the guards, all of the mi-go townspeople who live in the mountain spaces/valleys, all the guards of the narrow crevices of the mountain. Hearing these words they bend their knees and are filled with remorse—stiffened and paralyzed. In this way the turning of the wheel of samsara is [made] like stone, in this way the turning of the wheel is transformed/magically halted and paralyzed. Like the quivering/moving mi-go, transform! Transform and halt. Transform confusion/bewilderment. Until one takes refuge they will not transform and will remain unliberated—like a knot." These words the Bhagavan said, bestowing them on Ayushmat Ananda. These words of the Bhagavan evidently deserve praise (Mi rgod rnam 'joms 1971).

The final part of the text is a short occult prescription,[3] providing the reader with a ritual they can perform to avoid falling into a similar situation as described in the sūtra. To "bind the mi-go," one treats donkey hair with asafetida (the dried latex of the Ferula plant, used in regional cooking and medicine) before weaving it into thread. A woman must perform the weaving; she cannot be menstruating and must first undergo a ritual purification. The thread is then made into a cloth, the end of it is cut off, and the spell is complete.

What needs to be remembered is that these mi-go are distinctly and clearly human; they are not ape-men or yetis or literal monsters, but they are people. And while they may be brave and fierce, they are also seen as malevolent, less than human. In the text, mi-go is used to refer to *all* of the villagers who occupied the remote mountain passage Ānanda and the Buddha passed through. These mi-go are bands and families of thieves, and the binding words the Buddha recites paralyzes all of the members of the mountain city of these thieves. It is worth noting here the relation between thievery, wildness, and living on borders and far-off places. This text establishes a number of the standard elements of mi-go, specifically, their immorality and dwelling outside conventional borders. It also brings the early brave and fierce implications into conversation with human nature; the actions of mi-go are so ulterior to the principals that organize human life they have ceased to be human.

The sūtra and its mantra of protection and binding inspired a tradition of tantric rites for binding mi-go. These rites are scattered throughout tantric traditions, but are generally mantras and related occult operations with the purpose of protecting travelers on journeys through the wilderness, "binding" would-be thieves (mi-go) in place. In the *Dpal E ka dza ti khrag gi rba klong gi rgyud* (*Ekajati's Whirlpool of Blood Tantra*) a tantric compendium devoted to the goddess Ekajaṭī one finds exactly these binding rites: travelers are instructed to seal themselves in the center of a pen in an empty field and chant a Sanskrit mantra to ensure they are not accosted during their travels through the lands of mi-go[4] (*Dpal E ka dza ti khrag gi rba klong gi rgyud*, 432.7-460.3). These spells are largely in line with the material in the sūtra, presenting the mi-go as a human being engaged in inhuman behaviors. They tend to allude specifically to travelers and traveling, and situate the mi-go in desolate areas. These mi-go endanger people and similarly violate normative moral and organizational standards necessary for human culture as we know it.

In contrast to the *The Dhāraṇī that Utterly Subdues Mi-go*, the mi-go found in certain medical texts is clearly a nonhuman being. Instead of an abstract label or moral repudiation, it is understood as a being with a physical, animal existence. The earliest references to mi-go as a literal monster occur in seventeenth and eighteenth-century medical texts. Tibetan medicine and Buddhist doctrine explicitly acknowledge and involve preternatural or "mythical" beings, but the mi-go is distinctly physical in these texts, treated often as a conventional animal, and not a numinous, spiritual being. Its flesh, blood, and furs are understood as physically substantial enough to be included in practical guides for doctors and pharmacists.

The *Shel gong shel phreng* (*The Crystal Ball and The Crystal Rosary*) (Bstan 'dzin phun tshogs 1970) is a set of two books consisting of a listing of the principal *materia medica* and an auto-commentary explaining the use, appearance, and nature of these substances. Written in the seventeenth century by physician Tenzin Phuntsok, these books document the plant, animal, and inanimate, substances employed in the treatment of disease and production of medicine. The "flesh" (*sha*) chapter begins with the section describing the appropriate medical uses of human flesh. Human flesh is said to be good for alleviating "ulcerations, tumors, and malignant cancers of the skin and other illnesses of the gDon [an illness bringing spirit] wind (rlung)" (Bstan 'dzin phun tshogs, 400). The following section lists a variety of "wild" animals, beginning with mi-go and including lions, tigers, bears, wild (*rgod*) pig and wild (*rgod*) goat, vultures, crows, and ravens: "These various meats dispel gDon caused sickness (*gdon nad*)" (400). Fortunately, this brief reference is expanded on: it has been illustrated explicitly in medical manuals designed to aid physicians in identification and proper application of medical substances.

Mi-go, therefore, are described and illustrated in medical texts and commentaries, alongside primates, herbs, and exotic birds. Here they are animals, connected intimately with humanity, but explicitly apart. An undomesticated variant of human, wild and only partly recognizable, in appearance and behavior, as somehow like us. Notably, the *Dri med shel gong shel phreng (The Pure Crystal Ball and Rosary)* provides illustrations of the substances and animals enumerated in the earlier text *The Crystal Ball and The Crystal Rosary*. This book, therefore, would have been an extraordinarily practical tool for a Himalayan physician potentially unfamiliar with obscure Indian and Chinese flora and fauna. *The Pure Crystal Ball and Rosary's* entry on the mi-go reads as follows:

> Mi-go are shaped like humans or [members of] the bear family. They live on mountains. They are large and very strong. It is known that their flesh is beneficial for the treatment of illnesses caused by the gDon [spirits]. Their flesh clears away imbalances of bile, and other illnesses of the liver. (Ye shes bstan pa'i rgyal mtshan 1971, 228)

While the earlier uses of mi-go morally castigate human beings as behaving inhumanely, the mi-go referenced in medical texts is an actual inhuman creature, a literal monster. This use symbolically compounds all of the implications we have seen mi-go carry up till now, border dwelling, norm challenging, uncivilized behavior, all made flesh: Here, this "monstrous" mi-go transforms what had historically been presented as cultural otherness into biological otherness.

There is one contemporary folktale regarding the mi-go that is especially important to touch on, not only because of its evident longevity and geographic distribution but also because it embodies the essential properties of the monstrous mi-go. In each of its versions, the mi-go are depicted as liminal beings, imitating humans while living on the borders of human settlements. They mimic and steal, and *try* to be human, but their disorderly attempts result in them stealing from the farmers and damaging their livelihood. The folktale tends to be used to explain what "happened" to the mi-go, and why people either do not see them or only see them very rarely. One particular account of the folktale, recorded on a Chinese website devoted to Tibetan culture (zw.tibetculture.org), describes the origin of the name of a lake on a nature preserve, but the lake itself seems to have been added to the folk tale later, ostensibly to explain the name of the eponymous lake (*mi rgod mtsho*). The lake in Garze, Sichuan, now called Mugecuo, is part of a large complex of nature preserves and natural springs.

> Once, long ago a tribe of mi-go lived on the back of a mountain, in a plain, near a farmland called gu ('*agu*). Every year the land was tended by humans, in the spring the fields were planted and in the summer they were weeded. Then, in the autumn, when it was time to gather the harvest, the mi-go would copy what they had seen the farmers doing, and would pluck the sprouts from the field before the farmers could pick them. This caused the farmers' harvest to be greatly reduced. One day the common men of the town got together and hatched a plan. They filled up large pots with beer, and some with honey and pork fat. Then taking up wooden swords and preparing some bundles they then went to the plains [where the mi-go dwelt] and pretended to drink from the jugs and became drunk, they smeared their mouths with only a fly's mouthful-worth of sticky animal-fat honey *chaang* (beer). Then, in the field, they brandished their wooden swords, pretending to fight one another, before dropping to the ground, and playing dead. Soon, they secretly snuck back to their town, leaving behind the bundles they had prepared, filled with real swords—not wooden ones. The mi-go did not know any better than to emulate the men, they accepted the deception of the men, and imitated it themselves. So, they drank the beer and the honey and fat. One by one the mi-go, having really drunk from the vessels became intoxicated. They then found the bundles that the men had left in the fields, and found the real swords, which they took up and began to swing. However, their eyes were daubed shut by the honey and animal fat they had consumed. They blindly swung their swords and killed each other—all except the chief of the mi-go tribe. The chief, seeing what had happened to his tribe, was overcome with emotion, and realizing he was about to cry sat atop a large rock and wept (this boulder is not far from *Bzhung bra aha*). He remained there, weeping, and his tears flowed into the gu plains, filling them and making a lake. Ever since then, because of these events, humans have called the lake, which is presently the town of Dartsedo

(famous for its sightseeing) the *mi rgod mtsho*, mi-go lake. ("Mi rgod mtsho yig gtam rgyud," n.d.)

A similar account is found in a letter written by the Tibetologist and aristocrat Prince Peter of Greece and Denmark. This account only features the first part of the story, and does not include the origin of the lake's name, the crying mi-go chieftain, or any overt geographic reference at all:

> A few days before Christmas 1951, Prince Peter of Greece sent a letter to the Calcutta *Statesman*. . . . He described some peculiar events that took place in a village close to Jalap La, in Sikkim. Having noticed that a yeti was frequently coming to drink water from their trough, the villagers filled it with *chang*—the local rice beer—instead of water. They were thus able to capture the drunken being and, after tying it up, they headed down south, intending to bring it to Kalimpong to exhibit it. But their plans changed abruptly when the yeti, sober again, was able to break the ropes and escape along the way. According to Prince Peter, the being was a monkey, and it might have provided some clues that would help answer puzzling questions posed by the famous and mysterious footprints found and photographed by Shipton during his 1951 Everest Expedition. (Sawerthal and Torri 2017, 131)

There is a third example of this story in an account from Shinya Lama Punyavajra, the third chief lama of the Boudhnath Stupa in Kathmandu (Nath 1994, 98), though this one is much briefer, and like the account Prince Peter provided, does not contain the ending section describing the formation of the lake. We see in all of these stories the same concern with wildness and civilization, with appropriate behavior and conflict on the outskirts of human society. These monstrous concerns are the core of the meaning of mi-go: near-human wildness, and social transgression.

Ultimately, mi-go in all of its Himalayan meanings speaks to the liminal space in-between humans and animals, wildness and social order. The mi-go is *not* a mi (human), but it must be *more* mi than a yak or a crow—after all, these animals don't have mi in their names. If they are undomesticated or particularly dangerous they may have a go, but they are not *so* closely connected with humanity as to have it in their own names. Every time mi-go is used it is used to describe people or things that are *like* people, but that have in some way violated or transgressed the basic rules of humanity, and so fail to really *be* human. In this way, mi-go tells us, among other things, what it means to be human, to be civilized, and how important limits, borders, and normative order is to our shared humanity.

MI-GO, TRANSGRESSION, MONSTROSITY, AND WILDMEN

In *Ten Theses on Monsters and Monstrosity*, Allen S. Weiss (2004, 194) writes, "Monsters are indicators of epistemic shifts." In this sense, monstrosity represents change or violation of conventionally accepted knowledge and wisdom. So, monsters represent transgressions and violations of accepted norms, moral standards, socio-cultural values, biology, and so on: The deformed "monster" of premodern medical teratology is a transgression of "healthy" physiology, the zombie is a violation of the duality of life and death, the sphinx or satyr is a challenge to conventional zoology. Monsters as symbols of social change, and thus transgression, are understood to be living, physical, violations of accepted natural and moral orders and law. They, by definition, straddle the norms and limits, the rules by which we live and organize our lives. Theorist Jeffrey Jerome Cohen expands on the role of the monster as "indicator" or symbol, pointing out that the monster is filled with cultural information:

> The monstrous body is pure culture. A construct and a projection, the monster exists only to be read: the *monstrum* is etymologically "that which reveals," "that which warns," a glyph that seeks a hierophant. Like a letter on the page, the monster signifies something other than itself: it is always a displacement, always inhabits the gap between the time of upheaval that created it and the moment into which it is received, to be born again. (Cohen 1997, 4)

Monsters are typically made *monstrous* by failing or violating one or more human norms or dictums: Too tall, too short, an unnatural combination or number of limbs, conjoined twins, too animalistic, too violent, too prone to laughter, incivility, cannibalism; the monster represents or enacts a transgression of our lived human norms through its behaviors and appearance. Monsters transgress norms and by violating them they function to establish normativity. Normativity, in philosopher Lorraine Daston's words, "is the quality of telling us what *should* be, as opposed to describing how things are." Human culture opposes theft, moves toward organization, and demands a degree of domesticity. Daston goes on to assert the universality of norms for humanity: "There is no known human culture, past or present, without any norms at all" (Daston 2019, 46). This is why understanding the history, nature, and implications of mi-go's specific violations of normativity is important: it tells us far more about humanity than it does about yetis or thieves.

In the folk tale above, the mi-go try to teach themselves to be human, but it is actually the mi-go who teach us how *not* to be human. All things called mi-go engage in some kind of violation of the normative bounds of human behavior, morality, and civility. As such they personify wildness or the inverse of human social order, which seeks to domesticate and civilize, to live in centralized settlements away from wild or unkempt borders. As wild beings, the mi-go show civilized humans what not to do and be, demonstrating the limits of their social lives.

In social function points to a connection between mi-go and a Western monster tradition: the wildman. The wildman is the name used to describe a culturally and geographically widespread "species" of monster: a humanlike thing, covered in fur, active on the outskirts of human culture. The wildman lives on the limits of society—sometimes human, sometimes animal—feasting on human flesh, foraging nourishment, and garbage (Dudley 1973, 7). The wildman, as a monster, also tells us about the limits of humanity and human norms: the limits of our settlements and civilizations, the edges of our accepted behaviors—even the limits of our human appearance. The wildman does not utterly violate these norms, but transgresses them *just* enough to draw our attention to them. They live on the margins of our society, not in space or beneath the ocean; they imitate our social behaviors; they are not wholly alien, but drink beer and raise children. Even in their appearance they are discernibly human like, but more hirsute. The wildman is a clear neighbor, an ancestor, and the fears and judgments the wildman provokes as a monster are therefore distinctly *human* fears. Like the mi-go the wildness of the wildman can be understood as "belonging to a set of culturally self-authenticating devices . . . they do not so much refer to a specific thing, place, or condition as dictate a particular attitude" (Dudley 1973, 7). In this case, the attitude is one of acceptable or normative humanity, the basic set of fluid norms and rules humanity relies on.

Wildman is a good option for a literal translation of mi-go; it connects the word and related monster to a wider monster tradition while roughly translating "undomesticated human." However, this translation occludes much of the historical and social information provided, and would seem to be less relevant for the thieves and brigands of the sūtras and tantras. Like the mi-go, wildmen live on boundaries, and represent violations of normative human order with their essential wildness. Wildness is what makes wildmen, and mi-go, monsters; this un-domesticity is a confrontation of human form and animal behavior, of the near-limits of the human social world. In *Myths of the Dog-man* David Gordon White (1991, 27) opines, "The Wildman almost always represents the image of the man released from social control, the man in whom libidinal impulses have gained full ascendency." In the same way, mi-go always denotes or implies transgressive wildness in opposition to normative humanity—whether as a literal monster or not—there is a perennial incivility and transgression of normative social order encoded in all uses of mi-go.

CONCLUSION

From disparate examples across the Himalayas and hundreds of years of textual tradition a clearer picture of humanity's collective concern and fear of violations of civility, and the boundaries of human life this fear implies, emerges. Wherever mi-go occurs, it occurs in close proximity to humanity. The monstrosity of yetis and mi-go is a lack of culture, an uncanny failure of something otherwise very human to ultimately be human, or for something human to stop or fail at human behavior. This is clearly evinced in the many interrelated uses of mi-go in the texts reviewed above. Throughout these uses, mi-go is consistently linked to a particular kind of violation of a normative order, always indicating a transgression of the boundaries of human social and behavioral norms. In this way, even when used in a rare positive context, like fierce or brave, mi-go still retains the implication of inhumanity and monstrosity. Mi-go speaks to the monstrous wildness that stands in contrast to the typical and acceptable in human life; it is the violation of the normative standards by which we define our humanity.

While largely ignored in Western research and theory this broader role of mi-go, as an indicator of transgression and near-humanity, is evident when examined in its traditional contexts in Tibetan literature and culture. It is important to note that the disparate textual examples presented in this chapter are from a fairly limited, though still neglected, corpus: Tibetan literature. This research has not taken into account non-Tibetan textual canons, or the innumerable oral traditions throughout the Himalayas currently mythologizing and theorizing mi-go. Yet even this limited selection of texts reveals a historically consistent meaning. A meaning that aligns well with Western attitudes surrounding the idea of monstrosity and monsters analyzed above but is otherwise inaccessible or ignored in existing scholarship. From its earliest uses and old Tibetan origins as an indicator of bravery, wildness, and later of theft and barbarous behavior, mi-go draws a line in the sand between the acceptable and human, and the uncivilized, wild, and barbarous. The later, and more familiar, mi-go of medical manuals and monster stories retains this meaning, symbolically embodying the limits of humanity in a near-human creature.

This is an important point of congruence between Tibetan and Western attitudes toward transgressions of social and moral boundaries. Mi-go clearly fulfills a very similar role in Tibetan thought as the wildmen and monsters defined in the Western theory discussed above. However, this role has gone largely unaddressed, with Western scholars and explorers only presenting and projecting their existing convictions and beliefs, while actively excluding centuries of existing local theory. In these scholarly works mi-go is at best roughly translated, generally alongside lists of other Himalayan names for "the yeti," a term that will also go undefined and unexamined. As the Tibetan sources presented above reveal, the meanings and uses of these otherwise unexamined names constitute discrete theories of morality and humanity. These theories, overlooked in favor of existing Western notions of "cryptids" and "missing links," provide subtle and valuable insights into the nature of humanity and morality as gleamed by Tibetan and Himalayan authors. These insights are clearly valuable ones, articulating many points of similarity between the intellectual traditions. Not least of which is the similarity between the uses of mi-go and monster which, in their perspective contexts, mean very similar things.

Like the term monstrosity, the term mi-go conveys a moral judgment, highlighting elements that fail to cohere with order, civility, and domesticity. Yetis and raucous laughter, and anything else mi-go, can all be thought of as monstrous because of how *close* to us they are. This recognition also tells us something about the nature of humanity: it highlights the central importance of normativity and domesticity in human civilization. Mi-go represents the symbolic violation of the norms of domesticated humanity.

So, mi-go certainly tells us something about Tibetan and Western ideas of monsters and humans, how disparate people observe and address similar transgressions and norms. But most significantly, mi-go tells us something about ourselves. It tells us something subtle, and perhaps unsettling, about human nature, and how close we all really are to inhumanity, to the collapse of our values and norms. To modify David Gordon White's (1991, 27) assertion quoted above, that "The Wildman almost always represents the image of the man released from social control" I would assert that the mi-go represents this image as well. Every mi-go is only a few transgressions away from the human; this is equally true for us humans, who are closer than it seems to a wild monstrosity kept at bay only by our collective acquiescence to human norms.

NOTES

1. In old Tibetan legal texts go is also used to refer to a professional military class, for example the "*rgod* of a hill fort" (Bialek 2018, 456), is used to identify the commander of a particular fortification.

2. For example, the martial arts master Klu bum Mi rgod, eponymous protagonist of a popular Tibetan Wushu novel (Nag po skal bzang 2013).

3. "This is the ritual: Mix asafoetida with donkey's hair [to make threads], and have a clean [ritually pure] woman spin the thread, while reciting twenty-one times the aforementioned [text]. When done [making the cloth] cut/discard the knot at

the end, then untie the separated knot. This is the Siddhi" (Mi rgod rnam 'joms 1971, 306).

4. A similar binding rite is found in another Tantric compendium of Ekajaṭī, *The Collected Wrathful Tantras of Ekajaṭī* (*Ral gcig ma'i drag sngags 'dus pa'i rgyud*, 92.2-102.2), while a translation of a mi-go binding ritual in the Tārā tradition can be found in Stephen Beyer's *Magic and Ritual in Tibet* (1973, 209).

Chapter 10

The Mesopotamian Demon Lamaštu and the Monstrosity of Gender Transgression

Madadh Richey

Matthew Lewis's 1796 gothic novel *The Monk* narrates the fall of its Capuchin protagonist, Ambrosio following his encounters with a boy named Rosario who turns out to be a demon in disguise. Derided in its day for its scandalous portrayals of incest and sexual violence, Lewis's "romance" is now recognized as a classic expression of queer horror and desire. As two recent articles from a trans studies perspective observe, a major aspect of Rosario's threat to Ambrosio lies in the former's being an ostensibly female person who presents as masculine when first encountered by Ambrosio and the reader (Marshall 2018, 31–7; Zigarovich 2018a, 90–1). This threat to the gendered order is so acute that, as Nowell Marshall observes (2018, 36), several modern commentators have found themselves attempting to reinscribe Rosario as "actually" female to quarantine his monstrous difference; Rosario, in such readings, becomes a "succubus who comes to [Ambrosio] in her own succession of deceptive veils" (Hogle 1997).

As most readers will undoubtedly know, the fashioning of demons as gender-transgressive is hardly unique to this particular eighteenth-century novel. Neither, though, is the strange desire to circumscribe the monster's threat as though proceeding from only one among several aspects of difference. In the present chapter, I address the Mesopotamian baby-snatching demon Lamaštu to problematize both the naturalizing of difference in the body and to ask why and in what contexts discursive arrangements around monstrous figures work to isolate and rehabilitate them. What emerges are insights not only on Lamaštu's discursive positionings but also on her potential for taking up and even taking on her specific manifestation of gender-transgressive monstrosity.

"KAMADME, DAUGHTER OF ANU, IS HER FIRST NAME"[1]: INTRODUCING LAMAŠTU

The demon Lamaštu is among the best known of subordinate supernatural entities from pre-Hellenistic Mesopotamia, thanks to a combination of visual art and textual sources that span the third through first millennia BCE. Visual art sources come exclusively in the form of small amulets, mostly made of various types of stone, that would have been worn or hung in domestic contexts. Over ninety amulets, originating from throughout modern-day Iraq, Syria, Israel, and Palestine, have been collected into a numbering system that scholars treat as canonical.[2] There are, however, "dozens of further amulets" (Panayotov 2015, 599) lying unpublished in museums and private collections, and publication of these will continue to extend our demonological insight.

The oldest amulets depicting Lamaštu tend to be schematic in nature.[3] Lamaštu herself is generally depicted in the center with very poorly defined features (nos. 17, 22, 40, 43, 51, 73). On some amulets, she has a bird-like head but is otherwise anthropomorphic (nos. 18, 32, 74); she is usually flanked by two animals who can often be identified as a pig and a dog despite their simplified anatomical rendering. Accessories are often incised next to her body, but these too are generally sketched rather than illustrated in detail. Two symbols that are often found are a triangle with an attached line and a hatched rectangle of sorts; parallels in later, more elaborate amulets, suggest that these are to be taken as representations of a spindle and a comb, respectively. The amulets frequently bear on their reverse either genuine cuneiform inscriptions or ancient pseudo-inscriptions—that is, signs that look like cuneiform text but that are meaningless, presumably included to lend the prestige of writing even in the absence of manufacturer literate ability (DeGrado and Richey 2017, 122–4).

In the late second and early first millennia BCE, Lamaštu representations become far more ornate and complex. Both the demon's features and her accessories are now intricately rendered, with hatching to mark the ribbing of her avian feet and wavy lines to suggest fur on her head and upper body. Lamaštu remains in the center, and she now often holds snakes, some of which even have multiple heads (nos. 23, 24, 36, 41, 55, 80, 81). In this period, the demon's breasts are often emphasized both in terms of detail and composition; in many exempla, she suckles a dog and a pig, both of whom are now unambiguously taxonomized. Lamaštu's accoutrements are scattered about her with a concentration and profusion suggesting *horror vacui*. Lamaštu is generally furnished with a donkey mount, who himself sometimes stands on a boat that sets sail facing right. Cuneiform inscriptions are to be found mainly on the reverse of these amulets, rarely on the obverse.

A small group of amulets includes additional figures that suggest by their inclusion an iconographically dramatized demonic conflict; these amulets can have either three or four horizontal fields or registers. The upper register usually contains, as might seem appropriate, astral and other symbols for such gods as Ištar, Šamaš, Sîn, and Nabû. Either below this, replacing it, or on the reverse may be a register including seven animal-headed protective figures. The next register is generally given over to a scene inclusive of both humans and supernatural entities; fish-cloak-wearing *apkallu* sages gather around a bed and attempt to heal a bedridden sick individual, while lion-headed *urigallu* demons guard the margins (see nos. 3, 4, 37, 61, 63, 64; cf. 77). In the lowest of three registers on these amulets, Lamaštu sets sail on a barque faced by a solitary demon, whose facial features are exaggeratedly canid and whose body often seems a mishmash of elements variously therio- and anthropomorphic. A second representation of what appears to be the same demon often peeks out over the top margin of the amulet, so that only his head is visible from the *recto*, but the *verso* sometimes includes a detailed incision of his hinder parts (nos. 1, 2, 58; cf. 29). This demon can be identified from texts on his own images as Pazuzu, well-known to both horror fans and the general public from the 1973 film *The Exorcist*. Despite his evil aspect in that film, Pazuzu is, in Mesopotamian texts and iconography, a fearsome but ultimately protective figure (DeGrado and Richey 2019; Heeßel 2002). Although he is potentially dangerous, his violence can generally be directed against other, more threatening demons. His conflict with Lamaštu is never described in texts, but the amulets juxtapose them as an opposing pair.

As mentioned briefly above, Sumerian- and Akkadian-language incantations against Lamaštu were often written in cuneiform script on the backs of these amulets. This is what originally made it possible for scholars to identify the main creature on the front as Lamaštu herself, as these spells both name the demon and describe methods for driving her away. A few stereotyped incantations recur constantly, and deviations from the norm are usually the result of poor copying or of substituting pseudo-inscriptions for true cuneiform. By the early first-millennium BCE, several of these stereotyped Sumerian and Akkadian incantations were collected together on clay tablet manuscripts with other spells and ritual instructions.[4] These tablet manuscripts came to follow one of two regular orders, three large tablets in length, that modern scholars now refer to as constituting the "*Lamaštu* series" (Farber 2014, 16–24; cf. Steinert 2016, 242). This series is one among several that were, in early first-millennium Assyrian and Babylonian contexts, copied in widespread standard editions; other such series include *Šurpu* "burning" and *Maqlû* "incineration."[5]

This background prepares one to assess Lamaštu with reference to both textual and visual art data. The broader context of ancient Middle Eastern studies illuminates the historical threads on which Lamaštu's characterizations draw, and looking to literary and specifically queer and trans theory can inform a contemporary understanding of her positioning and resonance within gendered systems of third—through first-millennium BCE Mesopotamia.

"LIKE A LEOPARD HER BACK IS SPOTTED"[6]: LAMAŠTU'S ANIMAL MONSTROSITY

Lamaštu is in many ways the prototypical monstrous demon, and scholars of the ancient Middle East have duly recognized her as such (Farber 1983, 444–5; 2014, 1–6; Wiggermann 2000, 224–36). Scholarly characterizations share a preoccupation with Lamaštu's theriomorphic features and especially her species hybridity. There is no denying that this is a significant element of Lamaštu's monstrosity. Lamaštu combines anthropomorphic, avian, and occasionally lupine features; although in earlier amulets she often does so in a vague, ill-defined way, first-millennium iconography standardizes her image. In later sources, Lamaštu nearly always has a lupine face, donkey ears, avian talons, and a humanoid upper body and upright posture.

In the incantations, Lamaštu is compared with several dangerous predators, including the *barbaratu* "she-wolf," *nēšu* "lion," and *nimru* "leopard."[7] These similes not only stress the fact that the demon poses a threat but that she should be linked with the inhuman, the bestial beyond human society. This exclusion is figured in terms of both species and space. It is no coincidence that, of the precise animal predators invoked, at least the leopard and the wolf appear to have been considered exotic or at least esoteric.[8] Throughout the incantations and rituals, Lamaštu is both said to come from the swampy, mountainous, or forested wilds beyond culture and she is begged to return whence she came. The texts abound with such phrases as *leqēši-ma ana tâmti šupur šadî* "Take her to the deep, and to the peak of the mountain" (*Lamaštu* II.145, ed. Farber 2014, 176–7). The bond between externalized animal and wilderness is occasionally even made through direct juxtaposition: *ana pan nammaššê ša ṣēri panīki šuknī*, the ritualist enjoins Lamaštu: "Head off toward the animals of the wilderness!" (*Lamaštu* I.198, ed. Farber 2014, 158–9). Lamaštu's belonging to these savage regions is also sometimes imagined in terms of ethnic or racial foreignness. Lamaštu is called both an "Amorite woman" (Farber 2014, 148–9, 288–9) and an "Elamite woman" (ibid., 154–5, 190–1) geographically divergent references to allegedly barbaric inhabitants living west and east of the Assyrian and Babylonian urban centers. In the context of the incantations, such formulations authorize an isomorphism between animal Otherness and human Otherness. Lamaštu's assorted modes of difference recursively enhance one another, and they instruct ancient audiences not only in her inhumanity but in the inhumanity of all of the analogs invoked.

In addition to the dangerous predators with whom she is compared, Lamaštu frequently associates with other animals, again in both text and iconography. Lamaštu often clenches serpents in both of her hands, and she is frequently surrounded by other poisonous creatures, such as scorpions and centipedes; these are species that were often opposed in ancient Middle Eastern pest incantations (recently George 2016, 98–118). Even the earliest visual art depictions show Lamaštu flanked by dogs and pigs, and in first-millennium iconography, she habitually suckles these two animals at her breasts (Wiggermann 2010). Several Mesopotamian texts suggest that pigs and dogs were considered to be unclean or despised, at least in certain contexts. A collection of popular sayings from Mesopotamia affirms that the pig is *lā qašid* "unholy," and that he is fecal, stinky, and polluting (VAT 8807 rev. III.13-14, ed. Lambert 1960, 215). In Mesopotamian art, pigs are distinctly hairy and are depicted as occupants of the swamp or objects of the hunt.[9] Dogs present a more complex case; they were certainly kept as pets, and ritual and other texts describe the use of real dogs and tiny dog statuettes to guard the Mesopotamian home (Farber 2007a; Watanabe 2017). Although political subordinates are often described as "dogs" in Mesopotamian literature and letters, there is less direct evidence for canines having been despised or disgusting (Breier 2013). Several passages from the Hebrew Bible, however, do invoke the dog as adjunct to death and folly and associate it with abhorrent practices and abject substances, including the eating of corpses and of the dog's own vomit (Breier 2017; see e.g., 2 Kgs 9:10; Prov 26:11). Such acts of ideological exclusion inform and sustain these animals' frequent affiliation with Lamaštu, and in turn her demonic character gains connotations of savagery and uncleanliness.

ARRAKĀ ŠUPRĀŠA UL GULLUBĀ ŠAḪĀTĀŠA: LAMAŠTU AS GENDER TRANSGRESSOR

So far, so pedestrian. In Assyriological scholarship, Lamaštu's demonic difference has been thinkable primarily in anatomical and animalistic terms, which reflects and recapitulates a trend in ancient Middle Eastern studies toward conceiving the monster chiefly as a body that can be taxonomized. A fixation on externalized difference and explicitly nonhuman Others has, however, obscured ways in which Lamaštu is abjected as though within humanity and specifically within a matrix of gendered beings.

As it turns out, the texts and visual art describing and combating Lamaštu figure her as one who transgresses Mesopotamian gender categories in several interlocking ways. One of these is Lamaštu's seeming resistance, presented in both visual art and text, to myriad grooming and dressing norms. The amulets uniformly depict Lamaštu as naked, with iconographic focus on her exaggerated breasts. Like the naked Early Christian martyrs described by Elizabeth Castelli (1991, 43), Lamaštu's nudity is "at once a sign of [her] own resistance to social power and a sign that females remain, at some level at least, inscribed as sexualized beings for male viewers[,] spectators[, and] readers." Lamaštu's nudity is also repeatedly stressed in the incantations, often with strongly marked verbal adjuncts that perpetuate her aura of dissolute and even violent impropriety. Texts outside of the standard series assert that Lamaštu's "underwear is stripped off" (*dādūša šaḫṭū*) or "clipped off" (*buttuqā*) (Farber 2014, 80–1, 298–9, 329). Both verbs connote not only a lack but an immodest lack produced by violent intervention, whether by the demon herself or some other party. Her grooming also leaves something to be desired, perhaps in several senses. Lamaštu's "hair is hanging loose" (*perassa waššarat*) (Farber 2014, 280–1, cf. *Lamaštu* II.86, ed. Farber 2014, 172–3, 238), suggesting a reversion to natural circumstances that simultaneously denies artifice and evokes tousled eroticism. Finally, in a notable passage, the demon's "fingernails are long" and "her armpits are unshaven" (*arrakā ṣuprāša ul gullubā šaḫātāša*) (*Lamaštu* I.109, ed. Farber 2014, 154–5, 211). Even lacking extensive evidence for regular body hair removal in Mesopotamia, these corporeal invocations together imply regimes of regulation that the demon has undercut. These regimes, of course, do not stand historically isolated but echo in those rhetorics that engineer horror from Dracula's fingernails "long and fine, and cut to a sharp point" (Stoker 1897, 20) and incarcerate animalized feminists as "hairy-legged zoo girls" (Herzig 2015, 116).[10]

These illustrations and descriptions suggest that Lamaštu's visual difference is conducted not only along species but also along gendered axes. Layering these additional axes on the analysis sensitizes the observer to ways in which Lamaštu's gendered transgressions shade into violence. As scholars in queer and trans theory have increasingly shown, gender transgression is rarely allowed to stand as neutral difference and is far more often cast as gender *aggression*, no matter how empirically innocuous the gender-transgressive individual. While such discourse frequently demonizes adult trans women as unstably violent and sexually threatening (Bettcher 2007), implicit claims to similar effect are nowhere more disconsonant and therefore nowhere more distressing than when these characterizations are weaponized against gender-transgressive *children*. Such an appalling incongruity is highlighted by Gayle Salamon's recent study of the 2008 murder of Latisha King, a black transgender junior high school student in Oxnard, California. Latisha, at age 15, was fatally shot in a school classroom by a classmate. This classmate, according to court testimony of observers, perceived her allegedly inappropriately gendered behavior of wearing eye shadow, her high-heeled boots, and her manner of walking and speaking to be threatening to his masculine, heteronormative "safety." As Salamon (2018, 5) summarizes in her introduction: "Violence justifies itself by characterizing non-normative gender as itself a violent act of aggression and reading the expression of gender identity as itself a sexual act" (see similarly Salamon 2010, 105).

While a fictional construct rather than a living subject, Lamaštu's expressions of non-normative gender and reactions to them operate similarly, both as a recursively sufficient rationale for her violence and as a justification for resistance to it. Several of the above-noted characterizations of Lamaštu as gender-transgressive index her threat in precise ways; for example, lack of grooming points toward the dangerous bestial, and lack of clothing both suggests a perilous eroticism and makes visible her deviant suckling of unclean creatures. On the whole, Lamaštu's inability to abide by feminine norms is understood to constitute an active threat against civilized society, but especially against its most treasured possessions—children. Lamaštu is never explicitly said to be barren, but scholars have long noted her particular fascination with pregnant women and with appropriating their children so that she might nurse them, lethally and with poison. The following is an example of such rhetoric from the standard incantation series:

The Daughter of Anu counts the pregnant women daily,
keeps following behind the ones about to give birth.
She counts their months, marks their days on the wall.
Those about to give birth she puts under a spell:
"Bring me your sons—I want to nurse them!
In the mouth of your daughters I want to place my breast!"

She holds in her hand fever, cold, chills and frost (. . .)
She spatters venom all over the place (. . .)
She indeed slays young men.
She indeed does violence to young women.
She indeed smites little ones. (from *Lamaštu* I.117–30, ed. Farber 2014, 154–7)

Lamaštu's fixations are depicted as transferred from pregnant mother to defenseless infant, the latter of whom is potentially done in by the demon's chilling diseases and poisons (Farber 2007b, esp. 141–5; Scurlock 1991, 155–9). This passage and others like it dramatize Lamaštu's gender transgression as a queer threat to what Lee Edelman (2004) and others have called "reproductive futurism," the political imperative to replicate oneself and thence produce public discourse as an anodyne refuge in which standards of decency and offense are calibrated to the imagined standards of the ostensibly pure child. To show how Lamaštu's deviations from appropriate femininity constitute such a threat, the texts must conceive an elaborate stalking and intimate transfer of fluids, presumptive perversions of motherly norms that proceed from the demon's very body.

The texts prescribe combating this violence in a complex way: one simultaneously casts Lamaštu out geographically and brings her conceptually *within* a system of properly gendered beings. In the parlance of Judith Butler (1993, esp. 121–4), the texts attempt to interpellate Lamaštu as a feminine entity. Interpellation involves the use of language and other symbolic structures to "hail" an individual as belonging to one of several classes, in queer theory usually one of several *gendered* classes. Going beyond simply addressing Lamaštu with feminine terms like "daughter" (*mārtu*), as the texts indeed do, the ritual elements of the *Lamaštu* texts enjoin the successive provisioning of the demon with several highly gendered items:

> May the magician, the exorcist Asalluhi give to you a comb, a brooch, a distaff, a rug, and a pin. (. . .) May you [Lamashtu] be anointed with oil (. . .) May you be shod with shoes. (from *Lamaštu* I:196–200, ed. Farber 2014, 158–9)

The specificity of these provisions is notable, as is the way in which they line up with accessories depicted on the amulets, as discussed above. Many—including the spindle and distaff, the brooch, and the pin—are not only civilizing in the sense of implying inclusion in a socioeconomic exchange system but are both highly and complexly gendered in Mesopotamian contexts (similarly Götting 2018, esp. 456; Quillen 2015, 480). The spindle and distaff, for example, are the proper possessions of someone who spins and weaves; as Louise Quillien (2015) recently shows, although first-millennium Mesopotamian textile professionals were often men, domestic textile production remained closely associated with femininity. Similarly, iconographic and burial data suggest a strong association of pins with feminine dress (Cifarelli 2018, esp. 83, 91–7).

Through the invocation of these associations, the rituals function as a dramatization of interpellation; the amulets, meanwhile, become a physically and temporally stable mnemonic that anxiously predicts Lamaštu's domestication. Taken together, the ritual-plus-iconographic discourse would thus have been available both to those experiencing ritual praxis and to observers of any Lamaštu amulets. The overall operation implied takes a demon who is breaking gendered norms and then tries to coerce her into following these norms. Because Lamaštu is imaginary, this does not do violence to the demon in any palpable way, but it does implicitly establish the monstrous nature of gender transgression and provide precedent for regulation of that expression within Mesopotamian society.

CONCLUSION: VOICING LAMAŠTU

In scholarship on gender and sexuality, whether in ancient or modern contexts, it is no longer sufficient merely to observe representations of gender transgression, nor even of concomitant representations of alleged solutions to this alleged problem. Moving beyond banalities requires asking where such simultaneous representations find their founding rationales and what they aim, consciously or covertly, to do. In answer, one might say that the discourse around Lamaštu posits that category disjunction and threats to society lurk not in every individual but rather in particular marked, demonic bodies. These bodies can allegedly be recognized by their external effect of hybridity, disorder, deviant maternity, and hypersexualization. The discourse reassures its targets by conveying that to contain gendered threats to society, one need only repair specific—and always corporeally distant—nonhuman bodies.

Such a discourse is an instantiation of what Jack Halberstam (1995, 187) has called the "easy morality of monstrosity versus humanity." One of Halberstam's core claims in his *Skin Shows* is that narratives that concretize monstrosity in the body alone are fundamentally conservative. Such narratives shore up an imaginary battlefront between society and the monstrous, and they suggest that one will always be able to recognize, across the trenches, foe from friend (see also Halberstam 2011, 181). The discourse around Lamaštu is making precisely these moves. By foregrounding the demon's gender transgressions and placing her in opposition to female domesticity and appearance, the discourse restricts gender transgression to the realm of the demonic. The cultural production around Lamaštu then serves a regulative function by erecting the impossible monstrous position as both a reassurance and a warning.

At this point in queer theory's development, though, it is a tedious truism that our categorizing schemas, including sex and gender, are constructed, contingent, and repressive. Using the trans, queer, and/or monstrous body solely to "reveal" that construction and repression does little more than make a theoretical mascot of a subjugated class. This class then continues to be treated merely as an object rather than a potential subject. What attention to monsters like Lamaštu could instead allow is the fashioning of personal, conceptual space for existence as one who unapologetically pushes toward discomfort, fascination, and even disgust—in other words, conceptual space for existence *as* the monstrous. The dual emphasis on gender transgression and gender interpellation in the discourse around Lamaštu finds a particularly productive intertext in the relatively recent tendency to articulate, claim, and re-deploy trans monstrosity. An early and powerful embodiment of this trajectory is Susan Stryker's "My Words to Victor Frankenstein above the Village of Chamounix," a record of a 1993 performance piece (Stryker 1994), often and increasingly reprinted and responded to in the queer and trans theoretical world.[11] In this piece, Stryker compares herself and specifically her somatic self-fashioning to that of Frankenstein's monster. The gendered expectations—or better interpellations—of social interaction need not be experienced as sites of shame (Stryker 2019, 40), but can rather be unleashed in transformative, self-preserving rage, rage that simultaneously contests patriarchal, cisgender, and heteronormative imperatives and articulates a living space for the gender-transgressive body.

Key for present context is that even though the science of trans body modification aims to produce "bodies that satisfy the visual and morphological criteria that generate naturalness as their effect" (Stryker 1994, 242), occupying a subject-position in relation to these modifications allows for the possibility or even the necessity of being "in an unassimilable, antagonistic, queer relationship to a Nature in which [one] must nevertheless exist" (ibid., 243). The discourse around Lamaštu attempts to habituate and normalize her in terms of gender but must acknowledge in the end that this process is enacted as a perpetual one; it is experienced as only iteratively effective, and thus ultimately ineffective. The prospect of Lamaštu's return must remain available that it be possible to attribute future misfortune, repeated on the communal and/or personal level, to her intervention. This tension between allegedly naturalizing act and impossibly unnaturalized target produces the possibility that the monster remains a monster, or in other words that monstrosity *is* a livable and even purposeful position.

This tension is not unique to the discourse around Lamaštu, but her particular power for enfleshing and empowering may be that, like the monologuing Frankenstein but unlike many Mesopotamian and other monsters, she is represented as speaking in her own voice even as civilized society attempts to both domesticate and exclude her. Lamaštu offers not just a lens through which to view monstrosity, gender transgression, and interpellation, but a voice that speaks and owns marginalized gender transgression as a place from which one can speak righteous rage, bred from the injustice of being cast out of heaven. In naming her difference, her grievance, and her peril, Lamaštu ultimately turns to stare her onlookers in the face: "*mārat Anu ša šamê anāku namurrāku*; I am the daugher of Anu from heaven," she says. "I am terrifying."

NOTES

1. *Kamadme mārat Anu šumša ištēn*, from *Lamaštu* I.1, ed. Farber 2014, 144–5. In several formulae throughout the standard first-millennium incantation

series (Farber 2014, and see below), Lamaštu has seven names, the first of which ties her to Anu (Sumerian An), a Mesopotamian high god of the sky. The reading of Lamaštu's Sumerian name as "Kamadme" is now demonstrated conclusively by George 2018.

2. Thureau-Dangin (1921, 171–83, nos. 1–18) initiated this convention, and it was codified and expanded first by Klengel (1960, nos. 1–44; 1963, nos. 45–50). Amulets published after Klengel's articles are assigned numbers in several subsequent publications mostly by Farber and Wiggermann according to the schema outlined in DeGrado and Richey 2017, 118 n. 49. Some Lamaštu amulets that have been newly published since Farber 2014 do not yet have widely accepted "Lamaštu amulet" numbers, for example, George's (2016, 52–3, pls. 137–39 [nos. 62–65]) publication of Martin Schøyen Collection (Oslo) MS 1913, 2049, 2779, and 2819. An amulet from Chatal Höyük now in the collection of the Oriental Institute Museum, Chicago as no. OIM A17367 is published by Götting 2019.

3. The schema in this and the following paragraphs is based on that of Wiggermann 2000, 217–24 and Farber 1983, 441–4. Eva Götting is preparing a book-length study of the Lamaštu amulets.

4. The edition of the Lamaštu series (see immediately below) is Farber 2014. Because the present contribution primarily addresses a non-Assyriological public, citations of texts and extracts direct one to Farber's edition, where manuscript information can be easily located (see especially ibid., 45–52), as can epigraphic and lexicographical notes with references to earlier scholarship.

5. The chief book-length study of magic in Mesopotamia is Schwemer 2007. Recent accessible English-language introductions include Abusch 2007; Schwemer 2015; and Zomer 2017. The series *Ancient Magic and Divination* (Leiden: Brill) regularly publishes new texts and studies.

6. *kīma nimri tukkupā kalâtūša*, from *Lamaštu* II.37, ed. Farber 2014, 122, 168.

7. A recent thorough study of animal similes and accomplices in Lamaštu material is Hirvonen 2019, which includes (at ibid., 324–30) full references for all of these similes. Mertens-Wagschal 2018 discusses the valence of lion and wolf in similar incantatory corpora.

8. As Hirvonen (2019, 328) notes, although the leopard (*Panthera pardus*) was native to Iraq, its reclusiveness seemingly resulted in minimal encounters with humans, hence its mysterious connotations. In addition to the sources cited in the previous note, Mesopotamian understanding of the leopard is summarized by Heimpel 1983 and Williams-Forte 1983. Iconography suggesting the leopard was paradigmatically exotic includes an eighth century BCE. Nimrud ivory depicting a foreign tribute bearer carrying a leopard skin and accompanied by a monkey and an oryx (MMA 60.145.11; Ivory, 7.6 x 13.5 cm.). The wolf, similarly associated with the nonhuman steppe rather than the relatively urbanized lowlands, is discussed by Weszeli 2016.

9. See, for example, the Sennacherib wall relief from the Southwest Palace at Nineveh, BM 124824 (ca. 700 BCE), depicting a pig with her piglets in the swamp.

10. In the cited volume, Herzig treats the 1970s social consternation over "Arm-Pit Feminism." The quotation given here appeared in print first in Quindlen's (2007)

thirty-year retrospective on the 1977 National Women's Conference and is attributed there simply to "one Texas legislator."

11. Stryker builds especially and notably on Stone 1991, esp. 299. Extensions of this argument are, appropriately, legion, and include Stryker's (e.g., 2019) own self-responses. One can consult recent work on this front in Dahl 2018; Hayward 2010; Weaver 2013; and Zigarovich 2018b. Popular articulations of this sentiment are also increasingly available, for example, McBee 2020.

Chapter 11

Topophilic Perversions
Spectral Blackface and Fetishizing Sites of Monstrosity in American Dark Tourism

Whitney S. May

Ptolemy's *Geography* (150 CE), a treatise on second-century cartographic practices, informs us that Roman mapmakers indicated unknown territories on their maps with the phrase, "Here there be lions" (Van Duzer 2014). At a time when lions presented formidable danger to anyone going off the beaten path, "Here there be lions" was meant to advise caution to those wishing to enter terra incognita. Over time and as more and more distant lands were discovered and mapped, the range of warning creatures grew to include the wondrous and terrifying new wildlife that cartographers encountered abroad: elephants, hippos, and walruses, for example, soon joined in the menagerie of navigational symbols for caution. When these marvels became familiar, Medieval and Renaissance maps added mythical creatures, thus giving rise to the cartographic phrase we know so well now thanks in part to the Hunt-Lenox Globe from 1510 (as well as *Star Trek II: The Wrath of Khan*): "Here there be dragons."

The practice of adorning the uncharted regions of maps with depictions of stalking dragons and fearsome sea monsters had more or less receded by the time the first European settlers arrived in what would become the United States. And yet the impulse to regard unmapped territory as monstrous is an enduring one that has always haunted the modern American imagination. Today, that impulse emerges in the practice, and depiction, of American dark tourism.

The already-thriving industry of American dark tourism has experienced a recent spike in popularity, with new television shows such as FX's *American Horror Story* and Netflix's *Dark Tourist* surveying its fictional and real reaches alike even as traditional haunted house attractions undergo full-contact revisions into "extreme" haunts like McKamey Manor in San Diego, where patrons pay—and sign release waivers—typically to be bound, forced to eat things such as rotten eggs, and placed in cages full of snakes (Cook 2015; Johnson 2018); or like Blackout of New York City, where visitors are made to watch and then abstractly participate in simulations of sexual assault while surrounded by what appear to be dismembered body parts (Brown 2012; Riviello 2017; "Blackout: The Show" 2019). Meanwhile, fresh ghost tours appear across the country in suspiciously, previously unhaunted locales. This all begs the question: what has prompted an upsurge in Americans seeking out—or more worryingly, constructing— sites of gruesome history in ever-increasing numbers? Something more insidious than lions or even dragons, no doubt. We've gone well beyond terra incognita to a place beyond even *terra obscura*. And one thing's for sure: here, there be monsters.

Although the practice of dark tourism goes back as long as written memory, the subject has only relatively recently become the focus of academic research. A. V. Seaton, then a professor of Tourism Marketing, entered it into critical discourse in 1996 when he coined the term "thanatourism" as a modernization of a specifically Romantic strain of thanatopsis, or the contemplation of death. "Thanatourism," as he defined it, "is travel to a location wholly, or partially, motivated by the desire for actual or symbolic encounters with death, particularly, but not exclusively, violent death, which may, to a varying degree, *be activated by the person-specific features of those whose deaths are its focal points*" (240, emphasis mine). It's on this last aspect that this chapter will focus: the human dimension of practicing dark tourism, especially where the dead are concerned, and especially when their deaths are fetishized and reconfigured by the living into an experiential, ultimately consumable product. While traveling to sites of suffering is a timeless practice that predates the Romantics even by Seaton's estimation, my interest here lies in dark tourism's more recent iterations, that is to say its multifarious, reconfigurational leverages as a symptom of late capitalism in line with Fredric Jameson's (1992) evaluations. If, following Earnest Mandel, Jameson describes late capitalism as "the purest form of capital yet to have emerged, a prodigious expansion of capital into hitherto uncommodified areas" (36), then the practice of dark tourism in a postmodern culture indicates that the outer edges of the map, the monstrous margins of American moral geography, have not been spared from the insatiable grasp of this most incessant form of commodification.

While Seaton implicates only "morbid fascinations with death" (1996, 240) as the unsavory impulses driving this market, this explanation lacks sufficient dimension to account for the effects of dark tourism that extend beyond the experience of a dark site—the aspect of the site that returns home with the dark tourist. Dark tourism constitutes a pilgrimage of sorts to sites steeped in what J. E. Tunbridge and G. J. Ashworth (1996) call "dissonant heritage," or the psycho-social consequences of (re)presenting the past as an attraction, especially where doing so distorts or displaces the truth for specific, typically marginalized groups. These are the "person-specific features" indicated by Seaton in his definition of thanatourism. Ashworth writes more specifically about "atrocity heritage" in his study of Holocaust tourism, which he notes is "both a highly marketable combination of education and enjoyment and a powerful instrument for the transference of political or social messages" (2009, qtd. in Sharpley 12).

An especially chilling example of dissonant heritage being animated—or rather, conjured—for consumers through spectral scripts lies in the reiterative "ghost" slave figure present in contemporary American dark tourism. In the interest of focus, I take as my case study the scripts of two ghost tours operating in Savannah, Georgia, as a means to examine the ways in which dark tourism featuring the "ghost" slave figure reconfigures the suffering of black bodies into commodities for modern purchase that echo the practice of slavery whose human narratives it so indiscriminately invokes and animatedly revises. In short, these tours "spectralize" the antebellum slave market for modern audiences by reformatting racialized assemblages into marketable myths about nationhood and citizenship that revise historical suffering and depravity for wholesale consumption. They additionally deploy white nationalistic messages in the interest of extending the regulation of black bodies beyond the earthly (fleshly) limits of slavery, and well into its afterlives. In short, this ghost story format animates both an incursion of the past on the present *and* future in the Derridian (1994) sense, as well as an indictment of these dark realities where racism, hyper-capitalism, and so many more of their terrible valences still hold sway over the American national identity. With all this in mind, it would appear that this national identity, as well as the dark tourism used to map out its moral geography, has an alarming potential to become an avenue for something even darker.

"SLAVE VAULTS" AND CHILD GHOSTS: TWO CASE STUDIES FROM SAVANNAH

Tiya Miles (2015) confides in *Tales from the Haunted South* that her descent into studying southern dark tourism began with a secret; mine began with a lie. Both brought us, naturally, to the same place.

Virtually every article and ad bearing a title like "America's Most Haunted Cities" ranks Savannah, Georgia, respectably alongside the likes of Salem and New Orleans. I found myself there at my first conference as a graduate student several years ago. Feigning illness to extricate myself from a spectacularly loud mixer at the conference hotel, I stole out to walk alongside the Savannah River and to catch some air and a moment of relative solitude. After a golden evening of wandering, sampling pecan pralines, and getting lost between Savannah's many squares, I went out that night in search of a distraction. What I found (after more pralines) was the Ghosts & Gravestones ghost tour. $20 later, I found myself along with a dozen or so others aboard a repurposed, black streetcar festooned with fake cobwebs and plastic spiders and worryingly called the "Trolley of the Doomed."

After a brief introduction from a tour guide in somber, Victorian attire, whom we were fervently encouraged to call the "Gravedigger," we were on our way. The Trolley of the Doomed wound through the same streets I'd walked in the daylight, which were now magically transformed by the night air and, probably, by the alternately dulcet and hair-raising tones of a Halloween soundtrack being piped through the trolley's stereo. Every few minutes, we'd stop for the Gravedigger to deliver a tragic tale about a specific location.

For example, one of our first stops was Savannah's "slave vaults," a series of four enormous hollows set deep into the brick wall of Factor's Walk, the "back side" of the businesses along River Street, which is the main tourists' thoroughfare along the river. Here, the Gravedigger pronounced, enslaved people taken off the ships entering the harbor were kept until they were separated and sold. Echoing the language of the Ghosts & Gravestones website, he intoned: "Many who visit [the vaults] have seen the shadows of slaves that were brought into the city by boat and others have heard the[ir] tormented moans" ("The Most Haunted Places in Savannah," 2019).

Like so many sites in this troubling genre of prepackaged ghost story, the Savannah "Slave Vaults" give up their secrets with just a little excavation; or rather, they give up their ghosts. Disturbed by these lines of narrative in 2011, a wholesome collaboration between the teenagers of a local youth group, the Savannah Research Library and Municipal Archives, and Georgia Southern University determined, after years of archaeological study, that there's no credible link whatsoever between the Cluskey Embankment Stores—the historical name for what Savanah ghost tours have theatrically renamed the "Slave Vaults"—and Savannah's ghastly history with the transatlantic slave trade. Instead, the archaeologists—both the professionally trained and the teenaged—uncovered over 6,700 artifacts and a far less insidious example of poorly documented public works history. It would seem that a dearth of formal historical documentation made space for an informal oral history: When asked about the origins of the slave pen myths, Savannah Research Library and Municipal Archives director Luciana Spracher had a ready theory: The tales were, according to her, "a common belief spread by local tour companies" (2014: qtd. in Curl). Despite the publication of the archaeological research about the debunked "slave vaults," the Cluskey Embankment Stores remain a popular stop on most of Savannah's ghost tour routes.

Alarmingly, this is just one of the many Savannah locales advertised along ghost tour routes as possessing "deep" connections to Savannah's slave trade, but whose validity simply cannot be verified, or rather, whose verification is avoided in the interest of burgeoning profits, whether for ghost tour companies or the businesses located at these conveniently haunted locations. Other such sites include various historical buildings, a supposed slave burial ground, and at least two of Savannah's twenty-one remaining squares, which are pointed out to tourists as former slave markets. Meanwhile, archival evidence of what occurred in colonial Savannah, and where these events *truly* took place remains in the form of shipping manifests, historical maps, and the like. But it seems that tourists, especially of the dark variety, prefer the myths, and so ghost tours revise history as needed to promote their industry. But sensationalizing slavery to these supernatural dimensions effaces the horror of slavery's ubiquitous cruelties. Further, it introduces something like flexibility to the historical record where slavery is concerned, rendering historical brutality—and truth itself—a plastic commodity in multiple senses. Attending to this rupture therefore becomes a priority for the writers of dark tourist scripts. Edward T. Linenthal's (2008) observations about the cognitive dissonance involved in managing southern plantations in the modern age seems appropriate here: these sites, he writes, are engaged in, "if not denial, then the transformation into something benign, through a minefield of monumental memory to the 'faithful slave' and the 'black mammy,' the *Gone With the Wind* fiction of slavery" (214). The result is another of dark tourism's paradoxes, highlighted cogently by Richard Sharpley (2009, 6): "It remains unclear whether dark tourism is tourist-demand or attraction-supply driven."

Although not on the Ghosts & Gravestones route, another of these haunted locales is a popular stop for competing for ghost tours and is a regular attraction for individual dark tourists. It also characterizes the imbricated and problematic supply/demand dynamic inherent to dark tourism. The Olde Pink House is a restaurant carved out of a 1771 mansion where, "it's said" that the ghosts of slave children taunt the guests and kitchen workers. (By the way, it's worth noting that none of the restaurant's marketing materials mentions these specific ghosts; the language of its haunting has been toned down, likely in the interest of moving a more palatable, family-friendly product, and the lurid details are left for the Gravediggers.) James Caskey (2013) devotes a chapter of his book *Haunted Savannah: America's Most Spectral City* to the ghosts specific to the Olde Pink House. To follow is an excerpt from this chapter, which details the account of Gail Thurmond, the

> talented and versatile piano player and vocalist who entertained diners for years in the [Olde Pink House's tavern]. But Gail was not just blessed with musical talent; she is one of the few people who are gifted with special "sight": the ability to see the spirit world. She claims to have seen a small African-American child in the tavern from time to time, or feel his presence. She even claims to have asked this small boy his name, and he replied "Magumbo."

My best archival sleuthing only returns one possibility for the origins of the word "Magumbo." It does seem rather unlikely, though, that a ghostly child from before the American Civil War gave, as his name, a nonsense safe-word invented by Krusty the Clown in an episode of *The Simpsons* from 2002. I have another theory, though: It's more likely that somewhere in the spectral game of telephone between the spirit child, Thurmond, and Caskey, that someone intended—or did not intend—to invoke the 1953 African safari film starring Clark Gable and Grace Kelly, *Mogambo*. In the film, the word "mogambo" is presented alternately as the Swahili words for "the Greatest," and then for "passion." The trailer for the film forces a heavy-handed connection between the word "Mogambo" and Africa, proclaiming: "Mogambo, unforgettable adventure in untamed Africa. Africa, known for centuries as 'the white man's graveyard.'"

One might imagine that the truth of the "Magumbo" ghost story is coming into clearer focus, but there's still one more problem: "Mogambo" is not a Swahili word at all. In keeping with Hollywood legend, the film's IMDb entry credits *Mogambo*'s producer Sam Zimbalist with inventing the title by modifying the name of the iconic, Latin-American themed, Sunset Strip nightclub Mocambo, because it sounded vaguely Swahili ("Mogambo (1953)"). Certainly, the absence of the word from the script itself supports one classic film buff's assertion that it was a cursory addition to the production, "likely in a 'now what the hell do we call it?' session before the crew for the 1953 adventure ever set foot in Africa" ("Mogambo" 2015).

Without a doubt, this *Mogambo* theory would be difficult to prove, especially where external factors might have motivated Ms. Thurmond's source amnesia with regard to the alleged enslaved ghost child's name. Nevertheless, the exploitative leverages of this tale are compelling, to say the least, and become more so when the trail of profit is followed. Caskey's book is sold for, on average, $17 in tourist shops throughout the city and the Olde Pink House chapter appears in fragments on various ghost-hunting websites, and in its entirety on the sites of at least two popular Savannah ghost tour companies. Only one is a copyright issue, though, because as it turns out, Caskey operates the other himself. At the time of this writing, his company averages 14 tours per week, in addition to 7 "Haunted Pub Crawls," all at $20 per adult ticket. No doubt, the unfortunate tale of "Magumbo" is disseminated to the patrons of each. Ms. Thurmond still performs at, and therefore likely draws income from, the tavern to which her ghost story brings business. The racialization of ghosts for profit, it seems, is something of a closed circle.

There's also something to be said for the "naming" of the "ghost" slave, something that echoes in one of the two contentions with which Sharon Patricia Holland (2000) foregrounds her book *Raising the Dead: Readings of Death and (Black) Subjectivity*: that "the (white) culture's dependence on the nonhuman status of its black subjects was never measured by the ability of whites to produce a 'social heritage'; instead it rested on the status of the black as nonentity" (15). In this instance, that the "ghost" slave receives this name almost like a dismissal is telling enough; that this name seems to be the haphazard assembly of various signals from popular culture, all as racist as the racing of the "ghost" slave, reveals much about the ways that white audiences (and mythmakers) replicate their own narratives, personal and historical—and in the space where these conflate, necroideological—into seemingly endless pop-cultural avenues. To borrow once more from Holland (2000, 18), "An old saying contends that you can tell the strength of a nation by the way it treats its poor; today, one can also ascertain its relative strength by examining the way a nation treats its dead."

HIEROGLYPHS OF THE SPIRIT: RACIALIZED ASSEMBLAGES IN THE STORIES WE TELL

So, what are we left with in these examples of dark tourism in Savannah? In the Factor's Walk "slave vaults," a set of perfectly innocent storage rooms receives a spectacularly distasteful revision by local ghost tour companies, despite an absence of evidence to support these adjustments or, by extension, of reverence for the history or truth. In the "Magumbo" tale, we have a fabricated word that enters the pop-cultural consciousness in 1953 as a false (and inherently racist) invocation of Africa, and a modern report that this word was uttered by a ghostly African or African-American enslaved child. In each, we have something like spectral blackface, wherein historical suffering is colonized and recoded for the entertainment and consumption of modern, paying audiences. If there are ghost stories to be found here, it's unclear where pop-culture ends and the stories begin, where the historical, systemic oppression and exploitation of people of color ends and the present, narrative oppression and exploitation of people of color begins. What *is* clear is that we seem to be more content to travel to supposedly "haunted" sites to commune with stylized ghosts than we are to confront the very real ones of our nation's past, or, in the Derridian (1994) sense of the *arrivant*, the ghosts of our future, especially where the discursive limits of these interactions are crossed, whether knowingly or unknowingly. Telling these stories and generating the ghosts that fill them becomes something of an ontological mapmaking project for a postmodern culture experiencing what Patrick West (2004) pithily calls "mourning sickness." Such a designation resonates well with Miles's determinations of racialized ghosts, where "the black ghost marks the demonic spirit of possession through which Americans transformed people into things" (2015, 17). Miles follows this line of inquiry further in *Tales from the Haunted South*, positioning antebellum nostalgia as the fulcrum upon which "ghosting" race or "racing" ghosts turns; rather than nostalgic, I read this process as a distinctly hypercapitalist one. Putting a price tag on these racialized configurations of dark tourism (both implicitly and explicitly generated or consumed by white dark tourists) carries with it a rather chilling assessment of the postmodern subject under a capitalist world system, who even in their ghost stories and how they handle their ghost stories cannot seem to imagine a life (or an afterlife) in which human beings are not, living or dead, haunted by the shadow of unfettered capitalism, a terrible reality that, as we know, Marx himself often described in spectral—thanatoptic—language.

Athinodoros Chronis (2005, 389) considers touristic landscapes coconstructive sites that serve a nationalistic function, where places are "symbolically transformed and used by service providers and tourists alike to negotiate, define, and strengthen social values of patriotism and national unity, in times when these values are most needed." This is an optimistic assessment, but one that carries darker value-strengthening potential when it comes to dark tourism, especially dark tourist attractions whose narratives are generated as a means of drumming up profit. Scripting these experiences to simultaneously titillate tourists and strengthen their ideas of "Americanness" is what Tim Edensor (2002, 85) calls "staging the nation." For the purposes of constraint, I've focused here on a slice of time, in the Foucauldian sense, and a slice of space; and a slice of the broader milieu of issues that haunt the American sociopolitical landscape. But if the Factor's Walk vaults and the "Magumbo" tale, just two of so many similar tales whose discussions would require a much larger type of project, are any indication of the dark tourism occurring across the country, then the nation we're staging is a deeply flawed one. It's also one that, whether intentionally or not, reinforces the harmful ideas about power, boundaries, and brutality against which we still struggle so fervidly.

In the spaces between all of these categories, there are "hieroglyphs." Discussing the physical marks left on enslaved people's bodies by those who harmed them in "Mamas's Baby, Papa's Maybe: An American Grammar Book," Hortense Spillers (1987, 67) reasons that the "undecipherable markings on the captive body render a kind of hieroglyphics of the flesh whose severe disjunctures come to be hidden to the cultural seeing by skin color." Spillers's discursive division of "flesh" and "body" allows her to explore the epistemological negation of black bodies that arise at the question of ethnicity. While Spillers follows this line of thought into intergenerational hieroglyphs of the flesh, this association lends itself remarkably well to similar divisions of "flesh" and "spirit," where each have become bound up in separate systems of power and profit. Alexander G. Weheliye (2014) carries the reframing of these structures forward in *Habeas Viscus: Racializing Assemblages, Biopolitics, and Black Feminist Theories of the Human.* By Weheliye's (2014, 113) estimation, "In contrast to bare life, biopolitics, and so on, habeas viscus incorporates the violent racializing assemblages that facilitate the continued conflation of Man with human while also pumping up the volume on the insurgent praxes of humanity composed of hieroglyphics of the flesh." Dark tourism that features "ghost" slaves, and the process of fabricating them, constitutes yet another of these racialized assemblages. In these dark touristic practices, hieroglyphics of the flesh mark black bodies as a form of capital in an antebellum commodity chain; hieroglyphics of the spirit translate these marks into spectral versions of material systems of slavery, even and *especially* after these have been terminated.

In addition to spatial delineations, Anthony D. Smith (1991, 16) indicates that nations "provide individuals with 'sacred centers,' objects and sites of spiritual and historical pilgrimage that help additionally demarcate the 'moral geography' of that nation." Smith's attention to moral geography is particularly appropriate for studying dark tourism, as these spaces tend to obfuscate accepted notions of morality and culpability. If a nation's moral geography can be mapped as surely as its physical geography, then the compulsion to make sense of both demonstrates Robert Tally Jr.'s (2019) theory of "topophrenia," wherein a relentless uneasiness and need to map—a cartographic imperative—animates the human experience. Tally defines topophrenia as "a 'placemindedness' that characterizes a subject's interactions with [their] environment, which is itself so broadly conceived as to include the lived space of any given personal experience . . . as well as the abstract space whose true representation is beyond any one individual's ken (a larger national, international, or ultimately universal space of a 'world system')" (1). Dark tourism, then, constitutes a need to navigate physical and moral space, to access and make sense of the monstrous perimeter of both and by extension to locate the subject's place within each. These sites become something like ceremonial reference points, which offer, according to Nuala Johnson (1995, 63), "points of physical and ideological orientation," often around which "circuits of memory" are organized." When it comes to dark tourism, especially that which inscribes "ghost" slaves into its cast of characters, these circuits of memory serve to replicate systems of slavery as capitalistic material and spiritual possession and, most troublingly of all, to normalize this practice into the future, as well.

A 2015 study of American teenagers noted that, after visiting dark tourist sites, respondents often began sentences in their reflections with the phrase "As an American." These responses "reinforce that certain responsibilities and behaviors were thought to be expected of a U.S. citizen" (Tinson et al. 2015, 869) and, beyond that, that sites of dark tourism become spaces where individuals orient themselves within the broader social and historical contexts of their national myths. These myths, it turns out, are populated by ghosts or in more insidious situations, by fabrications of ghosts. They also discursively reanimate and repackage the oppressions of slavery in postbellum Savannah in ways that re-inscribe the lineages of those oppressions back into the American imaginary under the guise of entertainment and for the purposes of turning a profit. David Coughlan (2016) observes in *Ghost Writing in Contemporary American Fiction* that "A nation and a national identity form by force of definitions along geographical, political, ethnic, religious, or cultural lines, and by force itself, so that the very concept of the nation itself is haunted" (7). In our haunted nation, we conjure our ghosts, not so much in the magical or spiritual sense, but rather in an authorial one wherein we ascribe complicated social and political meanings to them, where, as the Ghosts & Gravestones homepage promises of its attraction, "reality and the supernatural collide."

CONCLUSION: DEAD LANDSCAPES, DEAD NATION

If a nation's iconic sites offer reference points for ideological and ontological orientation, then sites of dark tourism exist at the furthest reaches of our nation's moral geography, where the ghosts that characterize them have taken the place of lions and dragons as indicators of what lies beyond that map's edges. These ghosts animate both an incursion of the past on the present, as well as an indictment of the future of its dark realities where racism, sexism, xenophobia, and so many more of hyper-capitalism's darker valences still hold sway over our national identity. That we utilize necroideologies to re-map living landscapes into dead ones fascinates Russ Castronovo (2001). His theory of necro citizenship makes space for these questions of "social death, the hauntings of memory, and disembodied citizens to the political forms of the U.S. democracy"; extending these concerns, he continues, "Citizenship is paramount among these forms, naturalizing the transformations of persons into official political entities as well as social corpses" (2001, xiii). Castronovo's theorizations about "necro ideology" chart the deployment of death and its attendant conditions in the shaping and maintenance of American citizenship in the nation's cultural productions. Our constructed ghosts, then, as cultural productions are merely manifestations of ourselves, a national splitting, in the Jungian sense, from the predatory impulses animated by capitalism. It's a split that conveniently liberates the history of capitalism from its imbricated history of racism, ensuring a worrying supply and a downright alarming demand in the present and future. It's only in interrogating this problematic commodity chain that we illuminate the danger for repeating the crimes of history that white audiences are invested in forgetting—in this case, the commodification and consumption of black bodies, however spectral they may be.

The popularity of dark tourism reveals a cultural obsession with dead landscapes, acknowledging at an industrial scale that our nation is brimming with them and the phantoms that haunt them, whether these are the ghosts of history or just ghost stories. In our haunted nation and in our haunted present, where #MAGAlomaniacal attempts to recast our history in the rose-tinted light of American exceptionalism, dark tourism becomes our point of access to the darkest reaches of our moral geography. And the ghosts that we write to haunt the edges of this map? Those remind us that here there has always existed something worse than lions and dragons, monsters or specters: here there's only us, searching for shadows in the dark.

Part III

MONSTERS TEARING DOWN THE GATES

Chapter 12

Finding Bigfoot

The Anthropological Machine and the Generation of Monsters

Timothy Grieve-Carlson

From its debut in 2011 to its end in 2018, Animal Planet's least-eponymous show, *Finding Bigfoot*, was one of the most popular programs in the channel's history. *Finding Bigfoot* was a reality show with a simple narrative format: in each episode, a crew of four Bigfoot hunters traveled to an area where encounters with hairy anthropoid monsters have been reported. Once on location, the crew held a public "town-hall"-style event where they solicited reports of Bigfoot sightings from locals. Recounting these personal narratives of sightings was often emotional for the witnesses, who volunteered to publicly relive a particularly traumatic or simply baffling moment of their lives. Tears were not uncommon, nor were sincere requests for an explanation from the investigators.

Following the town hall, episodes proceeded with an investigation in the area where they have received the most sighting reports. This was always a rural or wild setting, and the investigation was often held at night. The investigators had a repertoire of techniques for tracking their quarry, but none was so well known or performative as what the investigators referred to as "doing a call." The style of call varied, but it was usually an extremely loud and drawn-out scream or howl into the darkness around them. Following the call, the investigators huddled in nervous anticipation of the response, and they often seemed to receive one: a scream, a howl, or a moan from somewhere deep in the distance, presumably from a Bigfoot who has been fooled into responding to what it thought was one of its own kind.

For all its modern gadgets, social-media-savvy investigators, and reality show performativity, *Finding Bigfoot* was just the latest expression of a very old and common story: the presence of a hair-covered, human-shaped monster who resides just on the edge of or far beyond human space, defined in this chapter as a "wild person." While the program certainly represented a crest of the popularity of Bigfoot-like monsters in the public imagination, it was by no means the first or most popular form of the image.

Bigfoot, our contemporary popular version of the wild person in the United States, is a relatively recent cultural phenomenon, arising in the late 1950s (Coleman 2003). American narratives of encounters with wild people, however, are much older, and can be located with some frequency in sources as early as the colonial period (Arment 2006). As the lens widens, it becomes clear that the image we associate with the word "Bigfoot" is by no means uniquely American or even a modern phenomenon. In terms of cultural, historical, and geographic range, hair-covered and human-shaped monsters are apparently ubiquitous: In Asia, there is the famous Himalayan Yeti, the Almas of Mongolia and Russia, the Yeren of central China, and the Orang-Pandek on the island of Sumatra. The indigenous people of Australia call them Yowie, while Europeans called them Wild Men or Wodewose. The different cultures of South and Central America have the Mapinguary in Brazil, the diminutive Didi in Guyana, and the Ucumar in Argentina and Chile (Sanderson 2006; Forth 2007).

The wild person is clearly not limited to places where proximity to nonhuman primates might inspire the image, nor does it seem bound by any other limits other than the presence of humans to encounter them. I am not the first scholar to recognize the ubiquity of these figures—as the anthropologist Gregory Forth wrote in a 2007 article on the proliferation of wild people across cultures, "western and non-western images of the wildman share many features, thereby suggesting variants of a pan-human archetype likely to find expression independently of individual cultures and histories" (Forth 2007, 262).

At the mention of a possible "pan-human archetype," it is important to acknowledge that these cross-cultural figures are presented here extracted from their contexts and stripped of the cultural worlds that they inhabit and sustain. There is an inadequacy, and perhaps a futility in trying to draw them all together here. However, I remain drawn to these similar figures *because* they have such various cultural contexts, and *because* these hair-covered and human-shaped monsters seem to step effortlessly between cultural worlds and historical periods as easily as they cross oceans and mountains. Gregory Forth pointed out this very dilemma in his article on the apparent ubiquity of wild people: "It should become clear how cross-cultural evidence and several methodological problems need to be addressed if these resemblances are to be explained" (Forth 2007, 262).

In the chapter that follows, with Forth's methodological problems in mind, I explore the meaning of the wild person with theoretical and methodological frameworks from monster theory, religious studies, and anthropology, before turning toward Giorgio Agamben's concept of the "Anthropological Machine" to analyze a specific encounter narrative: the famous Bigfoot encounter of William Roe. This chapter starts with Forth's initial question: why does the image of the wild person occur so frequently across cultures and throughout history? The answer, I suggest, is that wild people are a ubiquitous presence because they trespass an essential boundary in our collective geography of thought. As we will see, it might be *the* essential boundary: the human, and everything else. Narratives of encounters with wild people like Bigfoot disrupt our capacity to distinguish humans from nonhumans, and in doing so, they trouble the essential category of the human.

Is there anything, then, that marks a "wild person" beyond the humanoid body covered in hair? Is there anything that each variety of the wild person mentioned above has in common beyond their shared appearance, which is already quite significant? There is, in fact, a common phenomenology to wild people traditions: the wild person *appears*. Wild people's traditions are constituted in cultural narratives of presence and encounter. As the act of "doing a call" on *Finding Bigfoot* suggests, cultural discourses of wild people reinforce this presence through certain practices, like the retelling of an encounter narrative, or through the solicitation of presence in practices like "doing a call."

Is the interdisciplinary framework of monster theory relevant here? As Jeffrey Kripal has pointed out, monster theory is perfectly suitable for analyzing monsters as a discourse, but its many insights seem to falter when they are pointed toward monsters that appear in the lives of real people. In his 2017 book *Secret Body*, Kripal points out some of the inadequacies of monster theory for looking at monsters that seem to share our world with us:

> Enter "monster theory," which looks at the narratives and images of the monster throughout Western history as a kind of recurring deconstruction and reconstruction of cultural and social categories. Here the monster is taken seriously, but only, as far as I can tell, as an unconscious Foucauldian discourse, Derridean deconstruction, or postmodern materialism.... And what of real monsters? By "real" I do not mean to point to some future biological taxon. I do not think that we will someday shoot a Sasquatch or net the Loch Ness Monster. By real I mean quite simply "really experienced," I mean "phenomenologically actual." I mean to remind us that many people, including many modern people, have experienced monsters not as "discourses" or as cultural "deconstructions," but as actual incarnate, discarnate, or quasi-incarnate beings. (Kripal 2017, 332–3)

The tension that Kripal points out, between fictional monsters and monsters really present, has not been lost on people who have encountered monsters.

The famous Canadian Bigfoot researcher John Green once quoted a witness as saying: "It's like you walking down a back alley and bumping into a Frankenstein monster. Everybody knows there's no such thing, but you've just seen him" (Zada 2019, 27). How should scholars treat such monsters really present? Much in the same way that my own discipline, the history of religions, tries to treat claims of religious experience without affirming or denying the ontological status of the divinities in question, I want to accept the basic validity of this experience *as an experience* without affirming or dismissing any ontological stance on the presences in question.

Such an approach requires two presuppositions. First, wild people *appear*: that is, narratives of wild person encounters refer to "really experienced" events. Second, these events and experiences have meaning; indeed, they contain a complex of meaning(s) that can be interpreted. At first glance, these two presuppositions might seem inconsistent, even contradictory. How should a theorist treat an event as "phenomenologically real," while simultaneously presuming that it represents a discourse that can be interpreted? The history of religions is full of examples. Catholics have long reported apparitional appearances of the Virgin Mary. As Robert Orsi reminds us, these appearances did not suddenly stop as modernity dragged on:

> Many times in the past 250 years since Hume's confident prediction that the gods really present would soon be forgotten, vast crowds have gathered at the places on earth where the Mother of God had appeared, sometimes to single visionaries, at other times to groups of people. (Orsi 2016, 48)

While scholars or scientists might disagree on the ontological status of the events that Orsi describes, these events *do occur*. In Kripal's terms, Marian apparitions are "phenomenologically actual." At the same time, her person tells us certain things about cultures in which she appears: it would be difficult to read the appearance of the "Blessed Virgin" without hearing something about cultural attitudes toward sexuality, not to mention things like gender, the status of children, codes of moral purity, and so on. The Blessed Virgin is both a phenomenologically real presence in this world and a tapestry of discourses, of *meanings,* that reveal important cultural patterns in the communities in which she appears.

Orsi's method in his 2016 book *History and Presence*, alongside Kripal's articulation of the phenomenological reality of certain monstrous presences, could present a viable approach for the analysis of monsters like wild people in religious studies. In *History and Presence*, Robert Orsi addresses a tendency in religious studies scholarship to derive the category of "religion" from Protestantism. In a field dominated by Protestant historiography and its emphasis on text, symbols, and belief, Orsi points out that the *presence* of the gods in people's real lives has been ignored in the largely Protestant academic study of religion. Primarily drawing on the history of Catholicism but with reference to other religions of presence, Orsi argues that the gods as immanent, tangible, and visible presences in the world are undeniable in many historical sources, and scholars of religion are obliged to attend to these presences.

Since the beginning of the modern study of religion, scholars have pointed out that people come face to face with gods and monsters in "uncivilized" societies or elsewhen. The Protestant origins of the study of religion looked down on these other traditions, while praising forms and practices that seemed familiar (Kippenberg 2002, 167). But there were exceptions. As Kripal acknowledges, "Historians of religion have long known, at least since Rudolf Otto's still unsurpassed *The Idea of the Holy* (1917), that the experience of horror often functions as a kind of potential or camouflaged numen" (Kripal 2017, 331). The gods appear to human beings, often in terrifying or bizarre forms.

Only recently has the academic study of religion acknowledged that modern people and yes, even some Protestants, have religious lives and worlds in which the gods are present (Orsi 2016, 40). This was not an easy sell: indeed, the very idea of being a "modern" person almost definitionally means living in a world completely bereft and independent of supernatural presences and agents (Orsi 2016, 41; Josesphson-Storm 2017). Nonetheless, gods, supernatural beings, and monsters continue to appear to us. People continue to come face to face with the Blessed Virgin, in her sacred grottoes in Lourdes and in new sites of Marian apparitions. This situation does not require that religious studies scholars assume that the appearance of the Blessed Virgin is "real." It requires an acknowledgment that she is present, that she is *here*, a much more subtle and intimate designation, requiring new methodologies.

Robert Orsi's gods and Jeffrey Kripal's monsters have much in common. Both are constituted *through* encounter, in moments of abundant or overwhelming presence. Like Robert Orsi's gods or the Blessed Virgin, the Kripalian monstrous body is replete with meanings, recalling Jack Halberstam's assertion that monsters themselves are "meaning machines" (Halberstam 1995, 21). Monster theory rightly recognizes the monstrous body as a text waiting to be read and interpreted, and in the act of interpreting the monsters (or gods) we encounter, we interpret the cultural worlds we build and inhabit.

What is demanded of scholars by stories of encounters with monsters like wild people is not another quixotic trip into the woods to "do a call." Rather, it is hermeneutical attention, the analysis of the *meaning* of these encounters. This exact point was made by the Oxford geneticist Bryan Sykes in his 2015 book *The Nature of the Beast*. In the book, Sykes surveyed genetic evidence for wild people like Bigfoot, which, he initially and gamely hypothesized, might represent relict populations of hominids. Sykes ultimately concluded that there was no genetic evidence for relict hominids, but the work concludes with a frankly stunning admission:

> Funnily enough, even though there were no anomalous primates among the hairs I tested, I think my view has altered more in favour of there being "something out there" than the reverse. This change of heart comes from speaking to several people . . . who have nothing to gain but have seen things, in good light while in the company of other witnesses, that are hard to explain otherwise. To automatically reject these accounts is just as blinkered as accepting that every broken branch has been snapped or twisted by a sasquatch. (Sykes, 311)

Rather than genetics, Sykes argues that it is the abundant evidence for the subjective experience of such presences that is the truly worthy object of study. For the geneticist looking at the wild person, it was the repeated narrative of encounter that compelled his attention and ultimately brought on a "change of heart." With Sykes's conclusions in mind, let us turn to the interpretation of the wild person directly.

THE ANTHROPOLOGICAL MACHINE

In her 2009 book *The Monkey and the Inkpot*, Carla Nappi considered the cultural roles of wild people in early modern China and central Asia. "Semianthropoid figures have appeared in Chinese literature for most of China's history," she noted, and she went on to suggest that these figures occupied an analogous role to Bigfoot in contemporary America. Wild people in both twenty-first-century America and sixteenth-century China provided "a medium for working out social and cultural anxieties[;] the study of humanoid creatures was also a study of the idea of humanity itself" (Nappi 2009, 124). From the perspective of monster theory, monstrous bodies are synthetic representations of thoughts, desires, and anxieties that we would have trouble thinking directly. What monstrous thought, or desire, or anxiety, could be so fundamental that it would arise independently in both twenty-first-century America and sixteenth-century China?

In his lectures at the College de France on the abnormal, Michel Foucault describes the monster in terms of transgression, betweenness, and the violation of taxonomies:

> The monster is essentially a mixture. It is a mixture of two realms, the animal and the human . . . of two species . . . of two individuals . . . of two sexes . . . of

life and death . . . finally, it is a mixture of forms . . . the transgression of natural limit, the transgression of classifications, of the table, and of the law as table: this is actually what is involved in monstrosity. (Foucault 2004, 63)

In reading narratives of encounters with wild people, we are looking at a very particular form of monstrous mixture: Lévi-Strauss might say that we are dealing with a monster whose territory lies somewhere between nature and culture, but perhaps more precisely and more symbolically significant, we are dealing with a monster who disrupts the boundary between humans and nonhumans.

Nonhuman primates have posed a problem for philosophy at least since Plato. In *Hippias Major*, Plato quotes Heraclitus saying that the most beautiful ape is hideous when compared to a human, in the same way that the wisest man is an ape before the mind of God (Corbey 2005, 8). Indeed, as an English verb, "ape" refers to a humiliating imitation. Plato is setting up a hierarchy that probably preceded him and would persist long after him. Christian thinkers like Augustine and Albert the Great read Plato alongside the book of Genesis, in which the separate acts of creation clearly reify the sharp boundary between humans and other animals. Through the medieval idea of *scala naturae* or "The Great Chain of Being," the European understanding of discrete, unchanging animal forms gradually leading to the human explained how similar two species could seem—like a moth and a butterfly—but ultimately, it was discontinuity that ruled the place between the species. The gap, then, between the human and the animal was already quite wide when Descartes planted a flag between the two that has never really been pulled up: humans are rational subjects, while animals are automatons, unfeeling, running on instinct rather than thought, and just as available for exploitation as a vein of iron ore (Corbey 2005, 22).

These centuries of human exceptionalism have been troubled by a mocking semi-anthropoid that the philosopher Giorgio Agamben has called "the apeman." This ape-man was haunting the Swedish taxonomist Carolus Linnaeus when he wrote, "Surely Descartes never saw an ape" (Agamben 2004, 23). Linnaeus was pointing out the obvious problem with any human/animal binary: when one impartially compares a human being and another primate, the continuity is so obvious that such a binary seems unstable or fragile at the very least, if not outrightly false.

While the distinction between human beings and other animals is not exclusively a "Western" or modern phenomenon, Raymond Corbey notes that the "idiosyncratic, extremely hierarchical character of Western views of apes . . . is brought out more clearly still when these views are compared with views and practice among such non-Western peoples" (Corbey 2005, 30). The Chinese gibbon is traditionally viewed rather highly as an "aristocrat" among animals, an inspiring link between humans and the rest of the world (Corbey 2005, 31–2). The same distinction remains, but in the history of China the gibbon is actually admired for marking it, and for suggesting continuity, while Europeans derided the ape for signifying human/animal continuity. Here, we can read Corbey alongside Carla Nappi again, who noted that Chinese wild people served the purpose of distinguishing humans and nonhumans by symbolically marking the difference. Europeans tried to sever any hint of continuity between the human and the animal, while early modern Chinese authors valued the possibility of continuity even while they expressed a similar tendency to distinguish the human from everything else.

This fundamental tendency among humans to distinguish themselves from their environment has been a primary theme of twentieth-century cultural anthropology. Edmund Leach summarized the central point of Lévi-Strauss's *Mythologiques* project as a prolonged meditation on the various ways in which humans, across the ethnographic record, have dreamed and schemed of an escape hatch from their animality: "Lévi-Strauss' central preoccupation is to explore the dialectical process by which this apotheosis of ourselves as human and godlike and other than animal is formed and re-formed and bent back upon itself" (Leach 1974, 36).

Since Lévi-Strauss, this elaboration of the nature/culture binary has been rightly critiqued and demonstrated to be more of a dense entanglement than anything resembling a neat opposition. Nonetheless, this synthesis of the ethnographic data demonstrates a persistent cross-cultural tendency among human beings to form cultural worlds that insulate them from the Outside: the "natural," the other, the animal. Lévi-Strauss's nature/culture binary, restated by Leach and corrected by a generation of cultural anthropologists, can be reframed and usefully redeployed here in terms of a consistent attempt by humans to *distinguish* themselves within their world. It is of critical importance here to clarify that "the human" itself is not a consistent or universal category. Indeed, following the work of Sylvia Wynter, we can see how certain expressions of the human can "overrepresent" and dominate others. Any local expression of the category requires rigorous scrutiny and contextualization (Wynter 2003).

In his 2002 essay "The Open: Man and Animal," the contemporary philosopher Giorgio Agamben outlined precisely *why* the distinction between human being and animal seems so aggressively sought out:

> It is as if determining the border between human and animal were not just one question among many discussed by philosophers and theologians, scientists and politicians, but rather a fundamental metaphysico-political operation in which alone something like "man" can be decided upon and produced. If animal life and human life could be superimposed perfectly, then neither man nor

animal—and, perhaps, not even the divine—would any longer be thinkable. (Agamben 2004, 21)

Agamben argues here that the human/nonhuman distinction is *the* conceptual ground for any further ontological elaboration. Before human beings can conceptualize their world, implement a system of knowledge, or organize themselves into a pattern of belief and behavior called culture, humans must meaningfully distinguish themselves from their environment and the other beings within it. Contrary to Lévi-Strauss's nature/culture binary, this binary distinction is neither total nor is it necessarily oppositional: humans inhabit, interact with, and indeed depend upon nonhumans. Agamben is arguing that their ability to do so rests on a capacity to set themselves apart—conceptually—by creating an artificial category for themselves: the "human."

Agamben elaborates a theoretical concept for manufacturing the category of the human that he calls "the Anthropological Machine." "*Homo sapiens*," he writes, "is neither a clearly defined species nor a substance; it is, rather, a machine or device for producing the recognition of the human" (Agamben 2004, 24). Agamben is suggesting here that "the animal" is a concept invented by human beings to define themselves against. For example, the concept of the human, which divides *Homo sapiens* from bonobos with an abyss of difference, while arranging bonobos and giant bivalve clams as categorically the same, is clearly more of a conceptual project than any kind of scientific or philosophically defensible position. Animality is a problem that humans have, against which they must constantly contrast themselves to create themselves.

In a world where Linneaus could simply refer Descartes to a monkey as a refutation of his philosophy, it is clear that humans tend to develop a conceptual grammar of difference to distinguish themselves and thereby generate the category of the human. Descartes was an extreme example, but as Lévi-Strauss's work suggests, there appears to be some version of this conceptual grammar across the ethnographic record. There are side effects to using this grammar, however, flotsam that drifts in the conceptual abyss between the human and the animal, which Agamben identifies as an "ape-man":

[The anthropological machine] functions by excluding as not (yet) human an already human being from itself, that is, by animalizing the human, by isolating the nonhuman within the human: *Homo alalus*, or the ape-man. (Agamben 2004, 37)

By *Homo alalus*, the ape-man, Agamben refers to Ernst Haeckel's hypothesized species of human before the evolution of language, a nonspeaking human. Agamben is suggesting that the creation of a synthetic category called "human," which separates us from animals, will necessarily generate its exception. If I might paraphrase Agamben, he suggests that the anthropological machine, when "activated," will not only generate humans: it also will generate the exception that proves the rule. It will generate humans in the mode of nonhuman. It will generate ideas and images of ape-men. If I might paraphrase Agamben rather aggressively: the anthropological machine will generate humans, but only if the places beyond their homes are haunted by Bigfoot.

As an illustration of some of the theoretical points made above, I would like to turn to a text considered to be among the best-documented Bigfoot encounters. The following is an excerpt from the text of a sworn affidavit signed in 1957 by William Roe in Edmonton, Alberta. On the day of the event, Roe had decided to use his day off from his job on a road-building crew to enjoy a hike in the Canadian woods. He came upon a clearing, where he saw a massive being that he did not recognize: "My first impression was of a huge man, about six feet tall, almost three feet wide, and probably weighing somewhere near three hundred pounds. It was covered from head to foot with dark brown silver-tipped hair. But as it came closer I saw by its breasts that it was female" (Sanderson 2006, 75–8). Being an experienced hunter with his rifle in hand, he crouched and observed the creature:

> The thought came to me that if I shot it I would possibly have a specimen of great interest to scientists the world over . . . I levelled my rifle. The creature was still walking rapidly away, again turning its head to look in my direction. I lowered the rifle. Although I have called the creature "it," I felt now that it was a human being, and I knew I would never forgive myself if I killed it . . . Just as it came to the other patch of brush it threw its head back and made a peculiar noise that seemed to be half laugh and half language, and which I could only describe as a kind of a whinny. Then it walked from the small brush into a stand of lodge-pole pines. I stepped out into the opening and looked across a small ridge just beyond the pine to see if I could see it again. It came out on the ridge a couple of hundred yards away from me, tipped its head back again, and again emitted the only sound I had heard it make, but what this half laugh, half language was meant to convey I do not know. It disappeared then, and I never saw it again. (Sanderson 2006, 75–8)

Agamben can help us understand several strange moments in William Roe's remarkable affidavit. Roe tells us that it was his feeling that the being before him was somehow human that prompted him to lower his rifle. In the book *Homo Sacer*, Agamben draws on the ancient Greek distinction between *zoē* and *bios*, roughly "noncitizens" and "citizens." *Zoē* are beings who are excluded from the political sphere, while *bios* refers to beings who comprise the body politic. As Agamben (1998, 12) puts it: "The fundamental categorial pair of Western politics is not that of friend/enemy but that of bare life/political existence, *zoē/bios*, exclusion/inclusion." For the ancient Greeks, nonhuman animals like livestock (or the "specimen" that Roe planned to shoot) do not have political rights, and therefore they cannot properly be "murdered," merely slaughtered as property. Inclusion in the political sphere, *bios*, is the only way to access a "right" to live. William Roe narrates an encounter with a being in transit from *zoē* to *bios* in real time, and he does so by describing his own moral calculation as he leveled and then lowered his rifle: "I would never forgive myself if I killed it."

The moment of *zoē/bios* transit is a common theme in American Bigfoot encounters, which are often reported by hunters and sportsmen who happen to be armed at the moment of encounter. In Charles B. Pierce's 1972 dramatic documentary *The Legend of Boggy Creek*, a hunter in the Arkansas bottomlands recalls his thought process during a wild person encounter: "If I'd of had my rifle, I believe I could have knocked him down easy. But I doubt if I would have, cause I kept thinking: there's just a chance, it might be a man. And if I'd of shot that thing and it turned out to be a man, I'd of had to live with that the rest of my life" (Pierce 1972). Like William Roe, the Arkansas hunter experienced a profound moral oscillation in the presence of the wild person, before ultimately calculating that such a killing might indeed be murder, unbearable to the conscience.

The act of vocalization is another element from William Roe's account that Agamben illuminates. When it opens its mouth, it does not simply grunt, roar, or growl. It seems to chatter, giggle, mumble: it vocalizes on a register that Roe calls "half language." There is an implicit yet indecipherable meaning in these vocalizations. Agamben's analysis of the human/nonhuman threshold intersects precisely with William Roe's account:

> What distinguishes man from animal is language . . . if this element is taken away, the difference between man and animal vanishes, unless we imagine a nonspeaking *man* . . . who would function as a bridge that passes from the animal to the human. The animal-man and the man-animal are two sides of a single fracture, which cannot be mended from either side. (Agamben 2004, 36)

Roe's wild person (though he calls the wild person "it," he recognizes her as female) opens her mouth but she does not speak, nor does she simply growl like an animal: she vocalizes her very betweenness, chattering in some unknown pidgin of the human and the nonhuman, her body and voice acting as a momentary bridge in that vast (conceptual) gulf between the human and everything else.

The image of the wild person, in Roe's account and for our analysis here, marks that vast gulf by standing within it, by drawing our nervous attention to the threshold that we have hastily and haphazardly constructed between "us" and the world. In aesthetic terms, the body and voice of Roe's wild person is demarcating the almost-human, "the uncanny valley." The ecological philosopher Timothy Morton directly connects the experience of the uncanny valley to something that Agamben might call an "ape-man" and I have called wild people:

> Somewhere in the Uncanny Valley are all the humanoid, hominid, hominin-type beings, beings we define as genetically close to us, or designed to resemble us. The theory runs that we are disturbed by them because they resemble us too closely. . . . Why are they in there? I think the defining characteristic is *ambiguity*. Are they related to me or not? When I look at them, they seem to have recognizable features. . . . And this is what really disturbs me about them: I might have more in common with them than I think I want to. When you start to think in this way, the valley becomes an artefact of anthropocentrism, racism and speciesism—of xenophobia, a fear of the "other," which is, often, really a fear of what we have in common with the "other." (Morton 2018, 174–6)

Our monsters are never distinct from the cultural worlds we inhabit, and any discourse of the "almost human" will incorporate local cultural xenophobias like racism and antiSemitism, as Morton suggests. William Roe's account is not exempt from this pattern. As he writes, "the shape of this creature's head somewhat resembled a Negro's" (Buhs 2009, 59).[1] Discourses of wild people, in America and elsewhere, frequently encode the local racist, antisemitic, or otherwise bigoted discourses of the cultures in which they occur. Especially in a post-Darwinian episteme, discourses of the "almost human" have been used to subjugate and target vulnerable groups of people. Agamben notes this as well: in his analysis of *Homo alalus*, he concludes that the end result of Haeckel's theory in the history of Europe was not a missing link, but a rampant anti-Semitism:

> To move our field of research ahead a few decades, and instead of this innocuous paleontological find [*Homo alalus*, the ape-man] we will have the Jew: that is, the non-man produced within the man . . . the man-ape, the *enfant sauvage* or *homo ferus*, but also and above all the slave, the barbarian, and the foreigner, as figures of an animal in human form. (Agamben 2004, 37)

For Agamben, European discourses of the "man-ape," the almost-man, *Homo alalus*, implicitly justified a "great chain of being" hierarchical structure, one in which antisemitic discourses will later locate Jewish people as "almost" human. This is not the case in every wild person narrative or tradition: wild person encounters and traditions are as varied as the cultures and histories they occur in, and a wild person tradition in contemporary North America, fascist Germany, or early modern China will not necessarily imbue an "almost human" with the same array of political meanings—but it is a dangerous and common political result of the idea of the "almost human" across cultures and throughout history (Jackson 2020).

I hope that Giorgio Agamben has the chance to read William Roe's affidavit, since it seems to enclose and disclose so much of his philosophy in just a few stunning paragraphs. To briefly summarize my reading of the body of the wild person: Agamben describes the anthropological machine as a conceptual framework for generating humans and reifying them against everything else. Lévi-Strauss's work indicates that some version of this basic human/nonhuman conceptual border occurs across cultures. Within this model of human/nonhuman distinction, objects or events in which this threshold is crossed hold particular significance. In our case, the image of a human in the mode of nonhuman, covered in hair, crossing the treeline at the edge of human space, evokes such a dense and generalizable array of meanings that some version of the image has appeared in a wide variety of cultural and historical contexts, wherever the synthetic boundary called "human" puts itself together.

The body of the wild person violates this fundamental distinction, evoking fear and awe in people like William Roe with its distorted shape, recognizably anthropoid yet faintly blurred by a coat of hair, and its voice, a chattering half-language between the roar of an animal and the sentences of *sapiens*. Wild people narratives are not functional, rather, they have a cause: the persistent attempt by different groups of human beings across cultures and throughout history to distinguish themselves from their environment through the elaboration of "the human" as a durable concept, or as Agamben calls it, "the Anthropological Machine." And the wild person still continues to fulfill itself in analysis: by violating the threshold between the concepts of human and nonhuman, the wild person reveals them to be simply that: concepts.

NOTE

1. This sentence is actually removed from the affidavit text provided in my 2006 reprint (and two other reprints I was able to access) of Ivan T. Sanderson's *Abominable Snowmen*, and I am grateful to Justin Mullis for pointing out this racist dimension of William Roe's encounter, which seems to have been deliberately obscured.

Chapter 13

Thomas Jefferson
The First Cryptozoologist?
Justin Mullis

According to a 2007 survey by Baylor University, roughly 13 percent of Americans believe in the flesh-and-blood reality of creatures such as Bigfoot, the Yeti, and the Loch Ness Monster ("Belief in Bigfoot"). While it is unclear how many of those millions of Americans actively search for these beasts those dedicated monster hunters who do frequently refer to themselves as cryptozoologists and their quarry as cryptids, both terms derived from cryptozoology: "the study of hidden animals."

Cryptozoology is a contested field. No university offers a degree in it and so the vast majority of self-professed cryptozoologists lack any formal academic training in those fields that intersect with their interests, such as zoology, paleontology, or evolutionary biology (Regal 2011, 173). Because their various hunts have failed to yield compelling physical evidence (i.e., a body) to prove the existence of any cryptid, cryptozoologists instead can only offer myths, legends, eye-witness accounts, and conjectures as proof of the beasts they seek. Eschewing the rigors of science, cryptozoologists publish for a popular audience rather than for experts resulting in the practice itself frequently being derided as a pseudoscience.

Historians attempting to trace the beginnings of cryptozoology typically locate the practice's origins in the mid-twentieth century when Belgian-French zoologist Bernard Heuvelmans (1916–2001), with deference to Scottish-born naturalist Ivan T. Sanderson (1911–1973), is believed to have coined the term (Poole 2011, 134; Regal 2011, 18–19).[1] The problem with this however is that the aims, aspirations, and methodologies of cryptozoology clearly predate the word itself in both fact and fiction. Heuvelmans acknowledged this crediting both the science-fiction work of authors such as Jules Verne and Sir Arthur Conan Doyle, as well as the research of Dutch zoologist A. C. Oudemans (1858–1943) with sparking his own interest in the subject of the hypothetical existence of fantastic beasts (Miller 2015, 149–51).

If cryptozoology does not begin with Heuvelmans and Sanderson, however, then where does one truly begin when looking for the historical starting point of the field? I would suggest one start with Thomas Jefferson (1743–1826): Founding Father of the United States, author of the Declaration of Independence, and third president of the United States. Yes, Thomas Jefferson also deserves recognition as one of the pioneers of cryptozoology.

There is no question that the labeling of Thomas Jefferson as a cryptozoologist is anachronistic. However, I contend that the benefits of looking at Jefferson as such a practitioner more than makes-up for any blurring of the linguistic timeline as doing so can provide one with valuable insight into the reasoning and impetus behind cryptozoology and what may motivate some people to go monster hunting.

THE POLITICS OF NATURAL HISTORY IN JEFFERSON'S TIME

To understand the cryptozoological activities of Jefferson one must start by first understanding the life and work of a very different man: mathematician and naturalist Georges-Louis Leclerc (1707–1788), the Count of Buffon. A member of the French Royal Academy of Science and the Royal Society of London as well the Curator of King Louis XV's Royal Botanical Gardens, Buffon was the eighteenth-century equivalent of a celebrity-scientist (Knapp 2019, 121–7). As Joe Hanson put it, imagine Buffon as "Carl Sagan in a powdered wig" and you'll be on the right track (Hanson 2015).

Buffon's magnum opus was a thirty-six-volume encyclopedia titled *Natural History: General and Particular* (1749–1788), which proclaimed to unveil "the true history of each thing" (Dugatkin 2009, 17). The book was a best-seller during its time, selling out in its first six weeks. Part of this can be attributed to the provocative nature of its contents, which included the first-ever attempt by anyone to put forth a completely secular scenario for the origin of the Earth. Buffon theorized that the Earth was formed when a comet struck the sun, tearing away pieces of it. These pieces had initially been white hot before gradually cooling to a point where life could form. Based on experiments he had conducted with heated iron spheres Buffon dismissed the then commonly held belief that the Earth was only around 6,000 years old and instead insisted that it must be many tens of thousands, if not millions of years older. Such heterodox conjectures landed Buffon in hot water with the Faculty of Theology in Paris and in 1764 he was accused of promoting atheism. Buffon finagled his way out of this charge by claiming that his idea regarding the origin of the planet was merely a thought experiment and that he had no interest in infringing upon the church's authority. However, modern historians of science generally agree that Buffon was, in all likelihood, an atheist (Rudwick 1985, 93–5; Switek 2010, 175, 277 n. 59; Knapp 2019, 125–6).

Cosmological conjectures aside the second most provocative aspect of *Natural History*, and what helped make it one of the most talked-about works of the eighteenth century, was Buffon's theory of American degeneracy. Stemming from his supposition that heat had been instrumental to the development of life on Earth, Buffon became one of the first naturalists to argue that the environment played a vital role in how various animals reached their present state. However, his ideas about how this worked are, by today's standards, a bit odd. According to Buffon animals which developed in parts of the world where it was warm and dry tended to be powerful, robust, and fertile while animals which developed in parts of the world which were cold and wet tended to be degenerate: which is to say that they were weak, cowardly, and infertile. Though Buffon would never set foot in the Americas he was nevertheless convinced that the entire New World was, essentially, one big cold wet swamp.[2] Ergo all American animals could be assumed to be smaller and more pathetic than the animals found in the Old World. Nowhere in America were there animals as large and impressive as the Old World's elephants and hippopotamuses, its lions or tigers. Likewise, animals that the New World did have—such as wolves and deer—were deemed inferior to their European counterparts.

Such scientific theorizing took on a political dimension as well since, for Buffon, human societies tended to mimic the animals they developed alongside, an idea that if not clear from Buffon's often purple prose, was unavoidable in *Natural History*'s copious illustrations. Most of these drawings were by artist Jacques de Sève, who, under Buffon's direction, frequently exaggerated the size and grandeur of various animals. Scholar of animal-human relations Boria Sax observes that Sève's illustration of a giraffe shows a specimen so large and robust that it looks more like a dinosaur (Sax 2018, 38).[3] In addition, Sève's depictions of the book's various beasts and birds find them not in naturalistic settings but rather inhabiting "landscapes filled with picturesque ruins, broken statues, pedestals and columns," castles, bridges, and ramparts: images associated with classical western civilization and republicanism (Semonin 2000, 132–3). The implication then regarding the fledging American colonies could not have been clearer. If American animals were degenerate, then so too would be any human society that sprung up alongside them.

Thomas Jefferson: Monster Hunter

In April 1775, the American Revolutionary War broke out, just one month after Thomas Jefferson—previously employed as a lawyer—was elected to the Continental Congress as the representative of Virginia. The following year he would draft the American Declaration of Independence. A graduate from the College of William & Mary in 1762, Jefferson studied mathematics and philosophy while developing a profound love of the sciences. As a result, he was already well acquainted with Buffon's *Natural History*, including its theory of degeneracy. Jefferson was also perceptive enough to realize that such conjecture posed a potential threat to American democracy in its libelous accusation of New World zoological impotency.

Though France served as America's primary ally during the Revolutionary War, officially entering it in 1778, this was not a decision that all French citizens uniformly supported. Historian Philippe Roger has shown that a significant cabal of French intellectuals opposed this intervention on the basis of Buffon's theory of degeneracy arguing that there was nothing to be gained from fighting over a land of sickly animals, noxious plants, and uppity colonists (Dugatkin 2009, 29). Concerns about the potential of America's natural resources among the French were real enough that in 1780 François Barbé-Marbois, then secretary of the French delegation in Philadelphia, sent out a questionnaire to various representatives asking them to inventory their state's flora and fauna. Jefferson's answer to this inquiry came in the form of his one and only book, *Notes on the State of Virginia* (1785), published two years after the end of the Revolutionary War and described by various historians as the most important book in American history prior to 1800 (Ibid., 68).

Jefferson was not the only Founding Father to repudiate Buffon's allegations of American degeneracy. Benjamin Franklin, Alexander Hamilton, and James Madison also all took up their pens against Buffon's claims, but only their pens. It was Jefferson alone who attempted to take the fight beyond the printed page and into the realm of hard science (Ibid., 47). Central to Buffon's argument had been the assertion that America boasted no large animals. If Jefferson was going to show Buffon, and the rest of the world, just how impressive he believed America, and by extension Americans, truly was then he was going to need animals that were larger and more awe-inspiring than any ever found in the Old World. In short, Jefferson was going to need monsters.

This set of circumstances resulted in Jefferson's first foray into cryptozoological speculation. In December 1781, while writing *Notes on the State of Virginia*, Jefferson learned that in 1739 French explorer Charles le Moyne had traveled down the Ohio River with a contingent of Algonquians and Iroquois, coming across a saltlick located in what is present-day Kentucky. There they discovered scores of gigantic bones; many eroding right out of the marshy ground. The Frenchman collected some of these strange bones including a 3½-foot long thigh, a single tooth weighing 10 pounds, and a tusk like that of an elephant. Because of this they designated this location as "the place where the elephant bones are found"; a description that would be reprinted on French maps of the New World for the next two decades (Kolbert 2014, 25–8; Semonin 2000, 88, 97).

These bones eventually made it back to France where they received the attention of the country's leading naturalists including Buffon who actually mentions them in his *Natural History*. Buffon agreed that the tusk and thigh bones were most likely those of an elephant, but the tooth gave him pause. This tooth was a molar, covered with sharp bulbous points, built for chewing. Modern elephants have no such teeth. Buffon's conclusion was that the knobby tooth must have come from a different animal, probably a hippopotamus (Hedeen 2008, 38).

Still in December 1781, Jefferson, deciding that he needed to examine these bones for himself, dispatched none other than legendary frontiersman Daniel Boone (1734–1820) to convey a letter to General George Rogers Clark (1752–1818), commander of the Army of the West, asking that he collect and send Jefferson some of these extraordinary bones. Clark agreed to the request but would not actually get around to it until February of 1784 (Semonin 2000, 184–5; Hedeen 2008, 65).

Upon having a chance to review the mysterious bones and grinding teeth, Jefferson—unsurprisingly—found that he fiercely disagreed with Buffon. In *Notes* Jefferson savagely attacks the French naturalist's conclusion that the bones belong to two different animals wryly noting that "wherever these grinders are found, there also we find the tusks and skeleton; but no skeleton of the hippopotamus nor grinders of the elephant. It will not be said that the hippopotamus and elephant come always to the same spot, the former to deposit his grinders, and the latter his tusks and skeleton?" (Jefferson 1785, 42).

Rather Jefferson felt that the only logical conclusion was that the bones belonged to a single hitherto unrecognized species, an opinion shared by Scottish anatomist William Hunter (1718–1783)—the personal physician of England's Queen Charlotte—who had also examined the fossils sent back to France. Hunter argued that not only were the bones and teeth from the same animal, which was neither an elephant nor a hippo but that the mystifying molars most closely resembled those of a carnivore. Hunter also felt that this American "monster" was related, in some way, to a similar elephantine creature whose remains had been discovered thawing out of the Siberian tundra in the early seventeenth century and called a "mammoth" by locals there. On the basis of this assessment, Hunter dubbed the mysterious creature the *Incognitum*—literally "Unknown Animal"—making it, semantically, the original cryptid (Semonin 2000, 137; Kolbert 2014, 27).

The idea of an unknown giant carnivorous monster similar to the Siberian mammoth, but hailing from the New World, excited Jefferson. Here, at last, was the kind of creature he needed to refute Buffon's libelous accusations of American degeneracy. The Incognitum also reminded Jefferson of a story he had heard sometime between 1775 and 1781 from "a delegation of warriors from the Delaware tribe" who said that the huge bones which had come from the lick were those of the "Big Buffalo" who "in ancient times" had "begun a universal destruction" of the local wildlife ultimately resulting in "the Great Man above" descending from heaven, armed with lightning, and slaughtering the whole heard until only a single "big bull" remained. This bull then fled "over the Ohio, over the Wabash, the Illinois, and finally over the great lakes, where he is living to this day" (Jefferson 1785, 40–1; Hedeen 2008, 26–7).

Folklorist Adrienne Mayor has documented that the Delaware were not the only tribe with stories associating the fossils at Big Bone Lick with monsters that had been wiped out by supernatural means (Mayor 2005, 1–72). Jefferson, however, was a deist which meant that while he did believe in a God who was the author of all creation he did not believe that this deity worked miracles or engaged in other forms of divine intervention (Holmes 2006). It was Jefferson's deism which led him to create the Jefferson Bible—a copy of the New Testament from which he excised all references to miracles including Christ's resurrection—as well as to deny the reality of extinction. In *Notes* Jefferson argues that "such is the economy of nature, that no instance can be produced of her having permitted any one race of her animals to become extinct; of her having formed any link in her great work so weak as to be broken" (Jefferson 1785, 54). Jefferson's skepticism regarding extinction was rooted in his belief that God had created the world as a machine so finely tuned as to never be in need of maintenance—hence no miracles. Therefore, if even one piece was to vanish—that is, go extinct—then the whole apparatus would break down and cease to function.

Furthermore, Jefferson reasoned that just because no one had ever seen a living Incognitum or mammoth—Jefferson would use the terms interchangeably—did not mean there were not any out there. As French historian of science Claudine Cohen muses, being "a good lawyer, Jefferson refused to accept negative arguments as proof" when considering the idea that monstrous creatures could be hiding "in the northern and western parts of America" (Cohen 1994, 86–7). In fact, the possibility seemed completely plausible to Jefferson since "those parts still remain in their aboriginal state, unexplored and undisturbed by us" (Jefferson 1785, 54). For Jefferson the reality of the Incognitum was a given, so much so that he included it on a list of known North American terrestrial animals published in *Notes* (Jefferson 1785, 49). All that remained now was the simple matter of finding one.

Though the Revolutionary War ended in 1783, the battle for America's dignity was still raging (Switek 2010, 174). Jefferson would soon be appointed ambassador to France, a job that would uniquely position him to confront Buffon face-to-face over the issue of American degeneracy. Jefferson, therefore, could not wait for some intrepid explorer to find him a living mammoth, he needed a bona fide example of American megafauna and he needed it now. And as it turned out, Jefferson knew exactly what animal might do the job. In the spring of 1784, just prior to his voyage to France, Jefferson tasked attorney general of New Hampshire John Sullivan with procuring him the skeleton, antlers, and skin of a suitably large moose and shipping them to him in Paris, making it clear that money was no object as the acquisition of such an animal was "more precious than you can imagine" (Dugatkin 2009, 96). Specifically, Jefferson wanted a moose so large that a European reindeer—which on average grow to about 4 ½ feet at the shoulder—could walk underneath it. Why? Because Buffon had greatly exaggerated the size and majesty of the European reindeer in his *Natural History* and Jefferson was eager to prove that the American moose was even greater (Ibid., 19–20).

As was the case with the Incognitum, Jefferson's conviction that he could locate such a monstrous moose was largely rooted in rumor and hearsay. Ezra Stiles, president of Yale, had told Jefferson that he had seen a *female moose calf* at least as tall as an adult male reindeer. Sullivan also spoke to local hunters who claimed they had seen adult male moose that stood 8 ½ to 10 feet at the shoulder while Sullivan himself claimed that in one Pequawket village he had seen an antler from a moose so large that it was used as a baby's cradle. A 1798 New York broadside upped the size of the average moose to 12-feet at the shoulder, or twice as tall as the largest adult male moose on record (Ibid., 91–4).

However, by late 1785, Sullivan had still not managed to locate such an oversized ungulate. By this point, Jefferson had finally managed to secure an audience with Buffon and the two men dined together at the Count's home in January of 1786. Even though Jefferson still did not have his moose, he nevertheless proceeded to lecture Buffon on the size and power of the animal. While skeptical of Jefferson's claims, Buffon was opened-minded which encouraged Jefferson's conviction that should Sullivan find him a suitably robust moose he could persuade Buffon to renounce his theory of American degeneracy.

Sullivan's team of contracted hunters finally managed to bag a moose for Jefferson in the winter of 1787, though it was only a seven-footer and the antlers were, somehow, lost in the process. Jefferson would not receive his moose skeleton and skin—along with the antlers of a different moose—until September 1788 at which time he had them sent straightaway to Buffon along with a note apologizing that the specimen was on the smaller side but assuring the Count that American moose did get much larger. How much of an impression Jefferson's moose made on Buffon, if any at all, is unknown. Within six months of receiving the moose, Buffon was dead—having never detracted his claim of American zoological inferiority.

A CRYPTOZOOLOGIST IN THE WHITE HOUSE

Though Buffon was now gone, Jefferson considered the issue of American degeneracy far from over. Jefferson returned to the United States in 1789 becoming the first secretary of state under President George Washington, a position he held until 1793. Jefferson began campaigning for the presidency in 1796 but lost to John Adams thus becoming the vice president in 1797. That same year, however, Jefferson was elected the third president of the American Philosophical Society, the foremost scientific organization in the United States at that time. Jefferson had been a member since 1780 and would remain president until 1819. It was during this period that Jefferson resumed his cryptozoological activities.

In the spring of 1796, several large fossil bones were uncovered in a West Virginia cave. The fossils were fragmentary consisting of only "a femur, radius, ulna, three claws and other miscellaneous foot bones" (Debus 2010, 38). Based primarily on the three tremendous claws, Jefferson deduced that the animal was a new species of enormous cat and immediately set to work preparing a formal scientific paper on it that he presented to the American Philosophical Society on March 10, 1797. Titled, "A Memoir on the Discovery of Certain Bones of a Quadruped of the Clawed Kind in the Western Parts of Virginia," Jefferson argued that the fossils belonged to a tremendous relative of the African lion. Using what Allen A. Debus describes as "error-prone, back-of-the-envelope type calculations" Jefferson estimated the size and weight of his hypothetical lion ultimately producing a beast which was "7-feet-high, and would weigh 2,000 pounds" at its most "monstrous" (Debus 2010, 39; Jefferson 1797) This is a good 4-feet taller and over 15-hundred pounds heavier than the largest adult male African lion on record. Because the longest of the three claws was 7 ½ inches Jefferson dubbed his new species *Megalonyx*; literally "Great-Claw" (Thomson 2008, 34–40).

As with the Incognitum, Jefferson did not believe that the presence of fossil bones meant that his Megalonyx was extinct and echoed his earlier deist conviction in the divine "economy of nature." Seeking further proof of the giant lion's continued presence in North America Jefferson, as he had with the Incognitum, cited as evidence Native American legends—"heretofore considered as fables" but having "regained credit since the discovery of these bones"—and petroglyphs which described and depicted an animal he thought sounded like and resembled an African lion. In addition, as with his giant moose, Jefferson also relied heavily on travelers' tales. In one account, from "little more than 30-years ago," Jefferson related how a "company of adventurers" had described hearing "terrible roarings of some animal unknown to them" which "went round and round their camp" with "eyes like two balls of fire" glowing in the night (Jefferson 1797).

Having outlined his evidence for the Megalonyx's existence, Jefferson concluded his paper with a renewed repudiation of Buffon's theory of American degeneracy. How could anyone claim that the New World was zoologically inferior to the Old when it boasted monsters such as the Megalonyx and the mammoth? And just like the mammoth, Jefferson was sure it was only a matter of time before a living specimen of his Megalonyx was obtained since much of the North American interior still remained unexplored and "there is surely space and range enough for elephants and lions, if in that climate they could subsist; and for mammoths and Megalonyxes who may subsist there. Our entire ignorance of the immense country to the West and North West, and of its contents, does not authorize us to say what it does not contain" (Ibid.).

In 1799, Jefferson published his paper, but now with a brief note appended to the end. This came about a result of Jefferson rediscovering, in the interim between his presentation and publication, an article among his files concerning the discovery of bones similar to those of his Megalonyx in Spanish Argentina. While the original scientists to examine these fossils also concluded, as Jefferson had, that these were the remains of a giant cat, a brilliant young French scientist, George Cuvier (1769–1832)—who was very much Buffon's successor in status and influence—used his new method of comparative anatomy to deduce that these bones came from a giant sloth which he dubbed Megatherium (Pimentel 2017, 152–96).

Jefferson was reluctant to acknowledge his mistake but eventually did. Nor would this be the last error of Jefferson's that Cuvier would bring to light. In the early nineteenth century, Cuvier would identify Jefferson's Incognitum as a type of prehistoric elephant which he dubbed the Mastodon; and like all pachyderms it was an herbivore. Cuvier would also be the first to make a compelling argument for the reality of mass extinction. This, however, was a reality that Jefferson had an especially hard time accepting.

Two years after becoming president of the United States in 1801, Jefferson succeeded in doubling the size of the country via the Louisiana Purchase. Jefferson did this in part because he believed that this newly acquired territory was the key to finding his much sought-after American megafauna. He shared this belief with the celebrated explorers Captain Meriwether Lewis and Second Lieutenant William Clark—the latter the younger brother of Jefferson's previous fossil emissary General George Rogers Clark—asking them to be on the lookout for any animals deemed "rare or extinct" (Thomson

2008, 59–60). Likewise in a February 1803 letter to a Parisian acquaintance Jefferson wrote that "it is not impossible that this voyage of discovery will procure us further information of the Mammoth and of the Megatherium" (Semonin 2000, 344).[4] Jefferson's reference to "the Mammoth and . . . the Megatherium" shows that while the president had recognized that his giant lion was actually a sloth, he still held out hope that it was a living species. Even after the Lewis and Clark expedition returned without any prehistoric monsters in tow, Jefferson remained resistant to the idea of extinction for most of his life finally acquiescing only three years before his death in 1826 (Hedeen 2008, 103–4).

Moreover, Jefferson's monster obsession was not without its political liabilities. In 1809, as Jefferson's presidency was coming to an end and he was working to assure that his fellow Democratic-Republican James Madison would become the next president, his political rivals in the Federalist party published the nineteenth-century equivalent of a political attack ad in the form of a poem lampooning Jefferson's preoccupation with extraordinary animals:

Go, wretch, resign thy presidential chair,
Disclose thy secret measures, foul or fair,
Go search with curious eyes for horned frogs,
Mid the wild wastes of Louisianan bogs;
Or Where the Ohio rolls his turbid streams
Dig for huge bones, thy glory and thy theme

W. J. T. Mitchell observes that Jefferson had hoped that the mammoth would serve not only as a biological refutation of Buffon's ideas but also become "the first symbolic 'political animal' of the United States, an emblem of Jefferson's vision of an ever-expanding continental empire of small farmers and artisans." Such a symbol was important since Jefferson "like . . . every American politician since, [aimed] to create the illusion that his party was above politics, and that his vision of a natural constitution would, like the paper constitution, provide a frame within which all parties could cooperate" (Mitchell 1998, 119).

THE FORGOTTEN CRYPTOZOOLOGIST

Despite all of this, Jefferson's work as a pioneering cryptozoologist has been largely forgotten.[5] However, in reflecting upon Jefferson's pursuit of hypothetical American megafauna it is impossible to ignore the degree to which the methodologies and assumptions employed by the Founding

Father regarding his belief in giant monsters roaming the unexplored regions of North America perfectly align with those employed by practicing cryptozoologists.

Like modern cryptozoologists, Jefferson relied heavily on the myths and legends of monsters told by indigenous peoples to support his assertion that such creatures actually exist as seen in his pursuit of the Incognitum, giant moose, and Megalonyx. While this type of ethno-knowledge has often proved helpful to field zoologists in identifying new species, cryptozoologists' assertion that all mythical and legendary creatures must be based on unknown real animals is both reductive with regards to understanding folklore and has so far failed to generate any worthwhile results in their various monster hunts (Naish 2017, 11–29).[6]

Along this same line, Jefferson's extensive use of anecdotal evidence of people's alleged sightings or encounters with unfamiliar animals, seen in the case of both the moose and Megalonyx, remains the foundation upon which the existence of most cryptids is based. When critics of cryptozoology point out that humans are not naturally good observers—let alone good at identifying wild animals when they have had no formal training in doing so—many modern cryptozoologists respond as Jefferson did in his day by reasserting both the witness's assumed familiarity with local wildlife and their general honesty as individuals—honesty here apparently precluding one's ability to make honest mistakes.

Additionally, there is Jefferson's argument that his monsters could be hiding in remote areas seldom visited by man. If this line of argument sounds familiar it is because it is still regularly marshaled by contemporary cryptozoologists to explain why they believe there is a chance of finding dinosaurs lurking in the jungles of Africa, sea monsters at the bottom of the ocean, or even a colony of Sasquatches in the deep Pacific Northwest woods (Heuvelmans 1995, 3–17; Heuvelmans 2007, 77–93).

But another prominent parallel between Jefferson and modern cryptozoologists is that in attempting to account for the existence of his various monsters Jefferson invoked what paleobiologist Darren Naish has termed the "prehistoric survivor paradigm" of cryptozoology in which various cryptids are identified as animals otherwise known only from the fossil record (Naish 2017, 38). Boria Sax notes that the willingness of cryptozoologists to claim that numerous supposed monsters are really prehistoric holdovers speaks to a general resistance among some to accepting the realities of geological deep time and mass extinction (Sax 2018, 169–72).[7] Jefferson shared these doubts largely as a result of his religious convictions and there is strong evidence to indicate that many in the cryptozoological community harbor similar faith-based misgivings (Laycock 2010; Regal 2011, 173; Poole 2011, 134–5; Loxton and Prothero 2013, 285–95, 308–9; Bielo 2016, 81–101).

Equally important as all of this however is the fact that Jefferson's cryptozoological pursuits were motivated, in part, by his deep and abiding love of science. Skeptics often defame cryptozoologists as harboring a fundamentally anti-intellectual mindset despite anecdotal evidence to the contrary (Naish 2017, 218–21). Jefferson was many things but he certainly was not anti-intellectual. As President John F. Kennedy once told a party of Nobel Prize laureates, they represented "the most extraordinary collection of . . . human knowledge that has ever been gathered together at the White House" since "Thomas Jefferson dined alone" (Anderson 2012, 283 n. 11).

So what did motivate Jefferson to go out and hunt monsters? As we have seen Jefferson's cryptozoological activities were primarily attempts by the Founding Father to exonerate America from Buffon's charge of zoological, and by extension national, degeneracy. In this vein, Jefferson's cryptids were, as geologist David Bressan put it, quite literally "patriotic monsters" (Bressan 2014). Furthermore, in his 2009 book *Bigfoot: The Life and Times of a Legend* researcher Joshua Blu Buhs characterized the debate over the existence of Sasquatch as a "contest for dignity" between the working class and academic elites. Historian of science Brian Regal came to a similar conclusion in his book *Searching for Sasquatch* (2011) arguing that cryptozoology represented the contested ground between amateur and professional science. Such theoretical frameworks apply perfectly to the case of Jefferson and Buffon. Buffon was a professional scientist while Jefferson an enthusiastic amateur. Buffon embodied the height of French aristocracy while Jefferson, despite accruing significant political power during his lifetime, nevertheless always saw himself as a simple blue-collar farmer.

But as the story of Thomas Jefferson as monster hunter reveals, this type of contest for dignity goes beyond individuals or even class structures. Cryptids can become symbols of national identity and the motivation for perusing them the desire to secure one's country's place on the world stage. The subject of the vitality of America's plant and animal life would remain a contested issue well into the early nineteenth century before finally being put to rest by the celebrated naturalist Alexander Von Humboldt (1769–1859) who was also a great admirer of Jefferson and spent a week with him at the White House in 1804 (Wulf 2015, 94–108). Ultimately it was Humboldt's meticulous fieldwork examining the flora and fauna of the New World, rather than Jefferson's posturing or monster hunting, which would strike the death blow to Buffon's theory of American degeneracy.

Today, few Americans are even aware of Buffon's slanderous science or the role it played in the origins of their country. Conversely, as historian W. Scott Poole observes, Jefferson's preoccupation with monsters "in early America" can be seen as the beginnings of what continues to be "a huge body of popular belief about other wondrous creatures of the New World, from

Big Foot to sea serpents, lake monsters, and lizard men" (Poole 2011, 12). In other words, it is Thomas Jefferson who can be credited with the very origins of cryptozoology.

NOTES

1. The question of who exactly coined the term cryptozoology—Heuvelmans, Sanderson or even possibly someone else—remains a controversial subject (Loxton and Prothero 2013, 16–17).
2. It probably didn't help matters that the nation's capital was actually built in a swamp (Wulf 2015, 98).
3. See Jay M. Smith's essay "Dreadful Enemies" for more on Buffon's theatrical description of various animals and how his description of one, the hyena, helped to create another cryptid: The Beast of Gévaudan (Smith 2016, 33–61).
4. In fact, Jefferson's conviction that his American monsters existed somewhere in the unexplored interior of America was a belief he had expressed as far back as 1784 in correspondence with Ezra Stiles (Mayor 2005, 57).
5. During the course of my research, I came across only a few works that made the connection between Jefferson and cryptozoology, and then only partially. On the subject of the Megalonyx, Debus writes that "Jefferson was a contemporary cryptozoologist" (Debus 2010, 40) while in a footnote Loxton and Prothero describe "Jefferson's speculation" that mammoths may have found refuge in the American interior an "example of cryptozoology" (Loxton and Prothero 2013, 371–2, no. 105). Most intriguing Heuvelmans, in a posthumously published work, wrote that Jefferson's methodology regarding the Megalonyx was "a perfect example of the cryptozoological approach" evidentially untroubled by the fact that all of Jefferson's conclusions about the animal were wrong (Heuvelmans 2007, 100).
6. While there is certainly some truth to the idea that every animal was a mythical animal before it was formally discovered by science, cryptozoologists badly misrepresent the reality of this fact as explained clearly and succinctly by paleobiologist Darren Naish in his book *Hunting Monsters: Cryptozoology and the Reality Behind the Myths* (2007).
7. Both Peter Dendle and Robert L. France have argued that cryptozoology as a whole can be seen as a result of a refusal to deal with the reality of extinction (Dendle 2006, 190–206; France 2017, 66).

Chapter 14

Shapeshifters and Goddesses

Gods, Monsters, and Otherness in the Mysticism of Gloria Anzaldúa

Stefan R. Sanchez

How does a monster become monstrous? How does a god become divine? I pose these questions as food for thought at the beginning of a journey through both the *otherworld* and the *otherworld* of Gloria Evangelina Anzaldúa. Anzaldúa is well known as a Chicana literary figure, as well as for her works of literary and cultural criticism in her early career. Her ideas contributed greatly to Chicana feminism and the shape of the contemporary Chicanx studies movement, as well as a significant portion of contemporary Latin American philosophy. *Borderlands/La Frontera* (Anzaldúa 1987), perhaps her most well-known work, contains descriptions of contact with divinities (later described in this chapter) and shamanic trance states, a fact that has historically been overlooked in the aforementioned academic circles. Anzaldúa herself was unhappy with the reception of *Borderlands*, stating in a 1993 interview that among the "unsafe" aspects of the text that do not get discussed is the "connection between body, mind and spirit . . . anything that has to do with the sacred . . . anything that has to do with the spirit" (Anzaldúa 2000, 24). Throughout Anzaldúa's works one will find references to not only the western philosophical canon but to western occultism, Mexican shamanism, new age spirituality, and folk Catholicism, all of which heavily informed her politics, activism, and literary criticism.

These largely ignored spiritual and metaphysical aspects of Anzaldúa's writing, however, are critical for understanding her larger discussions of individual identity in conflict, as they deal primarily with the other as a breach in curated narratives of common experience. These breaches in curated experience largely express themselves in ways that are often termed "supernatural."

Anzaldúa uses this term to describe both mystical experiences and that which society has repressed:

> Humans fear the supernatural, both the undivine (the animal impulses such as sexuality, the unconscious, the unknown, the alien) and the divine (the superhuman, the god in us). Culture and religion seek to protect us from these two forces. The female, by virtue of creating entities of flesh and blood in her stomach (she bleeds every month but does not die), by virtue of being in tune with nature's cycles, is feared. (Anzaldúa 1987, 17)

Thus, this chapter will largely serve as a dissection of this taxonomy of the "supernatural" appearing in Anzaldúa's *Borderlands/La Frontera*. For the purposes of this chapter, I will define the "Anzaldúan supernatural" as *the category of events, objects, processes, or entities which break perceived uniformity of the natural world, where "natural" refers to societal and religious normality as opposed to any objective notion of nature.* What is most interesting is that Anzaldúa's monstrosity just as often is found within the individual as with some outside force. Perhaps due at least in part to the apparent internality of these gods and monsters, most of Anzaldúa's interpreters have read encounters with these entities as metaphorical. I would encourage the reader to view them as mystical experiences that permeated the life of this author and activist, not only for the sake of accurate historical interpretation but because of what these entities would seem to imply for the human condition when read in this way. The gods and monsters Anzaldúa finds herself confronted by and eventually becoming, while quite real and traumatic to experience, usually arise from within herself and, for her, are present in everyone.

The formulation inherent in this taxonomy is vitally important to understanding Anzaldúa's use of the monstrous in her larger work and can illuminate how taxonomic notions of "gods" and "monsters" more generally can be used in interpreting human experiences. In this chapter, I will explore the motif of the other-within-the-self through three manifestations of the Anzaldúan supernatural which would seem to have been the most important to her own sense of identity. First is the Shadow-Beast, the principle undivine figure within the self. Second are god(esses), several of which are venerated throughout Anzaldúa's writing, but only one of which I will focus on, that being *Coatlicue*, the Aztec earth mother. Third, I will examine the *nagual*, the shapeshifter, as occupying a third space between the undivine and the divine. In doing so, I will attempt to show the usefulness of Anzaldúan monstrosity and divinity as a lens through which to examine individual identity in conflict, and the processes of fragmentation and unification which they represent.

THE CAGE: THE ANZALDÚAN SUPERNATURAL AND THE SOCIAL CONSTRUCTION OF THE NATURAL

Anzaldúa's life was complicated by medical, cultural, and spiritual strife. She was born in 1942 with an extremely rare hormonal condition which caused her to menstruate at the age of three months, which plagued her with health complications through the duration of her life (Anzaldúa 2000, 38). Throughout her life, she was criticized by her family for her interest in literature and creative writing, activities which in much of Chicanx culture were, and often still are, thought of as masculine pursuits at best, and impractical at worst (251). This was made worse by cultural clashes with her identity as a Chicana and as a lesbian in an era when the overlap of these discourses was rather turbulent (Anzaldúa 2015, 147). Her writing attempts to answer the adversities she experienced at the hands of both her home life and her wider cultural ecosystem, both in terms of Chicanx culture, and American culture more broadly.

Anzaldúa's childhood is characterized by religious and cultural hybridity, as well as religious and cultural othered-ness, in her 1987 volume *Borderlands/La Frontera* she describes her experiences growing up, "listening to the voices of the wind as a child and understanding its messages." She cites this sort of experience as common for many people of Mexican descent, but not talked about because it does not fit into either the curated reality of the church or that of "white rationality"—two things that she often wrote about as essentially interchangeable (Anzaldúa 1987, 36). Anzaldúa's personal system seeks to underline experiences such as this, which would conventionally be labeled as supernatural, and then expand the category of the supernatural beyond its traditional limits, essentially identifying the supernatural with the other.

Anzaldúa's taxonomy presents us with a supernatural comprised of two primary nodes: the *undivine*, which is carnal, animalistic, or otherwise so different from our notion of the "human" that it seems irreconcilable; and the *divine*, characterized by "superhuman" and godly forces that arise from within us (though this idea will be somewhat problematized later), which is human, or human enough, but too powerful to be controlled. The Anzaldúan supernatural presents a world wherein the world of the supernatural is the world of the "other," whether that be ghosts, shapeshifters, gods, and the like; or rabid dogs, racial minority status, or a woman's menstruation. Anzaldúa's implied "natural" would then be the loose consensus of cultural dominance, which in itself is ill-defined, has many layers, and is inherently precarious at its ontological roots. In this way, the Anzaldúan supernatural points to a similar "abiding sense of precariousness and insecurity built into the order of things" which Timothy Beale describes in his analysis of monstrous deities in the Near East in *Religion and Its Monsters* (2002, 21). However, while the monstrous reality must be repeatedly defeated or kept in Beale's schema, Anzaldúa's framework would appear to recognize the supernatural, those apparent abominations before order, the monstrous as beneficial to those who would acknowledge and embrace it.

For Anzaldúa, we, the uninitiated masses, are not supposed to remember otherworldly events we may experience (1987, 36). We ignore, we repress, we *cage* mystical experience, relegating it to the realm of the "supernatural" as previously defined. Experiences of the supernatural, whether they are more mystical or worldly, are relegated to what I will call the "otherworld." By the other-world, I mean the "world" or conceptual realm inhabited by those things which are not "allowed" by the institutionally constructed norms, *the world of things which are othered*. Note that I have intentionally stated that the otherworld is the category of things that are *othered* and not things which are *other*. I insist, as does Anzaldúa, that the other is created, not essentially other—even in regards to events that seem to exist outside of "rational" time and space. Otherness, for Anzaldúa is embodied by the divine and undivine, and expressed within the self, more often than not. The mechanics of this will become clear in the next sections as we explore, the Shadow-Beast, the principle figure of the undivine.

THE SHADOW-BEAST, *THE UNDIVINE*

The term "Shadow-Beast" appears frequently in Anzaldúa's writing but is only ever defined in snippets. As previously quoted, man's Shadow-Beast—woman—is a projection of his "recognized nightmarish pieces," the sight of which sends him into "a frenzy of anger and fear" (Anzaldúa 1987, 17). This concept is based on the Jungian archetype of the shadow, which Anzaldúa references in *Borderlands/La Frontera*, describing it as "the unsavory aspects of ourselves" (17). Jung (1980, 35) explains that the shadow is "a living part of the personality and therefore wants to live with it in some form. It cannot be argued out of existence or rationalized into harmlessness." Jung, however, also described a transformative aspect to the shadow. One always meets one's own shadow first in the process of meeting oneself (35). For Jung, confrontation with the shadow is a necessary step to know oneself through a painful experience that is like, "a tight passage, a narrow door, whose painful constriction no one is spared who goes down to the deep well. But one must learn to know oneself in order to know who one is" (36).

Building on Jung's vision, Anzaldúa's Shadow-Beast is a version of the shadow that is its own agentive organism. It visits Anzaldúa in her dreams and visions, takes over her body, and communicates with her through this process. Within Anzaldúa's framework, the Shadow-Beast is one of many "imaginal figures" that make up the individual, of which the conscious "I" is only a part (Anzaldúa 2015, 36). All members of this multiself inhabit a state of simultaneously literal and metaphorical existence with the distinction between the two mattering very little (177).[1] Anzaldúa attributes the qualities of the Shadow-Beast to the fact that it embodies our defensive, protective, and animalistic behaviors, what she calls the *undivine* in her concept of the supernatural. Any threat to the individual's perception of the world or the sense of identity "enrages [the] Shadow-Beast, who views the new knowledge as an attack on [one's] bodily integrity" (147). The Shadow-Beast is survivalistic, instinctual, and animalistic; it does not mesh with our idea of human, with "rationality." It is not concerned with objects in the world, it exists to protect the subject.

Like Jung's shadow, Anzaldúa's Shadow-Beast serves an important function. It is only beastly because it is a subject made into an object, it is those aspects that keep us alive and take care of basic needs, the *animalistic*. It is only shadow for the reason that Jung's shadow is shadow; it is the repressed and abused parts of the self—impulsive, instinctual, and unresolved—which then repeats these patterns for the sake of survival, out of fear. We are trained to fear what happens when the Shadow-Beast breaks out, but it is only in this lack of resolution and acceptance that the shadow finds monstrosity. Anzaldúa, therefore, finds that the solution to the presence of this wild, imaginal beast is to ally with it and find power in the monstrous and ally with what has been caged, much as Jung suggests one must reconcile with the shadow. Simple suppression is no solution. Indeed, the Shadow-Beast must be confronted to move past ignorance of the self (Anzaldúa 2015, 74–5).

For Anzaldúa, therefore, there would appear to be power in what is caged. The Shadow-Beast is dangerous—it is painted as a wild monster for a reason, but it would seem that Anzaldúa does not view restraining the beast as the solution to the problem of the beast's danger. Faced with our fear of the violent monster that rattles the cage of its signification, "we try to make ourselves conscious of the Shadow-Beast, stare at the sexual lust and lust for power and destruction that we see on its face, discern amongst its features the undershadow that the reigning order . . . projects on our Beast . . . we try to waken the Shadow-Beast inside us" (Anzaldúa 1987, 20). Anzaldúa describes this painful process as one that many do not wish to undertake and may even have difficulty with, but the monstrous is ultimately the ally. In her attempts to reconcile with the monster, Anzaldúa describes being "dragged underground by cold, clammy hands" while stared at by "lidless, serpent eyes" (20). Despite the harrowing confrontation with the Beast, however, she embraces the power that it holds and represents. Shadow-Beast is described as hating any sort of restraint placed upon the self, lashing out violently to protect the individual, thus making the Beast a useful part of the personality (16). The awakening of the Shadow-Beast which Anzaldúa describes may be viewed as a sudden resurgence in raw, animal instinct.

This return to instinct, for Anzaldúa, is the basis of the fully realized human, exemplified by the shapeshifter, as will be discussed later. To pave the way for understanding of the shapeshifter later, however, one must be familiar with an emergent property of this awakened animal instinct, referred to as *la facultad*, literally "the faculty," or "the capacity" (Anzaldúa 2000, 122). *La facultad* is broadly the faculty of experiencing the otherworld; it is a sixth sense described as "the capacity to see in surface phenomena the meaning of deeper realities, to see the deep structure below the surface" (Anzaldúa 1987, 38). What is most interesting is that Anzaldúa describes *la facultad* as a sense that is more likely to manifest in those who are marginalized or live in constant fear; those relegated to the "otherworld," therefore, are most likely to develop this sense for the otherworld. The marginal otherworlder is forced to develop this capacity out of self-preservation, as a sort of danger sense (38–9). This is instinct manifesting beyond standard human capacity, this is the realm of the undivine gaining superhuman (read: divine) power. The movement of the undivine Shadow-Beast toward the divine will be discussed in the later section on the shapeshifter. Just as the one possessed of the Shadow-Beast gains strength from confronting the Beast and embracing it, the otherworlder is more likely to acquire this otherworldly power. Initiated through loss of innocence, the *undivine* animal instinct becomes a superpower, with sensitivity to danger being only the beginning.

The Shadow-Beast and its animalistic-instinctual nature, therefore, show a danger of monstrosity arising from within the self in response to adversity in response to breaks in normalcy and safety; it then further entrenches, becoming an antagonist to its host and causing said host to act monstrously themselves in its attempts to survive the ordeal. Whether this is treated as a metaphor or a literal monster possessing the individual, the Anzaldúan notion of the Shadow-Beast places the danger of the undivine within the human individual, but also offers power in reconciliation of that break. Its capabilities can even be utilized by the individual upon such reconciliation. Anzaldúa offers here is an opportunity to turn away from the historical demonization of the carnal and animalistic and to find benefit in the fact that we are, biologically, beasts. However, examination of Anzaldúa's goddess, her principle representation of the divine, will reveal a number of aesthetic ties to the Shadow-Beast that cannot be ignored, and which signal the full relationship between the two, later expressed in the later section on the shapeshifter. In the next section, I will explore Anzaldúa's divine figure in the form of her gnosis of *Coatlicue*. The reader will note that this theme of fusion between animalistic and godly that would seem to be indicated by *la facultad* does not disappear. In fact, our introduction to the Anzaldúan divine will serve to problematize the differences between god and monster, toward a more complex, if somewhat unnerving self-construction.

GODDESS COATLICUE, THE DIVINE

Coatlicue—known by a variety of names such as "Serpent Skirt," *La Tonantzin*, the Great Mother, or the "monster who swallows the stars"—is treated by Anzaldúa as a central aspect of reality that represents both creator and destroyer, while acting as her personal savior from the brink of insanity (Anzaldúa 1987, 46). Traditionally, *Coatlicue* is the Aztec earth goddess, who is decapitated by her daughter in a familial conflict and resurrects in a monstrous state—her head replaced with two giant snakes, her arms becoming two additional snakes, and her feet replaced with eagle's talons. While there are certainly greater and lesser goddesses that Anzaldúa propitiates in her personal system and which act as various reflections of philosophical and cultural inquiry, *Coatlicue* is the primary goddess.

Anzaldúa's account of *Coatlicue* revolves around her own experience of a condition called *susto* (lit. fright), usually translated as "soul loss," wherein the soul is "frightened out of the body" (48). Accounts of this condition vary across different Latin American cultures, and a lengthy discussion of the symptoms and mechanics of *susto* is beyond the scope of this chapter.[2] For the sake of brevity, I will simply include Anzaldúa's description of the symptoms which she attributes to the condition. She describes "sweating . . . a headache, [unwillingness] to communicate [and being] frightened by sudden noises" as her primary symptoms (Anzaldúa 1987, 48), along with a profound existential malaise. Eventually, she finds herself pulled into the underworld, travel to which is common in cures for *susto* (48). Here she is forced to confront a mirror, where she sees the visage of the goddess reflected back at her:

> I don't want to see what's behind Coatlicue's eyes, her hollow sockets. I can't confront her face to face; I must take small sips of her face through the corners of my eyes, chip away at the ice a sliver at a time. Behind the ice mask I see my own eyes. They will not look at me. [I look like I'm pissed off, look at this resistance][3]—resistance to knowing, to letting go . . . I am afraid of drowning. Resistance to sex, intimate touching, opening myself to the alien other where I am out of control, not on patrol (48).

Here, Anzaldúa interprets her experience as working through her own personal damages, staring *Coatlicue* in the face, at the power that is "greater than the conscious I" (50). Locking eyes with the Ancient Goddess, she pleads that

Coatlicue take control of her identity and put things right, setting aside the conscious "I" in an effort to cure her condition.

"I'll take over now," the goddess tells her (51). She then describes another set of teeth in her mouth, the breath being pulled out of her, and "the heart in [her] cunt starts to beat." She is surrounded by light. She collapses in on herself and sees an opening in the rock face upon which her spirit stands: *Coatlicue* has been released. "Someone in me takes matters into our own hands—over my own body, my sexual activity, my soul, my mind, my weaknesses and my strengths. Mine. Ours. Not the heterosexual white man's or the colored man's or the state's or the culture's or the religion's or the parents'— just ours, mine" (51). The pieces of her soul rush back, completing her being; she states, "I am no longer afraid." Yet, she describes something more; after this encounter, a presence which grows stronger, "thicker," every day—a thousand sleepless serpents' eyes, staring out into the night. She describes this awareness as her "vigilance."

In this moment, there is a blurring between the categories of *undivine* and *divine* per Anzaldúa's description. Anzaldúa's taxonomy of the supernatural places figures such as *Coatlicue*, as "divine," superhuman entities; despite this placement, there is an animalistic quality, both in terms of the intense sexual nature of the experience and the fact that the experience is linked to the presence of serpents' eyes, which are present in her visions of the Shadow-Beast as well. Anzaldúa describes *Coatlicue* as the "incarnation of cosmic processes" and within her image are contained "all the symbols important to the religion and philosophy of the Aztecs" (46). In particular, she is described as fusing the following oppositional concepts: "the eagle and the serpent, heaven and the underworld, life and death, mobility and immobility, beauty and horror." In this way, *Coatlicue* can be read similarly to Tanya Luhrmann's portrayal of "the Goddess" in her ethnographic study of magical practitioners, *Persuasions of the Witch's Craft* (1989). Luhrmann writes that the "Goddess" is "a spiritual embodiment, or interpretation of natural process," which is characterized as one of three ways to understand the "chaotic darkness" common to the systems of ritualized magic examined during her time studying in England in the 1980s (92). "The Goddess," Luhrmann writes, "is dissolution. The very nature of the concept entails the interconnectedness from all things" (94). The core of the "chaotic darkness" by Luhrmann's observation is "that to enter the chaos is to empower oneself" (97). Similarly, Anzaldúa's communion with Coatlicue is one meant to empower herself and to grant unity of the self through unity with the cosmos. This is not a pleasant cosmic union, but rather a *necessary* one, echoing what some scholars identify as "shamanic dismemberment" performed to be remade into something greater (Eliade 1989, 108–9).

Whereas the undivine by way of the Shadow-Beast presents the emergence of monstrosity from within the self through fragmentation, the divine by way of the goddess *Coatlicue* presents both an escape and an opportunity for growth. I would argue, however, that this growth fundamentally takes place by contact with the monstrous. Anzaldúa's Shadow-Beast and Coatlicue are both associated with the symbolism of the gaze of serpent eyes, and *Coatlicue's* animalistic qualities link her with the undivine as part of her divinity. Furthermore, Anzaldúa's goddess is described in terms of a totality of cosmic process, just as Luhrmann's Goddess or "darkness" is, and it is this union of the cosmos that creates a superhuman figure incorporating the animalistic: *Coatlicue* is not only a humanoid goddess figure but also incorporates serpent and eagle imagery into her visage. These animal features and the sexual nature of her presence as described by Anzaldúa demonstrate that she clearly has undivine aspects, though she is ultimately divine. Within Anzaldúa's framework, the animalistic is meant to be *undivine, and yet the divine makes use of it*. *Coatlicue's* serpentine eyes are both the eyes of an animal and the eyes of a goddess. If the *divine* has access to the *undivine*, and the *undivine* would seem to have access to the *divine*, as in the earlier section on the Shadow-Beast, then Anzaldúa draws into question the presence of a divider at all.

As seen in Anzaldúa, therefore, divinity creates unity by first playing upon the fragmentation created by the monstrous. Or perhaps one could interpret divinity as creating the monstrous to induce said fragmentation, similarly to the classical monsters that were considered omens of divine outrage.[4] Indeed, this would make sense given *Coatlicue's* monstrous aspects, where we see Anzaldúa fundamentally incorporating the undivine originally intended to be its opposite. By a similar token, the undivine is demonstrated to possess powers that hint at divinity. The true difference between the principle monster and the principle deity in Anzaldúa's writing, and perhaps even the difference between monstrosity and divinity as a whole, lies not in its essence, but rather in how it manifests the supernatural, that is, how it breaks uniformity of experience. It would seem that Anzaldúa's dichotomy between the undivine and the divine is an intentionally false one, set forth to be problematized. In the following section, I will explore further the dissolution of the dichotomy of divine and undivine, between Shadow-Beast and Goddess, between monstrosity and divinity.

SHAPESHIFTERS, MAGICIANS, RESONANCE, OBLITERATION OF CATEGORIES

Beyond these divine/undivine figures, Anzaldúa describes in her writings a three-tiered cosmos represented by a tree, with the trunk representing the middle world or our human world. Represented by the roots of the tree is the underworld, and the branches of the tree represent the sky world (Anzaldúa 2015, 25–6). In the underworld, one can find "earth energies, animal spirits, and the dead who have not moved on to the next level of existence" while in the sky world, one may find "noncorporeal energies, spirits who are gods and goddesses, spirits of the dead who have progressed beyond the land of the dead" (25–6). Furthermore, Anzaldúa comments that the underworld itself is the soul's perspective of the world, and that one journeys to the underworld to retrieve the pieces of the soul that may be lost, as they would be through *susto*, the frightening of the soul from the body as discussed before. According to Anzaldúa, "these three interconnected, overlapping worlds are the same place" (26). The tree reaches deep within the psyche, to the deep reaches of the *less-than, the animal, the undivine* (the underworld), as well as far out to the *more-than, the cosmic, the divine* (the sky world). Despite this, everything on the tree happens simultaneously, causing an erasure of the boundaries between self, other, and world, because these boundaries are arbitrary.

Within this system representing both the cosmos and the self, Anzaldúa introduces the *nagual*, the guardian or totem spirit that acts as a bridge between the two, and thus as a bridge between the undivine and the divine, allowing the individual to benefit from both. The term is derived from indigenous *Nahua* belief structures, representing the ability to shapeshift into one or more animals. According to philosopher James Maffie in his book *Aztec Philosophy* (2014), the term is often used to refer to a deeper unconscious transformative power or spirit that is more magical or extraordinary than the standardly visible expression of life, *tonal or tonalli* (38). Anzaldúa is given to translate this term as "totem spirit" or "guardian" (Anzaldúa 2015, 27). Anzaldúa acquired this *nagual* in the form of a snake, which is the primary shape that she associates with shapeshifting experiences. More specifically, she experienced *la víbora, the viper*. As a child, on a cotton ranch, she was bitten by a rattlesnake.

> I barely felt its fangs, Boot got all the [poison][5] . . . my animal counterpart . . . since that day I've sought and shunned them. Always when they cross my path, fear and elation flood my body. I know things older than Freud, older than gender. She—that's how I think of la Víbora, Snake Woman . . . . Forty years it's taken me to enter into the Serpent, to acknowledge that I have a body, that I am a body and to assimilate the animal body, the animal soul. (Anzaldúa 1987, 26)

Like her experiences with the Goddess and the Shadow-Beast, we again see the imagery of the snake. Anzaldúa's goddess is associated with snake imagery and now so is her shapeshifter spirit, her *nagual*. However, one must also note that the snake has a connection to the Shadow-Beast as well. Anzaldúa refers to her Shadow-Beast as a human-serpent *thing* with "lidless serpent eyes . . . cold clammy moist [hands] dragging us underground, fangs barred and hissing." Further, when seeking reconciliation with the Beast, she asks, "How does one put feathers on this particular serpent" (1987, 20)?[6] This shows the *undivine* nature of the *nagual*, connecting it not only to the *undivine* as an animal but to the ultimate expression of *undivinity* in humans, the monster dwelling within oneself. In this analysis, the Beast itself shares much symbolism with *Coatlicue* in its depiction, particularly the need to face its visage in the mirror, and the unmistakable imagery of "serpent eyes."

The *nagual*, therefore, cannot be categorized as wholly divine or undivine and simultaneously cannot be excluded from either. Anzaldúa's description of the power of her shapeshifted form in *Light in the Dark/Luz en lo Oscuro* would seem to support this dual nature:

> I'm aware of my breath and my heartbeat, but nothing else. Time collapses. My body shifts gears. [My body][7] becomes part of, merges with, "disappears" into my surroundings. When my consciousness flows out into an animal, it becomes my vehicle, to feel, touch, hear, taste, and smell in the underworld and otherworld. This real/imaginal animal initiates me into these worlds via its perspective and "language." (2015, 27)[8]

The key here is the use of the term "otherworld." While the underworld is the realm of the undivine and basic, and the sky world is the realm of the divine, and complex, the otherworld exists in association with both (27).

The concept of *la facultad* from my discussion of the Shadow-Beast and the undivine becomes relevant here. Anzaldúa in her earlier writing explains *la facultad* as a heightened sensory capacity stemming from trauma, which I maintain is the beginning of the undivine survivalistic animal (the Shadow-Beast) developing into the *divine*. In later writing, however, the meaning of *la facultad* is expanded to reference not merely a sixth sense, but the capacity to carry/be *nagual* or otherwise to be a shapeshifter (Anzaldúa 2015, 26). Further, one of the powers of the *nagual* is to sense the *otherworld*, which she defines as everything in association with the nonstandard reality. *Undivine* animal instinct, therefore, makes way for *divine* perception and power. Describing the relationship between the bodily, particularly sexual, and mystical forces, Jeffrey J. Kripal (2017, 63) states that "radio was made for the radio signal, and vice versa." Just as with the radio signal, there would seem to be a made-for-ness in the relationship between the animalistic *undivine* and the godly *divine*. They are inseparable and cannot be understood without the other. If we take Anzaldúa's example, this trait would seem to be true of monstrosity and divinity as well.

BOLT CUTTERS FOR THE CAGE

Where does the shapeshifter or *nagual* leave the concepts of monstrosity and divinity then? If (1) the role of the monstrous undivine is to break uniformity through fragmentation by testing weaknesses and points of stress in one's construction of reality and (2) the godly divine's role is to create unity from these fragmentations by mending cracks and creating better structures, then (3) the shapeshifter represents command of this process, an understanding of the principles of fragmentation and unity that results in one simultaneously being monstrous and godly. Indeed, there is a link in Anzaldúa's writing between possession of the heightened instinct *la facultad* and possession of the *nagual*. This link becomes especially pronounced in her later writings, where she makes explicit the links between the two (Anzaldúa 2015, 26).

This linkage is further enhanced through Anzaldúa's incorporation of divinity via another serpent goddess, *Cihuacoatl*. Anzaldúa describes *Cihuacoatl* as the antecedent to *La Llorona,* the wailing ghost woman of Mexican folklore (2015, 166). *La Llorona* was originally human, but her trauma transformed her into something supernatural. Sometimes she snaps and drowns her children, sometimes her husband is the one who drowns her children, causing her to snap and kill him, but in most cases she is transformed by the abuse of her husband, a trauma which transforms her into a supernatural creature. While most describe *La Llorona* as a child-abducting monster, often to their children so as to keep them from wandering around at night, Anzaldúa describes her as searching for pieces of herself, represented by her children, much as Anzaldúa had to undergo reassembly as the result of *susto* (1987, 38). *Cihuacoatl/La Llorona* represents, for Anzaldúa, "not the root of all evil, but instinctual knowledge and other alternative ways of knowing that fuel transformation" (2015, 121).

If we read the divine as a catalyst for unity and growth by way of fragmentation, and the animalistic undivine as that which actually sparks this fragmentation, then the shapeshifter is a sort of monstrous, divinized human. By this I mean, as one who understands the processes of unity and fragmentation, the shapeshifter taken as either monster or ally (for Anzaldúa it is most likely meant to be read as both, a divine monstrofication of sorts), can be the author of these forces for good or ill. This concept reflects Kripal's "mytheme" of *authorization*, which is characterized by an understanding of the forces which author our responses to the world, giving way to a measure of control over them, literally a breaking free of limiting forces. Kripal's "mythemes" are based on his study of people who have had recurring paranormal experiences or encounters with otherworldly entities and ultimately found meaning in them. He explains that authorization means "we do not need to be puppets at the mercy of some neurological programmer, or for that matter the authoritarian dictates of some sky-god . . . we can recognize that we are pulling our own strings, that the angels and aliens *are us*" (Kripal 2015, 28). The antagonist of the Anzaldúan story is not the monsters, but the system that would keep us from recognizing the utility of the monstrous, and its use in the human ecosystem.

CONCLUSION: FRAGILE REALITY, ROBUST IDENTITY

Charles H. Long uses the concept of the *rupture of myth* to explain the point in a myth wherein an a-priori, unexpressive, and basal world suddenly begins to change (Long 1995, 34). Long describes creation stories by the use of this principle; however, it is also reflected in Anzaldúa's concept of the supernatural, particularly as it relates to humans, gods, and monsters. Silencing or caging builds a need to express—to prove one exists and to escape the cage (35). In this way, through her discussion of the supernatural, Anzaldúa is creating something akin to the rupture of myth.

Anzaldúa attempts to show us that the order of things—to once again echo Beale's analysis of the mythological cycles of the Ancient Near East—is precarious and inherently unsustainable to a degree (Beale 2002, 21). However, as reflected in Anzaldúa's schema, this is the point. Reality does not abide stagnation. What is perhaps most interesting about Anzaldúa's mysticism and concept of the supernatural, however, is that control of one's life comes through a process of monstrofication. Through embracing the "other" within the self, one embraces an outer reality which exists independently of the self. This process then allows one to become a divinized monster, a rupture of myth in one's own right.

This process of monstrofication, of breaking through the cage of naturalness imposed by rationality, can be seen throughout Anzaldúa's work. It can be seen in her political philosophy of *nepantleria* (lit. worker of liminal space), wherein the primary goal is to guard the sacredness of the emergence of new modes of identification and knowledge, as well as to "guard against reproducing exclusions based on racial and class identity" (Anzaldúa 2015, 83). She describes *nepantleros* and *nepantleras*, adherents to this philosophy, seeing through "our own cultural conditioning and dysfunctional values" (83). The monsters of our social sphere for Anzaldúa must be confronted and dealt with, not simply the ones contained to our psyche.

Whether the gods and monsters of Anzaldúa's world are literal or figurative is the wrong question—she would certainly say so, at any rate. Rather, the Anzaldúan supernatural is built upon the dominant societies assumptions of what is natural, or more accurately, what is normal. From within those assumptions—which may be socially enforced or internalized—monsters arise, and gods subsequently descend upon those monsters to bring them into the ranks of divinity. Amid all this, we attempt to understand the nature of these entities in our own lives, literally or figuratively, and attempt to inhabit the third space of the shapeshifter—the divinized monstrosity.

NOTES

1. See also Corbin (1972, 8).
2. More detailed explanation of *susto* may be found in Rubel et al. (1984) and Knab (1995).
3. *Miro que estoy encabronada, miro la Resistencia.*
4. The term "monster" originally derives from the Latin *monstrum*, which refers to a sort of omen or message which serves to reveal divine will or judgment. For a detailed analysis of the etymology of the term "monster," see Beal (2002, 4–5).
5. *Veneno.*
6. This is a reference to Quetzalcoatl, the Aztecan god of life, and clearly a plea to create divinity from the undivine.
7. *Mi cuerpo.*
8. See Long (1995, 51) for an approximation of language. Here Anzaldúa is describing a code-shift in her subjectivity.

Chapter 15

The Monster Within
Rape and Revenge in Genesis 34
Leland Merritt

During the 1970s and 1980s, horror fans were obsessed with the "Rape-and-Revenge" subgenre that dominated ticket sales and video rentals. Movies such as *The Last House on the Left* and *I Spit on Your Grave* offered audiences an interesting, albeit gruesome question: What would you do if you or someone you loved was raped and left for dead? The films depict horrific scenes of violence that would leave our protagonist either dead or not far from it. However, the final act of these exploitation films would thrill audiences with violent revenge that would philosophically "fit the crime." Yet, these films do not let the audiences off easily. Whether it is Töre promising to build a church as reparations for his violence in Ingmar Bergman's *The Virgin Spring* or Jennifer entering a church and asking for forgiveness for what she is about to do in *I Spit on Your Grave*; the audience is left to decide if these acts of violence are justified or monstrous.

While "Rape-and-Revenge" films have been popular for the last half century, film is not the first medium to ponder these questions. The question of violence as retribution to rape is present even in the Hebrew Bible. In particular, Genesis 34 recounts the story of Dinah's rape at the hands of the local prince and the subsequent revenge brought on by Dinah's brothers. In the same way that the horror movies ask if the revenge creates monsters of the protagonists; Genesis 34 asks if the brothers' actions are worth the trouble that they will bring. This chapter will argue that Genesis 34 is a "Rape-and-Revenge" story that utilizes horror to demonize Israel's enemies while offering a complicated portrayal of its heroes. While pondering the principal of *lex talionis* with images of extreme violence, the text's complex morality begs the questions: What is the cost of vengeance? Who are the monsters in the text?

A basic definition of what constitutes a Rape-and-Revenge story is quite simple: A Rape-and-Revenge story must contain a rape and a retributive action because of that rape. This broad definition allows for a lot of variance among its media representations, and while many of its iterations fall into the horror genre,[1] Rape-and-Revenge is not itself a genre. Rather, it is a narrative structure (Read 2000, 25). While the events that take place in a Rape-and-Revenge narrative are certainly horrifying, that alone does not make them "horror films." In fact, Rape-and-Revenge films have appeared in American cinemas since the dawn of the silver screen. Films such as D.W. Griffith's 1919 film *Broken Blossoms* or Alfred Hitchcock's 1929 film *Blackmail* were using themes of rape-and-revenge before sound came to the cinema.

It is clear that Genesis 34 fits the basic definition of a Rape-and-Revenge narrative. Shechem, prince of the city "Shechem," rapes[2] Dinah in verse 2 and Dinah's brothers kill Shechem, his father, and the men of the city in verses 25–27. The Rape-and-Revenge cycle is completed. However, it is not just the fact that a character is raped and the rape is avenged that makes this classification interesting. Genesis 34 utilizes themes that are common within other Rape-and-Revenge narratives. This chapter will look at three films in conjunction with Genesis 34. The films are Ingmar Bergman's 1960 film *Jungfrukällan* (English: *The Virgin Spring*), Wes Craven's 1972 film *The Last House on the Left*, and Meir Zarchi's 1978 film *I Spit on Your Grave*.

I have chosen these three films, not only because of their mark on popular culture[3] but also because these three films utilize the Rape-and-Revenge narrative structure in a similar way to Genesis 34. Understanding these films offers a new way to understand and interpret the themes of the passage. There are four major themes: country versus city, the sympathetic monster, deceit and castration, and the monstrous actions of our heroes. All four of these themes are central parts that make up the Rape-and-Revenge cycle in these four narratives.

COUNTRY VERSUS CITY

The rural versus urban divide is not new to the world. It seems to be a central fear in every culture and expresses the fear of the unknown outsider. In fairy tales, the protagonist must travel through the dark forest to get to the next village. However, dark things live in the forest. There is a fear of that which is not like us. People in the city look down on country folks as uneducated, simple-minded inbreds who eat roadkill. On the other hand, people in the country view city dwellers as amoral snobs. The city is where you are mugged; you do not have to lock your doors at night in the country. These stories create monsters out of the other. Carol Clover states, "[In horror films,] country people live beyond the reaches of social law. They do not observe the civilized rules of hygiene or personal habit. If city men are either clean-shaven or wear stylish beards or moustaches, country-men sport stubble. . . . The typical country rapist is a toothless or rotten-toothed single man with a four-day growth" (Clover 2015, 125). The narratives portray the country bumpkin as monstrous other. They are human, but something is not quite right.

In *The Virgin Spring*, the goat herders are wearing dirty rags. Their smiles reveal missing and crocked teeth. This is contrasted by the fancy dress that Karin wears. The whiteness of her hair and cleanness of her dress represent her purity, whereas the goat herders' black and dirtied clothes represent their evil. "What is threatening about these little uncivilities is the larger uncivility of which they are surface symptoms. In horror, the man who does not take care of his teeth is obviously a man who can plunder, rape, murder, beat his wife and children, kill within his kin, commit incest, and/or eat human flesh" (Clover 2015, 126). The goat herders do not come from a village or a city; they come from the hinterland. They are abject. Thus, the goat herders are a people who are not bound to a law. This is the city dweller's fear of the country. The rural country is a land that is not held to the same laws as the city.

The Last House on the Left follows *The Virgin Spring*'s demonization of the other but reverses the location. In this instance, the Collingwoods live out in the country, while the monstrous other resides in the city. The opening credits of the movie are peaceful shots of nature before focusing on the Collingwood's country home. The opening scene is a dialogue between Dr. John Collingwood and his wife, Estelle. Dr. Collingwood sits in his chair, reading the newspaper, when Estelle asks him "What's new in the outside world?" He responds, "Same old stuff, murder and mayhem." This innocuous conversation sets the stage for the movie. The outside world is "murder and mayhem" and it is about to be brought to the front door of the Collingwood's home. As the scene develops, Mari enters the room ready to meet her friend for a concert in the city. Contrasting *The Virgin Spring*'s emphasis on the daughter's purity, Mari is wearing red, and her parents comment on how she is not wearing a bra. Craven is playing with the emphasis of virginal purity in *The Virgin Spring*. Whereas, Karin in *The Virgin Spring* wore a bright dress and was riding into town to deliver candles to a church; Mari is wearing red and going into town to see a band named Bloodlust. "Aren't those the guys who dismember chickens?" asks Dr. Collingwood. "They only did that once" Mari responds. Craven's point is clear. Just because the daughter is not as pure as Bergman's Karin; the rape is not any less brutal. Differences aside, the monstrous other is still present in *The Last House on the Left*. Mari's parents are clearly loving toward their daughter, and they will not stop her from going to the concert, but not without noting their concern. There is a distinction between the Collingwood's peaceful, country home, and the urban neighborhood where chicken-dismembering bands play heavy metal. In the city, the girls will meet Junior whose years of drug abuse have dissolved much of his mind. His teeth are crooked, and his speech is slow. The gang's hideout is dirty with a single mattress on the floor where the single female member services the group's leader, Krug. A stark contrast to the Collingwood's well-ordered house.

Perhaps, of the three movies, the contrast between city and country is most palpable in *I Spit on Your Grave*. The movie begins with shots of Jennifer leaving her New York City apartment, wearing a nice dress. Upon arrival in the country town, she meets three of the four-gang members at a gas station. Johnny, the leader of the gang, works as a gas station attendant and pumps Jennifer's gas, while Stanley and Andy (both unemployed) wrestle in the yard. This scene is full of economic undertones. Jennifer is a New York socialite dress in a clean dress while Johnny is a blue-collar worker, covered in grease. Jennifer's first meeting with Matthew, the mentally disabled grocery delivery boy who is the fourth member of the gang, focuses again on the economic contrast between the two. After Matthew comments that Jennifer "comes from an evil place," Jennifer gives him a tip and remarks, "Here's a tip from an evil New Yorker." "I've never gotten a tip like that before!" shouts Matthew. *I Spit on Your Grave* equates the city with riches and the country with poverty. As Carol J. Clover states, "To be from the country is, by the same token, to be poor" (Clover 2015, 120). While the other films also contain the economic divide (Töre's prosperous farm versus the poor goat herders and the nice Collingwood, country home versus the dilapidated apartment of runaway convicts), it is consistently evident in *I Spit on Your Grave*.

Genesis 34 is a text driven by the conflict between pastoral nomads and established villages. In the same way, the city people fear the country and country people fear the city, Villages feared pastoral nomads. Bible scholars, Matthews and Benjamin, speculate on the dangers that pastoral nomads posed to villages. "If foreign herders passed unchallenged through their land, important military information might be transmitted to an enemy, or scarce natural resources might be exhausted . . . foreign herders might engage in raiding or other unsanctioned activities which would drain the local economy" (Matthews and Benjamin 1993, 55). In the mind of the villagers, pastoral nomads are the monstrous other. Note that the rapists in *The Virgin Spring* are goat herders and the gang in *The Last House on the Left* disguise themselves as traveling salesmen. The fear of the itinerate stranger is well established in horror.

Genesis 34 is a text that is highly concerned about the purity versus impurity of the monstrous other. Similar to the films, economic issues define the conflict. For the villagers, the conflict with pastoral nomads is an economic issue. Herders could raid, steal, encroach upon local resources, control trade routes, or share important information with one's enemies. On the other hand, a covenant with a group of herders could be economically advantageous (Matthews and Benjamin 1993, 53–5). Hamor and Shechem portray these concerns during their marriage negotiations with the family of Jacob. Hamor's appeals to the economic side of the sons of Jacob by describing the economic benefits of marrying Dinah to Shechem (Genesis 34:10). Shechem is willing to set the bride price as high as they want to convince the brothers (Genesis 34:14). The economic inequality ultimately will not matter because the brothers of Dinah will take all of the city's wealth during their destruction (Genesis 34: 27). While in the films, the poor rape the rich, Genesis 34 is the opposite. The local village leadership rapes a young girl from the nomads outside of the city. While the films seem to be concerned about an attack on traditional family values, Genesis 34 seems concerned about an attack on Israelite purity.

SYMPATHETIC MONSTERS

A common theme in all four of these narratives is the complicated rapists. The narratives are centered on the monstrous other, but the stories bring out a human element. There remains sense of regret among (at least one member of) the rapists. However, the narratives do not let these characters off the hook. The wages of rape is death and in each of these narratives, a rapist will regret his actions but the regret is not enough to keep him alive. Jeremy Morris argues that according to the principles of *lex talionis*, a crime must be appropriately punished. "By acting in a certain way toward others, I am accepting that others can act in that way toward me. If I murder . . . then I should be treated as a murderer. In murdering I have chosen murder as the rule, and so I may be justly killed" (2012, 46). In the eyes of Rape-and-Revenge narratives, if one rapes then they have chosen violence as the rule, and may be justly killed. Their level of regret is not taken into consideration by the avengers.

In *The Virgin Spring*, one of the three goat herders is a young boy around the age of ten. While he does not sexually assault Karin, he does participate in trapping and seizing her. After the two men rape and beat her, the men tell the boy to remain there while they go destroy the evidence. The boy waits, staring at Karin's lifeless body, as it begins to snow. He tries to bury her by covering her in dirt but quickly gives up and runs away. Later, Töre offers the goat herders shelter, the boy's guilt begins to manifest. He spills his dinner and is sent to bed. Once in bed, he continues to look on with a distorted face that portrays his guilt. Once the killing begins, the boy will run to Märeta for protection. Töre rips the boy from his wife, lifts him above his head and throws him across the room, killing him.

The Last House on the Left, which is highly influenced by *The Virgin Spring*, also focuses on one of the rapist's son. However, in *The Last House on the Left*, the son is in his twenties. Still, throughout the film, the narrative reveals the verbal, emotional, and physical abuse that Junior experienced at the hands of Krug, Junior's father. Junior is also addicted to heroin, and his mental capabilities are clearly not all there. After the rape scene, while the other rapists are disposing of Phyllis, Junior is left guarding Mari. She attempts to convince Junior that they should run away together and get married. Junior considers this, not realizing Mari is deceiving him to get away. At his weakest moment, Mari does escape, only to be caught by the rest of the gang. Junior does attempt to redeem himself by shooting at his father during his struggle with Mr. Collingwood. Junior's shot misses. Krug turns his attention to his son and with one last string of emotional abuse convinces Junior to shoot himself in the head. Junior would never be able to rid himself of his father's control over him. Even though Junior is not killed by the Collingwoods, his death is still justified by the narrative structure.

In Genesis 34, Shechem brutally rapes Dinah in verse 2. The rape is described with a string of three verbs. "When Shechem, son of Hamor the Hivite, prince of the land, saw her, he took her (ויקח אתה) and he layed her (וחשכב אתה), and he raped her (ויענה). Verse three complicates the narrative's portrayal of Shechem with another string of three verbs. "And his soul was drawn (ותרבק) to Dinah, daughter of Jacob, he loved (ויאהב) the girl, and he spoke tenderly (וידבר על-לב) to the girl." The three verbs in verse three contrast the verbs in verse 2. The one who just raped Dinah is now claiming that he loves her. Susanne Scholz explains Shechem's actions as typical of rapists. "Feminist scholarship discloses that rapists often try to appear 'normal' after the rape, especially in situations of acquaintance rape. Differentiating between 'hostility rape' and 'sexual gratification rape,' feminist scholars explain that the latter is the more ambiguous and confused one" (Scholz 2000, 141). Therefore, Shechem's love for Dinah is better explained as guilt for his actions. His proclamation to marry her is a way to soothe over Dinah and to keep the peace between the village and the pastoral nomads outside the walls. Hamor's opening statement during the marriage negotiations mentions Shechem's desire for Dinah (verse 8). Shechem is willing to pay anything for the marriage present as long as they give Dinah as his wife (Verse 12). Once the brothers agree to the marriage terms, Hamor and Shechem do not delay because "he was delighted with Jacob's daughter" (verse 19). However, Shechem's love means nothing to the sons of Jacob. Shechem's love for Dinah does not change the fact that he raped her. In verses 26–28, the brothers kill Hamor and Shechem, plunder the city, and take all the wealth of the city (including the women and children). In the minds of Dinah's brothers, the Hivites' rape of Dinah justifies their plundering of their village: A violent act for a violent act. How Shechem feels about Dinah has no bearing on the punishment.

CASTRATION AND CIRCUMCISION

Above, I argued that these narratives are structured as a city vs. country (or village vs. pastoral nomads) conflict. While there is an "us vs. them" component, Rape-and-Revenge always involves a gendered conflict. Even when the rape is male-on-male (see *Deliverance* 1972) the act of being raped is connected to emasculation. Carol Clover (2015, 160) notes the play between city/country and femininity/masculinity in *I Spit on Your Grave*:

> She is a woman because she is from the city. There has always been a strong hint of the unmasculine in the attributes ascribed to urban folk in a country setting. Even when they are tall and healthy, city men are seen as appearance-concerned, trinket-laden physically weak and incompetent, queasy about the hard facts of rural life, unfamiliar with weapons and fearful of them, overly dependent on the buyable services of others, and even under duress, given to tears . . . The sense of effeminacy that has always attended the worry about hypercivilization is now manifest in a "naturally" rapable female body.

For Clover, Jennifer is raped because she is a woman, but also "a woman because she is raped" (Clover 2015, 160). Rape is about one's power over another. In Rape-and-Revenge narratives, those who are raped are portrayed as being softer, weaker, and more feminine. In *The Virgin Spring* and *The Last House on the Left*, the fathers are portrayed as being rich and thus out of touch with the realities of physical hardship. Within these stories, they are symbolically castrated because of their failure to protect the women of their house. Jacinda Read suggests, "In other words, for female characters rape is represented as both a result of, and a violation of, their femininity and for male characters as a violation of their masculine ability to protect women" (Read 2000, 94). In these narratives, to rape one's daughter is to castrate the father.

For Read (2000, 94), there is still a difference between the castrated male and the raped female: "While women's responses to rape are often shown to result in an unnatural rejection of feminity that must be rectified, men's responses to rape are shown to arise out of nothing more than natural and normal masculine behavior." These narratives portray men and women's revenge quite differently. The men will resort to brutal violence, while the women will use deceit to level the playing field.

In *The Virgin Spring* and *The Last House on the Left*, the mourning fathers enact their revenge by directly coming face to face with their daughter's rapists. Töre walks into the room where the three goat herders are sleeping, wakes them, and engages in a knife fight with them. The knife symbolically penetrating the two older men before Töre seizes the boy. In *The Last House on the Left*, Dr. Collingwood's weapons of choice are a shotgun and a chainsaw. Dr. Collingwood thrusts the chainsaw toward Krug in a phallic manner.

The women in these narratives utilize deception to exact their revenge, though no less violently. In *The Last House on the Left*, Estelle Collingwood meets Weasel in the kitchen while her husband prepares in the basement. She pretends to seduce Weasel and leads him outside to a nearby lake, promising that she did not want her husband to hear. Once at the lake, Estelle performs fellatio on Weasel and as he nears climax, she bites down, disarming Weasel of his weapon.

In a similar manner, Jennifer uses her femininity to deceive her rapists into a trap. At the start of her revenge, she calls the grocery store to have Matthew deliver groceries to her cabin. Upon his arrival, Jennifer appears next to a tree wearing only a white cotton robe. Her stance resembles "Aphrodite on the half shell." She acts as a siren promising Matthew pleasure, but luring him into pain. Barbara Creed (1993, 129) describes her as "dressed in the garb of a priestess or nymph." Matthew shouts that he hates her, but she begins to disrobe and walks further into the forest. Matthew follows her next to a tree, where they begin to have intercourse. As Matthew approaches his climax, Jennifer wraps a noose around his neck and trips a rope trap, causing Matthew to hang from a tree, naked. In the following scene, Jennifer approaches Johnny at his gas station. She talks him into getting into the car with her. Johnny follows her because he believes that she really wanted it (Clover 2015, 117). She takes him back to her cabin, draws a bath, and services him with her hands. As he climaxes, Jennifer reaches next to the tub, grabs a knife, and castrates Johnny. With two members of their gang now missing, Stanley and Andy decide to finish what they started, but Jennifer uses deception one more time. While Andy is ashore, Jennifer, wearing a bikini, swims out to Stanley's boat, climbs aboard, making sure to show off her derrière in the process. This shot reeks of the male gaze, but Jennifer uses it to her advantage. Stanley, stunned by Jennifer's forwardness, loses his baring and gives her the upper hand.

In Genesis 34, the men of Jacob's family are castrated. The act of rape was an attack on the men's ability to protect the women of their household. "Rape in the world of the Bible was not simply an act of sexual violence, but a political challenge to the father of a household" (Matthews and Benjamin 1993, 178). While the sons of Jacob will use brutal violence in verses 25–28, they utilize feminine deceit similar to the women in *The Last House on the Left* and *I Spit on Your Grave*. Notably, the family of Jacob are pastoral nomads. In foreign lands, pastoral nomads were at a disadvantage when negotiating with villages. Shechem's rape of Dinah is symbolic of the Hivite's power over the family of Jacob. Estelle Collingwood and Jennifer Hills use sexual seduction to lure their victims into their trap. Similarly, Dinah's brothers use the promise of marriage to their sister and their daughters to deceive Shechem and Hamor. For the sons of Jacob, circumcision was a purifying ritual that would combine the two families. Circumcision was a mark of their kinship (Eilberg-Schwartz 1990, 164). Shechem and Hamor blinded by their sexual and economic desires miss the trap in front of them. The Hivites believed that circumcision had made them pure in the eyes of the sons of Jacob; instead, it made them vulnerable. Every male in the city was incapacitated by the surgery; thus, the city was left unprotected and, to use Clover's language (2015, 160), rapable. The principle of *lex talionis* prevails, a castration for a castration.

THE MONSTER WITHIN

With the revenge finished, the Rape-and-Revenge cycle is complete. However, these narratives do not end with the final knife thrust into the remaining rapist's heart. For the films, the camera keeps rolling, and Genesis 34 proceeds. These narratives are not simply *lex talionis* stories. The narrative always asks the question, "Was this justified or has the protagonist become the monster?" In *The Virgin Spring,* Töre looks at what he has done, as the camera shows shots of his victims lying in cross formations. He falls to his knees and begs for God's forgiveness. He then marches with his family to where his daughter's corpse lays. He vows to God that he will build a church there and as he picks up his daughter, a spring shoots forth from the ground. The family washes their hands in the spring, symbolically cleansing themselves. Heller-Nicholas notes: "The violence and cruelty of Karin's rape and murder supposedly corresponds with the intensity of Töre's bloodlust. In turn, this facilitates the impact of his spiritual conversion at the film's conclusion at the discovery of the "virgin spring" (Heller-Nicholas 2011, 23). *The Virgin Spring* is about the transformation of a law-abiding, Christian, family man into a violent monster, and then back again.

The Last House on the Left does not offer the same redemption to the Collingwoods. The police arrive just as Estelle kills Sadie and Dr. Collingwood mutilates Krug with a chainsaw. The final shots of the film are of the Collingwood's wrecked living room. John Collingwood sits on a turned over couch, looking down at his chainsaw, when Estelle comes over to comfort him. The only sound is John's heavy breathing. The deputy comes over and takes the chain saw from him, and the camera focuses in on Dr. Collingwood's disgusted face. He does not know what he has become. In contrast to its predecessor, no church will be built and no spring will flow forth. "Craven's rejection of a happily-ever-after universe is an ethical statement in its own right. . . . In *The Last House on the Left*, violence begets more violence, and an assumption that 'good' will triumph over 'evil' has been exposed as naïve in the world in which it is set" (Heller-Nicholas 2011, 38). In *I Spit on Your Grave*, before Jennifer begins her revenge, she dresses in all black, drives to a church approaches the Cross, gets on her knees, and says, "Forgive me, forgive me." In the final shot of the film, Jennifer escapes on a motorboat, but as she speeds away, her face is stoic as she ponders her actions. The credits begin to roll. In a world run by *lex talionis*, Jennifer's actions are justified. Yet, the director does not let Jennifer celebrate nor does the audience cheer.

Genesis 34 proposes the same question as the films: "Are the brothers' actions justified?" According to the principle of *lex talionis*, the answer is yes. However, Genesis 34 offers an alternative view through Jacob's only words in the chapter: "You have brought trouble on me by making me odious to the inhabitants of the land, the Canaanites and the Perizzites; my numbers are few, and if they gather themselves against me and attack me, I shall be exterminated, both I and my house" (Verse 30). Jacob is describing himself as a monster in the eyes of the inhabitants of the land. Noel Carroll's (1990, 26) seminal work "The Philosophy of Horror" argues that a monster is horrifying when it induces fear and disgust. In verse 30, the Canaanites have witnessed the destructive nature of the family of Jacob. Jacob's sons have killed every male in the city, plundered the city, captured the women and children, and stolen all of its wealth. In her tremendous article on horror and rape/revenge in Judges 4–5, Rhiannon Graybill notes that rape is a result of warfare in the book of Judges. "Sexual violence as a weapon of warfare is widely attested in ancient literature and contemporary reality. . . . This lawlessness frequently means violence against female bodies" (2018, 20). This same lawlessness is present in Genesis 34. The brothers' answer to the rape of their sister includes the rape and kidnapping of the Hivite women (Verse 29). In search of retribution, they have become monsters.

The Jacobite nomads are clearly a violent threat that must concern the other inhabitants in the land. However, for Carroll, it is not just the threat that creates a monster; the monster must also disgust its viewers. Jacob states, "You have brought trouble on me by making me rancid (ינשיאבהל) to the inhabitants of the land." The root שאב is used in the Hebrew Bible to describe the rotting flesh of dead fish and spoiled food.[4] Jacob's description here is to conjure up the image of dead flesh baking in the hot sun. Images of Dracula's cold flesh, the rotting corpses of zombies, or Frankenstein's bolted-together beast convey horror. They are both threatening and disgusting.

However, it is what people do to monsters that concerns Jacob most: "My numbers are few and they will gather together against me and they will smite me and they will exterminate me, both I and my house." Jacob's imagery brings to mind the image of the angry crowd surrounding Frankenstein's monster in Universal's *Frankenstein* (1931). Jacob's numbers are few and he now has enemies on all sides. His sons, through their deceit and violence, have tainted any political or economic treaties that Jacob had hoped to make. If the inhabitants band together, there is no stopping them from utterly ruining the house of Jacob. Thus, Jacob must ask his sons, "Was this worth it?"

Jacob's sons respond in a fashion that exhibits *lex talionis*, "Should our sister be treated like a whore?" (Verse 31). Thus, verses 30 and 31 act as two opposing thesis statements for the two sides. Verse 30 argues that peace must be maintained, even at the cost of our daughters. While verse 31 argues that the wages of rape is death. Yet, the text does not answer which side is correct. The chapter ends, and the issue is left unanswered. Just as Dr. Collingwood is left staring at his chainsaw and Jennifer is left pondering her actions, the text leaves the reader pondering the question, "Who is the monster?"

In conclusion, it is unquestionable that Genesis 34 fits the narrative Rape-and-Revenge structure. Shechem rapes Dinah in verse 2 and her brothers enact their revenge in verses 25–28. However, by analyzing Genesis 34 in light of other Rape-and-Revenge narratives (namely *The Virgin Spring*, *The Last House on the Left*, and *I Spit on Your Grave*), the text's major themes are enlightened and explained. The text is not simply a story of a girl who is raped and her brothers' vengeance. Genesis 34 is a narrative about the complicated nature of *lex talionis*. The brothers were well within their rights to avenge their sister's honor. Yet, at what cost does it come? Friedrich Nietzsche (1998, 68) famously said, "He who fights with monsters should be careful lest he thereby become a monster. And if thou gaze long into an abyss, the abyss will also gaze into thee." Genesis 34 does not answer this question but allows the readers to consider the consequences and decide for themselves.

NOTES

1. Jacinda Read, *The New Avengers: Feminism, Femininity, and the Rape-Revenge Cycle* (New York: Manchester University Press, 2000) criticizes Carol J. Clover, *Men, Women, and Chain Saws: Gender in the Modern Horror Film* (Princeton, NJ: Princeton University Press, 2015), for only discussing horror movies that fit the Rape-and-Revenge structure. Further, Read criticizes Barbara Creed, *The Monstrous-Feminine: Film, Feminism, Psychoanalysis* (New York: Routledge, 1993) for

creating all *femme castrarices* as the "monstrous-feminine" thus categorizing all rape-and-revenge narratives as horror films.

2. Scholars have debated whether or not Dinah is actually raped. Lyn M. Bechtel, "What If Dinah Was Not Raped," *JSOT* 62 (1994), is right to point out the group dynamics of Shechem's actions in Genesis 34. However, Yael Shemesh, "Rape Is Rape Is Rape: The Story of Dinah and Shechem" rightly argues that Genesis 34 uses the same language that other rape narratives use.

3. *The Virgin Spring* won the Academy Award for Best Foreign Language Film in 1961.

4. See Ex. 7:18,21; 8:10; 16:20; Is. 50:2.

Chapter 16

"Monsters among Us"
The Cathartic Carnage of American Horror Story

Heidi Ippolito

While psychiatrist Ben Harmon (played by Dylan McDermott), quoted above, sees storytelling as a way to "control" or "cope with" fear, the hit television show *American Horror Story* (2011–present) aims not to mute our fears but to release, unmask, and identify with the American monsters that walk among us and live inside us. Created by Ryan Murphy and Brad Falchuk, *American Horror Story* (*AHS*) is an anthology series that first aired in 2011 on FX, and has since spawned a total of nine seasons, with four more seasons scheduled to air in the coming years.[1] Each season tells a self-contained story with different settings and characters, though many of the same actors are cast in multiple seasons, appearing and reappearing each year in fresh costumes and wigs—an ever-changing costume party for those repeatedly cast in Murphy's extravagant world of horrors. The first season (*Murder House*) begins in a haunted Los Angeles Victorian mansion and subsequent seasons reposition into new settings and plotlines: in sequence, season 2: *Asylum*, a 1960s mental institution; season 3: *Coven*, a witch coven in New Orleans; season 4: *Freak Show*, a 1950s traveling "freak show";[2] season 5: *Hotel*, the paranormal-prone Hotel Cortez in Los Angeles; season 6: *Roanoke*, a nightmarish reenactment TV show in Roanoke County; season 7: *Cult*, the aftermath of the 2016 presidential election; season 8: *Apocalypse*, an apocalypse orchestrated by the Antichrist; and season 9: *1984*, a 1980s summer camp that homages the slasher genre. Each semi-historical (or future) setting wields brutal carnage and ruthless dark humor to cathartically address the historical and contemporary traumas that flow from the veins of America's past and present. In other words, *AHS* provides therapy through entertainment, an invitation to be amused and as well as challenged. Polarizing ideas of good and evil are punctured, allowing for a communal experience with the wounds of humanity that move beyond categorical straight-jackets.

With its biting allegorical commentary and pastiche tones, *AHS* is part of a long legacy of complex, postmodern television monsters—*Buffy the Vampire Slayer* (1997–2003), *Supernatural* (2005–2020), *True Blood* (2008–2014), *The Vampire Diaries* (2009–2017), *The Walking Dead* (2010-present)—but its success has also helped to birth a new brood of supernatural shows that feature flawed, sympathetic characters—for example, *The Magicians* (2015–2020), *Lucifer* (2015–present), *Stranger Things* (2016–present), *A Discovery of Witches* (2018–present), *The Order* (2019–present), *The Witcher* (2019–present)—as well as remakes and reboots of *The X-Files* (2016–2018), *Charmed* (2018–present), *The Chilling Adventures of Sabrina* (2018–present), *Legacies* (2018–present) *Roswell, New Mexico* (2019–present), and *Nancy Drew* (2019–present).

In his book *Monsters in America*, W. Scott Poole presents monsters as "part of the genetic code" of our nation that "raise questions about . . . what we mean by the phrase 'American history'" (Poole 2018, 18, 22). Poole asserts that "monsters walk among us," not as psychological metaphors or media-imposed narratives, but as dangerous and enticing sirens who woo us into engaging with the bloody histories that fertilize American soil (24). Within this interpretation, *AHS* continues this project of presenting American history as "a quest . . . that will both terrify and fascinate" (15). Not only does the show take the supernatural and the ineffable seriously, but it also gestures audiences toward the acceptance of those who live within our national borders but are still deemed "Other." Each season of the show presents monsters as "meaning machines" that both define and defy what it means to be human (Halberstam 1995). The show's ability to embody and manipulate traditional "monster" categories (the witch, the ghost, the vampire, the zombie, etc.) reflects Jeffrey Jerome Cohen's notion that monsters do not fit "the Aristotelian taxonomic system" (Cohen 1996, 6).

However, as revealed in *AHS*, neither does America. Our country is a broken and mutating family made up of Others who have the potential to be accepted beyond monstrous stereotypes, as well as familiar faces whose friendly masks have fallen away in light of historic horrors. *AHS* breaks open a new traumatic narrative in each season, spilling blood and entrails out of the screen and onto living room floors. The show begins with marital infidelity that leads to death and familial destruction (*Murder House*) and subsequently moves on to expose: truth and lies found in both religion and science (*Asylum*); the enslavement of Black people and oppression of women (*Coven*); respect, visibility, and equality demanded by those who defy categories of American "normalcy" (*Freak Show*); vaccination, uncontrollable addictions, and spread of disease (*Hotel*); historical trauma inflicted on Indigenous lands and the people who return to exact vengeance (*Roanoke*); the fears and frustrations surrounding the 2016 presidential election (*Cult*); the ever-present potential of a global nuclear war (*Apocalypse*); and a commentary on the treatment of veterans and the way religious beliefs are wielded as an ethical shield (*1984*). While each season uncovers new sources of American monstrosity, they often haste through intense suffering into pseudo-happy endings. This structure results in a viewing experience that allows audiences to cathartically encounter the underbelly of American evils.

The persistent incursion of dark, monstrous (and often teen-oriented) television reflects a desire from American audiences (and creators) to have critical encounters with supernatural entertainment. But *why* do we enjoy watching a chilling assortment of references to America's unpleasant past (and, often times, present)? Why are viewers drawn to seeing historical trauma (racism, homophobia, serial murders, cruel medical experiments, Indigenous genocides, school shootings, etc.) flash across the screen? Tn *The Philosophy of Horror*, Noël Carroll defines this "paradox of horror" as "the question of how people can be attracted by what is repulsive" (Carroll 1990, 160). Carroll concludes that "contemporary horror fiction" is consistently popular due to a combination of "curiosity and fascination" that is able to "articulate the widespread anxiety of times of stress" (213). Horror stories drape the allure of curiosity over deeper discomforts. Categorical abominations stitch the strange and familiar together, creating hybrids that both draw *and* repel the gaze. Ravenous werewolves, mindless zombies, and hideous witches reflect a collective "uncertainty about living in the contemporary world" (213) as well as a fear of what the future holds. This often drums up nostalgia for the past, "when things seemed stable and a sense of certainty prevailed" (214). And yet, historical places and figures are often at the center of such dreadful tales, leaving no time or place without blood-smeared hands.

AHS combines nostalgic aesthetics with present anxieties to boil a unique American concoction of paradoxical horror. Fear of the past, present, and future collides with characters that defy categories, demanding a fresh interpretation of what it means to watch horror stories in the age of digital streaming services and social media. In this chapter, I will compare *AHS* to the vision of an ideal tragedy set out in the writings of Aristotle. Not only does *AHS* complicate our ideas of Aristotelian catharsis, but it also demonstrates why television (supernatural television in particular) is an ideal medium for this type of narrative. The popularity of *AHS* indicates that American audiences want to have these difficult conversations about our national sins (racism, sexism, ableism, etc.), even if we find them gruesome. Between horrified gasps and fingers rushing to cover our eyes, the bloody subjects often found in *AHS* are at once relatable and repellant. The supernatural settings provide a distancing safeguard (we are not in the "real" world), but the show's focus on ordinary human experiences makes these monstrous characters irresistibly relatable. While it is not a new impulse to locate the real within the unreal (fairy tales and horror stories have existed throughout human history), the current wave of supernatural horror television provides a unique insight into the multifaceted mind of how Americans understand and reckon with themselves.

THE VIOLENCE OF AMERICAN CATHARSIS

There is much that could be said (and has been said) on how *AHS* deals with the complicated "monstrosity" of gender, race, sexuality, disability, ageism, mental illness, class divides, politics, and sexual violence in the United States (Earle 2019; Iftene 2015; Janicker 2017; King 2017; LeBlanc 2018; O'Reilly 2019; Taylor 2012). Recently, viewers and critics have become especially vocal about the tendency for mainstream shows to use horror and fear as entertainment, particularly the graphic use of rape in *AHS,* as well as shows such as *Game of Thrones* (2011–2019), *The Handmaid's Tale* (2017–present), and *True Blood* (2008–2014). But concerns regarding violence and exploitation on television are hardly new. The complex relationships between culture, art, violence, exploitation, and mass media are beyond this chapter's scope, but these factors certainly play a role.[3] In Poole's words, "It would be too simplistic to view monster tales as simply narratives in service of American violence" (20).

Instead, this chapter will focus more broadly on *AHS*'s overall ability to facilitate cathartic experiences through gory, visually iconic, semi-satirical television. Admittedly, the show takes full advantage of classic horror tropes and current cultural trauma to achieve its goal, but its deliberate irreverence reveals self-awareness and nuance rather than unbridled exploitation. In the words of TV critic Emily Nussbaum, the show is "rude"—it is "brazen and crude and funky" in a way that pushes against a "demand for politeness," erasure, and silence (Nussbaum 2014). Ultimately, *AHS* irreverently couples extreme violence, rude humor, and cultural awareness in an earnest attempt to platform marginalized identities and expose injustices.

The vulgar and colorful cast of blood-soaked characters in *AHS* lures viewers into shock-value entertainment that masks a deeper therapeutic significance. Each collection of stories gruesomely rips open the narrative seams our country has so carefully stitched into Franken-stories such as the American Dream, the Nuclear Family, and the Pursuit of Happiness. Patriarchal bread-winners cheat, dream homes are haunted, ambitions of fame end in murder and damnation, and romantic hopes are dashed by greed and bigotry. By exposing the underbelly of these iconic American ambitions, viewers must face the complex innards that make up our patchworked history: stolen Indigenous lives and lands, generations of kidnapped, enslaved, and oppressed Black lives, repression of female voices, disregarded people with disabilities and non-neurotypicalities, and an impossible expectation for individual success undergirded by a toxic dependence on capitalistic structures. These are just *some* of the nightmares that stare at us when we awaken from these hollow American Dreams.

In discussing American fantasies and nightmares, we might ask, "what does it mean for something to be 'American'?" (Earle and Clark 2019, 5). Harriet Earle and Jessica Clark tease out this question in their article on *AHS* for the *European Journal of American Culture*. For Earle and Clark, the show "creates a gruesome patchwork of the most interesting and degenerate parts of American public history, the parts of American life that horrify and titillate" (7). In fact, much of the success of the show builds on "the American cultural obsession with the dark and depraved" (ibid.)—depraved injustices that range from historical abuses of unchecked mental institutions to present-day bigotry surrounding the 2016 presidential election. In Nussbaum's words: "It's why we watch through our fingers, squinching our eyes. Why go to the circus if there's no chance of blood?" (Nussbaum 2014). The extreme content of *AHS* allows confrontation with these bloody transgressions, past and present, but also engenders compassion toward misunderstood individuals, which we often deem as Other.

The monsters in *AHS* are terrifying because we, the audience, are complicit in their perpetuation. For example, in the show's inaugural season, *Murder House*, Dr. Ben Harmon, his wife Vivian (Connie Britton), and daughter Violet (Taissa Farmiga) relocate as a way to move on from miscarriage and infidelity. However, their newfound haunted Los Angeles home seems to drag them deeper into the woes that many American families face: financial ruin, extra-marital affairs, depression, suicide, and home invasion. The show's third season follows a coven of witches in present-day New Orleans, but they are not the only group of local women who commune with the supernatural. The (primarily white) witches at Miss Robichaux's Academy must also contend with the high voodoo priestess, Marie Laveau (Angela Bassett), and her fierce protection over New Orleans' Ninth Ward. Initially presented as a story about outcast women and their struggle against patriarchal norms, this season concocts a disturbing brew of American racism and slavery, steeped in the complicated and often violent relationships between Black and white women.

AHS problematizes modern binaries by normalizing the Other through engaging storytelling and well-developed characters. Instead of pitting villains against heroes, the show teases out conflicts within similar groups. Instead of *controlling* these cultural fears, the show forces viewers to *face* the horrors of our American wrongdoings. Control is further relinquished in the patchwork of voices featured throughout the entire series; marginalized queer identities, people of color, people with mental and physical disabilities and differences, and women of a certain age take the spotlight, reminding us that the American stage must widen to accommodate all types, especially in light of its restrictive history.

ARISTOTLE'S *KATHARSIS*, REIMAGINED

What makes *AHS*, as a television show, particularly suited to telling these American monster stories? A peek into the crypt of the classics, to Aristotle's definition of tragic storytelling in his *Poetics*, is helpful here. For Aristotle, the successful effect of poetic tragedy is "universality" as well as "purification" or *katharsis* of "pity and fear" through a story that admirably imitates life on a grand scale (Aristotle, trans. 1996, 13–16). There has been much debate on the interpretation of *katharsis*, but translator Malcolm Heath's view is that, for Aristotle, *katharsis* does not get rid of emotion but "gets rid of an emotional excess" to achieve "a balanced state" that "mitigat[es]" "inappropriat[e]" feelings (xxxix–xl). Though it seems far-fetched to attain a balanced emotional state in our current American climate,[4] the ultimate cathartic goal in *AHS* is not to achieve social stasis, but to encounter explosive confrontation. A reoccurring character arc in almost every season is that of an intense revelation: in *Murder House*, Ben Harmon's daughter, Violet, must face her rotting corpse to come to terms with her death and current ghostly state; "Lobster Boy" Jimmy Darling (Evan Peters) falls in love with a con artist whose partner murders and mutilates members of Jimmy's troupe in *Freak Show*; and in *Hotel*, Detective John Lowe (Wes Bentley) investigates a string of murders, unconscious of his involvement in the crimes until it is too late. Each season ends on a seemingly balanced note, but not all of these characters find peace in their lives (most notably, Detective Lowe, who is gunned down by the police). In *AHS*, therefore, catharsis is not achieved by providing a gleeful Hollywood ending, but by brutally reflecting the complex unpredictability of life. Each season wraps up neatly, imposing an ending that is more contented than "happy," but within which exists a residue of the story's unpleasantness. There are no simplistic endings with wholly resolved problems, but rather an acknowledgment of discomfort and difficulty. This discomfort also lodges itself in the viewer, allowing the catharsis to live on past the show's final note.

While *AHS* provides for the viewer an Aristotlean catharsis—one in which emotions are not resolved, but balanced—it also works against Aristotle's notion that such stories must be anchored in "universality" rather than the "particular individual" (16). According to Aristotle, specificity is best left to the "lampoonists" of comedy, and "those who use spectacle to produce [a monstrous] effect" are working far outside the realm of tragedy (16; 22). *AHS,* however, challenges both of these assumptions. It blends historical fact and fiction in both broad and precise strokes to produce specific characters and settings that are entirely unique and engrossing to the viewer, while also using its signature dark humor to be unabashedly lampoonish and monstrous.

For example, the Hotel Cortez in *AHS*'s fifth season *Hotel* has all the trappings of a glamorous Los Angeles institution of a bygone era that has rotted away with the onslaught of modernity's Instagram influencers, competing Airbnb rentals, and harsh Yelp reviews. In a general sense, therefore, it resembles any number of seedy hotels that attract drug addicts, secret affairs, and naïve foreign tourists. More specifically, the Hotel Cortez draws clear inspiration from the Hotel Cecil in Los Angeles, a famed 1924 landmark connected to the Black Dahlia murder, "the Nightstalker" serial killer Richard Ramirez, and the mysterious death of a guest in 2013 (Barragan 2019). There is also a clear nod toward H. H. Holmes's notorious hotel built during the 1893 World's Fair in Chicago, full of labyrinth hallways that lead to nowhere and tortured bodies sealed behind brick walls.[5] Holmes himself seems to inspire *Hotel*'s "James Patrick March" (played by Evan Peters), an American serial killer prototype who continues his murderous rampages in ghost form, mentoring and hosting homicidal protégés such as Richard Ramirez, Aileen Wuornos, John Wayne Gacy, Jeffrey Dahmer, and the Zodiac Killer. The Hotel Cortez, therefore, is both a vague landmark and a vibrant home to a particular cast of living and undead characters: a timelessly chic vampire heiress (Lady Gaga), an eccentrically confident transgender bartender who makes amends with her estranged son (Denis O'Hare), an emotionally needy drug addict (Sarah Paulson), an unraveling detective (Wes Bentley), and a brood of sadistic serial killer ghosts, among others. Historically "real" serial killers dine with fictional detectives and vampires, an artistic choice that promises to reveal hidden bloody secrets within America's already bloody history rather than abide by perfect documentary accuracy.

Additionally, while *AHS* contains fundamental Aristotelian elements such as "astonishment," "reversal," "recognition," and "suffering" (17–20), it deftly bends his rules calling for a "well-constructed" plot with a clear beginning, middle, and end (10). Aside from season eight, *Apocalypse* (which continues storylines from *Murder House* and *Coven*), each new season of the show presents a self-contained story that begins in the first episode and ends in the last. However, each season takes on a distinctive flavor of storytelling, weaving multiple timelines, characters, and flashbacks that muddle the clarity of classical Aristotelian tragedy. Most notably, *AHS*'s sixth season, *Roanoke*, critiques current reality television by presenting a show within a show about another show within a show. The first six episodes of *Roanoke* are a dramatic reenactment series titled *My Roanoke Nightmare*, while the final six episodes go behind the scenes of the series' doomed sequel reality show (*Return to Roanoke: Three Days in Hell*) using found footage from smartphones, hidden cameras, news footage, and internet clips. In his article "Beginning, Middle, End of an Era: Has Technology Trumped Aristotle?," Richard J. Allen also questions the "universality of the accepted formulas for dramatic [three-act] structure" as dictated by Aristotle (Allen 2013, 10). Audiences will always crave traditional storytelling structures, but the success of streaming platforms, DVR, smartphones, and digital downloads "have altered the way we view television" and, according to Allen, "are likely changing ... the entire concept of storytelling" for future generations of TV viewers (11). In response to the evolving landscape of television distribution, shows are written in a variety of bingeable forms (miniseries, episodic, anthology, etc.). *AHS* takes on the season-long anthology format, allowing for semi-Aristotelian endings to each season while also fulfilling the digital desire for never-ending, consumable stories. In other words, *AHS* provides satisfactory endings, but the deeper tales of American woe promise to return at the premiere of each new season.

BINGEING CATHARSIS THROUGH RELATABLE CHARACTERS

AHS's embrace of the anthology format makes it especially poised to deliver catharsis to the twenty-first century. As a medium, television (particularly with narrative-driven, episodic shows) can respond with near-immediacy to current events and cultural trends. While the internet possesses the same instantaneous quality, the storytelling mode of television delivers curated voices that contribute to the cultural conversation. Journalist and author Michael Wolff compares TV's "grand narratives" with the "moralistic intensity" of the internet: while the current "Golden Age of Television" caters to an audience that embraces "moral relativism" and celebrates human nature as "complex," online moralism releases its fury in the form of mass public shaming, Reddit trolls, Twitter feuds, and Facebook politics (Wolff 2017, 91; 190–2). Even though many television audiences participate in binge-watching, they are generally *conscious* of what they binge. Internet users, on the other hand, *passively* scroll through their feeds as mobile couch potatoes.[6] Curated, *quality* storytelling seems to be the key here: TV viewers gravitate toward quality stories (even when binged) and are more actively involved in the stories they consume.

While passive internet users may scroll past historical violence and national conflict, cathartic television like *AHS* confronts its viewers directly.

The unique and outlandish characters on *AHS* are not strictly good, evil, logical, or irrational; they express complex human emotions and distinct experiences, even when portraying something nonhuman. For Aristotle, a tragic character requires "goodness," "appropriateness," "likeness," and "consistency" (Aristotle, 24). Like any well-written show, *AHS* has characters who behave consistently, but I doubt Aristotle would approve of the overall likeness, goodness, and appropriateness of the vampires, witches, demons, circus performers, and ghosts who fill the starring roles. Just as monstrous revivals take on the flavor and likeness of their cultural context, *AHS* reimagines classic creatures instead of sticking merely to the standard tropes. Lady Gaga's vampiric Countess, for instance, trades in fangs and capes for disco couture and midnight movies at the Hollywood Forever Cemetery (funded by a dwindling fortune built on old movie stars in the twenties and later depleted by Bernie Madoff).

While much of this break with Aristotle's appropriateness and likeness can be attributed to the passage of time, the wily reversals of goodness (and permeation of badness) move beyond orthodox depictions of clear-cut characterization. It is tough to define any character as purely virtuous or depraved in *AHS*. Pushed beyond desperation in the haunted woods of *Roanoke*, Lee Harris (Adina Porter) is a murderous, alcoholic ex-cop but also an affectionate and sacrificial mother. Tate Langdon (Evan Peters) enters *Murder House* as a kind but troubled teen; slowly, the season exposes him as a disturbed school shooter, sadistic killer, and the rapist of his girlfriend's mother. Even for the most horrific characters, each of these "monsters" gets to tell their story, allowing viewers to look upon their actions with compassion (some more easily than others). Whether they are strictly *human* may be up for debate, but their *humanity* is not. Postmodern monsters complicate modern notions of what it means to behave rationally or be a good person. Instead of abiding by Aristotle's universal plots and clear-cut characters, the monsters on *AHS* weave lightness, darkness, comedy, and tragedy into an assemblage built on dramatic tension and released through dark humor.

The layered casting, anthology structure, and self-aware humor of *AHS* cause the audience to see their own stories in these unlikely characters. Riffing off of Bertolt Brecht's *Verfremdungseffekt*, also known as *distancing effect* or *alienation effect*, the show uses the same actors to play various characters in different seasons. These casting choices are aware of their alienating effects: viewers can relate emotionally to the fictional characters as well as disconnect and engage as fans of their favorite reoccurring actors. The oscillation between detachment and reattachment once again engenders *active* TV viewership. Furthermore, by recycling the same bodies throughout the series, reoccurring faces in *AHS* become ubiquitous faces of the masses. Jessica Lang or Evan Peters may be heroic one season and devilish the next. Each season reminds us that monsters are not easily recognizable, and that innocence can be hidden behind a monstrous mask. These shapeshifters represent the array of schizophrenic personalities and potentials within all of us. We should not be so quick to judge our neighbors—they could be Satan or Savior.

These dichotomies are found not only in our neighbors but also in our own homes. Each "monster" in *AHS* ultimately finds meaning and purpose within the families and communities that accept them. The unconventional and traditional families featured in the show include the biological or nuclear family (*Murder House, Hotel,* and *Roanoke*), families fostered by difference and sameness (*Asylum, Freak Show,* and *1984*), sisterhood as family (*Coven*), and families formed around devotion (*Hotel, Cult,* and *Apocalypse*). Throughout each season, institutional power (church, government, science, the nuclear family) and individual agency (self-interest and self-reliance) are nothing but a house of mirrors; disintegrating illusions of wealth, power, fame, and the individualistic American Dream.

In *Asylum*, for example, institutional figures such as Dr. Oliver Thredson (Zachary Quinto), Dr. Arthur Arden (James Cromwell), and Monsignor Timothy Howard (Joseph Fiennes) are later revealed to be a twisted serial killer posing as a therapist, a Nazi doctor performing gruesome experiments on the patients, and a cowardly, amoral priest who puts papal ambitions ahead of ethical choices. Rather than care for the patients at Briarcliff Manor (those who society has tossed aside), these men abuse their power to satisfy their own needs, crumbling any sense of trust in American religious and medical institutions. Despite these cruelties, victims from *AHS* redeem their suffering through camaraderie and solidarity. From the ashes of apocalyptic tragedy rise affectionate communities, personal relationships, and familial bonds. Battles between good and evil turn out to be battles between loyalty and betrayal; forgiveness and isolation; communal purpose and individual power.

CONCLUSION: ON-SCREEN CATHARSIS IN VIRTUAL SPACES

The monsters and their cobbled communities on *AHS* may look grotesque or sometimes act cruelly, but they should be viewed with cautious empathy. Metaphorically, the show sees America as a family—the citizen-relatives we are stuck with, for better or worse. As American audiences, we must admit responsibility for our monstrous actions and hold each other accountable while also allowing for inevitable mistakes. Poole critiques the simplistic understanding of "horror narratives" as providing "societ[al] catharsis" or "group therapy," and warns that these monsters should not be "reduced to the story of psychic wounds opened by national traumas" (24). However, in an age of curated storytelling, social media fandom, and virtual communities, we should not so quickly dismiss the curative exposure generated by on-screen stories. The show goes beyond splashy entertainment and one-time catharsis; the narratives stick with viewers long after bingeing the show. Fans are active and vigilant, often remixing and commenting on the show while embracing its characters and aesthetics. The creation and circulation of memes is a significant way viewers engage their TV obsessions while also critiquing aspects of the show they find problematic. This kind of virtual engagement resurrects cathartic themes beyond the TV screen and breathes new life into the mutable screens of sharing, posting, and reproducing.

AHS, in all its aggressive gore, is cathartically satisfactory because it confronts current and historical American horrors while also engendering empathy toward fellow humans on an individual and communal level. The show offers bold and timely critiques of issues that demand justice, gives visibility to identities that have long suffered erasure, and provides emotional guidelines toward living a compassionate life. Unlike Aristotle's categorical goodness and structural clarity, contemporary American audiences need a different kind of tragedy—namely, the extreme terror and dark irreverence of the horror television anthology—to bring about catharsis. This is not a cathartic return to Aristotelian balance or normalcy, but a catharsis that brings a confrontation with "the haunted house" of "the American past" (Poole, 24). In other words, we should embrace these monsters through the lens of Poole, not Aristotle. By unleashing confrontation, catharsis, and the uncertainty in the face of the unknown, *American Horror Story* may be breeding a monstrous audience, as it does not have ultimate control over its viewers. We can only hope that these fan-monsters give and receive empathy before devouring each other.

NOTES

1. Nine seasons have aired at the time of submission, but the bulk of this chapter focuses on the first eight seasons.

2. The term "freaks" was popularized by Tod Browning's 1932 film of the same name (*Freaks*), about a traveling circus and its sideshow performers. Though the term has been primarily understood as a derogatory slur, *AHS*'s fourth season (*Freak Show*) is seemingly attempting to reclaim the word. However, even with the best intentions, it is problematic for those outside the disability community to use the word, so for the remainder of this chapter, I will only use it when referencing the show's season four title.

3. In response to critiques of (some) of his shows as insensitive, Ryan Murphy continues to work toward producing "television as advocacy" by incorporating more diverse creative teams (Nussbaum, 2018).

4. I am not implying that the stress of America in the twenty-first century should be seen as *more* traumatic compared to other periods but that there is an undeniable anxiety underlying the current American experience, just as there always has been. The American present continues to face a war over its own past: some see a nation tilled on stolen lands and deeply steeped in white supremacy; others carry a sense of national pride and American exceptionalism.

5. The full exploits of H.H. Holmes are historically contested, but his notoriety as "the first American serial killer" has reached common lore, and recent revival has been instigated by Erik Larson's popular book, *The Devil in the White City* (2003).

6. Television audiences (including those watching stream-able, internet-distributed television) and internet users are not distinct groups; most people embody both of these roles to varying degrees. Likewise, there are, of course, TV viewers who watch passively and internet scrollers who are incredibly active. This topic is complex and evolving quickly, and it requires further nuanced conversations about the relationships between television and virtual spaces.

Chapter 17

To Eat or to Be Eaten—*CHEW*
A New Study between the Beast and the Sovereign

Elena Pasquini

Monsters are a beautiful, artistic means by which humans are allowed to question their own humanity, and explore how it is created and how it is maintained. The man-eater monsters specifically create a literary and philosophical space where the human is not at the top of the food chain; thus it is not the most powerful being, and positions it in a much more precarious condition. This displacement creates an action-reaction that pushes on the boundaries between the monsters and the humans, often blurring those same boundaries or even making them difficult to see at all.

This chapter analyzes the work of writer John Layman and artist Rob Guillory in the comic *CHEW* published by Image Comics between 2009 and 2016, which has since been collected into twelve volumes. What makes this comic interesting compared to other superhero comics is that all superpowers in this universe are related to food in one way or another. *CHEW* allows the man-eater monster to appear in a new narrative medium, while at the same time positions itself in a long literary tradition surrounding the idea of man as wolf. The philosopher Jacques Derrida justifies the importance of "the wolf" in literature because it holds a special privilege in human imagination (the scary, big bad wolf, strong and cunning) and it is part of how humans define and rewrite themselves. Derrida (2009, 9) writes, "in a fantasy, a narrative, a mytheme, a fable, a trope, a rhetorical turn, where man tells himself the story of politics, the story of the origin of society, the story of the social, construct, etc.: for man, man is wolf." As evidenced in this quote from Derrida, literature and language have an important role in defining humanity, oftentimes through the construction of an opposite or counterpart. This counterpart, however, does not just stand still as a semiotic reality but will attack and threaten the human into action. The monster is the abject, a part of humanity that is divided from it, but which, at the same time, cannot be completely refused. It is the man wearing a wolf mask to disguise himself so that man can find himself in the mask and through it. Using the detailed study of *CHEW* as a case study, this chapter examines the importance of language and the power that certain words create in human society. This study draws on the theories of Jacques Derrida on language and the use of imaginary monstrous figures, like the *wolf*, both in the essay collection *The Beast and the Sovereign* (2009–2011) and the essay "The Animal That Therefore I Am (More to Follow)" (2002). In particular, this chapter takes inspiration from Derrida's study of the Latin proverb *homo homini lupus* (man is wolf for another man) and uses *CHEW* to explore what it means to be human by identifying three "wolves" inside the comic. Each "wolf" reveals a facet of how humans fight to establish their sovereignty and how this fight produces both gods and monsters.

THE MONSTROSITY OF TONY CHU

Before diving into our discussion of monstrosity, Derrida, and Chu, it is important to lay the groundwork by explaining in detail *CHEW*'s setting and superpower mechanics. This framework is important to understand how the protagonist, a special agent of the law for the department of Food and Drug Administration (FDA), Tony Chu, finds himself in a liminal space between the categories of human and monster. The story is set in the contemporary United States but in an alternate timeline with significantly advanced science. In this reality, cyborgs and other advanced technological dreams are common, and the reader is confronted with superheroes and super villains. Their powers are all related to the use, manipulation, and/or consumption of food. For example, the individuals known as *xocoscalpere* can mold chocolate into a form that subsequently works like the real thing—for example, if they make a replica of a sword or a gun it is as lethal as a real weapon; those known as *cibovoyant* can see a person's future by biting them; a *cibosensor* can describe food so vividly that it feels like actually eating the food they are describing, and so on. The powers shown in the series are varied, and while most seem positive or quietly innocent at a first glance, all can be wielded to achieve negative outcomes: the *xocoscalpere* creates deadly weapons; the *cibosensor* can cause nausea and food poisoning if they want, and so forth. None, however, are as peculiar as agent Tony Chu's power. As seen in *Volume One: Taster's Choice* he is a *cibopath*—an invented word which uses the Italian word *cibo*, meaning food, and the ancient Greek *pathos*, meaning to suffer or to feel.

In the context of the narrative, therefore, he has the power to gain information from anything consumed about its life and death. When Tony is presented to the reader, Guillory and Layman emphasize the trouble such power creates for the character with two simple panels. First, the illustrator shows Tony eating an apple while behind him a scene in an orchard takes place with people gathering apples in a fruit basket. The scene behind Tony is an illustration that explains how his power creates pictures in his head that retell the history of what he is consuming, that is, the apple has been picked from the orchard. In the following panel, Tony is seen biting a hamburger. Tony's expression is almost tearful; behind him a crying cow is being bludgeoned to death with a hammer while blood gruesomely splatters on the sides. If an apple is consumed, the information is simple: where it grew, what products were used, who picked it, and so on. If an animal is consumed, their fears and pain at the moment of the slaughter is also read, seen, and felt by the cibopath (Layman and Guillory 2009).

As illustrated in the panels in the first volume, the emotional aspect of consuming another being, with the necessity of killing, is something that Tony cannot escape. Tony is always hungry, explains Layman; his power makes a fundamental act such as eating extremely difficult for the protagonist to enjoy, making him reluctant to eat at all, let alone show or use his power. What is noteworthy is the fact that Tony's power does not stop at regular food: anything that can be eaten can give Tony a reading, including humans. At the end of the first chapter, therefore, Tony's power is exposed because the protagonist is forced to make a choice between the collective good of giving closure to the families and a self-protecting silence to not expose his cannibalistic power. While in a restaurant, Tony has an unexpected reading of the cook when a drop of his blood ends up in Tony's plate. It reveals to the agent that the cook is actually a serial killer. This moment introduces a difficult moral quandary for Tony: on the one hand, if he confronts the killer, his power will be discovered and complicate his life; on the other hand, if he does not intervene, the cook will continue to kill and his victims will not have the justice they deserve.

From the beginning of the comic, with Tony's confrontation with the murderer, the reader is asked to pay attention to the complexity of how we define the monstrous: who is the monster and who is the human? On the page, there are two monsters facing each other in a black alley. One possesses a superpower making him technically more than human; the other, while unquestionably a human being, is morally a monster because he has broken a critical social pact by killing. The killer does not know who, or what, Tony really is and decides to take his own life in an attempt to block the course of justice and punishment. He believes that in killing himself, he will bring his victims as anonymous passengers with him, for without sharing their names or where their remains are, they will be forever lost. However, Tony's cibopath powers can render this final choice completely meaningless. Tony does not need the killer alive to obtain the information he needs; he can decide to cannibalize the corpse of the serial killer to bring peace and justice to the victims. The price, however, is high, as doing so would mark Tony as a cannibal, which is a fundamental taboo in most human societies, including that of the narrative itself.[1] Tony, however, breaks the law and eats part of the cook to discover where his victims are located—an act that violates his oath as a member of law enforcement and humanity, but which is performed out of compassion toward the victims. In this moment, Tony becomes monstrous. By overstepping his own society's taboo of cannibalism, Tony voluntarily steps out of the realm of law and acceptance and enters into a space that can be considered monstrous.

Tony's monstrosity in the stand-off is portrayed via the unique medium of graphic novels with a powerful use of colors and zooming in and out of the panels. Tony is presented on the left, gun out and ready to shoot; the serial killer on the right with a kitchen knife in hand. The unbalance of power between the two is clear already and will be further amplified in the moment of Tony's cannibalism. The panels alternate from zooming in on one of the characters, then switching to place both characters in the frame. The frequent switches of perspective work to create a faster pace in this scene, while the predominantly gray color palette references noir films. The serial killer then cuts his own throat to escape justice, but in his illustration, Guillory focuses on Tony being covered by a splash of bright red blood that breaks the monotony of the grays. On the next page, the panels are more focused and the flow of the graphic narrative is slower. After showing the killer struggling and holding his own throat in pain and shock to make his survival instinct made prominent, the whole focus is again still on Tony. Guillory zooms his illustration specifically on Tony's salivating open mouth, which is the panel's central feature, while the rest of the face is mostly cut by the frame. In the final panels, the reader sees only Tony's back as the frame slowly zooms out, leaving Tony alone in the dark alley. Continuing the largely monochromatic gray color palette references the corpse being consumed by Tony, and there is only a small splattering of red blood and the written sound of chewing (Layman and Guillory 2009).

This introduction to Tony Chu and his first use of powers is visceral, violent, and animalistic. The graphic novel goes out of its way to signify how, once used, Tony's power challenges his humanity. Everything is silent, and there are no other beings—human or animal—that witness this confrontation. The scene at the end, with a banal and empty street view could almost make us doubt there is any life at all if not for the vibrant "chomp" written in color: there is life because someone (something) is eating, consuming, and absorbing another something (someone). In short, the scene suggests that perhaps Tony is a monster, a freak, an outcast, and Tony's status as a pariah becomes the key theme of the graphic novel. *CHEW* goes deeper, however, than simply stating Tony is or is not a monster; rather, it considers monstrosity as something largely socially constructed through what Derrida has called the sovereignty of naming—who gets to name, who is named, and what is the relationship between the two. Exploring how *CHEW* reflects Derrida's theories concerning naming and sovereignty can help us understand how powerful language is and how influential it is creating a society. Art in general, and the graphic novel in particular with the use of both verbal and visual languages, can help us to catch a glimpse of what it means to be human, and how humans are named either as divine or monstrous.

DERRIDA AND THE SOVEREIGNTY OF NAMES

This first chapter of the *CHEW* series clearly sets the mood and highlights some of the questions about what it means to be human or monster that become central to the rest of the paper. Questions about specific definitional boundaries and where to draw the line, if there are any, are examined and re-examined. This violent world and the primordial eating-consuming cycle that defines the comic is part of a long tradition of literature that is influenced by the Latin saying: *homo homini lupus*, "man is wolf for another man" (Derrida 2009, 9–11). This Latin phrase has its first written referenced in Plautus's *Asinaria*, but has a lengthy history after that in such work as the writings of Erasmus and Hobbes's *Leviathan*. The aphorism encapsulates a series of questions that help to question and illuminate the human-monster relationship. In the beginning of *The Beast and the Sovereign*, Derrida analyzes this particular man-wolf-man saying to show how it uses language to create the "*human*" through specifically identifying and declaring its sovereignty over the "*other*." For Derrida, the category of the other is generally reserved for animals and the "God," creating a schema and hierarchy, but to such logic we can also include the category of the "monster." All three of these beings are defined by their relationship to the human as being "nonhuman," and thus belong to a sphere outside what can be considered humanity. Derrida claims that God and animal have a specific position in the schema, the first of superiority to the human and the second as an inferior being compare to the human that can be illustrated as God> human> animal, a theo-anthropo-zoological schema (Derrida 2009, 13). In adding the monster to Derrida's schema, there is a problem of where to locate it. The category is not as fixed as the others, but in a way it is fluid, it can be both superior and inferior in relation to the human. The monster, therefore, rotates around the human redefining the boundaries that defy both the human and the monster. The two push and pull each other sometimes toward the god, sometimes closer to the animal, sometimes battling for the middle. Language, in particular, creates the human and parallels the monster, forcing them to battle for the affirmation of their sovereignty against each other and helping to define their boundaries.

Reflecting Derrida's claims surrounding the power of language to accept or reject someone's sovereignty, and, therefore, their humanity, is Tony's main character arc. This particular scene featuring Tony via an examination of Derrida's discussions of the intersection between sovereignty and language. In Derrida's study, the sovereign is defined as: "in the broader sense of the term, is he who has the right and the strength to be and to be recognized as himself, *the same, properly as the same of himself* [author emphasis]" (Derrida 2009, 66). It is, therefore, a proclamation of the self that at the very core is performed by the act of naming oneself as oneself. However, this act requires the complicity of the other that has to accept such affirmation and thus confirm the power of it (Derrida 2009, 68). It is a dual exchange between the self and the other, each other having the power to affirm and destroy the naming.

Humans have used other humans to create and collectively accept their sovereignty, and have further used literature and art (something that is a creation of humanity) to justify it. In his essay, "The Animal That Therefore I Am (More To Follow)," Derrida analyzes how Western society justifies its own privileges and sovereignty by looking at the creation of man and language in Genesis. The power of God is performed not just by creating all things, but also by naming them. The latter ability is shared with humankind. To further his point, Derrida compares two different translations of Genesis translated by Édouard Dhorme and André Chouraqui,to show how a simple change between the passages creates a powerful challenge in the hierarchy of God-human-animal. Derrida considers this:

> For one must indeed specify that that story is a second "Heading" [. . .] The man who, in that rendering, calls the animals by name, is not only Adam, the man of the earth, the husbandman [*glébleux*]. He is also Ish preceding Ishah, man before woman. It is the man Ish, still alone, who gives names to the animals created before him: "The husbandman cried out the name of each beast," one translation (Chouraqui) says; another (Dhormes): "Man called all the animals by their names" (Gen. 2:20). (Derrida 2002, 384)

In this passage, Derrida points out that what we have now are translations, leaving ample room for interpretations and changes. In fact, he carries on explaining how the two French translations of this passage (Gen 2:20) create a very different perception of the power and position of humanity, Adam, in the creation and ruling of the world. In Dhorme's version, Derrida explains how the power of ownership over all things gets transferred from God to man by sharing the names of all things which allows man to rule. In Chouraqui's version, it was only after the human was created that God decides that it will be Adam who names all other beings (Derrida 2002, 385–6). In the first version, there is a certain level of equality between all things named by God; in the second, the animal is constructed as an extreme other, and the divisions between human and animal are made even stronger, because humans have direct ownership of the other. Derrida points out that it is the power of language which creates this hierarchy from God to mankind to animal and that its ultimate function is as a justification to establish whose power is the strongest. God has the potential not only to create and name but also to destroy, punish, and kill both humans and animals; similarly, man has the same power over the animal, as evidenced by his practice of naming everything and also consuming it. Derrida calls this a theo-anthropo-zoological schema in which humans sit exactly in between the God and the animal, sharing characteristics of both (Derrida 2009, 13).

Receiving a name then implies the necessity of a superior force that allows a being to be itself. Therefore, if Genesis is considered not just a religious scripture, but also a piece of literature in which humans validate their own sovereignty by literally naming themselves, then humans claim the superior force, positioning themselves as closer to God in the schema. Through language and literature, humans reinforce their position in the hierarchy, but also express their greater proximity to God than to the animal. This cycle also exposes the fragile place of humanity—the paradox that humans can take on the role of both animals and gods, depending on the use of language itself.

The category of the monster is deployed in a similar way to the other two categories of animal and god. In art, all three have the role of defining and outlining what a human is and even more *how* a human is a human. As mentioned before, the monster's fluidity makes its positioning in the schema difficult but not dismissible. The monster is sometimes above the human, almost god like, like the Titans of the ancient Greek mythology; sometimes it is like an animal like the figure of the kraken or the werewolves of folklore; sometime the monster is a mirror, a distorted equal to the human as the aliens in Octavia Butler's *Bloodchild* (1984). In all these cases, the monster is fundamental for the human to define, understand, and label what it really means to be human and how to protect that status. As suggested by Cohen (1996, 4), "the monstrous body is pure culture. A construct and projection, the monster exists only to be read." Because Derrida's human is constructed through gaining the power of naming, so the monster, like the animal, is a crucial component in producing that construction. Thus, humans need to feel threatened by the monster and ritualistically name it through language in art and literature to secure their sovereignty. Returning to Tony Chu and the narrative arc of the *CHEW* series, we see this constant exploration and extrapolation of sovereignty and naming through characters that surround Tony. As reflected in the Latin proverb of *homo homini lupus*, this is accomplished in large part through the placement of three "wolves"—three individuals who have a role in defining the character of Tony Chu through their ability to deploy names. These wolves, as illustrated in the next three passages threaten Tony's humanity either by language and/or brutal force, threatening to relegate him into three different categories: the first character considers him an outsider, a freak of society, a lesser human; the second considers him a rival, a potential god-like monster; the third instead sees him as an inferior, a monster closer to an animal to be used and abused. None of them consider him a human but something other than human. These characters perfectly parallel Derrida's schema of the God-human-animal while Tony is at the same time the monster and the human who is pushed and pulled, moved in and out of the categories by others.

THE EVERYDAY WOLF, MIKE APPLEBEE

The first wolf who calls into question Tony's humanity and attempts to label him as "monster" is his boss at the FDA, Mike Applebee. Layman and Guillory make Applebee quite unlikable: a middle-aged man, very sweaty, and clearly a bully. Tony already feels his monstrous power as a threat to his humanity, something placing him in the liminal category between human and animal. Before meeting another cibopath, Tony never knew who he was or how to call himself: He was unnamed and therefore unable to locate himself within the schema. Applebee takes advantage of this state and tries to position Tony in the inferior category of the tripart theo-anthropo-zoological schema by referring to Tony as a "freak" or a "freakshow." By offering this title, Applebee forces Tony to see his diversity as a negative trait. Applebee feels entitled from both his position as captain and as a "regular" human, to push Tony outside the human category thanks to the power evoked by the simple word "freak." The term "freak" refers to the cannibalistic aspect of Tony. It is the thing that makes him a wolf himself, a threat and something to avoid and cast out, an expendable being.

Upon meeting another cibopath and realizing his true nature and potential, however, Tony has an option that was not previously open to him. This encounter means that Tony must claim a term for himself: either the scientific and validating cibopath or the derogatory freak. The label "cibopath" creates an alternative to "freak," because while Tony behaves cannibalistically, he does so to maintain human justice. At some level Applebee acknowledges this; as much as he hates Tony's "freakish" nature, he knows how useful Tony is and never allows him to suppress his power with beetroots—the natural suppressant for Tony's power—because Tony needs his power to be useful to the FDA. His worth, therefore, is linked paradoxically to the same trait which Applebee uses to define him as inhuman. When Tony accepts his identity and names himself as a cibopath, seeing his "monstrosity" in a positive, or potential positive, light, the word freak loses all its power and so does Applebee. Tony frees himself by precariously positioning himself between human and animal, paradoxically accepting this same position.

THE WOLF WITH NO NAME: THE VAMPIRE

Tony's sovereignty to determine his own name is again challenged when he encounters the second "wolf": a character called "the Vampire," who is a hyper-representation of the cibopath. The Vampire embodies the "monster" fully, seeing himself as stronger and above humanity. Throughout the series, he tries to label Tony with the same name by pushing the protagonist outside the human and into the monster. This is evidenced in the Vampire's narrative construction: he is the only character without a human name because he has claimed for himself the title of Vampire. By naming himself, he proclaims his sovereignty not just above his enemies, but also above humanity and human society as well; he is superhuman because he is the monster that eats humans. Layman and Guillory make this clear when they first introduce the Vampire to the reader and Tony himself in *Volume Two: International Flavour* (Layman and Guillory 2010).

After a security guard dies mysteriously, Tony decides to use his power and bites the victim to get an impression of his last moments alive. The image created in Tony's head is of the man, scared, with his neck exposed mere seconds before being bitten by another human who possesses long, sharp canines teeth just in the moment before piercing the neck—classic image most readers will associate with vampires, Tony stammers while claiming that vampires do not exist. This is an ironic statement coming from a character who has just consumed the flesh of a dead body to gather such information. In this way, Layman uses the power of language and associations with the word "vampire" to amplify meaning. In picking a monster terminology "vampire" over the more scientific word "cibopath," Layman's villain makes a calculated move that brings us back to Derrida's analysis of the *homo homini lupus*. Derrida explains that "whenever man does not make known to man who or which he is, he becomes wolf" (Derrida 2009, 61). This demonstrates that the wolf is any human that does not show or proclaim himself or his humanity to another man, but rather hides it to gain some form of advantage. It emerges from the liminal space of the unknown which generates an immediate fear and terror because of his unknown nature.

Wolf, therefore, is always the big bad wolf, the fear, the monster; the Vampire is not really a vampire, as the *lupus* is not a real wolf but a man. He dresses, acts and names himself a vampire to create fear and position himself above the rest. The Vampire is actually an extremely powerful cibopath who has discovered the full depth of such power. He has discovered that cibopaths can obtain the skills and all knowledge of another humans if they consume enough of their blood and flesh (Layman and Guillory 2010). The Vampire has collected and eaten not just regular humans but specifically other superhumans, becoming a wolf to his own people to rise above them. In assimilating all these powers, the Vampire has projected himself out of the human category, but instead of plummeting into the animal category, he has risen closer to the status of God in the theo-anthropo-zoological division. Thus, the name given by his parents before such transformation is completely lost to the reader and all other characters. The Vampire is the wolf that evokes himself with language and actions, killing and consuming all inferior beings. His god-like nature is clear in Guillory's drawing, which mimics Leonardo da Vinci's The Last Supper in terms of arrangement.

The scene is set in a space observatory. The Vampire is at the center of the image seated at a table with a high pile of ribs in front of him and his followers gathered around him. Like Jesus, the Vampire's arms are open inviting his followers (twelve of which are clearly drawn and highlighted) to join him (Layman and Guillory 2015). His speech on the next page again recalls the last supper when Jesus invites his followers to eat his body and blood through the bread and the wine, consuming a part of God. The Vampire instead demands his followers sacrifice themselves to him, in this way they are going to become one with him and so one with the divine. While Jesus is a god, the Vampire is a monster god.

Layman and Guillory build on the Vampire's identity as a monster god in his destruction at the hands of Tony. Similar to how Jesus's death was ordained by God, another monster who shares the same power, Tony, is responsible for the destruction of the Vampire. As in a fight between Titans or ancient gods, Tony and the Vampire fight in *Volume Ten: Blood Puddin'* (Layman and Guillory 2015). Tony is victorious both practically (he kills the Vampire) and metaphorically in the struggle between human and monster that the Vampire has forced upon him. If the Vampire has the power to affirm himself, so does Tony. More importantly, Tony has finally realized he has the power to refuse being categorized by others, and he can name himself, performing his own sovereignty like the Vampire has. Tony will not eat the Vampire, and will not gain all the Vampire's knowledge, powers and skills and thus he will be neither god like nor monster like. What's more, he refuses to let the Vampire finish his life in the schema he has created for himself, moving him from above the human to below it, closer to the animal.

After the fight, the Vampire remains the center of attention: his eyes completely black, his vampire teeth showing in a bright smile. He is dying, but he still does not think he has been defeated. He tells Tony that he will achieve immortality through him, as he wrongly assumes Tony will claim his rightful reward as the stronger cibopath by eating the Vampire. In the following panel, Guillory moves the focus to a wider scene with Tony and the Vampire at the center, but also introducing the presence of animals—in this case rats (Layman and Guillory 2015). The Vampire stubbornly believes that as he has performed the role of the wolf thanks to his intelligence and strength, so the new more powerful wolf (Tony) will carry on the traditional act: eating, consuming, and assimilating. Tony refuses, though, and interrupts this cycle.

Guillory positions the reader's eyes at the level of the rats which frame the scene while Tony is showing the Vampire that he is not interested in the schema of the strongest. Tony explains that this is the Vampire's end, he is going to die but Tony will not eat him, the rats will. All the Vampire's powers are now useless, immobilized as he falls into the zoological part of the schema. The Vampire is not going to be eaten by the strongest, his rival and the winner, but by another animal that society detests even more than the wolf. With this ending, Guillory and Layman use Tony's choice to reintegrate the Vampire into the cycle of the world, in its very visceral, primordial structure. Tony proclaims his humanity by using a human system of justice and not the monster's: he kills the threat to humanity, the terrorist on the outside, protecting the human sovereignty and its law. The Vampire is not reintegrated into the human category either. Being fundamentally human, as Tony, the Vampire now neutralized should be brought to justice and be judged by the human law in a courtroom. However, Tony refuses the humanity of the Vampire altogether, and he himself, as an active member of the human sovereignty, proclaims his own justice and proceeds to punish him himself. This vigilante trope is typical of the superhero arc and, in this study of human sovereignty and the monster, it highlights the arbitrariness of law and justice all together.

The problem of justice or being right has been pushed forward so far by the analysis of the wolves in the comic and deserves further expansion. It is possible to ask again of Derrida's interpretation of *homo homini lupus* what justice and power seems to be in this scenario. The *lupus*, the wolf, is both cunning and strong, and the power of its violence is not really in question. Derrida connects two sentences that in French, Italian, and other romance languages create an interesting flux which is embodied in the word "wolf" as evocation of the big bad wolf. To overcome is "avoir raison de" meaning to overcome someone or something and "avoir raison" is also "have reason" to be right against an opponent (Derrida 2009, 7). The two phrases, therefore, verbally link "to be right," as in correct, with "to overcome" by strength. Derrida explains that a link is created, therefore, with the reason for the strongest being embodied in *homo homini lupus* and traditionally confused with "being right" through the centuries: might makes right, so to speak. However, Derrida stresses this should not be considered logically, morally correct. Being the strongest should not be confused with being in the right. It is an interpretative creation of language, but not a real ethical dogma. The Vampire represents this interpretation of the reason of the strongest, however, because he proclaims himself other than human, wearing the mask of the wolf. It is easier, therefore, to take it back and destroy him.

THE HIDDEN WOLF: DAN FRANKS

If the Vampire is nameless, this third wolf has a typical human name: Dan Franks. This sets him apart from the food reference in Tony Chu's name or the nature-based surname of Applebee. He is the man par excellence, entirely removed from association with nature or such. More importantly, he is the representation of toxic masculinity which is never referred to as monstrous but only as human. Franks is never once called a monster or a freak, but his violence is as terrible, maybe even more brutal, than the Vampire's. He is the example that Layman and Guillory give as the real *lupus*, the strongest man that believes to be right by the nature of his strength. In his study, Derrida adds to the God-human-animal schema an extra division inside the category of human itself, using Rousseau's terms from *The Social Contract*: man is divided by the nature of his sovereignty into chiefs and cattle, masters and servants, because fundamentally someone has to follow the strongest sovereign (Derrida 2009, 11–13). In *Volume Five: Major League CHEW*, Dan Franks believes himself to be a chief: he is a strong, manly man; he likes sports (he is a sports journalist) and he should get the girl because this is how it should be. But he does not get the girl. It is Tony, the skinny man, the weird one, the monster, who gets the girl (Amelia) (Layman and Guillory 2011). For a man like Franks this makes no sense; why she picks a lesser man like Tony completely escapes him.

The incapacity to self-criticize and the level of entitlement leads Franks to plot revenge against Tony, the monster. If with Applebee, Tony was pushed toward the animal through teasing, Franks throws the protagonist into the category without blinking. Tony becomes the animal (the cattle) without any possibility to escape. Franks chooses to exploit Tony's power for his personal gain. As a sports fanatic and a journalist, he decides that the best way to make money would be to write a book about the sexual deviances of famous baseball players. To do so, he force-feeds Tony, a bit like a goose, but with body parts of dead players to obtain the information he needs to become rich. This powerful act of monstrosity is captured in a final panel of Franks that appears at the end of the chapter. When Franks decides he has had enough of Tony, he does not kill him or set him free but decides to sell him to the highest bidder. Dan performs human exploitation over another human to the fullest potential.

A two-page illustration shows Tony beaten, blooded, and tied to a chair that is suspended above a stage in a theater. The audience is full of people watching, while Franks is standing proud and dominant on the stage next to Tony. Tony is clearly just an object and framed no better than any other animal: tied up like a piece of meat and ready to be sold for the best price. At the auction, Guillory depicts many references, both historical and fictional, to characters who have perpetuated the philosophy of amoral domination and manipulation: One bidder has a swastika tattooed on his shaved ahead, and another is the Devil himself. In the spread, the most important and scariest figures are Franks and the Devil (Layman and Guillory 2011). Franks is smiling, in control and drawn with completely black eyes, symbolizing his lack of soul and thus humanity. Perfectly opposite to him, the big full face of the Devil peers out of the right side of the frame. But the Devil, with his pink, heart-shaped eyes, does not seem to be looking at Tony but gazes more directly at Franks. The Devil is also smiling, mirroring Franks's pleasure over the situation that he himself may have orchestrated. They are both enjoying the monstrosity of the human exploitation of another human, the violence of the strongest over another being that should be respected as such. Franks never received the name "monster" or "freak" himself, but his evil nature is undeniable. Even if Layman never writes the word "evil" or "monstrous," Guillory reveals these aspects of Franks's character through the images.

CONCLUDING THOUGHTS

Through the exposition of the three wolves in light of Derrida's theo-anthropo-zoological schema, the comic *CHEW* can be understood as an exploration of the construction of monstrosity through shifting understandings of sovereignty to name and the identification of the "wolf." As Cohen explains, "the monster's very existence is a rebuke to boundary and enclosure" that the human desperately tries to convince itself it has against the other and which makes them who they are (Cohen 1996, 7). The three wolves (and Tony himself as both human and monster) break and make the boundaries of humanity to show how this category is not fixed but in constant movement. While it is tempting to place the monster as synonymous with animal, as revealed through our exploration of *CHEW,* the theo-anthropo-zoological schema actually welcomes the monstrous in the middle. The monster, as this essay has tried to show, seems to orbit around the human world, moving fluidly between the god and animal categories. In this way, it forces and helps the human to confront its own instability, its paradox, and contradictions. Cohen claims that the purpose of the monster is to constantly ask us why we create them (Cohen 1996, 20). *CHEW* exposes that it is the human who can answer, saying that the monster has been created so that the human can create (and recreate) himself. If a human is a god, a man, or a wolf, the monster does not know because they are both always a problem of language and how the human and the monster decided to nominate themselves for the next turn, the next battle.

NOTE

1. For a study of cannibalism in real-world cultures, see Beth A. Conklin, *Consuming Grief—Compassionate Cannibalism in an Amazonian Society* (Austin: University of Texas Press, 2001).

Bibliography

Abusch, Tzvi. "Witchcraft Literature in Mesopotamia." In Gwendolyn Leick, editor, *The Babylonian World*. New York: Routledge, 2007: 373–85.
Agamben, Giorgio. *Homo Sacer: Sovereign Power and Bare Life*. Translated by Daniel Heller-Roazen. Stanford, CA: Stanford University Press, 1998.
Agamben, Giorgio. *The Open: Man and Animal*. Translated by Kevin Attell. Stanford, CA: Stanford University Press, 2004.
Allen, Richard J. "Beginning, Middle, End of an Era: Has Technology Trumped Aristotle?" *Journal of Film and Video* 65:1–2 (2013): 9–22.
Anderson, John G. T. *Deep Things Out of Darkness: A History of Natural History*. Los Angeles: University of California Press, 2013.
Anzaldúa, Gloria E. *Borderlands/La Frontera: The New Mestiza*. San Francisco, CA: Spinsters/Aunt Lute Book Company, 1987.
Anzaldúa, Gloria E. *Interviews/Entrevistas*. Edited by AnaLouise Keating. New York: Routledge, 2000.
Anzaldúa, Gloria E. *Light in the Dark/Luz en lo Oscuro: Rewriting Identity, Spirituality, Reality*. Edited by AnaLouise Keating. Durham, NC: Duke University Press, 2015.
Aristotle. *Poetics*. Translated by Malcolm Heath. New York: Penguin Books, 1996.
Arment, Chad. *The Historical Bigfoot: Early Reports of Wild Men, Hairy Giants, and Wandering Gorillas in North America*. Landisville, PA: Coachwhip Publications, 2006.
Arnold, Kenneth. [1952] *The Coming of the Saucers*. Reprint. Point Pleasant, WV: New Saucerian Books, 2014.
Arnold, Sarah. *Maternal Horror Film: Melodrama and Motherhood*. London: Palgrave Macmillan, 2013.
Asma, Stephen T. *On Monsters: An Unnatural History of Our Worst Fears*. New York: Oxford University Press, 2009 [2011, 2016].

Associated Press. "'Buck Rogers' Flight Stirs Conjecture: Others Confirm Sky Mystery." *The Press Democrat*, June 27, 1947. https://www.newspapers.com/clip/45923156.

Associated Press. "'Moth Man' Sighted." *Beckley Post-Herald*, November 17, 1966. https://www.newspapers.com/clip/45920919.

Association of Religion Data Archives. "Belief in Bigfoot" (Baylor Religion Survey, Wave 2, 2007). http://www.thearda.com/quickstats/qs_43.asp.

Aziz, Abuali Alibhai. Sermon (*wa'z*). Delivered in Chicago on 15th April 1982.

Badley, Linda. *Film, Horror, and the Body Fantastic*. Westport, CN: Greenwood Press, 1995.

Barbera, Joseph. "The Id Follows: *It Follows* (2014) and the Existential Crisis of Adolescent Sexuality." *International Journal of Psychoanalysis* 100:2 (2019): 393–404.

Barragan, Bianca. "Downtown LA's Creepy Hotel Cecil Set to Finally Reopen in 2021." *Curbed LA*, September 3, 2019. https://la.curbed.com/2019/9/3/20847705/hotel-cecil-reopen-skid-row-housing-trust-hotel.

Bauman, Richard. "Verbal Art as Performance." *American Anthropologist* 77:2 (1975): 290–311.

Beal, Timothy K. *Religion and Its Monsters*. New York: Routledge, 2002.

Bechtel, Lyn M. "What If Dinah Is Not Raped? (Genesis 34)." *Journal for the Study of the Old Testament* 62 (1994): 19–36.

Bekkum, Koert van, Jaap Dekker, Henk van de Kemp, and Eric Peels, editors. *Playing with Leviathan: Interpretation and Reception of Monsters from the Biblical World*. Themes in Biblical Narrative 21; Leiden: Brill, 2017.

Bell, Karl. *The Legend of Spring-heeled Jack: Victorian Urban Folklore and Popular Cultures*. Woodbridge: Boydell Press, 2017.

Bettcher, Talia Mae. "Evil Deceivers and Make-Believers: On Transphobic Violence and the Politics of Illusion." *Hypatia* 22:3 (2007): 43–65.

Beyer, Stephan. *The Cult of Tārā: Magic and Ritual in Tibet*. Berkeley, CA: University of California Press, 1973.

Bhandari, Sushil et al. "Genetic Evidence of a Recent Tibetan Ancestry to Sherpas in the Himalayan Region." *Scientific Reports* 5:9 (November 2015): 1–9.

Bialek, Joanna. *Compounds and Compounding in Old Tibetan: A Corpus Based Approach*. Marburg: Indica et Tibetica Verlag, 2018.

Bielo, James S. "Creationist History-Making: Producing a Heterodox Past." In Jeb J. Card and David S. Anderson, editors, *Lost City, Found Pyramid: Understanding Alternative Archaeologies and Pseudoscientific Practices*. Tuscaloosa, AL: University of Alabama Press, 2016: 81–101.

Blackburn, Lyle. *The Beast of Boggy Creek: The True Story of the Fouke Monster*. San Antonio, TX: Anomalist Books, 2012.

"Blackout: The Show." *The Blackout Experience*, 2019. http://www.theblackoutexperience.com/2019halloween.

Blake, Linnie. *The Wounds of Nations: Horror Cinema, Historical Trauma and National Identity*. Manchester: Manchester University Press, 2008.

Blatty, William Peter. *On the Exorcist from Novel to Film*. New York: Bantam Books, 1974.
Bloom, Harold, editor. *Stephen King*. Philadelphia, PA: Chelsea House, 2007.
Blouin, Michael J. "'A Growing Global Darkness': Dialectics of Culture in Goddard's *The Cabin in the Woods*." *Horror Studies* 6:1 (2015): 83–99.
Bod ljongs nag chu sa khul gyi lo rgyus rig gnas. Nag chu rdzong: Nag chu sa gnas srid gros lo rgyus rig gnas dpyad gzhi'i rgyu cha rtsom sgrrig khang, 1992. TBRC ID: W00EGS1016733.
Bowring, Richard John. *The Religious Traditions of Japan, 500–1600*. Cambridge: Cambridge University Press, 2005.
Bras mo ljongs kyi gnas yig. Edited by Bkra shis tshe ring. Gangtok, Sikkim and Dharamsala: Jointly published by Namgyal institute of Tibetology, Deorali, Gangtok and Amnye Machen Institute, Dharamsala, 2008. TBRC ID: W1KG818.
Breier, Idan. "Representations of the Dog in Seventh-Century BCE Assyrian Letters." *Journal of Northwest Semitic Languages* 39:2 (2013): 19–36.
Breier, Idan. "'Who Is This Dog?' The Negative Image of Canines in the Lands of the Bible." *Ancient Near Eastern Studies* 54 (2017): 47–62.
Bressan, David. "Thomas Jefferson's Patriotic Monsters." *Scientific American*, May 15, 2014. https://blogs.scientificamerican.com/history-of-geology/thomas-jeffers on-8217-s-patriotic-monsters.
Brown, August. "Terror Creeps Into the Mind." *The Los Angeles Times*, October 26, 2012. https://www.latimes.com/archives/la-xpm-2012-oct-25-la-et-1026-night-b lackout-20121026-story.html.
Bryant, M. Darrol. "Cinema, Religion, and Popular Culture." In John R. May and Michael Bird, editors, *Religion in Film*. Knoxville: University of Tennessee Press, 1982: 101–14.
Bstan 'dzin phun tshogs. *Dri med shel gong dang dri med shel phreng dang lag len gces bsdus*. Tashigang: Lcags po ri par khang, 1970. TBRC ID: W23762.
Buell, Denise Kimber. "Hauntology Meets Posthumanism: Some Payoffs for Biblical Studies." In Jennifer L. Koosed, editor, *The Bible and Posthumanism*. Atlanta: SBL Press, 2014: 29–56.
Buhs, Joshua Blu. *Bigfoot: The Life and Times of a Legend*. Chicago: University of Chicago Press, 2009 [2010].
Butler, Judith. *Bodies That Matter: On the Discursive Limits of "Sex."* New York: Routledge, 1993.
Capper, Daniel. "The Friendly Yeti." *Journal for the Study of Religion, Nature & Culture* 6:2 (2012): 71–87.
Capper, Daniel. *Learning Love from a Tiger: Religious Experiences with Nature*. Berkeley, CA: University of California Press, 2016.
Carroll, Noel. *The Philosophy of Horror, Or, Paradoxes of the Heart*. New York: Routledge, 1990.
Cartmell, Deborah, editor. *A Companion to Literature, Film, and Adaptation*. Wiley Blackwell, 2012.

Caskey, James. "One of America's Most Haunted." *Haunted Savannah: America's Most Spectral City*. Savannah: Manta Ray Books, 2013.

Castelli, Elizabeth. "'I Will Make Mary Male': Pieties of the Body and Gender Transformation of Christian Women in Late Antiquity." In Julia Epstein and Kristina Straub, editors, *Body Guards: The Cultural Politics of Gender Ambiguity*. New York: Routledge, 1991: 29–49.

Castronovo, Russ. *Necro Citizenship: Death, Eroticism, and the Public Sphere in the Nineteenth-Century United States*. Durham, NC: Duke University Press, 2001.

Cave, Janet, Laura Foreman, and Jim Hicks, editors. *Mysteries of the Unknown: Hauntings*. Richmond, VA: Time-Life Books, 1989.

Childress, David Hatcher. *Yetis, Sasquatch, & Hairy Giants*. Kempton, IL: Adventures Unlimited Press, 2010.

Choden, Kunzag. *Bhutanese Tales of the Yeti*. White Lotus Press, 2007.

Chronis, Athinodoros. "Coconstructing Heritage at the Gettysburg Storyscape." *Annals of Tourism Research* 32:2 (April 2005): 386–406.

Cifarelli, Megan. "Gender, Personal Adornment, and Costly Signaling in the Iron Age Burials of Hasanlu, Iran." In Saana Svärd and Agnès Garcia-Ventura, editors, *Studying Gender in the Ancient Near East*. University Park: Eisenbrauns, 2018: 73–107.

Clover, Carol J. *Men, Women, and Chain Saws: Gender in the Modern Horror Film*. Princeton, NJ: Princeton University Press, 1992 [2015].

Cohen, Claudine. *The Fate of the Mammoth: Fossils, Myth, and History*. Chicago: University of Chicago Press, 1994.

Cohen, Jeffrey Jerome, editor. *Monster Theory: Reading Culture*. Minneapolis, MI: University of Minnesota Press, 1996.

Coleman, Loren and Jerome Clark. *Cryptozoology A-Z: The Encyclopedia of Loch Monsters, Sasquatch, Chupacabras, and Other Authentic Mysteries of Nature*. New York: Simon & Schuster, 1999.

Coleman, Loren. *Bigfoot! The True Story of Apes in America*. New York: Paraview Press, 2003.

Coleman, Loren. *Mothman: Evil Incarnate*. New York: Cosimo Books, 2017.

Coleman, Loren. *Mysterious America: The Ultimate Guide to the Nation's Weirdest Wonders, Strangest Spots, and Creepiest Creatures*. New York: Paraview Pocket Books, 2007.

Conklin, Beth A. *Consuming Grief – Compassionate Cannibalism in an Amazonian Society*. Austin, TX: University of Texas Press, 2001.

Cook, Morgan. "McKamey Manor 'Victim' Speaks Out." *The San Diego Union-Tribune*, October 30, 2015. https://www.sandiegouniontribune.com/news/watchdog/story/2015-10-30/mckamey-manor-victim-speaks-out.

Corbey, Raymond. *The Metaphysics of Apes: Negotiating the Animal-human Boundary*. Cambridge: Cambridge University Press, 2005.

Corbin, Henry. *Mundus Imaginalis or the Imaginary and the Imaginal*. Translated by Ruth Horine. Zurich: Golgonooza Press, 1972.

Coughlan, David. *Ghost Writing in Contemporary American Fiction*. London: Palgrave Macmillan, 2016.

Cowan, Douglas E. *America's Dark Theologian: The Religious Imagination of Stephen King.* New York University Press, 2018.
Cowan, Douglas E. *Sacred Terror: Religion and Horror on the Silver Screen.* Waco: Baylor University Press, 2008.
Cowan, Douglas E. *Magic, Monsters, and Make-Believe Heroes: How Myth and Religion Shape Fantasy Culture.* Berkeley, CA: University of California Press, 2019.
Creed, Barbara. *The Monstrous-Feminine: Film, Feminism, Psychoanalysis.* New York: Routledge, 1993.
Csapo, Eric. *Theories of Mythology.* Oxford: Blackwell, 2005.
Curl, Eric. "Report: No Evidence Savannah Vaults Housed Slaves." *Savannah Morning News*, January 9, 2014. https://www.savannahnow.com/news/2014-01-09/report-no-evidence-savannah-vaults-housed-slaves.
Curtis, Barry. *Dark Places: The Haunted House in Film.* London: Reaktion Books, 2008.
Dahl, Ulrika. "(The Promise of) Monstrous Kinship? Queer Reproduction and the Somatechnics of Sexual and Racial Difference." *Somatechnics* 8:2 (2018): 195–211.
Daston, Lorraine. *Against Nature.* Cambridge: The MIT Press, 2019.
Dawkins, Richard. *The Selfish Gene.* Oxford: Oxford University Press, 1989.
Debenat, Jean-Paul and P. H. LeBlond. *The Asian Wildman: Yeti, Yeren & Almasty: Cultural Aspects & Evidence of Reality.* Hancock House, 2014.
Debenat, Jean-Paul. *The Asian Wild Man: Yeti, Yeren, & Almasty, Cultural Aspects & Evidence of Reality.* Blaine, WA: Hancock House, 2014.
Debus, Allen A. *Prehistoric Monsters: The Real and Imagined Creatures of the Past That We Love to Fear.* Jefferson, NC: McFarland, 2010.
Dégh, Linda and Andrew Vázsonyi. "The Hypothesis of Multi-Conduit Transmission in Folklore." In Dan Ben-Amos and Kenneth S. Goldstein, editors, *Folklore: Performance and Communication.* Paris: Mouton, 1975: 207–54.
DeGrado, Jessie and Madadh Richey. "An Aramaic-Inscribed Lamaštu Amulet from Zincirli." *Bulletin of the American Schools of Oriental Research* 377 (2017): 107–33.
DeGrado, Jessie and Madadh Richey. "The Aramaic Inscription of the Ashmolean Musuem Pazuzu Statuette and Ancient Middle Eastern Magic." *Semitica et classica* 12 (2019): 17–64.
Dell, Christopher. *Monsters: A Bestiary of the Bizarre.* London: Thames & Hudson, 2016.
Dendle, Peter. "Cryptozoology in the Medieval and Modern Worlds." *Folklore* 117:2 (August 2006): 190–206.
Derrida, Jacques. *The Beast & the Sovereign.* London: The University of Chicago Press, 2009.
Derrida, Jacques. "The Animal That Therefore I Am (More to Follow)." Translated by David Wills. *Critical Inquiry* 28:2 (Winter 2002): 369–428.
Derrida, Jacques. *Specters of Marx: The State of Debt, the Work of Mourning, and the New International.* Translated by Peggy Kamuf. Abingdon: Routledge, 1994.

Desmond, John M. and Peter Hawkes. *Adaptation: Studying Film and Literature.* McGraw-Hill, 2006.

Dge Thub bstan chos grags. "Lha 'dre zhes pa don du yod pa yin nam." In Nawang Tsering Shakspo, editor, *Lo 'khor gyi deb: Shes rig me long.* Leh: Jammu and Kashmir Academy of Art, Culture, and Languages of Leh, Ladakh, 1998: 60–80.

Dhakal, Shiva. *Folktales of Sherpa & Yeti.* Adapted by Yuyutssu R. D. Sharma. New Delhi: Nirala, 2017.

Dika, Vera. *Games of Terror: Halloween, Friday the 13th, and the Films of the Stalker Cycle.* Rutherford, NJ: Farleigh Dickinson University Press, 1990.

Dimmitt, Cornelia and J. A. B. van Buitenen, editor/translator. *Classical Hindu Mythology: A Reader in the Sanskrit Purāṇas.* Philadelphia, PA: Temple University Press, 1978.

Doak, Brian R. *Consider Leviathan: Narratives of Nature and the Self in Job.* Minneapolis, MI: Fortress Press, 2014.

Dotson, Brandon. "Hunting for Fortune: Wild Animals, Goddesses and the Play of Perspectives in Early Tibetan Dice Divination." *Études Mongoles & Sibériennes Centrasiatiques & Tibétaines* 50 (2019). https://journals.openedition.org/emscat/3702.

Douglas, Mary. *Purity and Danger: An Analysis of the Concept of Pollution and Taboo.* New York: Routledge, 2002.

Dudley, Edward J. and Maximillian E. Novak. *The Wild Man Within: An Image in Western Thought from the Renaissance to Romanticism.* Pittsburgh, PA: University of Pittsburgh Press, 1973.

Dugatkin, Lee Alan. *Mr. Jefferson and the Giant Moose: Natural History in Early America.* Chicago: University of Chicago Press, 2009.

Duojie. "Renlei you yeren ma?" In Yuan Xiaowen, editor, *Zangyi zoulang: wenhua duoyangxing, zuji hudong yu fazhan.* Beijing: Minzu Chubanshe, 2010: 591–603.

Durkheim, Emilé. *The Elementary Forms of Religious Life.* Translated by Karen E. Fields. New York: Free Press, 1995.

Durkheim, Émile. *The Rules of Sociological Method.* Edited by Stephen Lukes. Translated by W. D. Halls. Free Press, 1982.

Earle, Harriet E. H. *Gender, Sexuality and Queerness in American Horror Story: Critical Essays.* Jefferson: McFarland & Co, 2019.

Earle, Harriet E. H. and Jessica Clark. "Telling National Stories in American Horror Story." *European Journal of American Culture* 38:1 (2019): 5–13.

Eck, Diana L. *Darsan: Seeing the Divine Image in India.* New York: Columbia University Press, 1998.

Edelman, Lee. *No Future: Queer Theory and the Death Drive.* Durham, NC: Duke University Press, 2004.

Edensor, Tim. *National Identity, Popular Culture, and Everyday Life.* Oxford: Oxford University Press, 2002.

Eilberg-Schwartz, Howard. *The Savage in Judaism: An Anthropology of Israelite Religion and Ancient Judaism.* Bloomington, IN: Indiana University Press, 1990.

Eliade, Mircea. *Shamanism: Archaic Techniques of Ecstasy.* London: Penguin Books, 1989.

Eliade, Mircea. *Myth and Reality*. New York: Harperbooks, 1963.
Ellis, Bill. *Raising the Devil: Satanism, New Religions, and the Media*. Lexington: University Press of Kentucky, 2000.
Ellis, Bill. *Aliens, Ghosts, and Cults: Legends We Live*. Jackson, MS: University Press of Mississippi, 2003.
Ema, Tsutomu. *Nihon Yokai Henkashi*. Tokyo: Chukōbunko, 2004.
Farber, Walter. "Lamaštu." *Reallexikon der Assyriologie und Vorderasiatischen Archäologie* 6 (1983): 439–46.
Farber, Walter. "Lamaštu and the Dogs." *Journal of Semitics* 16 (2007a): 635–45.
Farber, Walter. "Lamaštu—Agent of a Specific Disease or a Generic Destroyer of Health?" In Irving L. Finkel and Markham J. Geller, editors, *Disease in Babylonia*, Leiden: Brill, 2007b: 137–45.
Farber, Walter. *Lamaštu: An Edition of the Canonical Series of Lamaštu Incantations and Rituals and Related Texts from the Second and First Millennia B.C.* Winona Lake: Eisenbrauns, 2014.
Fiddler, Michael. "Playing *Funny Games* in *The Last House on the Left*: The Uncanny and the 'Home Invasion' Genre." *Crime, Media, Culture* 9:3 (2013): 281–99.
Forth, Gregory. "Images of the Wildman Inside and Outside Europe." *Folklore* 118:3 (2007): 261–81.
Foucault, Michel. *Abnormal: Lectures at the College De France, 1974–1975*. Edited by Valerio Marchetti and Antonella Salomoni. Translated by Graham Burchell. London: Picador, 2004.
France, Robert L. "Imaginary Sea Monsters and Real Environmental Threats: Reconsidering The Famous Osborne, 'Moha-Moha', Valhalla, And 'Soay Beast' Sightings Of Unidentified Marine Objects." *International Review of Environmental History* 3:1 (2017): 63–100.
Frankfurter, David. "Awakening to Satanic Conspiracy: *Rosemary's Baby* and the Cult Next Door." In David M. Eckel and Bradley L. Herling, editors, *Deliver Us From Evil: Boston University Studies in Philosophy and Religion*. London: Bloomsbury Publishing, 2011: 75–86.
Freud, Sigmund. *The Uncanny*. Translated by David McClintock. New York: Penguin Books, 2003.
George, Andrew R. *The Queer Art of Failure*. Durham, NC: Duke University Press, 2011.
George, Andrew R. *Mesopotamian Incantations and Related Texts in the Schøyen Collection*. Bethesda: CDL Press, 2016.
George, Andrew R. Kamadme. "The Sumerian Counterpart of the Demon Lamaštu." In Greta Van Buylaere, Mikko Luukko, Daniel Schwemer, and Avigail Mertens-Wagschal, editors, *Sources of Evil. Studies in Mesopotamian Exorcistic Lore*. Leiden: Brill, 2018: 150–7.
George, Andrew R. "Appendix 2. The Neo-Babylonian Amulet." In Marina Pucci, editor, *Excavations in the Plain of Antioch, Volume 3. Stratigraphy and Materials from Chatal Hüyük*. Chicago: The Oriental Institute, 2019: 303–4.
Gilmore, David G. *Monsters: Evil Beings, Mythical Beasts, and All Manners of Imaginary Terrors*. Philadelphia, PA: University of Pennsylvania Press, 2003.

Godfrey, Linda S. *The Beast of Bray Road*. Black Earth, WI: Prairie Oak Press, 2003.
Goldhaber, Michael H. "Attention Shoppers!" *Wired*, December 15, 2017. https://www.wired.com/1997/12/es-attention.
Götting, Eva. "Lamaštu: Ikonographie einer altorientalischen Dämonin." Magisterarbeit, Freie Universität Berlin, 2009.
Götting, Eva. "Arcane Art: Some Thoughts on the Perception of the Magico-Religious Imagery of Lamaštu-Amulets." In Barbara Horejs et al., editors, *Proceedings of the 10th International Congress on the Archaeology of the Ancient Near East*. Wiesbaden: Harrassowitz, 2018: 456–66.
Grafius, Brandon R. *Reading Phinehas, Watching Slashers: Horror Theory and Numbers 25*. Lanham, MD: Lexington Books/Fortress Academic, 2018.
Grafius, Brandon R. *Reading the Bible with Horror*. Lanham, MD: Lexington Books/Fortress Academic, 2019.
Grafius, Brandon R. "Text and Terror: Monster Theory and the Hebrew Bible." *Currents in Biblical Research* 16:1 (2017): 34–49.
Grant, Barry Keith, editor. *The Dread of Difference: Gender in the Horror Film*. Austin, TX: University of Texas Press, 1996. [Second Edition 2015.]
Graybill, Rhiannon. "Day of the Woman: Judges 4–5 as Slasher and Rape Revenge Narrative." *The Journal of Religion and Popular Culture* 30:3 (2018): 193–205.
Graybill, Rhiannon. *Are We Not Men?: Unstable Masculinities in the Hebrew Prophets*. New York: Oxford University Press, 2016.
Greenberg, Harvey R. "Reimaging the Gargoyle: Psychoanalytic Notes on *Alien*." In Constance Penley, Elisabeth Lyon, Lynn Spigel, and Janet Bergstrom, editors, *Close Encounters: Film, Feminism, and Science Fiction*. Minneapolis, MI: University of Minnesota Press, 1991.
Halberstam, Judith/Jack. *Skin Shows: Gothic Horror and the Technology of Monsters*. Durham, NC: Duke University Press, 1995.
Hanson, Joe. "Thomas Jefferson And the Giant Moose." *It's Okay To Be Smart*, June 29, 2015. https://www.youtube.com/watch?v=7lwRZ6AUY44.
Hattori, Yukio. *Henkaron Kabukinoseishinshi*. Tokyo: Heibonsha, 1975.
Hayward, Eva. "Spider City Sex." *Women & Performance* 20 (2010): 225–51.
Hedeen, Stanley. *Big Bone Lick: The Cradle of American Paleontology*. Lexington: University Press of Kentucky, 2008.
Heeßel, Nils P. *Pazuzu: Archäologische und Philologische Studien zu einem altorientalischen Dämon*. Leiden: Brill, 2002.
Heimpel, Wolfgang. "Leopard. A. Philologisch." *Reallexikon der Assyriologie und Vorderasiatischen Archäologie* 6:7–8 (1983): 599–601.
Heller-Nicholas, Alexandra. *Rape-Revenge Films: A Critical Study*. Jefferson, NC: McFarland, 2011.
Herzig, Rebecca M. *Plucked: A History of Hair Removal*. New York: New York University Press, 2015.
Heuvelmans, Bernard. *On the Track of Unknown Animals*, 3rd edition. New York: Routledge, 1995.
Heuvelmans, Bernard. *Natural History of Hidden Animals*. New York: Routledge, 2007.

Heyes, Michael E. "Domestication in the Theater of the Monstrous: Reexamining Monster Theory." *The Journal of Gods and Monsters* 1:1 (2020): 36–53.
Hirvonen, Joonas. "Animals and Demons. Faunal Appearances, Metaphors, and Similes in Lamaštu Incantations." In Raija Mattila, Sanae Ito, and Sebastian Fink, editors, *Animals and their Relation to Gods, Humans and Things in the Ancient World*. Wiesbaden: Springer, 2019: 313–43.
Hogle, Jerrold. "The Ghost of the Counterfeit–and the Closet–in The Monk." *Romanticism on the Net* 8 (1997): n.p.
Holland, Sharon Patricia. *Raising the Dead: Readings of Death and (Black) Subjectivity*. Durham, NC: Duke University Press, 2000.
Holmes, David L. *The Faiths of the Founding Fathers*. New York: Oxford University Press, 2006.
Huber, Toni. *The Cult of Pure Crystal Mountain: Popular Pilgrimage and Visionary Landscape in Southeast Tibet*. Oxford: Oxford University Press, 1999.
Hur, Nam-Lin. *Death and Social Order in Tokugawa Japan: Buddhism, Anti-Christianity, and the Danka system*. Cambridge, MA: Harvard University Asia Center, 2007.
Iftene, Daniel. "Sexual Monstrosity in Contemporary Cult TV Series: The Case of the American Horror Story." *Ekphrasis. Images, Cinema, Theory, Media* 15:1 (2016): 37–47.
Imām Shāh, Pīr. vs 1865/1808-9 ce. *Moṭo Dasimo Avatār*, Manuscript KH 534. London: The Institute of Ismaili Studies.
Imām Shāh, Saiyad et al. *Mahān Isamāīlī Dharmapracārak Saiyad Imāmashāh ane Bījā Dharmapracārak Saiyado Racit Gīnānono Sañgrah*, Vol. 4. Muñbai: Isamāīlī Prīnṭīñg Pres, 1954.
Imām Shāh, Saiyad. *Moṭo Dash Avatār*, 2nd edition. Muñbai: Dhī Khojā Sīñdhī Prīnṭīñg Pres, 1923.
Inagaki, Taiichi. "Publicity of Konjaku-Monogatari-shu From the Muromachi to the Middle of the Tokugawa Era." *Studies in Language and Literature* 22 (1992): 101–18.
Ingebretsen, Edward J. *At Stake: Monsters and the Rhetoric of Fear in Popular Culture*. Chicago: University of Chicago Press, 2001.
Ingersoll, Ernest. *Dragons and Dragon Lore*. Escondido, CA: Book Tree, 1999.
Jackson, Shirley. [1959] *The Haunting of Hill House*. Reprint. New York: Penguin, 2006.
Jackson, Zakiyyah Iman. *Becoming Human: Matter and Meaning in an Antiblack World*. New York: New York University Press, 2020.
Jameson, Fredric. *Postmodernism, Or, the Cultural Logic of Late Capitalism*. Durham, NC: Duke University Press, 1992.
Janicker, Rebecca. *Reading American Horror Story: Essays on the Television Franchise*. Jefferson, NC: McFarland, 2017.
Jefferson, Thomas. "A Memoir on the Discovery of Certain Bones of a Quadruped of the Clawed Kind in the Western Parts of Virginia." *Transactions of the American Philosophical Society* 4 (1799): 246–60.
Jefferson, Thomas. "Notes on the State of Virginia: Electronic Edition." Philadelphia, PA: Prichard and Hall, 1788. https://docsouth.unc.edu/southlit/jefferson/menu.html.

Johnson, D. M. "The 'Phantom Anesthetist' of Mattoon: A Field Study of Mass Hysteria." *The Journal of Abnormal and Social Psychology* 40:2 (1945): 175–86.
Johnson, Jessica. "Legal, Modern Day Torture House McKamey Manor." *Hidden San Diego*, 2018. https://hiddensandiego.net/mckamey-manor.php.
Johnson, Nuala. "Cast in Stone: Monuments, Geography, and Nationalism." *Environment and Planning D: Society and Space* 13:1 (1995): 51–65.
Johnson, Richard. "The Story So Far: And Further Transformations." In David Punter, editor, *Introduction to Contemporary Cultural Studies*. Harlow: Longman, 1986: 277–313.
Josephson-Storm, Jason. *The Myth of Disenchantment: Magic, Modernity, and the Birth of the Human Sciences*. Chicago: The University of Chicago Press, 2017.
Jung, Carl Gustav. "The Archetypes of the Collective Unconscious." In Herbert Read, Michael Fordham, Gerhard Adler and William McQuire, editors, R. F. C. Hull, translator, *The Collected Works of C.G. Jung*. New York: Pantheon Books, 1980.
Kalmanofsky, Amy. *Terror All Around: The Rhetoric of Horror in the Book of Jeremiah*. New York: T&T Clark, 2008.
Karmay, Samten Gyaltsen and Yasuhiko Nagano. *A Survey of Bonpo Monasteries and Temples in Tibet and the Himalaya*. Osaka: National Museum of Ethnology, 2003.
Karmay, Samten Gyaltsen. *The Arrow and the Spindle: Studies in History, Myths, Rituals and Beliefs in Tibet*. Kathmandu: Mandala Book Point, 1998.
Kato, Suichi. *A History of Japanese Literature: The First Thousand Years*. Tokyo: Kodansha International, 1979.
Keel, John A. *The Mothman Prophecies*. New York: Tor, 2013.
Keetley, Dawn. "Introduction: Six Theses on Plant Horror; or, Why are Plants Horrifying?" In Dawn Keetley and Angela Tenga, editors, *Plant Horror: Approaches to the Monstrous Vegetal in Fiction and Film*. London: Palgrave Macmillan, 2016: 1–30.
Kelle, Brad E. "Dealing with the Trauma of Defeat: The Rhetoric of the Devastation and Rejuvenation of Nature in Ezekiel." *Journal of Biblical Literature* 128:3 (2009): 469–90.
Kewon, Damien. *A Dictionary of Buddhism*. Oxford: Oxford University Press, 2004.
King, Stephen. "Sometimes They Come Back." In Stephen King, *Night Shift*. New York: Signet, 1978: 143–70.
King, Stephen. *It*. New York: Signet, 1980.
King, Stephen. "The Body." In Stephen King, *Different Seasons*. New York: Signet, 1982a: 293–438.
King, Stephen. "Rita Hayworth and the Shawshank Redemption." In Stephen King, *Different Seasons*. New York: Signet, 1982b: 15–110.
King, Stephen. *The Tommyknockers*. New York: Signet, 1987.
King, Stephen. *Needful Things*. New York: Signet, 1991.
King, Stephen. "Rainy Season." In Stephen King, *Nightmares and Dreamscapes*. New York: Pocket Books, 1993: 453–79.
King, Stephen. *Insomnia*. New York: Gallery, 1994.

King, Stephen. *Desperation*. New York: Viking, 1996.
King, Stephen. *Bag of Bones*. New York: Gallery, 1998.
King, Stephen. [1983] *Pet Sematary*. Reprint with a new introduction. New York: Pocket Books, 2006.
King, Stephen. "N." In Stephen King, *Just After Sunset: Stories*. New York: Pocket Books, 2008: 272–351.
King, Stephen. *Duma Key*. New York: Pocket Books, 2008.
King, Stephen. *Just After Sunset: Stories*. New York: Pocket Books, 2008.
King, Stephen. *Under the Dome*. New York: Gallery, 2009.
King, Stephen. *Danse Macabre*. Revised edition. New York: Gallery, 2010.
King, Stephen. *Revival*. New York: Gallery, 2014.
King, Stephen. *The Bazaar of Bad Dreams*. New York: Scribner, 2015.
Kippenberg, Hans. *Discovering Religious History in the Modern Age*. Translated by Barbara Harshav. Princeton, NJ: Princeton University Press, 2002.
Klengel, Horst. "Neue Lamaštu-Amulette aus dem Vorderasiatischen Museum zu Berlin und dem British Museum." *Mitteilungen des Instituts für Orientforschung* 7 (1960): 334–55.
Klengel, Horst. "Weitere Amulette gegen Lamaštu." *Mitteilungen des Instituts für Orientforschung* 8 (1963): 24–9.
Knab, Timothy J. *A War of Witches: A Journey into the Underworld of the Contemporary Aztecs*. San Francisco, CA: Harper San Francisco, 1995.
Knapp, Sandra. "Comte de Buffon: A Grand Theorist." In Robert Huxley, editor, *The Great Naturalists*. London: Thames & Hudson, 2019: 121–7.
Kolbert, Elizabeth. *The Sixth Extinction: An Unnatural History*. New York: Henry Holt and Co., 2014.
Komatsu, Kazuhiko. *An Introduction to Yōkai Culture: Monsters, Ghosts, and Outsiders in Japanese History*. Tokyo: Japan Publishing Industry Foundation for Culture, 2017.
Konita, Seiji, editor. *Shirei Gedatsu monogatari kikigaki*. Tokyo: Hakuzawasha, 2012.
Kripal, Jeffrey J. "Better Horrors: From Terror to Communion in Whitley Strieber's *Communion* (1987)." *Social Research* 81:4 (Winter 2014): 897–920.
Kripal, Jeffrey J. *Mutants and Mystics: Science Fiction, Superhero Comics, and the Paranormal*. Chicago: The University of Chicago Press, 2015.
Kripal, Jeffrey J. *The Secret Body: Erotic and Esoteric Currents in the History of Religions*. Chicago: The University of Chicago Press, 2017.
Kunsang Choden. *Bhutanese Tales of the Yeti*. Bangkok: White Lotus, 1997.
Kunzang Choden. *Folktales of Bhutan*. Bangkok: White Lotus, 1994.
Kyrou, Ado. *Le Surréalisme au Cinema*. Paris: Le terrain vague, 1963.
Lambert, Wilfred G. *Babylonian Wisdom Literature*. Oxford: Clarendon, 1960.
Landes, Richard A. *Encyclopedia of Millennialism and Millennial Movements*. New York: Routledge, 2000.
Laycock, Joseph P. "A Search for Mysteries and Monsters in Small Town America." *Smithsonian Magazine*, July 11, 2018. https://www.smithsonianmag.com/travel/monster-festival-pilgrimage-small-town-america-180969568.

Laycock, Joseph P. "The Secret History of the 1928 Exorcism in Earling, Iowa." In Adam Possamai and Giuseppe Giordan, editors, *The Social Scientific Study of Exorcism*. Cham: Springer Press, 2020: 17–32.

Laycock, Joseph P. "Mothman: Monster, Disaster, and Community." *Fieldwork in Religion* 3:1 (2009): 70–86.

Laycock, Joseph P. "The Religious Struggle Over Cryptozoology." *Science + Religion Today*, February 18, 2010. http://www.scienceandreligiontoday.com/2010/02/18/the-religious-struggle-over-cryptozoology.

Layman, John (writer) and Rob Guillory (artist). *CHEW: Volume One: Taster's Choice*. Berkeley, CA: Image Comics, 2009.

Layman, John (writer) and Rob Guillory (artist). *CHEW: Volume Two: International Flavour*. Berkeley, CA: Image Comics, 2010.

Layman, John (writer) and Rob Guillory (artist). *CHEW: Volume Five: Major League CHEW*. Berkeley, CA: Image Comics, 2011.

Layman, John (writer) and Rob Guillory (artist). *CHEW: Volume Ten: Blood Puddin'*. Berkeley, CA: Image Comics, 2015.

Leach, Edmund. *Claude Lévi-Strauss*. New York: Viking Press, 1974.

LeBlanc, Amanda Kay. "'There's Nothing I Hate More than a Racist:' (Re)Centering Whiteness in *American Horror Story: Coven*." *Critical Studies in Media Communication* 35:3 (2018): 273–85.

Lévi-Strauss, Claude. *The Raw and the Cooked*. New York: Harper & Row, 1969.

Lindahl, Jared R. "The Ritual Veneration of Mongolia's Mountains." In José Ignacio Cabezón, editor, *Tibetan Ritual*. New York: Oxford University Press, 2010: 225–46.

Linenthal, Edward T. "Epilogue: Reflections." In James Oliver Horton and Lois E. Horton, editors, *Slavery and Public History: The Tough Stuff of American History*. Chapel Hill: University of North Carolina Press, 2008: 213–24.

Long, Charles H. *Significations*. Aurora, CO: The Davies Group Publishers, 1999.

Lovecraft, H. P. "The Call of Cthulhu." In S. T. Joshi, editor, *The Call of Cthulhu and Other Weird Stories*. New York: Penguin, 1999: 139–69.

Lovecraft, H. P. "At the Mountains of Madness." In S. T. Joshi, editor, *The Thing on the Doorstep and Other Weird Stories*. New York: Penguin, 2001: 246–340.

Lovecraft, H. P. *The Fiction: Complete and Unabridged*. New York: Barnes & Noble, 2010.

Loxton, Daniel and Donald R. Prothero. *Abominable Science! Origins of the Yeti, Nessie, and Other Famous Cryptids*. New York: Columbia University Press, 2013.

Luhrmann, Tanya Maya. *Persuasions of the Witch's Craft: Ritual Magic in Contemporary England*. Cambridge, MA: Harvard University Press, 1989.

Maffie, James. *Aztec Philosophy: Understanding a World in Motion*. Boulder, CO: University Press of Colorado, 2014.

Marshall, Nowell. "Beyond Queer Gothic: Charting the Gothic History of the Trans Subject in Beckford, Lewis, Byron." In Jolene Zigarovich, editor, *TransGothic in Literature and Culture*. New York: Routledge, 2018.

Marzouk, Safwat. *Egypt as a Monster in the Book of Ezekiel*. Tübingen: Mohr Siebeck, 2015.

Matthews, Victor H. and Don C. Benjamin. *The Social World of Ancient Israel: 1250-587 BCE*. Peabody, MA: Hendrickson Pub, 1993.

Mayor, Adrienne. *Fossil Legends of the First Americans*. Princeton, NJ: Princeton University Press, 2005.

McBee, Thomas Page. "The Monster in All of Us." *Out*, February/March 2020: 9–11.

McHugh, James. *Sandalwood and Carrion: Smell in Indian Religion and Culture*. Oxford: Oxford University Press, 2012.

Meldrum, Jeff. *"Sasquatch Field Guide" (laminated brochure)*. Blue Lake, CA: Paradise Cay, 2016.

Meldrum, Jeff. *Sasquatch: Legend Meets Science*. New York: Tom Doherty Associates, 2006.

Mertens-Wagschal, Avigail. "The Lion, the Witch, and the Wolf: Aggressive Magic and Witchcraft in the Old Babylonian Period." In Greta Van Buylaere, Mikko Luukko, Daniel Schwemer, and Avigail Mertens-Wagschal, editors, *Sources of Evil: Studies in Mesopotamian Exorcistic Lore*. Ancient Magic and Divination 15. Leiden: Brill, 2018: 158–69.

Meurger, Michel and Claude Gagnon. *Lake Monster Traditions: A Cross-cultural Analysis*. London: Fortean Tomes, 1988.

"Mi rgod bcings ba'i le'u sde dgu pa." In R*al gcig ma'i drag snangs 'dus pa'i rgyud*. Rnying ma rgyud 'bum, Volume 42, 92.2-102.2. Thimpu: National Library, Royal Government of Bhutan, 1982. TBRC ID: W21521.

"Mi rgod byad bcings bya ba'i le'u." In *Dpal E ka dza ti khrag gi rba klong gi rgyud*, Rnying ma rgyud 'bum, Volume 42, 432.7-460.3. Thimpu: National Library, Royal Government of Bhutan, 1982. TBRC ID: W21521.

"Mi rgod byad chings kyi le'u sde gsum pa." In *Dpal gnod sbyin zla gsang dmar po'i rgyud*. Rnying ma rgyud 'bum, Volume 42, 703.6-834.4. Thimpu: National Library, Royal Government of Bhutan, 1982. TBRC ID: W21521.

"Mi rgod mtsho yig gtam rgyud." (n.d.) September 13, 2017. http://zw.tibetculture.org.cn/history_1/history/201709/t20170913_4346272.htm.

"Mi rgod rnam 'joms." In *Mdo Mang* vol. 2 Varanasi: s.n., 1971: 303–6.

Mikles, Natasha L. "The Monstrous and the Moral: Interpreting King Yama's Narratological Arc in Returner Literature." *Revue d'Etudes Tibétaines* 55 (2020): 385–408.

Miles, Tiya. *Tales From the Haunted South: Dark Tourism and Memories of Slavery from the Civil War Era*. Chapel Hill: The University of North Carolina Press, 2015.

Miller, John. "Zooheterotopias." In Mariangela Phalladino and John Miller, editors, *The Globalization of Space: Foucault and Heterotopia*. Brookfield, VT: Pickering & Chatto, 2015: 149–64.

Mitchell, W. J. T. *The Last Dinosaur Book: The Life and Times of a Cultural Icon*. Chicago: Chicago University Press, 1998.

"Mogambo (1953)." *Internet Film Database*, accessed April 17, 2020. https://www.imdb.com/title/tt0046085/?ref_=tt_pg.

"Mogambo." *Movies A La Mark: With a Cast of Thousands*. 2015. https://moviesalamark.com/2015/05/30/mogambo.

Momin, Wafi A. *The Formation of the Satpanth Ismaili Tradition in South Asia*. PhD dissertation, The University of Chicago, 2016.

"MonsterTalk: Transcript for 'Hop Springs Eternal'." February 6, 2013. https://www.skeptic.com/podcasts/monstertalk/13/02/06/transcript.

Mori, Masato. "Konjaku Monogatari-Shū: Supernatural Creatures and Order." *Japanese Journal of Religious Studies* 9:2 (1982): 147–70.

Morris, Jeremy. "The Justification of Torture-Horror." In Thomas Fahy, editor, *The Philosophy of Horror*. Lexington: University Press of Kentucky, 2012: 42–56.

Mortensen, Eric D. "Boundaries of the Borderlands: Mapping Gyelthang." In Stéphane Gros, editor, *Frontier Tibet: Patterns of Change in the Sino-Tibetan Borderlands*. Amsterdam: Amsterdam University Press, 2019: 115–39.

Mortensen, Eric D. "Pasum Tso: The Tributaries of Tibet's Religious Folklore." *Harvard Asia Quarterly* 3:2 (1999): 36–42.

Mortensen, Eric D. "Prosperity, Identity, & Intra-Tibetan Violence, and Harmony in Southeast Tibet: The Case of Gyalthang." In Ben Hillman and Gray Tuttle, editors, *Ethnic Conflict and Protest in Tibet and Xinjiang*. New York: Columbia University Press, 2016: 201–22.

Morton, Timothy. *Being Ecological*. London: Pelican Books, 2018.

Nag po skal bzang. *Klu 'bum mi rgod*. Zi-ling: Mtsho sngon mi rigs dpe skrun khang, 2013.

Naish, Darren. *Hunting Monsters: Cryptozoology and the Reality Behind the Myths*. London: Sirius Publishing, 2017.

Nakamura, M. Kyoko. *Miraculous Stories from the Japanese Buddhist Tradition The Nihon Ryoiki of the Monk Kyokai*. London and New York: Routledge Taylor & Francis Group, 1997.

Napier, John. *Bigfoot: The Yeti and Sasquatch in Myth and Reality*. New York: E. P. Dutton, 1973.Nappi, Carla. *The Monkey and the Inkpot: Natural History and Its Transformations in Early Modern China*. Cambridge: Harvard University Press, 2009.

Nath, Tribhuvan and Madan M. Gupta. *On the Yeti Trail: the Search for the Elusive Snowman*. New Delhi: UBSPD, 1994.

Nebesky-Wojkowitz, René de. *Where Gods are Mountains: Three Years Among the People of the Himalayas*. Translated by Michael Bullock. London: Weidenfeld and Nicholson, 1956a.

Nebesky-Wojkowitz, René de. *Oracles and Demons of Tibet: The Cult and Iconography of the Tibetan Protective Deities*. Graz: Akademische Druk und Verlagsanstalt, 1975 [reprint Delhi: Book Faith India: 1996] [1956b].

Nickell, Joe. *Real-life X-files: Investigating the Paranormal*. Lexington: University Press of Kentucky, 2001.

Nietzsche, Friedrich Wilhelm. *Beyond Good and Evil: Prelude to a Philosophy of the Future*. Translated by Marion Faber. New York: Oxford University Press, 1998.

Norman, H. C. "The Kalki Avatāra of Viṣṇu." In *Transactions of the Third International Congress for the History of Religions*, Vol. 2. Oxford: Clarendon Press, 1908: 85–9.

Notkin, Deborah L. "Stephen King: Horror and Humanity for Our Time." In Tim Underwood and Chuck Miller, editors, *Fear Itself: The Horror Fiction of Stephen King (1976–1982)*. New York: New American Library, 1982: 131–42.

Nussbaum, Emily. "The New Abnormal." *The New Yorker*, December 8, 2014. https ://www.newyorker.com/magazine/2014/12/08/new-abnormal.
Nussbaum, Emily. "How Ryan Murphy Became the Most Powerful Man in TV." *The New Yorker*, May 7, 2018. https://www.newyorker.com/magazine/2018/05/14/how-ryan-murphy-became-the-most-powerful-man-in-tv.
O'Flaherty, Wendy Doniger. *Hindu Myths*. Harmondsworth: Penguin Books, 1975.
O'Flaherty, Wendy Doniger. *The Origins of Evil in Hindu Mythology*. Berkeley: University of California Press, 1980.
O'Reilly, Jennifer. "'We're More than Just Pins and Dolls and Seeing the Future in Chicken Parts': Race, Magic and Religion in *American Horror Story: Coven*." *European Journal of American Culture* 38:1 (2019): 29–41.
Ōkata, Yōji, editor. *Shin Kasane Gedatsu Monogatari*. Ōsaka: Mizui Shoin, 1985.
Orsi, Robert A. "The Problem of the Holy." In Robert Orsi, editor, *The Cambridge Companion to Religious Studies*. New York: Cambridge University Press, 2012: 84–108.
Orsi, Robert. *History and Presence*. Cambridge: Harvard University Press, 2016.
Otto, Rudolph. *The Idea of the Holy*. Translated by John W. Harvey. New York: Oxford University Press, 1923.
Panayotov, Strahil V. "Review of Walter Farber, *Lamaštu*." *Bulletin of the School of Oriental and African Studies* 78 (2015): 599–600.
Pimentel, Juan. *The Rhinoceros and the Megatherium: An Essay in Natural History*. Cambridge, MA: Harvard University Press, 2017.
Pinkowitz, Jacqueline. "Down South: Regional Exploitation Films, Southern Audiences, and Hillbilly Horror in Herschell Gordon Lewis's *Two Thousand Maniacs!* (1964)." *Journal of Popular Film and Television* 44:2 (2016): 109–19.
Pippin, Tina K. *Apocalyptic Bodies: The Biblical End of the World in Text and Image*. London: Routledge, 1999.
Poole, W. Scott. *Monsters in America: Our Historical Obsession with the Hideous and the Haunting*. Waco, TX: Baylor University Press, 2018 [2011].
Possamai, Adam. "Sociological Interpretations." In Joseph P. Laycock, editor, *Spirit Possession around the World: Possession, Communion, and Demon Expulsion Across Cultures*. Santa Barbara, CA: ABC-CLIO, 2014: 317–20.
Pourcher, Pierre. *The Beast of Gevaudan = La bête Du Gévaudan*. Bloomington, IN: AuthorHouse, 2006.
Quillien, Louise. "Invisible Workers: The Role of Women in Textile Production during the 1st Millennium BC." In Brigitte Lion and Cécile Michel, editors, *The Role of Women in Work and Society in the Ancient Near East*. Berlin: de Gruyter, 2015: 473–93.
Ramanujan, A. K. "Three Hundred Ramayanas: Five Examples and Three Thoughts on Translation." In Paula Richman, editor, *Many Ramayanas: The Diversity of a Narrative Tradition in South Asia*. Berkeley, CA: University of California Press, 1991: 22–49.
Rampa, T. Lobsang. [1959] *Doctor from Lhasa*. New Brunswick, NJ: Inner Light Publications, 1990.

Raphael, Rebecca. "Monsters and the Crippled Cosmos: Construction of the Other in *Fourth Ezra*." In Daniel C. Harolow, Karina Martin Hogan, Matthew Goff, and Joel S. Kaminsky, editors, *The 'Other' in Second Temple Judaism: Essays in Honor of John J. Collins*. Grand Rapids, MI: Eerdmans, 2011: 279–301.

Read, Jacinda. *The New Avengers: Feminism, Femininity, and the Rape-Revenge Cycle*. New York: Manchester University Press, 2000.

Regal, Brian. *Searching for Sasquatch: Crackpots, Eggheads, and Cryptozoology*. New York: Palgrave Macmillan, 2011.

Reider, Noriko. "The Emergence of Kaidan-shu: The Collection of Tales of the Strange and Mysterious in the Edo Period." *Asian Folklore Studies* 60:1 (2001): 79–100.

Reinarz, Jonathan. *Past Scents: Historical Perspectives on Smell*. Champaign: University of Illinois Press, 2014.

Reuchung Rinpoche. "The Life of the Great Physician-Saint gYu-thog Yon-tan mGon-po." In *Tibetan Medicine*. Berkeley: University of California Press, 1976.

Ricoeur, Paul. "Evil, a Challenge to Philosophy and Theology." Translated by David Pellauer, *Journal of the American Academy of Religion* 53:4 (December, 1985): 635–48.

Riviello, Alex. "How the 'Blackout' Haunted House Turned My Life into a Real Horror Movie." *Film: Blogging the Reel World*, May 18, 2017. https://www.slashfilm.com/blackout-haunted-house-experience/2.

Roberts, Michael. "The Mi-go." *Poetry* 49:4 (1937): 191–2.

Rubel, Arthur J., Carl W. O'Nell, and Rolando Collado Ardón. *Susto: A Folk Illness*. Berkeley, CA: University of California Press, 1984.

Rudwick, Martin J. *The Meaning of Fossils: Episodes in the History of Paleontology*, 2nd edition. Chicago: University of Chicago Press, 1985.

Sadaradīn, Pīr and Imām Shāh, Saiyad. *Bāvan Gāṭī tathā Vīs Ṭol*, 1st edition. Muñbai: Dhī Khojā Sīñdhī Prīṇṭīñg Pres, n.d.

Sadaradīn, Pīr. *Nāno Das Avatār*, 3rd edition. Muñbai: Dhī Khojā Sīñdhī Prīṇṭīñg Press, 1929.

Sadaradīn, Pīr. *Mahān Isamāīlī Sañt Pīr Sadaradīn Racit Gīnānono Sañgrah*, Vol. 1. Muñbai: Isamāīlī Prīṇṭīñg Press, 1952.

Sakakura, Honda and Kawabata Yoshiaki, editors. *Konjaku Monogatari-shū Honchō sezoku bu san*. Tokyo: Shinchōsha, 1981.

Salamon, Gayle. *Assuming a Body: Transgender and Rhetorics of Materiality*. New York: Columbia University Press, 2010.

Salamon, Gayle. *The Life and Death of Latisha King: A Critical Phenomenology of Transphobia*. New York: New York University Press, 2018.

Sanderson, Ivan T. [1961] *Abominable Snowmen: Legend Come to Life*. Kempton: Adventures Unlimited Press, 2006.

Sano, Shōeki. "Nigiwahigusa." In *Nihon Zuihitsu Zenshū*, vol. 18. Tokyo: Kokumin Tosho, 1929.

Sawerthal, Anna and Davide Torri. "Imagining the Wild Man: Yeti Sightings in Folktales and Newspapers of the Darjeeling and Kalimpong Hills." In Markus Viehbeck, editor, *Transcultural Encounters in the Himalayan Borderlands:*

Kalimpong as a "Contact Zone." Heidelberg University Publishing (2017): 121–48.
Sax, Boria. *Dinomania: Why We Love, Fear And Are Utterly Enchanted By Dinosaurs*. London: Reaktion, 2018.
Schmalzer, Sigrid. *The People's Peking Man: Popular Science and Human Identity in Twentieth-Century China*. Chicago: University of Chicago Press, 2008.
Scholz, Susanne. *Rape Plots: A Feminist Cultural Study of Genesis 34*. New York: Peter Lang Inc., International Academic Publishers, 2000.
Schwemer, Daniel. *Abwehrzauber und Behexung: Studien zum Schadenzauberglauben im alten Mesopotamien*. Wiesbaden: Harrassowitz, 2007.
Schwemer, Daniel. "The Ancient Near East." In David J. Collins, editor, *The Cambridge History of Magic and Witchcraft in the West, From Antiquity to the Present*. Cambridge: Cambridge University Press, 2015: 17–51.
Scurlock, JoAnn. "Baby-Snatching Demons, Restless Soul and the Dangers of Childbirth: Medico-Magical Means of Dealing with Some of the Perils of Motherhood in Ancient Mesopotamia." *Incognita* 2 (1991): 137–85.
Seaton, A. V. "Guided by the Dark: From Thanatopsis to Thanatourism." *International Journal of Heritage Studies* 2:4 (1996): 234–44.
Semonin, Paul. *American Monster: How the Nation's First Prehistoric Creature Became a Symbol of National Identity*. New York: New York University Press, 2000.
Shackle, Christopher and Zawahir Moir. *Ismaili Hymns from South Asia: An Introduction to the Ginans*. Richmond: Curzon, 2000.
Shams, Pīr. *Vāek Moṭo (Vel Sāthe) tathā Satagur Nuranā Vīvā*, 2nd edition. Muñbai: Dhī Khojā Sīndhī Prīnṭīñg Press, 1917.
Shams, Pīr. *Mahān Isamāīlī Sañt Pīr Shams Racit Gīnānono Sañgrah*, Vol. 2. Muñbai: Isamāīlī Prīnṭīñg Press, 1952.
Sharpley, Richard. "Shedding Light on Dark Tourism: An Introduction." In Richard Sharpley and Philip R. Stone, editors, *The Darker Side of Travel: The Theory and Practice of Dark Tourism*. Bristol: Channel View Publications, 2009: 3–22.
Shelley, Mary W. *Frankenstein, or, The Modern Prometheus*. London: Henry Colburn and Richard Bentley, 1831.
Siiger, Halfdan. "'The Abominable Snowman': Himalayan Religion and Folklore from the Lepchas of Sikkim." In James F. Fisher, editor, *Himalayan Anthropology: The Indo-Tibetan Interface*. New York: Walter de Gruyter, 1978: 421–30.
Smith, Anthony D. *National Identity*. London: Penguin, 1991.
Smith, Jay M. "Dreadful Enemies: The 'Beast,' the Hyena, and Natural History in the Enlightenment." *Modern Intellectual History* 13:1 (2016): 33–61.
Smith, Jay M. *Monsters of the Gévaudan: The Making of a Beast*. Cambridge, MA: Harvard University Press, 2011.
Smith, Jonathan Z. *Imagining Religion: From Babylon to Jonestown*. Chicago: University of Chicago Press, 1982.
Smith, Jonathan Z. *Drudgery Divine: On the Comparison of Early Christianities and the Religions of Late Antiquity*. Chicago: University of Chicago Press, 1990.

Smith, Jonathan Z. "Religion, Religions, Religious." In Mark C. Taylor, editor, *Critical Terms for Religious Studies*. Chicago: University of Chicago Press, 1998: 269–84.
Smith, Jonathan Z. *Relating Religion: Essays in the Study of Religion*. Chicago: University of Chicago Press, 2004.
Snellgrove, David. *Buddhist Himalaya*. Kathmandu: Himalayan Book Sellers, 1995 [1957].
Spillers, Hortense. "Mama's Baby, Papa's Maybe: An American Grammar Book." *Diacritics* 17:2 (Summer 1987): 64–81.
Steinert, Ulrike. "Review of Walter Farber, *Lamaštu*." *Zeitschrift für Assyriologie und vorderasiatische Archäologie* 106 (2016): 240–51.
Stine, R. L. *The Abominable Snowman of Pasadena*. New York, NY: Scholastic Inc, 2015.
Stoker, Bram. *Dracula*. New York: Modern Library, 1897.
Stone, Allucquére Rosanne (Sandy). "The *Empire* Strikes Back: A Posttranssexual Manifesto." In Julia Epstein and Kristina Straub, editors, *Body Guards: The Cultural Politics of Gender Ambiguity*. New York: Routledge, 1991: 280–304.
Strassberg, Richard E. *A Chinese Bestiary: Strange Creatures from the Guideways Through Mountains and Sea*. Berkeley, CA: University of California Press, 2002.
Strawn, Brent A. "Comparative Approaches: History, Theology, and the Image of God." In Joel M. LeMon and Kent Harold Richardson, editors, *Method Matters: Essays on the Interpretation of the Hebrew Bible in Honor of David L. Peterson*. Atlanta: SBL Press, 2009: 117–42.
Stryker, Susan. "My Words to Victor Frankenstein above the Village of Chamounix: Performing Transgender Rage." *GLQ* 1:3 (1994): 237–54.
Stryker, Susan. "More Words about 'My Words to Victor Frankenstein.'" *GLQ* 25:1 (2019): 39–44.
Surya, Das. *The Snow Lion's Turquoise Mane*. San Francisco, CA: HarperSanFrancisco, 1992.
Suzuki, Shōsan. *Inga monogatari*. Tokyo: Daibunkan, 1918. https://dl.ndl.go.jp/info:ndljp/pid/915767/4.
Switek, Brian. *Written in Stone: Evolution, the Fossil Record, and Our Place in Nature*. New York: Bellevue Literary Press, 2010.
Sykes, Bryan. *The Nature of the Beast: The First Scientific Evidence on the Survival of Apemen into Modern Times*. London: Coronet, 2014.
Sykes, Bryan. *Bigfoot, Yeti, and the Last Neanderthal: A Geneticist's Search for Modern Apemen*. Newburyport, MA: Disinformation Books, 2016.
Tally Jr., Robert T. *Topophrenia: Place, Narrative, and the Spatial Imagination*. Bloomington, IN: Indiana University Press, 2019.
Taylor, Daniel C. *Yeti: The Ecology of a Mystery*. Oxford: Oxford University Press, 2017.
Taylor, Tosha. "Who's Afraid of the Rubber Man? Perversions and Subversions of Sex and Class in *American Horror Story*." *Networking Knowledge: Journal of the MeCCSA Postgraduate Network* 5:2 (2012): 135–53.

"The Most Haunted Places in Savannah." *Ghosts & Gravestones Official Website.* https://www.ghostsandgravestones.com/savannah/haunted-places. Accessed March 6, 2019.

Thomas, William I. and Dorothy Swaine. *The Child in America: Behavior Problems and Programs.* New York: Alfred A. Knopf, 1928.

Thomson, Keith. *The Legacy of the Mastodon: The Golden Age of Fossils in America.* New Haven, CT: Yale University Press, 2008.

Thureau-Dangin, François. "Rituels et Amulettes contre Labartu." *Revue d'assyriologie et d'archéologie orientale* 18 (1921): 161–98.

Tibbetts, John C. and James M. Welsh. *The Encyclopedia of Novels into Film,* 2nd edition. New York: Checkmark, 2005.

Tinson, Julie S., Michael A. J. Saren, and Bridget E. Roth. "Exploring the Role of Dark Tourism in the Creation of National Identity." *Journal of Marketing Management* 31:7–8 (2015): 856–80.

Tsering Thakchoe Drungtso, and Tsering D. Drungtso. *The Tibetan-English Dictionary of Tibetan Medicine and Astrology.* Dharmsala: Drungtso Publications, 2006.

Tucci, Giuseppe. *The Religions of Tibet.* Translated by Geoffery Samuel. Berkeley, CA: University of California Press, 1980.

Tunbridge, J. E. and G. J. Ashworth. *Dissonant Heritage: Managing the Past as a Resource in Conflict.* Chichester: John Wiley & Sons, Ltd, 1996.

Turner, Victor. *The Forest of Symbols: Aspects of Ndembu Ritual.* Ithaca: Cornell University Press, 1967.

Tyler, Royall. "The Tokugawa Peace and Popular Religion: Suzuki Shōsan, Kakugyō Tōbutsu, and Jikigyō Miroku." In Peter Nosco, editor, *Confucianism and Tokugawa Culture.* Princeton, NJ: Princeton University Press, 1984: 92–101.

Upādhyāy, Ved Prakāsh. *Kalki Avatār aur Muhammad Sāhab,* Reprint edition. Koṭā, Rajasthan: Khālid Buk Ḍipo, n.d.

Van Duzer, Chet A. "Bring on the Monsters and Marvels: Non-Ptolemaic Legends on Manuscript Maps of Ptolemy's Geography." *Viator* 45:2 (2014): 303–34.

Vlček, Emanuel. "Old Literary Evidence for the Existence of the 'Snow Man' in Tibet and Mongolia." *Man* 59 (1959): 133–4.

Vlček, Emmanuel. "The Diagnosis of the 'Wild Man' according to Buddhist Literary Sources from Tibet, Mongolia and China." *Man* 60 (1964): 153–5.

Watanabe, Chikako E. "Association of the Dog with Healing Power in Mesopotamia." In Yağmur Heffron, Adam Stone, and Martin Worthington, editors, *At the Dawn of History: Ancient Near Eastern Studies in Honour of J. N. Postgate.* Winona Lake: Eisenbrauns, 2017: 689–97.

Weaver, Harlan. "Monster Trans: Diffracting Affect, Reading Rage." *Somatechnics* 3:2 (2013): 287–306.

Weheliye, Alexander G. *Habeas Viscus: Racializing Assemblages, Biopolitics, and Black Feminist Theories of the Human.* Durham, NC: Duke University Press, 2014.

Weiss, Allen S. "Ten Theses on Monsters and Monstrosity." *TDR/The Drama Review* 48:1 (2004): 124–5.

Wenner. E.T.C. *Myths and Legends of China.* London: George G. Harrup and Co., 1922.

West, Patrick. *Conspicuous Compassion: Why Sometimes It Really Is Cruel to Be Kind.* Civitas: Institute for the Study of Civil Society, 2004.
Weszeli, Michaela. "Wolf (Werwolf)." Mesopotamien. *Reallexikon der Assyriologie und Vorderasiatischen Archäologie* 15:1–2 (2016): 124–7.
White, David Gordon. *Myths of the Dog-Man.* Chicago: University of Chicago Press, 1991.
Wiggermann, Frans A. M. "Lamaštu, Daughter of Anu: A Profile." In Marten Stol, editor, *Birth in Babylonia and the Bible: Its Mediterranean Setting.* Groningen: Styx, 2000: 217–49.
Wiggermann, Frans A. M. "Dogs, Pigs, Lamaštu, and the Breast-Feeding of Animals by Women." In Dahlia Shehata, Frauke Weiershäuser, and Kamran V. Zand, editors, *Von Göttern und Menschen. Beiträge zu Literatur und Geschichte des Alten Orients. Festschrift für Brigitte Groneberg.* Leiden: Brill, 2010: 407–14.
Wiggins, Steve A. *Holy Horror: The Bible and Fear in Movies.* Jefferson, NC: McFarland & Co., 2018.
Wiggins, Steve A. "Good Book Gone Bad: Reading Phinehas and Watching Horror." *Horizons in Biblical Theology* 41:1 (2019): 93–103.
Wiggins, Steve A. "The Theological Origins of Horror." Forthcoming In Brandon R. Grafius and John W. Morehead, editors, *Theology and Horror.* Lanham, MD: Lexington Books/Fortress Academic, 2020.
Williams-Forte, Elizabeth. "Leopard. B. Archäologisch." *Reallexikon der Assyriologie und Vorderasiatischen Archäologie* 6:7–8 (1983): 601–4.
Williams, Tony. *Hearths of Darkness: The Family in the American Horror Film.* Madison, NJ: Farleigh Dickinson University Press, 1996. [Updated Edition: Jackson, MS: University Press of Mississippi, 2014.]
Wolff, Michael. *Television Is the New Television: The Unexpected Triumph of Old Media in the Digital Age.* New York: Portfolio, 2017.
Wood, Robin. "An Introduction to the American Horror Film." In Jeffrey Andrew Weinstock, editor, *The Monster Theory Reader.* Minneapolis, MI: University of Minnesota Press, 2020, 108–35.
Wood, Robin. *Hollywood from Vietnam to Reagan...and Beyond.* Revised and expanded edition. New York: Columbia University Press, 2003.
Wulf, Andrea. *The Invention of Nature: Alexander von Humboldt's New World.* New York: Penguin Random House, 2015.
Wynter, Sylvia. "Unsettling the Coloniality of Being/Power/Truth/Freedom: Towards the Human, After Man, Its Overrepresentation–An Argument" *CR: The New Centennial Review* 3:3 (2003): 257–337.
Yamada, Frank M. *Configurations of Rape in the Hebrew Bible: A Literary Analysis of Three Rape Narratives.* New York: Peter Lang Inc., International Academic Publishers, 2008.
Ye shes bstan pa'i rgyal mtshan. *Dri med shel phreng nas bshad pa'i sman gyi 'khrungs dpe mdzes mtshar mig rgyan.* New Delhi: International Academy of Indian Culture. Satapitaka series, v.82, 1971. TBRC ID: W1PD6.
Yoshida, Kōichi, editor. *Inga Monogatari, Hiragana Bon.* In *Koten Bunko* vol. 182. Tokyo: Koten Bunko, 1962.

Zada, John. *In the Valleys of the Noble Beyond: In Search of the Sasquatch.* New York: Atlantic Monthly Press, 2019.
Zigarovich, Jolene. "Transgothic Desire in Charlotte Dacre's *Zofloya*." In Jolene Zigarovich, editor, *TransGothic in Literature and Culture.* New York: Routledge, 2018a: 77–96.
Zigarovich, Jolene. "The Trans Legacy of *Frankenstein.*" *Science Fiction Studies* 45:2 (2018b): 260–72.
Zomer, Elyze. "Zauberei (witchcraft). A. In Mesopotamien." *Reallexikon der Assyriologie und Vorderasiatischen Archäologie* 15:3–4 (2017): 222–4.

FILMOGRAPHY

Alien. Directed by Ridley Scott. Brandywine Productions, 1979.
The Blair Witch Project. Directed by Daniel Myrick and Eduardo Sánchez. Haxan Films, 1999.
The Cabin in the Woods. Directed by Drew Goddard. Mutant Enemy, 2011.
The Dark Tower. Directed by Nikolaj Arcel. Columbia Pictures, 2017.
The Green Mile. Directed by Frank Darabont. Castle Rock Entertainment, 1999.
The Grudge. Directed by Takashi Shimizu. Ghost House Pictures, 2004.
It. Directed by Tommy Lee Wallace. Green/Epstein Productions and Lorimar Television, 1990.
It. Directed by Andy Muschietti. New Line Cinema, 2017.
It: Chapter Two. Directed by Andy Muschietti. KatzSmith Productions, 2019.
It Follows. Directed by David Robert Mitchell. Animal Kingdom, 2014.
Ju-on. Directed by Takashi Shimizu. Pioneer LDC, 2002.
The Legend of Boggy Creek. Directed by Charles B. Pierce. Howco International Pictures, 1972.
Maximum Overdrive. Directed by Stephen King. De Laurentiis Entertainment, 1986.
Misery. Directed by Rob Reiner. Castle Rock Entertainment, 1990.
Mogambo, directed by John Ford. Metro-Goldwyn Mayer, 1953.
Pet Sematary. Directed by Kevin Kölsch and Dennis Widmyer. Alphaville Films, 2019.
Ringu. Directed by Hideo Nakata. Basara Pictures, 1998.
The Shawshank Redemption. Directed by Frank Darabont. Castle Rock Entertainment, 1994.
The Shining. Directed by Stanley Kubrick. Warner Bros., 1980.
Stand By Me. Directed by Rob Reiner. Columbia Pictures, 1986.
Star Wars. Directed by George Lucas. 20th Century Fox, 1977.
The Witch. Directed by Robert Eggers. Parts and Labor, 2015.

TELEVISION

A Discovery of Witches. Sky One, 2018–present.

American Horror Story. FX, 2011–present.
Buffy the Vampire Slayer. The WB, 1997–2001. UPN, 2001–03.
Charmed. The CW, 2018–present.
Finding Bigfoot, Animal Planet. Aired 2011–2018.
Game of Thrones. HBO, 2011–2019.
Legacies. The CW, 2018-present.
Lovecraft Country. 2020. "Whitey's on the Moon." HBO. August 23rd.
Lucifer. Fox, 2016–2018. Netflix, 2018–present.
Nancy Drew. The CW, 2019-present.
Roswell, New Mexico. The CW, 2019–present.
Stranger Things. Netflix, 2016–present.
Supernatural. The WB, 2005–2006. The CW, 2006–2020.
The Chilling Adventures of Sabrina. Netflix, 2018–present.
The Handmaid's Tale. Hulu, 2017–present.
The Magicians. Syfy, 2015–2020.
The Order. Netflix, 2019–present.
The Vampire Diaries. The CW, 2009–2017.
The Walking Dead. AMC, 2010–present.
The Witcher. Netflix, 2019-present
The X-Files. Fox, 1993–2002. Fox (revival) 2016–2018.
True Blood. HBO, 2008–2014.

Index

ableism, 227
abundant events, 15–16
Adams, John, 192
Aetherius Society, 15
Aga Khan III, 76
Algonquians, 188
Alien (film), 8–9, 18
Alma (creature), 172
Amabie (*yokai*), 5–6
America, 164, 166–67, 176, 185, 187–88, 190–93, 197, 214, 225–36
American Horror Story (television show), 157
Amida Buddha, 92–93
amulets, 89, 146–47, 150, 155
Angrboða, 16
antisemitism, 14, 182
Argentina, 172
Aristotle, 230–33, 235
Asuras, 70
Augustine, 177
availability heuristic, 22

Bag of Bones (novel), 26
Barker, Gray, 43, 56
Battle of Sekigahara, 81
Bazaar of Bad Dreams, The (book), 24
Beal, Timothy, 9, 15
Beast of Gevaudan, 42, 51, 54–55, 197

Behemoth, 4, 31
beyul (concealed valley), 108
bigfoot, 5, 44–45, 58–59, 171–83, 185
bigfoot, Patterson sighting, 45
Black Dahlia murder, 231
blackmail, 214
Blair Witch Project, The (film), 19–20
Bloom, Harold, 24
bokon (departed soul), 80
Boone, Daniel, 189
borei (departed spirit), 80, 86
Brahma, 71
Brazil, 172
Bride of Frankenstein, The (film), 3
Broken Blossoms (film), 214
Buddhism, 4, 10, 14, 79–81, 83–91, 94, 117–24, 128–30, 134–35
Buffon, Comte de. *See* Leclerc, Georges-Louis
Butler, Judith, 152

Cabin in the Woods (film), 26, 38
Canada, 180
cannibalism, 240, 244, 250
Carrie (film), 32
Catholicism, 11, 174–75, 199
Chile, 172
China, 4, 6, 71, 84, 114, 117, 124, 136, 172, 177–78, 183

Chokyi, Lingza, 10
Christianity, 29, 81, 86, 90, 150, 177
Cihuacoatl, 210
Civil War, 162
Coatlicue, 200, 204–9
Cohen, Jeffrey Jerome, 6–8, 10, 27, 29, 30, 32, 129, 226, 243, 249–50
Cold War, 50
COVID-19, 5, 128
cryptozoology, 12, 50, 111, 113, 142, 185, 189, 196
Cthulhu, 9, 18
Cuvier, George, 193

Dahmer, Jeffrey, 231
Daityas, 6
Danavas, 6
Daniel (book of the Bible), 76
danka system, 80, 90–94
Danse Macabre (book), 18
Dark Tourist (television show), 157
Dark Tower, The (film), 21
Darwin, Charles, 182
Dawkins, Richard, 41, 43–47
Deliverance (film), 219
Derrida, Jacques, 159, 164, 173, 237–38, 241–45, 248–49
Descartes, René, 177, 179
Desperation (novel), 17
Devil, the, 249
dharma protectors, 123
Didi (creature), 172
Different Seasons (novel), 20
divination, 103
Dog-Man, 114, 140
Dogman (cryptid), 50
Douglas, Mary, 117, 123, 128
Doyle, Arthur Conan, 185
Dracula, 31, 150, 222
dragons, festival, 12
Durkheim, Émile, 9, 12–14

Eliade, Mircea, 5, 9, 206
Ellis, Bill, 14
England, 42, 189

Enuma Elish, 31, 121
Erasmus, Desidarius, 241
Exodus (book of the Bible), 224
Exorcist, The (film), 16, 30, 147
Ezekiel (book of the Bible), 31, 34, 38

Facebook, 128
Fenris Wolf, 16
Finding Bigfoot (television show), 171, 173
Flatwoods Monster, The, 52
folk religion, 103, 110
Foucault, Michel, 164, 173, 176
Fouke Monster, the, 6, 13–14
Fouke Monster Festival, 5, 10, 13
France, 42, 54, 187–89, 191, 196
Frankenstein (novel), 16
Frankenstein's monster, 153–54, 174, 222–23
Franklin, Benjamin, 188
Freaks (film), 235
Freud, Sigmund, 31–33, 208

Gabriel (angel), 66–67
Gacy, John Wayne, 231
Garuda, 59, 133
Gelugpa tradition, 104, 112
Genesis (book of the Bible), 213–24, 242–43
Genji monogatari (*The Tale of Genji*), 85
Germany, 183
ghosts, 79–96, 157–68, 226, 231
Ginans, 63–78
Green Mile, The (film), 21
Guyana, 172

Halberstam, Jack, 153, 175, 226
Halloween (film), 34
Hamilton, Alexander, 188
Hansel and Gretel, 20
Hariti, 4
harpies, 129
Haunting of Hill House, The (novel), 18
Heaven's Gate, 15

Hebrew Bible, 149, 213, 220
Hel, 16
Heraclitus, 177
Heuvelmans, Bernard, 185–86
Hinduism, 4, 7, 63–65, 70, 74–77
Hitchcock, Alfred, 214
Hobbes, Thomas, 241
Holmes, H. H., 231, 236
Holocaust, The, 159
homophobia, 227
Hosea (book of the Bible), 31
Humboldt, Alexander Von, 196
Hunter, Wiliam, 189

ikiryo (living spirit), 80, 85, 87–88
India, 4, 74, 76, 84, 114, 117, 124, 129, 135
Inga monogatari, 95
Iraq, 146, 155
Iroquois, 188
Isaiah (book of the Bible), 37, 224
Islam, 63–65, 73–76, 117
I Spit on Your Grave (film), 213–14, 216, 219–23
Israel, 146, 213, 217
It (film), 23, 26
It (novel), 18–20, 24–25
It: Chapter Two (film), 23
It Follows (film), 26, 34

James, William, 9, 36
Japan, 4, 5, 38, 79, 81, 84, 94
Jefferson Bible, 190
Jeremiah (bible book), 31, 34–35
Job (book of the Bible), 4, 37, 39
Judaism, 29, 182
Judges (book of the Bible), 222
Jung, Carl, 202–3
Ju-On (film), 26
Jurassic Park (film), 7

kaidan (strange tales), 81
Kali, age of, 64, 66–67, 71–73
karma, 88, 93
Kasane (ghost), 79, 88, 91–93

Keel, John, 43, 50, 56, 58–59
Kennedy, John F., 196
King, Stephen, 17–27, 36
Konjaku monogatari-shu, 79–80, 83–86, 88–89, 93
Koyasan (mountain), 89
kraken, 243
Kripal, Jeffrey, 10–11, 13, 173
Kyokai, 80

Lady Gaga, 233
La Llorona, 210
lamas, 108
Last House on the Left, The (film), 33, 213–16, 218–23
Last Supper, The, 246
Laveau, Marie, 229
Leclerc, Georges-Louis, 186–96
Legend of Boggy Creek, The (film), 5, 12, 52, 181
leprosy, 122
Leviathan, 4, 16, 29, 31, 36–37, 39
Lévi-Strauss, Claude, 177–79, 183
Lewis and Clark expedition, 194
Linnaeus, Carl, 9, 177, 179
Lizard Man, 52, 58
Loch Ness Monster, 173, 185
Loki, 16
Losar, 118, 123, 125, 128
Lotus Sutra, 4
Lovecraft, Howard Philips, 9, 19, 132–33
Lovecraft Country (television show), 4
lu (snake beings), 119, 122

Mad Gasser of Mattoon, Illinois, 43, 55
Mahdi, the, 65, 76
Madison, James, 188, 194
Magumbo (film), 162
Mahabharata, 63
Mapinguary (creature), 172
Marx, Karl, 164
Maximum Overdrive (film), 21
memes, 41, 44–46
Mexico, 201

Midgard Serpent, 16
millenialism, 63
Misery (film), 21
moja (deceased person), 80
Mongolia, 124, 172
Monk, The (novel), 145
MonsterQuest (television show), 50
moral panic, 14, 58
Mothman, 12–14, 43, 50, 52, 56–59
Mothman Prophecies, The (book). *See* Keel, John
Muhammad (prophet), 64, 66–67, 71, 74

nagas, 122
nags myi rgod (wild man), 98–99, 110, 131–44
nagual, 200, 208–10
Nash, Ogden, 5
Night of the Living Dead (film), 36
Nihon ryoiki, 79–80, 82, 84–86, 88–89, 92–93
Numbers (book of the Bible), 32, 37
Nyingmapa tradition, 112

Oiwa (ghost), 91
Ojoyoshu (The Collection of Rebirth Stories), 93
Orang-Pandek (creature), 172
Orsi, Robert, 11, 15
ostension, 44, 53
Otto, Rudolf, 11, 175
Oudemans, A. C., 185

Padmasambhava, 128
Pakistan, 117
Palestine, 146
Pazuzu, 147
Penny Dreadfuls, 56
Pet Sematary (book), 21
Plato, 177
Psalms (book of the Bible), 37
Ptolemy, 157
Puranas, 65, 68

QAnon conspiracy theory, 14

Quetzalcoatl, 212
Quran, 66

racism, 182, 227
Raelianism, 15
Ramayana, 63
Ramirez, Richard, 231
Rampa, Lobsang, 131, 133
rei (ghost), 80
Returners, 15
Revival (novel), 17
Rice, Ann, 22
Ricoeur, Paul, 65, 67
Ringu (film), 26
Rousseau, Jean-Jacques, 248
Rudra, 4
Russia, 172
ryo (ghost), 80

Sagan, Carl, 186
samsara, 134
Sanderson, Ivan T., 183, 185–86
Sasquatch, 5, 10, 111, 113, 173, 176, 195–96
Satanic Panic, 14
self-immolation, 4, 6
sexism, 227
Shawshank Redemption, The (film), 20–21
Shining, The (film), 21
Shiva, 77
Simpsons, The (television show), 162
skinwalkers, 50
slavery, 163, 165–66, 226, 229
Smalltown Monsters (television show), 50
Smith, Jonathan Z., 7, 8
Spring-heeled Jack, 14, 42, 55–56
Stand by Me (film), 20
Story of the Salvation of a Ghost, A, 93
Strieber, Whitley, 13, 15
succubus, 145
Sumatra, 172
Suzuki, Shosan, 79–81, 83, 86–88, 91, 94

Syria, 146

Tantra, 4, 117, 119, 135, 140
Tarasque, 12–13, 16
Teresa of Avila, 10
Texas Chainsaw Massacre (film), 33
Three Jewels of Buddhism, 123
Tibet, 97–116, 118, 128, 131–44
Titans, 243, 246
Tokaido Yotsuya kaidan, 91
tulku (reincarnated lama), 108
Turner, Victor, 9
Twain, Mark, 7
Two Thousand Maniacs (film), 39

ubume (monster), 84
Ucumar (creature), 172
UFOs, 43, 50–51, 56, 59
UFOs, flying saucers, 51
Under the Dome (novel), 17, 26
United States, 149, 157, 172, 186, 194, 238

Vajrapani, 4
Vajrayana. *See* Tantra
vampire, Gorbals, 14
vampires, 14, 22, 226, 231, 233, 245–49

Vedas, 69–71
Verne, Jules, 185
Virgin Mary, 15, 174–75
Virgin Spring, The (film), 213–19, 223–24
Visnu, 63–65, 67–70, 72, 76

Washington, George, 192
wendigo, 50
werewolves, 227, 243
wild men, 140, 142, 172
Witch, The (film), 20
witches, 226–27
witch trials, 14
Wuornos, Aillen, 231

X-Files, The (television show), 26

Yama, 15
Yeren (creature), 172
Yeti, 111, 114, 131–35, 138, 141–42, 172, 185
yokai, 5, 80
Yurei jobutsu no koto, 92

Zodiac Killer, The, 231
zombies, 222, 226–27

About the Editors and Contributors

EDITORS

Natasha L. Mikles is lecturer at Texas State University in San Marcos where she teaches courses on Tibetan and Chinese religion in their newly created religious studies major. She has published in several major journals in the fields of Tibetan studies and religious studies, including *Material Religion*, *Revue d'Etudes Tibétaines*, and *Culture & Religion*. Beyond these articles, Natasha is also developing a monograph based on her original translations and research on King Gesar's journey to hell and the epic's participation in Tibetan Buddhist culture. Natasha currently serves as the editor for *The Journal of Gods and Monsters*.

Joseph P. Laycock is associate professor of religious studies at Texas State University. His recent publications include *Speak of the Devil: How the Satanic Temple Is Changing the Way We Talk about Religion* (2020) and *The Penguin Book of Exorcisms* (2020). He is also a coeditor for the journal *Nova Religio*.

CONTRIBUTORS

Frank F. Chu has an MA in Buddhist Studies, an MSc in Japanese society and culture, and is currently a PhD candidate in Japanese studies at the University of Edinburgh. His main research focuses on the ideologies and social orders reflected from the popular ghost (*yūrei*) stories of Tokugawa Japan (1603–1868).

About the Editors and Contributors

Douglas E. Cowan is a professor of religious studies at Renison University College in Waterloo, Canada. He has written several books including *Sacred Terror: Religion and Horror on the Silver Screen*, *America's Dark Theologian: The Religious Imagination of Stephen King*, and, most recently, *Magic, Monsters, and Make-Believe Heroes: How Myth and Religion Shape Fantasy Culture*.

Brandon R. Grafius is an associate professor of biblical studies at Ecumenical Theological Seminary, Detroit. His most recent books are *Reading the Bible with Horror* (Lexington Books/Fortress Academic), which was nominated for a Grawemeyer Award in religion, and a handbook in the Devil's Advocate series on the film *The Witch* (Auteur Publishing/Liverpool University Press). He is coediting (with John W. Morehead) the *Oxford Handbook of Biblical Monsters*, scheduled for publication in 2023.

Timothy Grieve-Carlson is a PhD candidate in the Department of Religion at Rice University, where his research focuses on religion and ecology in American history. Timothy holds graduate certificates from the Center for Critical and Cultural Theory, the Center for Teaching Excellence, and for the study of Gnosticism, Esotericism, and Mysticism in the Department of Religion at Rice. His doctoral work explores the role of environmental knowledge and miraculous phenomena in the apocalyptic discourses of early Pennsylvania.

Heidi Ippolito is a third-year PhD student in the Joint Doctoral Program at the University of Denver and Iliff School of Theology. She holds an MLitt in theology, imagination, and the arts from the University of St. Andrews in Scotland and a BA in cinema-television (critical studies) from the University of Southern California. Compounded by her background working in the entertainment industry, Heidi focuses on the intersections between religion, fandom, social media, monster theory, and emergent forms of on-screen storytelling in TV, film, and video games.

Whitney S. May, MA, is pursuing her PhD in American Studies at the University of Texas and serves as an adjunct lecturer for the Departments of English at Texas State University and Literature at Southern New Hampshire University. Her primary research interests include Gothic and nineteenth-century horror literature as well as depictions of the doppelgänger in horror fiction and in popular culture. Her recent related work has been published in *Gothic Studies*, *Supernatural Studies*, and *The Edgar Allan Poe Review*, as well as in *Circus Space: The Big Top on the Big Screen* (McFarland Press, 2020).

Leland Merritt is a current PhD student in Hebrew Bible at Claremont School of Theology. His research interests include intertextuality, scribal culture in the ancient Levant, ancient Near Eastern literature, and horror in the Hebrew Bible. His forthcoming chapter "Making the End of the World Great Again: *Birdbox*, Borders, and the Refugee Crisis" will be published in *Seeing the Apocalypse: Essays on Bird Box*. He has spoken at several regional and national conferences including the annual Society of Biblical Literature. His dissertation focuses on horror theory in rape-and-revenge narratives in the Hebrew Bible with an in-depth focus on Judges 19.

Wafi A. Momin is head of Ismaili Special Collections Unit at the Institute of Ismaili Studies in London, where he also teaches in its educational programs. He holds a doctorate in South Asian languages and civilizations from the University of Chicago. His research interests include Ismaili history and thought, Islam in South Asia and its interaction with other religious traditions, and literary and manuscript cultures in India during the early modern and colonial periods.

Eric D. Mortensen is a professor of religious studies at Guilford College where he teaches courses on Tibetan and Himalayan religions, East Asian religions, and method and theory of comparative religion. For thirty years, he has regularly spent extended periods in Tibet and Yunnan where he conducts fieldwork on Tibetan and Naxi folklore and religion.

Justin Mullis holds a master's degree in religious studies from the University of North Carolina in Charlotte and is currently a PhD candidate in American culture studies at Bowling Green State University in Ohio where he is working on an expanded version of the essay presented here. His research interests—scholarly and otherwise—include cryptozoology, Japanese pop-culture, and the work of H. P. Lovecraft and related writers. His published work includes "Notes from the Land of Light" (*Kaiju and Pop-Culture*, McFarland Press, 2017), "Cryptid-Fiction! Science-Fiction and the Rise of Cryptozoology" (*Paranormal and Popular-Culture*, Routledge, 2019), "The Lurker at the Threshold of Interpretation" (*Theology and H. P. Lovecraft*, Lexington Books, forthcoming), and "Fear, Fairies and Fossils" (*Arthur Machen: Critical Essays*, Lexington Books, forthcoming).

Elena Pasquini is a scholar of comparative literature. After her first degree at the University of Florence in English, Japanese and Portuguese language and literature, she moved to Scotland. There, she obtained a second degree at the University of Aberdeen in English literature and literature in a world context and a master in fantasy literature at the University of Glasgow. During her studies, she developed a particular interest in monsters and monster theory which has no preference of medium: literature, manga, comics, and films are all considered sources for her study.

Madadh Richey is a postdoctoral research associate in Hebrew Bible at Princeton University and received her PhD in Hebrew Bible and the ancient Near East from the University of Chicago. She writes on art and texts illuminating the religions of the Late Bronze and Iron Age Middle East, especially the Levant and Mesopotamia.

Stefan R. Sanchez is a PhD student in Rice University's Department of Religion specializing in shamanism and comparativism, with particular focus on Native American and Latin American philosophy and mysticism, as well as cultural and religious hybridity. He holds MAs from Texas State University and Rice University in applied philosophy and ethics, and religion, respectively.

Rohit Singh earned his PhD in religious studies from UC Santa Barbara. He is currently a Buddhist studies lecturer at UNC Greensboro. His research specializes in three areas: the ethnography of Tantric rituals, astrology in Vajrayana Buddhism, and Buddhist-Muslim interactions in the Himalayas.

William Blake Smith is an independent writer and researcher. His work has been published in *Fortean Times*, *Skeptical Inquirer*, *Skeptic Magazine*, and *Weird Tales*. He is also the host and producer of the long-running podcast *MonsterTalk: The Science Show About Monsters*.

Lee Weiss is a PhD student in religious studies at Temple University. His research explores Tibetan Buddhism, comparative philosophy, and magic and occultism, with a particular focus on Tantric philosophy and Georges Bataille.